D0457476

WEDGWOOD

Also by Brian Dolan

Exploring European Frontiers

Ladies of the Grand Tour

WEDGWOOD
The First Tycoon

Brian Dolan

[Viking]

VIKING
Published by the Penguin Group
Penguin Group (USA) Inc., 375 Hudson Street, New York, New York 10014, USA
Penguin Group (Canada), 10 Alcorn Avenue, Toronto, Ontario, Canada M4V 3B2
(a division of Pearson Penguin Canada Inc.)
Penguin Books Ltd, 80 Strand, London WC2R 0RL, England
Penguin Ireland, 25 St. Stephen's Green, Dublin 2, Ireland (a division of Penguin Books Ltd)
Penguin Books Australia Ltd, 250 Camberwell Road, Camberwell, Victoria 3124, Australia
(a division of Pearson Australia Group Pty Ltd)
Penguin Books India Pvt Ltd, 11 Community Centre, Panchsheel Park, New Delhi—110 017, India
Penguin Group (NZ), Cnr. Airborne and Rosedale Roads, Albany, Auckland, New Zealand
(a division of Pearson New Zealand Ltd)
Penguin Books (South Africa) (Pty) Ltd, 24 Sturdee Avenue, Rosebank, Johannesburg 2196,
South Africa

Penguin Books Ltd, Registered Offices: 80 Strand, London WC2R 0RL, England

First published in 2004 by Viking Penguin, a member of Penguin Group (USA) Inc.

10 9 8 7 6 5 4 3 2 1

PHOTOGRAPH CREDITS
All photographs courtesy of the Wedgwood Museum Trust Limited, Barlaston, Staffordshire,
England, with the exception of the following: Fig. 10: *Joseph Priestley*, attributed to Ozias
Humphrey (British, 1742–1810), oil on canvas, 30¼" x 35⅛", Chemists Club Collection, Chem-
ical Heritage Foundation, Philadelphia, PA, USA, photo by Will Brown. Courtesy of the
Chemical Heritage Foundation Image Archives. Fig. 15: V&A Images/Victoria and Albert Mu-
seum. Fig. 18: Sir Joshua Reynolds, Jane Hamilton, wife of 9th Lord Cathcart and her daughter,
Jane, © Manchester Art Gallery. Fig. 22: Lemuel Francis Abbott, portrait of Matthew Bolton,
Birmingham Museums & Art Gallery.

LIBRARY OF CONGRESS CATALOGING IN PUBLICATION DATA
Dolan, Brian.
    Wedgwood : the first tycoon / Brian Dolan.
      p.   cm.
    Includes bibliographical references and index.
    ISBN 0-670-03346-4
    1. Wedgwood, Josiah, 1730–1795. 2. Potters—Great Britain—Biography. 3. Industrialists—
Great Britain—Biography. I. Title.
    NK4210.W4D65 2004
    338.7′665′092—dc22
    [B]   2004049633

This book is printed on acid-free paper. ∞

Printed in the United States of America
Set in Requiem
Designed by Jaye Zimet

To Professor Robert A. Hatch
and
M. Ismael Boulliau,

Sine qua non

"for health, happiness, Fame & every thing desirable in this sublunary world"

—Josiah's toast to his friend and partner,
Thomas Bentley, 17 December 1774

Preface

When the Soviet Communist Party disbanded in 1991 and the USSR collapsed, Western visitors flooded through the doors of Russia's museums in unprecedented numbers. The State Hermitage in St. Petersburg, long recognized as the country's premier museum, was at the time the world's largest museum, yet its extensive collections were relatively unknown to all but its curators and the KGB. When waves of Western visitors began to arrive, however, they meandered through galleries of Rembrandts, Rubens, and gilded grand ballrooms to an exhibition that the curators called "the museum's special pride": a spectacular display of some 950 pieces of eighteenth-century Wedgwood pottery.

The Wedgwood Collection is an elaborate dinner and dessert service intended for fifty guests, known as the "Green Frog Service," since the border pattern of each piece is decorated with a small green frog, representing the name of the area in a palace where the service was needed: La Grenouillière ("the frog marsh"). It was commissioned in 1773 by Catherine the Great and to this day, with a few exceptions of pieces on touring exhibitions, remains intact. From a room in the middle of the museum in St. Petersburg, visitors can admire over one thousand two hundred different views of English gardens, country homes, and scenes of industrial progress in eighteenth-century Britain printed on each piece, epitomized by the picture of Josiah Wedgwood's own home—a symbol of his own success as an artist, scientist, and entrepreneur—on a large oval serving dish.

Before sending Catherine's completed service to Russia in 1774,

Wedgwood displayed it in his London showroom and issued tickets to the public for private viewings. It caused a sensation. Carriages created a roadblock on Greek Street, in Soho, and spectators crowded around to catch a glimpse of the exhibition through the storefront windows as much as to gaze at Wedgwood's aristocratic patrons, who included Queen Charlotte, the wife of King George III.

Catherine the Great's order is extraordinary not only because each piece is unique—specially prepared by an artist for that service only—but because the Russian monarch wanted the individual scenes to symbolize the commercial strength and the individual liberty of the inhabitants of the country she so admired. Wedgwood's pottery became emblematic of Catherine's belief that beauty and utility could come together when artists and industrialists were supported by an enlightened government and not neglected under a reign of absolutism and despotism. Ironically, Josiah Wedgwood, who nearly went bankrupt completing her order, did not share her view that he lived under such an "enlightened" government. The personal, religious, and political struggles he encountered throughout his life served to remind him how difficult life was for those born without the privileges of inherited wealth. While an optimist, who dreamed that a Utopian future would eventually emerge from the wars and revolutions he witnessed throughout his life, he never forgot what the world looked like when he was a child.

Josiah was born on 12 July 1730, the twelfth child in a family of struggling potters in a small village in the hills a hundred miles north of London. He grew up surrounded by families who lived by their crafts. Everyday items—butter cups, knives, shoes, soap—were made in thatched cottages and sold in local markets. Most people in Britain and its young colonies ate off wooden plates and drank from metal mugs, not least since rough dirt roads across the country smashed brittle glass and earthenware en route to other markets. Only aristocrats owned the much-admired porcelain cups and saucers that the East India Company recently brought back from China, and they preserved the tea they sipped in padlocked tins to prevent servants from stealing a pinch of the £60 per pound ($100 in today's terms) luxury. Making a life as a potter was difficult. When Josiah was nine, his father died, bankrupt. Life's prospects for the youngest son—small and sickly—were not inviting.

Yet, with a determination to overcome seemingly impossible hurdles and the enduring love and support from his wife, Sally, he grew to become one of the world's most successful industrialists ever. Upon his death on 3 January 1795, Josiah was worth £600,000 (equivalent to around $100 million today), making him the twenty-fourth richest man in eighteenth-century Britain. A self-taught student of the Enlightenment, he was a rationalist who engaged in countless scientific experiments to improve his craft. He built one of the first factories in the world, which he named "Etruria," symbolizing the rebirth of an ancient and highly valued form of art. He was one of the first to employ Adam Smith's notion of the "division of labor"; he invented the precursor to the punching-in clock; he built a model community to house his employees and a health care program that saw them through retirement.

The Green Frog Service was the most ambitious order Josiah Wedgwood agreed to fill, and it is the most celebrated single commission on display today; but it is only one of many well-known wares that he designed and completed during his life. The first order to make his name famous was the "Queen's Ware" tea set he provided for Queen Charlotte in 1765; there followed a succession of innovations in materials and design that revolutionized the art and industry of pottery. That the business he started 250 years ago still exists today (though no longer family-owned), and that his own style of pottery is still admired for its elegance and quality, is only added testimony to his talent and commitment.

By any historical measure, Josiah Wedgwood's accomplishments are astonishing, but he achieved what he did with the help of the friends and family that surrounded him. In his early years, before he embarked on business for himself at twenty-nine years old, he saw a model of success in his two uncles, and received the crucial financial boost to set him on his way from the dowry of his cousin, Sally, whom he married at thirty-three. Drawing on extended family archives, this biography of Josiah Wedgwood offers the first detailed, intimate portrait of one of the world's most well known entrepreneurs, the first tycoon.

❧

While researching this book I have amassed a debt of gratitude to many friends, archivists, librarians, and museum curators who helped me along the way. Helen Burton at the Keele University Special Collections was tireless in her assistance and skillful in helping me navigate the Wedgwood archive; I am grateful to the Trustees of the Wedgwood Museum Trust,

Barlaston, for permission to consult and quote from the Wedgwood
Archival Collection, and to Gaye Blake Roberts and Lynn Miller for their
kind assistance when I worked at the Wedgwood Museum in Barlaston. I
offer a special thank you to Lynn Miller for taking the time to read the
manuscript and offer excellent suggestions on textual points and illustrations, most of which the Wedgwood Museum has also kindly provided.
Hilary Young at the Victoria & Albert Museum, Hugh Torrens at Keele
University, Michael Greenslade at the William Salt Library in Stafford,
the staffs at the Staffordshire Record Office, the Stoke-on-Trent City
Archives, Hanley Library, Cambridge University Library, the British
Library, the John Rylands Library in Manchester, and the London Library
deserve special recognition for their repeated help during my visits.

For providing manuscript material from which, in instances, I am
permitted to quote, I wish to thank RJ Chamberlaine-Brothers at the
Warwickshire County Council Record Office, Rachel Watson at the North-
hamptonshire County Council Record Office, S. Williams at the Hert-
fordshire County Council Archives, the Wiltshire County Council Record
Office, Claire Sawyer at the Bedfordshire County Council Record Office,
Christopher Whittick at the East Sussex Record Office, David Reeve at
the Dorset County Council Archives, Dr. Mike Rogers of the Lincolnshire
County Council Archives, and Richard Childs at the West Sussex Record
Office.

Friends and colleagues have always provided invaluable input: at the
Department of History and Philosophy of Science at Cambridge University, I thank Jim Secord and Simon Schaffer for their dedication to and
passion for exploring the history of Enlightenment science and society;
Henry Atmore (whose own interest in Etruria catapulted me into the
project with stimulating discussions at the start); as well as Dave Abram-
son, Shelley Adler, Will Ashworth, Paul Blanc (with special thanks for
access to his rare books on the history of occupational health), Robin
Boast, Jeff Brautigam, Mike Bravo, John Brewer, Roger Cooter, Janet
Dolan, Nancy Ernst, Sandra Evans, Bob Hatch, Gale Hennelly, Stephen
Jacyna, Kathy Keenan, Nick King, Nat Marshall, Jim Moore, Iwan Morus,
Carole Paul, Joad Raymond, Janet Todd, Sue Woolsey, and others I'm
no doubt forgetting who have all helped me along one way or another,
especially by reading drafts and talking biography. Additionally, the schol-
arship of certain individuals deserves special attention from anyone interested in the history of the Wedgwood business: Dr. Neil McKendrick's

pioneering articles, which he began in the 1960s, and Robin Reilly's magnum opus, the two-volume collector's edition of *Wedgwood*, a history that runs up to 1986, with its incredible wealth of illustrations. More recently, Gaye Blake Roberts of the Wedgwood Museum has been writing about hidden nuggets of Wedgwood history which she often publishes in *Etruria*, the magazine of the Wedgwood International Society, and *Ars Ceramica*, published by the Wedgwood Society of New York.

I would also like to thank my new colleagues at the University of California, San Francisco, for helping us (my wife and me, not Wedgwood and me) to settle in so comfortably.

I am grateful for the continued encouragement of Peter Robinson and Kathy Anderson, and for the interest and skill of Rick Kot and Hilary Redmon at Viking.

Finally, two special acknowledgments. First to my mother, Janet, who provided invaluable assistance in organizing materials and proofreading during the last few months of writing, not least braving the January Midlands wind to revisit many of the original sites in Staffordshire. Second to Dorothy Porter, for being as interested and as committed as ever in the desire to understand and cheer for the prospects of the youngest offspring in a large family.

Contents

Preface   ix

Currency Conversion and Costs ca 1760   xvii

Wedgwood Family Tree   xix

PART ONE: *Rivalry, 1730–1763*

1   A Place for Thomas   3

2   A Will and a Prayer   10

3   "Creators of Fortune and Fame"   19

4   A Potter and a Gentlewoman   31

5   Discipline and Dissent   42

6   "Dues & Demands"   57

7   The *Racehorse*   64

8   By the Docks   77

9   Paradise Street   87

10   "Improveable Subjects"   97

11   "O Grief of Griefs"   107

PART TWO: *History, 1764–1769*

12   Recipe for Success   123

13   Fit for a King and Queen   132

14   The Vexed and the Virtuosi   142

CONTENTS

15 "Exquisite Models"   151
16 The Creators of Beauty   158
17 An Afflicted Heart   167
18 The Arts Reborn   177

PART THREE: *Rebirth, 1769–1776*

19 Ingenious Working People
    and Formidable Opponents   193
20 French Frippery and Russian Husks   203
21 Wanting Air for Sally   211
22 "All the Gardens in England"   223
23 "Off for the Cherokee Nation"   233
24 Poison and Porcelain   238
25 Mad Ministers   250
26 The *Philosophes* and Plaster Shops of Paris   257
27 A Poor Regiment   264

PART FOUR: *Wealth, 1776–1795*

28 *Arrivistes*   275
29 Renewed Grief   287
30 "But Half Myself"   292
31 "A Storm Is Gathering"   296
32 "Some Plan of Life"   303
33 The "Giant Malady"   312
34 "To Mix Again with Their Original Clay"   322
35 "Unremitting Fires"   324
Epilogue   332

    Notes   341
    Bibliography of Works Cited   379
    Index   389

Currency Conversion and Costs
ca 1760

£ s d

£1	=	20 shillings (s)
1s	=	12 pence (d)
21s	=	1 guinea

Calculations estimating today's economic value:

To convert eighteenth-century values to modern UK estimates and U.S. dollars
   Multiply £1 × 70 for £   (i.e., £5 = £350)
   Multiply £1 × 100 for $ (i.e., £5 = $500)

This approximation does not accurately reflect the fluctuating and relative market value of wages or different commodities which help to define "wealth" or standards of living, nor does it take into account the overall proportion of net national income, which is why Josiah Wedgwood's personal worth, estimated at £600,000 at his death, should not be considered simply 70 or 100 times that today, but closer to the status of today's billionaire.

Average income 1760		*In today's £*	*In today's $*
Lords:	£10,000+ annually	£700,000+	$1,000,000+
Knights:	£6,000 annually	£420,000	$600,000
Gentlemen:	£2,000 annually	£140,000	$200,000
Manufacturers (silk):	£300 annually	£21,000	$30,000
Clergy:	£100 annually	£7,000	$10,000
Skilled laborer:	8s week	(£28/week)	($40/week)
Unskilled laborer:	2s week; 1d hour	(£7/week)	($10/week)

Expenses:

Rent for small manufactory . . . £15 annually

Bread . . . . 1d–3d per lb.

Beer . . . . 1d per pint

Tea . . . . 10s–20s per lb.

Wedgwood Family Tree

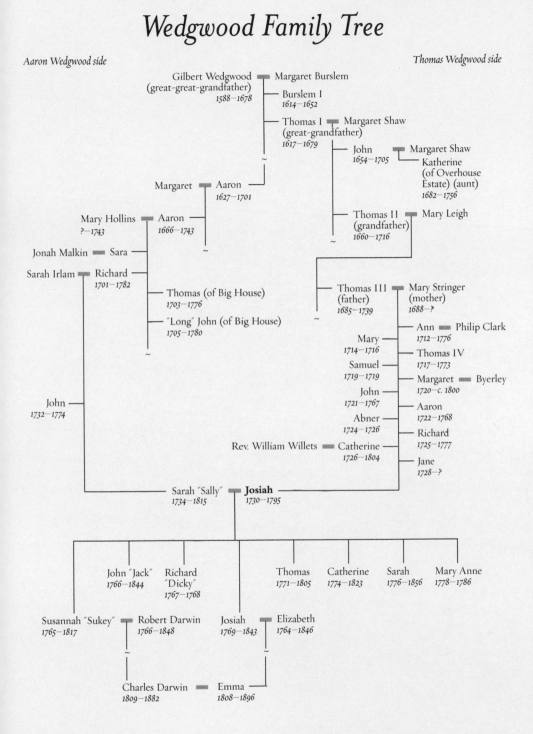

Aaron Wedgwood side

Thomas Wedgwood side

Gilbert Wedgwood ▬ Margaret Burslem
(great-great-grandfather)
1588–1678

Burslem I
1614–1652

Thomas I ▬ Margaret Shaw
(great-grandfather)
1617–1679

John ▬ Margaret Shaw
1654–1705
Katherine
(of Overhouse
Estate) (aunt)
1682–1756

Margaret ▬ Aaron
1627–1701

Mary Hollins ▬ Aaron
?–1743   *1666–1743*

Thomas II ▬ Mary Leigh
(grandfather)
1660–1716

Jonah Malkin ▬ Sara

Sarah Irlam ▬ Richard
1701–1782

Thomas (of Big House)
1703–1776

"Long" John (of Big House)
1705–1780

Thomas III ▬ Mary Stringer
(father)   (mother)
1685–1739   *1688–?*

Ann ▬ Philip Clark
1712–1776

Mary
1714–1716

Thomas IV
1717–1773

Samuel
1719–1719

Margaret ▬ Byerley
1720–c. 1800

John
1721–1767

Aaron
1722–1768

Abner
1724–1726

Richard
1725–1777

Rev. William Willets ▬ Catherine
1726–1804

Jane
1728–?

John
1732–1774

Sarah "Sally" ▬ **Josiah**
1734–1815   *1730–1795*

John "Jack"   Richard
1766–1844   "Dicky"
              1767–1768

Thomas   Catherine   Sarah   Mary Anne
1771–1805 *1774–1823* *1776–1856* *1778–1786*

Susannah "Sukey" ▬ Robert Darwin   Josiah ▬ Elizabeth
1765–1817   *1766–1848*   *1769–1843* *1764–1846*

Charles Darwin ▬ Emma
1809–1882   *1808–1896*

PART I
Rivalry
1730–1763

1

A Place for Thomas

A month before his ninth birthday, Josiah Wedgwood stood against brisk winds in the graveyard at his father's funeral. One imagines how the melancholic mood was a scourge to the family, becoming as familiar as the feeling of the soggy ground beneath their feet. Funerals were all too frequent. Mary had already stood over the graves of two young daughters and two sons. Now she and her eight children, the youngest being Josiah—or "plain Jos," as he referred to himself—once again mouthed somber hymns and thanked the preacher for his avuncular comforts. The father, Thomas, was fifty-two when he died. In 1739, this was an average life span for those fortunate enough to outlive adolescence, though Thomas considered himself above average in many respects. After all, he had come from a family that owned much of the land in the area of Burslem in Staffordshire, where generations of Wedgwoods, some more privileged than others, were born and laid to rest.

❧

The 1730s opened in peace and promise. Benjamin Franklin began the *Poor Richard's Almanack* in Philadelphia; John Kay patented his "flying shuttle," a landmark in textile mass production, leading some to dream of building large mills; Voltaire wrote *Lettres sur les Anglais*, championing democratic government; and David Hume developed his empiricist philosophy in his *Treatise on Human Nature*. The decade ended with trouble when England declared war with Spain, one of many wars that would haunt the rest of the century.

Such events seemed a world away from the small village of Burslem, which was tucked off a well-worn road that cut through the West Midlands, carrying travelers from the capital to the bustling port of Liverpool and the mercantile center of Manchester. It was here, in the northern part of Staffordshire, rippling with hills and valleys, often windswept and scraped by heavy, steely clouds, that a group of medieval Benedictine monks once attempted to tame the uncultivated meadowland, building an isolated monastery and clearing modest stretches of granges and crofts to cultivate wheat.

In the hundred-year period spanning the 1400s and 1500s, one man acquired much of the sloping ground of Burslem, and to declare his presence he adopted the place name, calling himself Thomas of Burslem. He had enough wealth, esteem, and land to guarantee that future sons would possess the honorable status of "gentleman" and "esquire." Eventually this privilege, benefitting directly from the expansive Burslem family properties, would pass on to Josiah Wedgwood's own family, due in part to the luck and in part to the shrewdness of great-great-grandfather Gilbert.

All Josiah's family knew how much Gilbert's life had changed their fortunes. Some listened to stories about him while harboring hidden feelings of resentment, others appreciated his good fortune. He was born in 1588, the youngest son of six, just a few miles north of Burslem. His father was a church administrator, his brothers were local husbandmen who lived in a single, small farmhouse. But Gilbert had energy and talent, and meant to make the most of the kind of life he was given; that life, he thought, revolved around pottery.

As a young man, Gilbert saw that most work available in the area was agrarian—rearing and shearing sheep, cultivating wheat, cattlekeeping and tanning. But one or two locals were working with clay. They dug the clay, and when the sun was out, dried it in "sun pans," forming it with their hands into coarse vessels for butter and beer—useful things for the farmers—and firing the pieces in a round, blackened oven, about as tall as a man, made of earth clod and fueled by coal from local pits. These men taught Gilbert that pottery required strength of both head and hand. One had to explore the dense woods and rocky ridges, prodding the "gouty, moorish, peaty black land" for raw material and then have the imagination to see finished forms in clumps of cold, wet earth. Gilbert was diligent, and he learned well. At that time, one could walk over a day in any direction and only meet a handful of potters—no more than about a hundred were working up and down the slopes of the region. But he became one of the best and was the first Wedgwood to be called a "Master Potter." Though there were never any guilds to enforce the status, this meant that he had learned all aspects of the craft, from collecting clay to firing it.

Not that it was a terribly technical craft. Gilbert's descendants would laugh about the crudeness of pottery and the fact that all it took back in his day was a shovel to dig the clay and coal and a simple oven. It was a romantic image—old Gilbert creating something from nothing. What made it even more romantic was that the rugged potter had married the beautiful and graceful Margaret Burslem.

This event perhaps chimed louder in the stories Josiah heard about great-great-grandfather Wedgwood than anything else. Her father was the wealthy Thomas Burslem, a descendant of the first Thomas of Burslem, and Burslem's principal landowner, having two large manor houses, hundreds of acres of meadowland, woods, and fields, and an income from farmer tenants and the family's new interests in coal mining. Margaret and Gilbert's first child, a son, was named Burslem Wedgwood, and Gilbert must have hoped that the union between these families would mean a new way of life for his children. In time, they inherited Overhouse Estate, and over 100 acres of land that formed the heart of Burslem passed into Wedgwood hands.

In a world that had barely moved beyond feudalism, where an extreme minority owned the majority of the land, the right of primogeniture was often ruthless in its execution; occasionally however, the weight of tradition shifts good fortune onto the shoulders of the unsuspecting. Gilbert and Margaret's eldest son, Burslem Wedgwood, had died young, and his inheritance passed to his younger brother, Thomas, Josiah's great-grandfather. Suddenly, at fifty-two years old, Thomas was the largest landowner in Burslem, a gentleman by title, who now lived in the prestigious manor house on the north hill overlooking Burslem and the shadowy green valleys of North Staffordshire. Along with the roomy timber-framed house, he had "barns, stables, outhouses, cowhouses, yards, folds, orchards, and gardens." He even had a "fish-pond and fish" out in front.

It was assumed that the eldest son would get first prize of the property, while the second son could be trained up in the family craft and prepared to make a living for himself. The other children, parents hoped, either married or at least found laboring jobs that would keep them fed. Before his unexpected inheritance, Thomas's place was therefore in his father's "pot-works." Gilbert sat his son down in his damp and dusty shed and trained him to work the clay—to feel it, to form it, and to fire it. In time, Thomas, dedicated as his father had been, became a master potter, taking on apprentices and journeymen, and expanding his craft. Gilbert taught his son not only the skills of the potter's craft but also the necessity of expansion—of always looking to acquire another acre, or an additional plot on which to build an additional workman's shed. The more ground one had, the more opportunity was at one's feet. The more elbow power one had to work it, the more potential there was for earning a better living. Thomas followed his father's instructions.

By the standards of seventeenth-century Burslem, Thomas was well accomplished by his fortieth birthday. He owned two small potteries—each with one mud-clod hovel and one gray stone "pot-oven"—one of which he inherited from his father. He soon bought a third.

Before moving into Overhouse Estate, Josiah's great-grandfather lived with his wife and father-in-law in the Churchyard House, a thatched country cottage at the bottom of a field on the south side of Burslem. A stone's throw between the little Burslem church toward the village and a rustic alehouse called the Crown and Mitre, the cottage sat in the oldest part of Burslem, the spot where monks had settled long ago. It was here that Thomas built himself some new "workhouses and pot ovens" with a "horse mill with the buildings thereto" on some uncultivated land he'd recently bought, adjacent to the house. This was now the master potter's main place of practice. Following tradition, Overhouse Estate would be destined for his eldest son, John; but his new, busy pottery was prepared as the inheritance for his second son, Thomas, who was here trained in the craft and, following in his father's footsteps, became "Master Potter." When this Thomas died, in 1717 the house and pottery near the church went to *his* eldest son, another Thomas. This was Josiah's father. The pottery that had been built two generations ago and passed from one Thomas to the next was known as the Churchyard Works.

The detached potwork in the somewhat removed southern fields of Burslem was built up over the sixty or so years from the time that great-grandfather Thomas had begun building it to the time Josiah's father died. Still the potters worked in dark hovels, old barns built alongside Church Lane, the winding dirt trail used by packing horses heading out from the village center and cows changing pastures. Josiah's father had three or four mud and stone sheds under thatched roofs. They were the "workhouses," whose clammy, gray, stained walls dripped with pungent condensation. Here mounds of unctuous rust-colored local clay, dug from a coal pit by a hired hand, were dumped into large square "slip-kilns," tin trays about ten inches deep, that were gently heated to steam off any water soaked within to give it the right feel before it was "beaten" and "turned." The other sheds he called "shops," and spent most of his waking hours stocking his "plank boards & shelves" with simple pots. The pieces were crooked and crude, even childlike to a later perspective. No one thought he was an especially gifted craftsman, even though he was a fourth-generation master potter. But competition to be the best was not a concern for him. To his mind, being a Wedgwood, a member of an established family with ties to the original Burslem, was more important than being identified as a master potter.

Thomas Wedgwood might have walked proudly around the village, his head high and his hand deep in his pocket, but in Josiah's own later assessment, his father—and his grandfather, for that matter—showed a profound lack of financial acuity, both wasting too much of their menial profits on unnecessarily high weekly expenses. They were uninspired and artistically lethargic. His father was satisfied with producing common black and mottled ware—simple in substance (no specially prepared clay) and design: baking dishes, jugs, porringers, and the like. The pieces were cheap and common; "he was apparently content to carry on the old fashioned peasant pottery," in the judgment of a later Wedgwood.

In the few years that Josiah's father and grandfather's trade overlapped—in the 1710s, before his grandfather's death in 1717, at fifty-seven—each mustered an annual trade worth a mere £36, from which everyday living expenses needed to be drawn. Later in life, long after brother Thomas pored over the account books, Josiah did some calculations of his own, casting a critical eye on those early days. He headed a piece of paper: "Men necessary to make an Oven of Black and Motled, per week, and other expenses." He added up what they paid for the clay, coals, couriers, packing straw, and labor: £4 5s per oven load. A crate of final goods was sometimes only worth £4, and often they could not get much more than one crate's worth into their one oven. Josiah calculated that the best any potworks in Burslem could do was to turn a profit of a mere six-teen shillings per week, and Josiah's father made even less. Regardless of the organization of the potworks and thus lack of innovation, Josiah still thought that with few minor adjustments his father or grandfather could have yielded a bit more profit, if even another five or six shillings a week—enough for one man's weekly wages. "The Wear and Tear," for instance, "and some other things, are rated too high," Josiah thought. The expenses could have been tightened up, "4l per Oven-full is thought to be suffi-cient, or more than sufficient, for the Black and Motled works of the largest kind." This was hardly the model of a successful business, or the figures that would allow one to be thought of as a gentleman. In fact, his father's income approximated the annual interest accrued from a landed gentleman's average income of £2,000 ($200,000) per annum; it was even well short of a country squire's salary at around £300 ($30,000) a year.

But day after day Thomas returned to the dusty workshops, where all Josiah's brothers and sisters spent long, laborious hours. The boys would pull leather straps to turn lathes for forming the contours of the clay and the girls dipped the pieces in glaze and fit handles onto mugs. The center-piece to one shed was Thomas's "throwing" wheel and rough, water-stained oak modeling tables. Everything, including the handles of the carving tools, was coated with a fine film of dark dried clay, like blood-stains.

The work that required the most muscle was performed just outside the sheds and across the mud yard, by horses turning a wooden "pug mill." Every other day, Josiah's brothers carried loads of clay from the slip kiln in the workshop to the mouth of the pug, an insatiable maw that swallowed up each shovelful, while fierce metal blades attached to a revolving shaft turned by the horses gnawed away at the clay, removing any air bubbles, and forcing it through a tube where the clay emerged as a condensed log, ready to be taken to the thrower's wheel. In the other corner of the yard, adjacent to the buildings and the coal fold, largely blocking any southern view of neighboring pastures, were the large brick ovens, the icons of the cottage industry that kept Josiah's family fed and clothed.

A footpath leading through a wooden gate embedded in the furze hedges on the north side of the potworks led the family to Burslem church, St. John's, where, in 1739, Josiah and his family stood outside, huddled around Thomas's freshly dug grave. Nearby were the gravestones of grandfather Thomas and great-grandfather Thomas. They had all been master potters, and they had all labored at and owned the adjacent potworks. But Josiah, the youngest son, was still too young even to begin working there. And none of those buildings behind him—now the largest pottery in Burslem—was ever bound to be his. The Churchyard Work had been passed along to Thomas, Josiah's eldest brother.

2

A Will and a Prayer

The winter that drifted into Burslem in 1739 was fierce. According to the weather logs, the freezing temperatures across England plummeted to depths never previously reached (−24°C in some parts by January 1740), setting a record that would not be surpassed for another two hundred years. Far away, in the "New World," where it was always hot according to seamen's stories, a war was being fought between England and Spain. It was a war of commercial rivalry, declared only a couple of months earlier after accusations that the English were smuggling goods and slaves, violating a twenty-year-old trade agreement. This was one of many wars that would come increasingly to affect the livelihoods of Burslem craftsmen and merchants. But right now, the wider world of political and commercial struggles was as far away from their minds as coconuts. The only thing that mattered to those in Burslem was the terrible winter that was gradually causing a Europe-wide famine.

Josiah and his family were forced to sit out the winter, huddled together under the frosty thatched roof of Churchyard House, where the curate had once lived. It was built along the bridleway next to the new potworks, and had been the Wedgwood family home since great-grandfather Thomas received it, along with 50 acres of meadow and pasture deemed to be "of great yearly value," as part of his wife Margaret's dowry in 1653. The timber-and-mortar–framed house, with two levels, was simple, unassuming, and "convenient"—"comfortable" was not a word that ever applied to common country cottages like this.

Since the days soon after great-grandfather Thomas moved in with his wife and father-in-law, Churchyard House was forever crowded with children. Josiah's older brothers and sisters were born while their aunts and uncles—their father's youngest siblings—were still growing up at the house. When Josiah was born here, in the shadows of the Elizabethan stone tower of St. John's Church, six, if not all seven, of his three sisters and four brothers were still living together. When their father died nine years later, his wife Mary and six of her children were still living in the house. Her eldest, Thomas, was twenty-three.

At night, Mary, Josiah's thirteen-year-old sister Catherine, and nineteen-year-old sister Margaret would slide the bed warmers under the blankets on the feather beds in both bedchambers—one for them, the other for the four boys. Still, the family awoke stiff and wheezing from the "intolerable smoke and stink" that lingered in the rooms when the night candles snuffed themselves out.

Downstairs, the largest room in the house was the kitchen. Six wooden chairs circled a large oak table, a walnut chest of drawers sat against the wall, cleavers and hammers hung on the walls, and "china" cups, saucers, and ale glasses were stacked on open shelves. The kitchen was for sitting, talking, and eating. Cooking went on in the "backhouse," a small earth shed out the back door.

During many evenings following his father's death, Thomas sat in his leather armchair in the kitchen in glacial silence, contemplating the weight of his new responsibilities. His life as head of the household and owner of the potworks was, he unhappily discovered, very difficult.

The days were long and dark. Josiah and his fourteen-year-old brother Richard made twice as many trips as usual to the coal fold next to the house, needing to feed the enormous open fireplace that dominated one whole wall of the kitchen. The crunch of each shovel must have rung like coins in Thomas's ears. Usually each delivery of coal, about 10s worth a week, was split between the workhouses and the home hearth, but not at the moment. Working life had practically numbed to a halt, and all the family could do was sit around the high, deep inglenook, which wafted waves of warm air around the ground floor and through the upstairs floorboards. It was frustratingly inefficient, not least because of gaps around the doors and windows.

Thomas was not a man to curse the ground, not when it yielded the raw materials for his family's own survival, but with the difficult turn of season and circumstances, it would be remarkable if he did not question

God's benevolence. Since the time when Gilbert first started the family on its endeavor as potters, Staffordshire had become a county as notable for its unique geology as for the common earthenware that it increasingly produced. Beneath Burslem lay "the vein of that clay for which this country is so famous," remarked a visitor in 1750. Famous was, perhaps, an overly generous characterization, but it was true that bricks, tiles, teapots, snuff boxes, and butter cups were delivered from here to places all around the country. "They bake 'em in kilns built in the shape of a cone which makes a very pretty appearance, there being a great number of them" in the area, the visitor thought. What the old miners called "coal measure," which formed a subterranean seam contiguous to the clay, fueled the kilns and ovens. These doubly rewarding natural resources supported the cultivation of the potter's craft.

Compared to the cost of the clay, coal was expensive—about twice as much. Each pannier of coal would cost about 3 pence on delivery ($3 today), but that was consumed cooking the day's meals. Heating the house for any lengthy duration, and providing the fuel for one burning of a kiln, could cost up to £1 ($100)—a hard week's earning for a man who dug the coal and clay from the ground.

Now the generous earth was frozen solid. The well next to the churchyard along with the natural spring that supplied it would not flow again for months. The eaves of the empty workhouses glittered with icicles. It was too difficult to shift the clay. The coal that was chiseled from local mines was consumed without yielding wares for the business, chalking up expenses without income. Thomas pored over the family account books, piecing together a history of evaporating finances. The death of his father and the abominable weather weighed on his mind, but more worrying in the long term was the realization that the potworks had never yielded much return while under his father's management.

❦

Burslem had not been a crowded place until recently; only a few hundred people living in cottages clustered along the slippery lanes surrounding the maypole. Lately, however, a stream of farm laborers into the area had rapidly turned this small village into a town. Suddenly there were four smithies, two butcher's shops, a joiner's, a cobbler's, a barber's, and a bakehouse. Most conspicuous was the smoke billowing from the twenty-three family potworks scattered about the hill and the mammoth "shord piles" where broken pieces of imperfect pottery were dumped. The loudest buildings were the nineteen alehouses packed mainly with men who worked in the potteries. Many were itinerant laborers and squatters who searched for butts of arable land and ended up cobbling together a living by digging for supplies of clay and working nearby mines.

When conditions were not so impossibly arctic, men dug holes all around Burslem. Sometimes they went to the meadows or wasteland, but more often they found it easier to edge away at a lane, since the ground was already worn and broken (hence the origin of the term "pothole"). People were liberally granted a "right" to do this, on very easy terms—a small rent charge or "fine"—which invited them to dig for clay, coal, and ironstone in such a manner. The digging created a curious sight, but travelers who cursed the treacherous paths quickly picked up on its benefits. Robert Plot, a passing naturalist and keeper of Oxford's Ashmolean Museum, who was researching a book on the "Natural History" of Staffordshire in the late 1680s, observed that "the greatest pottery they have in this county is carried on in Burslem, where for making their several sorts of pots they have as many different sorts of clay which they dig round about the town all within half a mile's distance."

Digging did not require any skill, only a shovel and a pannier for carrying the clay to the potter, who would pay three or four shillings per load. Hired hands who worked *within* the pottery demanded higher wages—labor costs were the major expense for master potters—since their jobs required a degree of training. For about seven shillings a week, peasants would grind flint, stock the kilns, and shovel coal. Artisans performed more skilled aspects of the craft, monitoring kiln temperature, mixing chemicals in the clay, and operating lathes; throwers worked the wheel, earning up to twelve shillings a week, along with modelers, moldmakers, and other apprenticed positions. "Packers"—often the potter's wife or daughter—loaded the goods in oak boxes and gave them to a constant line of men for delivery. To Plot's amazement, these "poor *Cratemen*" would then strap on a pair of loaded pistols and "carry them on their *backs* all over the *Countrey*, to whome they reckon them by the piece," earning perhaps five or six shillings each week of their absence.

Josiah was forever disturbed by the laborers' brutal conditions. Contemplating what life had been like when his father was in his prime, raising the family and running his potworks, he talked to older potters and created a vivid picture in his mind, jotting notes on a piece of paper. The image was not very attractive—all muddied bodies and blackened hands. There was "only one horse and one mule kept" in the village, he wrote; "No Carts scarcely in the Country." The roads, of course, were too rough, pitted, and mired for them to work anyway. "Coals carried upon Men's Backs." It was the only way. Josiah was certainly not alone in thinking that the conditions were "mean and poor."

By the time of his father's death, there were more beasts of burden around, more laborers camped in lumpy tenements, and more hollows scored into the earth. When dusk crept into the valley telling everyone it was time to quit work, tired patrons piled into the Jolly Potters, the Turk's Head, the Red Lyon, among all the other pubs where "they make an excellent quick sort of drink"—noted a thirsty Robert Plot—discouragingly called "Dredge Malt," a brew of oats and barley. "Meety noice and verry strung" was the drink, written the way the Burslem accent was spoken ("mighty nice and very strong"). As their pennies dwindled and more beer was drunk, the songs—usually ending with the slurred cheer "Up the Potter!"—got louder and brawls more frequent. The person who characterized the laborers' living conditions as "mean and poor" thought no more highly of their behavior, declaring that "the manners of the inhabitants were not superior to their habitations; and their pleasures and amusements at their wakes and holidays were gross and brutal." During rowdy seasonal festivals, the Burslem "wakes," the workers were entertained by mountebanks, and "bull and bear-baiting, as well as cock-throwing, were in high favor."

John Tellwright and "Ralphy" Leigh were two local potters who grew up with Josiah. Much later in life, the two met up at the Turk's Head with a local historian who asked them to reminisce about their youth. They downed a few jars of gin "whoile we tawken oud matters o'er," said John, in his strong Burslem accent. "Coom, sup it Rafy. Ere's to thee." The account of their remarkable conversation is worth quoting.

> "If you remember Ralph, those old potters couldn't find two ha'pennies to rub together to make a start in their trades," said Tellwright.
> "Yes, that's very true," remembered Ralph. "Although they pretended they were the best and could make the best, the result was that in the end they achieved nothing. And even before they could begin they were beaten by their bad habits."

"The old master potter was a companionable man," Tellwright added. "Very much one of the boys and part of the crew—men who liked a good time."

"They were that, Mr Tellwright. Just as soon as they had placed the ware in the ovens, off they'd go and make straight for ye alehouse on Swan Bank. And there they'd drink n' drink 'til the ware would be ready to be taken out, or so they thought, relying on guesswork and the state of intoxication they found themselves in. The master potters always took their laborers with them to the alehouse, and when they were all half drunk, many a row and fight would break out, each man taking his turn in the arena, arguing over whose turn it was to pay. And when they eventually returned to their oven with sore heads, all their pots would be spoiled."

While Josiah's father was not a gifted potter and possessed no innate talents for managing his small family trade, he would never tolerate the wasted expense of a full kiln's yield owing to drunken irresponsibility. He believed in strict codes of conduct, and the prominent Puritanical values that he was raised with were passed on to his children. Josiah himself was irritated by the stench of ale reeking from steamy pubs, the gambling scrums, and the evening idleness of those who never gave a minute's thought to the progress of the potter's craft. For many difficult years when Josiah himself was trying to enter the trade he would hang his head and lament of how he was "teazed of my life with dilatory, drunken, Idle, worthless workmen."

Josiah was not the first to express this sentiment, of course. He had already heard it repeated by his father and then his brother, both of whom elaborated on the differences between respectable craftsmen and unprincipled hired hands. Skilled craftsmen—those who created the wares rather than merely dug for the raw material—were taught to take pride in their responsibilities. A boy hoping to enter the trade would sign an elaborate and formal parchment agreement that laid down the rules of his apprenticeship, committing him to "behave and demean himself toward his said master" and that "at Cards, Dice, or any other unlawfull Games he shall not Play; Taverns or Ale Houses he shall not haunt or frequent; Fornication he shall not Commit, Matrimony he shall not Contract . . ." He was to enter a new social world and remain separate from the sphere of vice that lingered in the muddy streets and blasphemous public houses.

Josiah's father was especially concerned to enforce an air of respectability amongst his immediate family, conscientious as he was about the yoke of gentility that bound together his patriarchal ancestors. He, of course, was no gentleman, nor was Josiah's brother. But it was in their blood, even if the material wealth passed over them. Besides, Josiah's grandfather *was* a gentleman, as well as churchwarden responsible for supplying bread and wine for midsummer parties, buying new Bibles, and tending the pulpit. This legacy mattered to Josiah's father. It affected the way he saw himself in Burslem. He wanted so desperately to be better than he was, to be treated like a gentleman as had his own father and not merely as a struggling master potter. He even devised his own display of noblesse oblige, laying out an extraordinary £7 to purchase a seat in the front pew of the parish church so that his neighbors and kinsmen sitting behind him would consider him "one of the gentry of the village."

Josiah had never met his grandfather—he was born too late—and he did not look at his father the way the previous generation had looked upon his grandfather. But if there was one thing that Josiah learned in his youth besides Puritan probity, it was that he inhabited a world very different not only from the one he saw on the streets but from that of his relatives up the hill at Overhouse Estate. The Wedgwoods at the top of the hill were distinguished by wealth from the Wedgwoods at the bottom of the hill, and the relations between them were beginning to be tenser than ever.

The complaints about the deleterious habits of the "lads" in the alehouses were not merely expressions of concern about lack of discipline creating difficulties for one's business. During particularly trying times, like the bleak winter that began in late 1739, these habits weakened the village as a whole. Throughout January and February, no one moved in or out of Burslem—the roads were impassable—and no one worked. It did not take long before all those "dilatory, drunken" men ran out of pennies and went hungry.

The village had in the past relieved its poor through its own parish vestry, distributing up to one shilling a week per pauper for food from a fund raised by charitable donations and levies on land. About one or two dozen people had been registered to receive help in this way at any given time over the last few decades; but when Burslem thawed out in April 1740, the destitute who survived emerged in unprecedented numbers—more than could be looked after with traditional poor relief. As trade began to creep forward again, the churchwarden and overseers devised a new system that would at once deter people from descending into bad habits and introduce discipline to that element of the community. Their first parish "poorhouse" for paupers opened in 1741. This "foul ward" for the haggard and indifferent was a grim element on a hill amongst the weary and distressed potworkers.

The poor harvests of 1740 kept the potters praying in the parish for divine intervention, and Josiah's brother Thomas at the empty kitchen table pondering the accounts. The 50 acres of land said to be "of great yearly value" that came with the Churchyard House and Works were not yielding the amount needed for the family's survival. That plot of land, "a croft or two of hay, one or more of oats and barley, and a cow, or a few sheep, grazing on the adjacent waste," usually offered a few extra bushels of food they could sell, along with a bit of extra beef and some moorland mutton for a few extra shillings. But in the tough seasons of 1739 and 1740, they wouldn't be selling anything for much money; a bushel of wheat was going for 4s, a calf for about 8s, and a pound of beef for a mere 2d. Even though their small-scale farming was supplemented by a minor income from renting an adjacent field and a tenement—something a few other master potters managed to do as well, and another mark of difference between the growing "employing class" and the hired hands—it did not add up to much. Worse yet, the debt father Thomas left behind was growing and brother Thomas was struggling to think of ways to improve business.

Securing reliable cash flow was never going to be easy. In 1740, the arrangement between the pottes and the "cratemen" who carried the wares to the customer took no invoice of goods with them, and upon returning "they rendered no account of sales effected, or of the expenses of their journeys, but merely emptied their pockets of what money was left." "Money" was often in the form of trade tokens representing the value of halfpennies and farthings—small change was scarce. More often, exchanges were made on trust, the potter paying the courier his wages of five or six shillings a week after his journey and reported sales, the money from which would only later, once the account was large enough, be collected. Seeing the implications of the system in his brother's trade, Josiah knew this was an appalling way to conduct business.

However, it was clear to Thomas that pieces of pottery were not enough to pay off his father's debt and provide for his family's future in the manner that would meet his father's wishes. Father Thomas's last will and testament stated that the property he inherited was to be used "in the bringing up of my younger children, and in raising the sum of £120, which I hereby charge my Real Estate with. And my will is that the said sum be equally divided amongst my six younger children, viz., Margaret, John, Aaron, Richard, Katherine [*sic*], and Josiah; and that in paying the said sums, the elder shall still be preferred to the younger." For Josiah and his brothers and sisters, £20 would have been ideal, but, Thomas was unable to raise the money to pay the legacies. He did not know how he was going to afford to "bring up the younger children," even without laying aside their inheritance. His father had already bound himself for the sum of £50 to his aunt Margaret in order to raise money to pay off previous debts in 1727, and the interest on that was still being collected. The will said that the executors had the power to mortgage the estate to raise money, but it was already mortgaged to the hilt. There were only dead ends.

Josiah knew times were tough, but he could not have known the extent of it. His mother, the daughter of a Unitarian minister from Newcastle, not only did her best to protect him from the harsh conditions that were at their door, she did what she could to help him prepare for a world where everyone was "preferred to the younger." As she did with her other children, she helped him learn to read and write, looking over his shoulder while he diligently practiced his script, repeating his signature to perfection. Josiah learned well, but however committed either he or his mother was to his education, it would soon move abruptly from the hearth to the workshop. Thomas needed the child's labor.

3
"Creators of Fortune and Fame"

Despite his family's best efforts, Josiah's muscles were forced to develop faster than his mind—that was the normal path followed by boys and girls born to a trade. Both his great-grandfather and his great-grandmother, formerly of Overhouse Estate, had tried their best to enrich the lives of the next generation, each setting aside legacies earning "interest therein determined and my said children educated," a firm provision distinguishing their wills from any other in Burslem at the time. Obediently but warmly acknowledging the "worldly and outward estate it hath pleased God out of his superabundant goodness to bestow upon me," great-grandfather and great-grandmother passed down the sentiments of duty, discipline, and determined improvement expressed by this Protestant ethic to Josiah's day, even though their financial legacies had grown too thin to support the weight of such pledges.

To be sure, Josiah's parents tried as hard as they could, through bonds and mortgages. Seven-year-old Josiah even followed in the footsteps of his elder siblings and one or two cousins and attended lessons at the school in Newcastle-under-Lyme. Burslem wouldn't have its own "English Charity Schoole" until 1749, and even then, "two parts of the children out of three are put to work without any learning." According to his teacher, Thomas Blunt, Josiah was "a fair arithmetician & master of Capital hand." Josiah's schooling was not to last, but at least he had had the benefit of learning the basics.

Early each morning Josiah began his routine by taking a thin brass wire and slicing off chunks of leathery clay from the weathering mound and carrying them on his shoulder into the workhouse. He lifted lumps the size of his head up high and whacked them down as hard as he could on to the bench. "Blunging" the clay in this way softened it, preparing it to be dried and sifted to remove clumps of dirt and pebbles. Next he brought it to a "beating board," where he "beat it till it be well mixed," then took it to "the waging board" where he would "wage it, i.e., knead or mould it like bread." "Waging," or "wedging," the clay removed air pockets, helping to improve its texture and malleability.

It was arduous physical work, strengthening his shoulder and back muscles while toughening the skin on his hands that were soon stained dirty red from working the iron-rich local clay. In the evenings, Josiah and his brother Richard emerged from the gritty workhouse hungry and exhausted after a twelve-hour day—six days a week in the summer. Rising food prices meant less real sustenance and yet demanded more intense work in the effort to survive. It was a vicious circle, and Josiah's whole family struggled to reach subsistence level.

Josiah's proud father would have been devastated to witness the family's struggles, though he knew before he died that he had not lived up to his own dreams. Now, the court magistrates were keeping a watchful eye on the family. Josiah's mother, Mary, had already traveled to Lichfield to stand before the bench in her neatest clothes and receive instructions about how to handle her late husband's struggling estate. She was to "administer all the goods, chattels, credits of the said deceased," they said. "And we require you to make a true inventory of all and singular the personal estate of the said deceased and a true account of your said administration and to exhibit the same into the registry."

Probate inventories of all the deceased's possessions were not unusual, but this particular inventory was to be prepared with an eye to carving up and selling things off to service debts owed. The gravity of the situation was made clear when two of father Thomas's appointed executors, Mary's brother Samuel and her nephew John Wedgwood, also stood before the magistrates and "judiciously renounced their right to the probate of the said will." They did not want to be involved with a bankrupt estate and one they knew could not pay the legacies.

Neither meant offense by renouncing their executorships—it was, indeed, "judicial" and prudent, on their behalf. Mary's brother was a physician in nearby Newcastle, with his own career obligations to worry about, and preferred not to be held responsible for his brother-in-law's estate, while John Wedgwood was preoccupied with his own pottery business. But of the two, it was John Wedgwood's decision to renounce his executorship that pained Josiah's brother the most.

"Long John," as he was called, on account of his lanky, gaunt stature—he was easily spotted walking through town a head above the men's dirty leather caps and the women's rustic shawls—was Josiah's cousin. He was thirty-five years old, about ten years senior to Thomas, and a potter. Long John and his older brother, another Thomas, were inseparable. They lived together, worked together, ate together, and planned their future together, which for most of their lives would have nothing to do with courting women or marrying. The brothers focused purely on becoming better potters than their father Aaron—an ambitious order. Unlike his cousin (Josiah's father), Aaron was a quality potter, who set high standards for the craft, and he trained his sons well since he knew training was the most important thing he had to offer. He was determined not to see his own sons left behind in a world that favored the eldest brother.

Cousins Long John and Thomas came from the side of the Wedgwood family that, stretching back to the time of Gilbert, had not inherited anything substantial by way of Burslem land and wealth. What they had was a talent for their business carefully cultivated out of a burning desire to create their own sense of worth.

Long John's success made his decision not to become involved with his uncle Thomas's ailing estate all the more delicate. Josiah's brother knew how much the community admired his cousins' enterprise and how much pride they took in their self-made accomplishment: even in the difficult year of 1740 they were still aggressively expanding. They "left their father's service, to commence business for themselves in Burslem," the local historian Simeon Shaw was told, relaying a sense of the respect they marshaled in town. "As there was not then an instance of any Master Potter, who did not most diligently apply himself to some branch of the business, usually throwing or firing, their well-known industry, experience, and ingenuity warranted the expectation of a portion of Success." This was a modest appraisal. Their "portion of Success" was the lion's share, and Josiah's family was all too aware of it.

The cousins might have once looked up the hill to Overhouse Estate envious of the family fortune that passed to the other side of the Wedgwood family, but they soon walked around town with the kind of prestige that eluded Josiah's father and brother. For two branches of a family that lived within a mile of each other, the relationship remained formal. There had been two instances of marriage between cousins from each side—two of Josiah's aunts from his father's side had married two of Aaron Wedgwood's most educated and accomplished boys, Dr. Thomas the younger and Richard, a master potter who died young. But now relations were cool.

Perhaps they could have worked together, tackled the problem of debt and a troubled trade through a family arrangement—it was the sort of solution commonly struck within families across England. But along with everything else, Thomas had inherited stubbornness from his father, and preferred to do things without their help. Long John and cousin Thomas likely did not give it much thought in 1740. They had new premises they purchased from an aunt of theirs for £280 ($28,000 today), and a new account book with crisp pages where they envisioned a profitable future.

The success of Josiah's cousins was not entirely due to their industry, however, but was tied to two mysterious Dutchmen who had moved to Burslem at the turn of the eighteenth century. The role that chance, deception, and innovation played in creating Long John and cousin Thomas's successful business would prove a valuable lesson to Josiah.

❧

When the two Dutch entrepreneurs first arrived in London they felt a vague sense of familiarity, even in a bustling city three times the size of Amsterdam. The newly crowned monarchs, William III and Mary II, were, of course, familiar—not least since William was the former Stadtholder of Holland. But John Philip Elers and his brother David also had family connections in London—an uncle who was a merchant involved with the China importing trade, and their father, who sold decorated glass and "East Indian rareities." London was a fast-growing, innovative city, with promising commercial prospects. Enticed by the example of their father and his brother, John Philip and David decided to try their luck, and by 1688 were managing their own silversmiths shop.

Amongst all that was going on, one thing allowed the foreigners to feel right at home: the fact that Londoners loved their new coffeehouses. Whether it was Miles' in Westminster or the Turk's Head down the road in the Strand, coffeehouses had become the place where all the wits and literati from Pepys to Pope would drink and debate. The Dutch brothers were intrigued by a new debate that emerged amongst arguments over natural philosophy, constitutional principles, and the future of the monarchy: it was whether or not this new drink called "tay, alias tee" was a good thing for the British people.

It seemed that no one was quite sure what to do with tea—sometimes the Englishmen would boil the leaves in water for a period before laying them on a wooden plate, buttering them, and eating them with knife and fork. Samuel Pepys had once left the Turk's Head for "Home—and there find my wife drinking of tee, a drink which Mr. Pelling, the Potticary, tells her is good for her cold and defluxions."

Whether or not it had medicinal qualities was partly the issue. Skeptics thought that, at up to £10 per pound, it was more likely that such ideas were promoted by nostrummongers wanting to cash in. They could point to a circular distributed by the London merchant Thomas Galway that seemed to promise just too much. "The drink is declared to be most wholesome, preserving in perfect health until extreme old age," Galway announced. Some nations, he added, known for their "knowledge and wisdom, do frequently sell it among themselves for twice its weight in silver," but his customers were encouraged to visit his place in Exchange Alley where they could get it for a bargain, by comparison. That was the entrepreneurial spirit that the Elers brothers applauded, yet public skepticism had still to be quelled. Even in about 1680 the London market for tea was glutted when the East India Company delivered just under 5,000 pounds of the leaf.

However, by the end of the decade, just as the Elers brothers were settling in their new home, the drink was finally beginning to catch on, and the Dutchmen wondered what all the fuss was about. After all, their homeland had introduced Europe to tea drinking and their Dutch compatriot Cornelis Bontekoe was even encouraging people to drink up to two hundred cups of tea a day "for health."

But they spotted something intriguing in the behavior of the tea drinkers, mainly wealthy women, who found the new tea shops a refreshing alternative to the men's coffeehouses and the "base, black, thick, nasty, bitter, stinking, nauseous Puddle Water." The Elers brothers watched women in silk camlets and satin laces sipping ample amounts of the "China Drink," while stroking with admiration the fine rose-colored "tee pots" that were also a new import from the East India Company. They were elegant: delicate, yet tough, with a smooth, unglazed satin finish.

The Elers brothers were amused by the site of such fixed admiration for the Chinese pot. In Holland—which was much more "modern" than England at the time—not only was drinking tea more common, but a number of manufactories had been established for decades to produce their own imitations of the teapot.

But the English market was lagging behind in all areas of the production of fine pottery. London dealers frequently complained about their inability to supply a growing market, especially in what they called "Dutch jugs," "stone bottles," and "China ware." "The potters made dishes and painted wares," explained one retailer in ceramic tiles to a 1673 committee for "encouraging manufactures in England," "but not the sixth part of what the shopkeepers vend." What the English potters did produce "was not so good as what came from Holland," and worse still, it was "double the price of what the Dutch made." There were even stories circulating of merchants going to Holland "to bring a person well skilled in that art" back to England for work. This why Uncle John Elers moved to London.

Nor were John Philip and his brother David going to let an opportunity like this pass them by. They were confident that they could improve on the rough brown earthenware mugs commonly used to serve ale or coffee. To do so, however, they needed some practical information about available raw materials and potworks and they needed to meet people who set themselves the job of improving the technical aspects of pottery. No one suited their needs better than John Dwight and his philosophically minded friends, who were involved with the recently established Royal Society, a "society of Experimenters in a Romantick Model."

John Dwight was an Oxford-educated lawyer who had acquired a passion for experimental chemistry from his tutor Robert Boyle, a regular attendee of the meetings at the Royal Society where small groups of gentlemen discussed the findings of their private philosophical investigations. Dwight's own experimental findings had recently attracted considerable attention, for he boastfully announced that he had discovered "the misterie of the stone ware" that was generating so much interest in London tea shops, and he was able to manufacture "an opacous redd and darke coloured Porcellane" in imitation of the Chinese pots. Thinking that this was going to make him a fortune, he took out two patents to protect his innovations.

For a couple of experimentally minded Dutch entrepreneurs (rumor had spread that they once trained with the eminent chemist Johann

Becher, who spent some years in the Netherlands working on a scheme to recover gold from silver by means of sea sand), Dwight was exactly the person they needed to meet, or at least, whose secrets they needed to steal. They considered themselves fortunate, therefore, when they had the chance to listen to Dwight discuss his chemical experiments as guests at a meeting of the Royal Society. Having absorbed information about different kinds of clay found locally around Britain, and about his technique for rendering it "opacous," the brothers suddenly disappeared. They had packed their belongings and headed for Staffordshire.

Since most Staffordshire potters made pots just where their fathers made them before, few of them realized that this particular area of England contained such rare deposits of clay. Informed travelers, however, were aware it was a special spot of earth, even if they cared not to theorize about the reasons why. Later, "natural historians" (historians of nature) would explain that the site of the potteries was prepared by nature for the staple they produced. God had provided the ground for their way of life. Geologists then told how epochs of land submergence and elevation had worn down the grit and limestone rocks to form clay, while the coal and ironstone seams that appeared in strata in hillsides mixed with the presence of different ores and minerals, particularly iron oxide, to render a unique composition and color to the clays. The red clays so striking within the Staffordshire landscape came from a geological formation now called the Etruria Formation that lies immediately above the coal measures. It is a formation unique to the English Midlands, which makes the clay there equally unique.

When the Elers brothers moved into Dimsdale Hall some time around 1698 and rented a potwork a mile away at Bradwell Wood that sat on a seam of rich, red clay, the potters in nearby Burslem were instantly intrigued. Both Dimsdale and Bradwell Wood were secluded, well off any regularly used road, and just within squinting distance of Burslem's hilltop. Day after day, curious eyes caught glimpses of the strangers' busy activities; they erected new kilns, spent hours on their land digging the clay, then disappeared into their workshop, always keeping to themselves. Brazen visitors to Bradwell, peering over shoulders hoping for a glimpse into their hideaway, were politely encouraged to leave.

It was "their extreme precaution to keep secret their processes," wrote Simeon Shaw, recording what people had said about their new rivals, "and jealousy lest they might be accidentally witnessed by any purchaser of their wares." The ale-fueled gossip about the Elers brothers' "precautions" grew extravagant. They had manufactured clay pipes which they ran underground from Dimsdale to the workhouses in Bradwell "to intimate the approach of persons supposed to be intruders," it was said. When they needed hired hands as extra labor, they resorted to "employing an idiot to turn the thrower's wheel, and the most ignorant and stupid workmen to perform laborious operations, and by locking up these persons while at work, and strictly examining each prior to quitting the manufactory at night, they protected their secrets." But soon their isolation was interrupted.

One day Burslem awoke to discover a soaring, dirty stain on the horizon. The sky above Bradwell Wood was thick with voluminous smoke. "The people of Burslem were then very much surprised with the smoke," Josiah was later told by one of the eyewitnesses, "and ran in great numbers to see what was the matter." As they approached, they observed that it was caused by the kilns, erupting like Vesuvius, exhaling billows of black, sooty, noxious fumes. The Elers brothers were on ladders, pouring buckets of salt from mounds into "feeding holes" built high into the sides of the tall bottleneck ovens. The salt quickly vitrified in the red-hot interior, coating the wares with what they called a "salt-glaze." The like had never been seen before.

The wares that emerged from the slowly cooling kiln were striking. The Elers brothers had produced high-quality, finely shaped white pitchers and dinner plates. From another kiln emerged something even more outstanding. They had successfully manufactured smooth, unglazed, matt-red colored teapots, remarkably similar to the imported Yi-Hsing teapots so popular in London, where their new products were shipped to be sold in their store at Poultney in Cheapside. Unbeknownst to anyone around Burslem other than the Elers brothers, the red wares were also remarkably similar to Dwight's "opacous red and darke coloured Porcel-lane."

Dwight was outraged when a correspondent wrote in to the Royal Society reporting on some new pottery he had just come across, made from a "soft oar like Clay." "I have this to add," the correspondent wrote; the clay "is as good, if not better, than that which is brought from the East Indies. Witness the Tea-Pots now to be sold at the Potters in the Poultney in Cheapside, which not only for Art, but for beautiful color, too are far beyond any we have from China. These are made of the English red clay in Staffordshire, as I take it, by two Dutch-men incomparable Artists."

How could it be, Dwight groaned, that two Dutchmen were celebrated in the pages of a journal published by the very society to which he had announced his discovery as a rival to the Chinese teapots? The Elers brothers, with their own interests in chemistry, might have received an invitation to one of the meetings and pried information from the members. More likely, they must have bribed his workman, John Chandler, for the secrets.

Dwight immediately filed a lawsuit, seeking "to hinder and restrayne them from making, practicing, imitateing, counterfeiting, and vending of the severall wares and Manufactures in the plaintiffs bill." But it was too late.

It appeared that the "idiot" employed by the Elers brothers in their covert workshop in Staffordshire had duped them: with deceptively vacuous eyes he had carefully observed all their actions, and each night set to work imitating their methods. Soon, through a string of spying and strategic collaboration to procure the precious red clay, similar wares were being produced by other Burslem potters, most prominently Aaron Wedgwood, Father of Long John and cousin Thomas.

꙳

The story that Josiah had heard offered many salient points to a young potter. It revealed that the "art and mystery" of experimental chemistry had been producing remarkable results, and that a potter benefits most from learning skills beyond those traditionally associated with his craft. It also showed how through espionage rivaling that of the Elers brothers, Josiah's cousins had profited from stealing secrets. Indeed, a few months after his original lawsuit, Dwight added Aaron Wedgwood and his two sons' names to the suit, citing their "unjust and injurious practises," assuming that they had also "insinuated themselves into the acquaintance of the said John Chandler and enticed him to instruct them and to enter into partnership together . . ." Dwight was onto a losing battle—he managed to reach an agreement with the Elers brothers but his patents were soon to expire, and the courts favored commercial competition over secretive monopolies.

The Elers' reign was to fare no better. They were at Bradwell Wood for under a decade before they had consumed all the accessible rusty clay on their plot of land and the increased competition from the Burslem potters, particularly the Wedgwoods, drove them out of business ("The Fulhamites can come and go, but Wedgwoods will go on forever," the family allegedly declared, alluding to Dwight, who was from Fulham, and his rivals). By the time Aaron Wedgwood died, in 1701, the Elers brothers had already disappeared as mysteriously as they had arrived. "Where they went he knoweth not," wrote Josiah, who posed the question to the old potter who relayed the story.

When Long John and cousin Thomas entered the family trade in the 1720s, their father Aaron was aggressively expanding, moving to new premises, building new kilns, and boldly seeking out that lucrative London market. He worked non-stop imitating and trying to improve the Elers brothers' "Red China Ware," concealing pieces he thought successful in the garret of his house. The sons followed suit, continuing to work closely together, knowing what feats could be accomplished when two brothers work in close partnership. That was something to which Long John and cousin Thomas were wholeheartedly committed: loyalty and dedication to each other, and to the family potworks. They determined that there were two areas of the potter's craft that outweighed all others: "throwing," forming the clay at the wheel, and "firing," controlling the heat and timing of the kiln. That was where the Elers brothers had been most guarded.

Operating the potter's wheel while forming a lump of clay with wet hands was one of the most skilled—and difficult—techniques of the craft. There were two ways to spin the disc on the wheel: by anchoring one foot for purchase and using the other foot to push a pedal on the "kick-wheel"; or by rigging a rope around a shaft and having an assistant (the Elers' "idiot," more commonly a child) hand-drive the wheel. The kick-wheel allowed the thrower to work autonomously, and proved cheaper and less challenging than having two people involved. Most potters preferred this, including the Wedgwoods on both sides of the family. Cousin Thomas focused his efforts on becoming the best thrower in Burslem, while Long John concentrated on becoming the best "fireman" in the trade.

All potters knew the importance of these skills and worried that unless they left their wares in the kiln for just the right amount of time at the right temperature, they would lose the entire kiln load. The transformation of earth to art that took place within the oven was a hidden process, the "misterie" of the craft, which, apprentices would learn, could only be controlled by experience, the tacit knowledge of the "fireman." Human error was costly. A week's worth of wares, a mound of coal, clay, work, and profits wasted. But to get it right—to experiment with new mixtures of clay, times, and temperatures (producing a recipe that someone either patents or steals)—meant gaining a margin of superiority over the neighbors and more profit.

The new process of fine salt glazing relied on knowing when the kiln reached very high temperatures; producing non-glazed wares, such as the red teapots or cream-colored "earthenwares," required lower temperatures. No thermometer had been invented that could be rigged up to the kiln for reading internal temperatures (though in 1740 Long John invented what he called "pyrometrical beads," clay pellets placed in the oven to help gauge the temperature by monitoring the change in their appearance). Next to the entry, which was bricked over after the wares were stacked along the interior, were holes where firemen shoveled in coal. Only experience and constant attention to the heat that blasted from these small apertures provided information about the internal condition of the kiln.

The quality of the wares was testimony to the two men's highly skilled abilities. Visitors and early historians of Burslem had a regular way of referring to cousin Thomas and Long John, "the one an excellent thrower, the other a most skilful fireman." As their reputations spread widely outside Burslem, their trade grew, and more than anyone else in Burslem their accounts were enriched with an "export" market, not only to London but all areas of England. In Simeon Shaw's estimation, the brothers provided "a most pertinent illustration, that every man is the maker or marrer of his own fortune; that, he who depends upon incessant industry and integrity, depends on patrons the most noble, the most exalted, and who never desert, but are the founders of families, the creators of fortune and fame, controuling all human dealings, and converting even unfavourable vicissitudes into beneficial results." The two men were local celebrities. They were the ones who set the standard for the other potters.

On 21 April 1743, their father Aaron died. The next day, their mother Mary died, and both were buried in the graveyard of St. John's Church, in a prominent place closest to the front door of the chapel (where they remain to this day). Their estates, lands, and potworks were distributed amongst their three sons. Long John and cousin Thomas's status edged one more step forward. Their brother, Richard, took his inheritance and pursued a new business venture as a cheese factor in Spen Green, about twenty miles north toward Manchester in the county of Cheshire. Josiah was twelve when he attended the funeral, and would soon be starting his formal apprenticeship under his brother. Or so he imagined. Long John and cousin Thomas had no children, they were still too busy with business, but their brother Richard did. Sarah was nine; along with her only brother she was set to benefit from her family's industrious success. For the side of the Wedgwood family that had once looked up the hill with envy at those who inherited much of Burslem's wealth, things were improving at pace. For Josiah and his family, however, prospects of improvement were still elusive.

4

A Potter and a Gentlewoman

I t was with great pride that on 11 November 1744, Josiah took a pen in
hand and approached the large vellum parchment spread out on the
table as his mother and brother looked on. Signing an apprenticeship
indenture was a moment that changed the lives of many fourteen-year-
old boys in the region of Burslem. They were often the privileged ones,
since other poverty-stricken families sent children as young as nine to the
workshops. It was a sign of prosperity to not begin a formal apprenticeship until later, a symbol of the success of the trade, and Josiah's family,
however dispirited, would not break with a proud tradition.

The indenture Josiah signed spelled out the responsibilities assigned
to him and his "Master," his brother Thomas. He was bound "to Learn his
Art, Mistery, Occupation, or Imployment of Throwing and Handleing,
which he, the said Thomas Wedgwood now useth, and with him as an
Apprentice to Dwell, Continue, and Serve from the day of the Date
hereof, unto the full end and term of five years." He was formally required
to protect the business of his master, "his secrets keep, his Lawfull Commands Every will gladly do; Hurt to his said Master he shall not do, nor
wilfully suffer to be done by others . . . the goods of his said Master he
shall not imbezil or waste, nor them Lend, without his Consent to any."
As was customary, he was forbidden from swearing, drinking, gaming, and
marrying, but will "Demean and behave himself." For his part, Thomas
"shall and will Teach and Instruct after the best way and manner he can"
and he was to provide "Meat, Drink, Washing and Lodging, and Apparell
of all kinds, both Linen and Woolen, and all other Necessaries, both in

Sickness and in Health." And so, it announced, "by the grace of God, King of great Brittain, and so forth," Josiah became an apprentice.

In a craft where secrets clearly meant so much, this formal document represented a bond of trust between master and apprentice. A new relationship was created, one enshrined in a legal and technical tradition. It did not matter that Josiah was the master's younger brother. What mattered was that Josiah had the opportunity to sign the document at all.

When Josiah watched his mother sign her name below his, and then his brother next to that, it meant they were agreeing to see him through this rite of passage. For Josiah, it brought on a subtle feeling of emotional comfort, a sense of stability in his life, prospects of future employment, and, above all, the pride and prestige that came with receiving skilled training in the craft.

To Thomas, it meant doing what he could to give Josiah the training he needed, but more important for him, it meant he had a boy who was bound "well and faithfully to serve." He needed all the help he could get. Josiah's other brother, Richard, who had just finished his apprenticeship with Thomas, decided that the pottery trade was not for him, and so enlisted in the king's army and became a soldier. His decision to join was timely. France had declared war on Britain in a fight over colonial possessions in the New World, while, more urgently for the Staffordshire community, the Young Pretender, Charles Edward Stuart, had in 1745 advanced his Jacobite army, aiming to overthrow the Hanoverian monarchy, all the way to nearby Derby. It is said that Richard hid in the hills and watched the army march toward London, listening to them sing their Jacobin songs, and was enthralled by witnessing their retreat to Scotland as the invasion of England was deemed a failure. But Richard's subsequent departure for the army turned out to be convenient in at least one respect. Churchyard House needed extra space since Thomas and his new wife, Isabel, had just had their first child, baby Thomas.

The family circumstances, however, gave Josiah's brother renewed cause for concern. He could give Josiah a start at the trade, teach him on the wheel that he was taught on, just like his father before him, but he could not guarantee him a future. The Churchyard Works trade had never adequately recovered from the difficult times following their father's death. Consequently, in 1742 Thomas had assumed the added burden of working at Overhouse Estate, on the northern ridge of Burslem Hill. By then, his younger brother/apprentice Richard was trained well enough to see through the day's work while Thomas walked up Church Lane, past his cousins' potworks, and up steep Shoe Lane to the russet-tinged fields called the Brownhills, where the Overhouse potworks were perched.

The house and estate were now owned by his aunt Katherine, the only child of John Wedgwood, who had inherited it when Josiah's grandfather, being the younger brother, inherited the Churchyard House and Works. She was an eccentric, if also admirably strong-willed woman. She was fifty-nine years old and had lived an unusual life. At twenty-five she married her forty-year old cousin, Richard, from the "Aaron" side of the family, who had benefited from the Elers brothers debacle and was running one of the most profitable potteries in Burslem after Long John and cousin Thomas. They had their first child the year they married, but exactly ten years later, Richard suddenly died, followed tragically the next year by her eleven-year-old son, who died of smallpox. The next year she married another, more distant, cousin, Thomas Bourne, and had a baby, Sarah, who didn't survive infancy. Her second husband died seven years later. She was now married for a third time, to a gentleman named Rowland Egerton, and they had no children.

Aunt Katherine certainly did not need to levy any rent from Josiah's brother for using the once profitable potworks that her first husband had built. She already leased much of the nearly 200 acres of land that comprised her estates, land that occupied views from all directions of Overhouse—the Oldfields to the northeast, the rugged expanses of Oxley Croft and Meadow Hill on the northern hilltop behind her, even dark and damp Dale Hall Crofts—all of which brought her a rent-related income of about £100 per annum. It was an income that allowed her to be charitable as well as a touch extravagant.

Aunt Katherine was the only "gentlewoman" in Burslem, and a local celebrity at that. She should have been able to look down upon everyone else in Burslem from breezy Overhouse, but she was often incommoded by the "vast volumes of smoke and vapours" billowing from the salt-glaze ovens down below, an irony she found amusing. She employed two women "servant maids" and a "serving man" to make her comfortable, commissioned expensive furniture, and rode through town in her private chaise, a rarity in these parts. But beyond all the pomp and ceremony, she was deeply committed to helping her family—all extended branches of it—as well as the community in any way she could. She was admired for her well-known charitable gifts to the poor and the parish. And she had no reservations in helping out her struggling nephew, Thomas, for whom she seemed to have special, if during her lifetime, silent regard.

His fortunes were bleak nonetheless. Each week the kiln from each of his two potworks produced another batch of plain butter pots and the cloudy, "mottled," black-speckled saucers and mugs. Profits were thin, no more than ten shillings a week, so he was unable to hire any additional help and had to rely on young inexperienced Josiah.

Despite all the customary duties between master and apprentice formally assigned within the indenture, the agreement between Thomas and Josiah was unusual in one respect: Josiah was not to get any pay. In return for his "training," he received no "earnest money," only his food, clothing, and lodging. Thomas was thus able to save on expenses—by now he was so short of cash he was preparing to borrow £100 from a Thomas Adams (who may have supplied the Wedgwoods with coal)—but this deprived Josiah of the opportunity to put anything aside for his own future ventures.

Whatever the physical strains of the job, it was no less difficult for Thomas when his thoughts drifted to Josiah's future. If the cries of baby Thomas didn't affect Josiah, they served to remind his brother that anything he had left of Churchyard House and Works upon his death was intended to go to his son. Josiah was facing a harder uphill struggle than even brother Thomas. Then tragedy struck.

❧

The Reverend Samuel Stringer, Josiah's Unitarian minister grandfather, preached a rational approach to life and so was especially preoccupied with finding ways to endure life's trials. The Stringers, like the Wedgwoods, were a pious family, but religion to them was more about reading than praying. Unitarians were different from followers of the Church of England. They didn't believe in the doctrine of the "original sin," for instance, nor did they believe in the Holy Trinity, that God's omnipotence was divided between a supreme Father, a separate "spirit," and a Holy Son. Instead, they believed there was only a divine "unity." It was irrational to believe otherwise, they argued. Even the recently deceased national hero Sir Isaac Newton believed that the doctrine of the Trinity was based on "two corruptions of Scripture" and should no longer be relied upon.

The Reverend taught his daughter Mary that "rational ethics"—knowledge based upon reason, experience, and experiment—was preferable to "dogma." She and her family believed in free enquiry, free worship, and voluntary prayers rather than thoughtless allegiance to a church. "God that made the World," wrote the prominent Quaker clothier John Bellers (a Dissenter with Unitarian sympathies) "dwelleth not in Temples made with Hands" but within everyone, everything, everywhere. To study *nature* was to seek the truth. To cleanse the body was to care for God's "temple."

This Unitarian philosophy encouraged individual resourcefulness and gave Mary a strong sense of ability and prudence. Even though Parliament had passed the Act of Toleration in 1689, allowing those with views that dissented from the established canon to preach in public, Unitarians still received short shrift from the authorities. They spread "damnable heresies," Anglican clerics cried. Josiah's grandfather remembered well the antiquated laws that quashed attempts at rational inquiry into how literally liturgies should be taken, and how learned as well as scientific men were eliminated by their investigations. He would shudder to think of the story of the eighteen-year-old medical student at Edinburgh who was overheard repeating some statements from a shallow infidel tract he had read, and was promptly arrested. Denied counsel, he admitted the charges made; but despite his repentance and pleas for mercy, he was hung. His was the last execution for heresy in Britain, and it happened when Mary was nine.

It would have been difficult for Reverend Stringer to spot much by way of progress a half century later. Unitarians of his generation still spoke quietly and cautiously, if firmly, about their views. Since no Unitarian Church was to be established until 1774, the most effective preaching was amongst one's own family and neighbors. It would prove to be even longer before Unitarians' beliefs were granted full "toleration"; but Josiah, like his mother, was already converted.

Josiah had grown up with what was deemed by metropolitan lawmakers as unorthodox, even dangerous, beliefs about God and His creation. Grandfather Stringer's guarded discussions might have celebrated rational principles of education for his daughter and her children, but because they were "dissenting" ideas, they also promoted a sense of segregation, making Burslem, and the five small towns clustered around it (later referred to as "the Potteries") feel all the more isolated. This was something that any Wedgwood who wanted to break beyond provincial prejudices and join the commercial world needed to overcome.

In 1744, Mary's faith in reason and rational care was fully tested when

Josiah contracted smallpox. Feverish and nauseous, Josiah was placed in what was once the "priest's chamber" for the parish chaplain, a fetid, air-less room. Mary had already lost five of her children to the disease, but Josiah would have been too ill to register his mother's fear that he as well might die.

Smallpox was the scourge of all England that no generation escaped, a disease that tormented villagers who suffered constant fear for their fate as they watched churchyards fill with corpses and friends fall ill with the familiar symptoms. Josiah had entered the "febrile state," following a pattern spelled out in a recently published and immensely popular bedside *Treatise on the Small Pox.* Beginning "with a coldness, shiverings, and shakings," he ran a fever and suffered aches in his back and joints, sending torrents of pain throughout his moist, emaciated body as it heaved to vomit. Entering the "eruptive" state, his skin became itchy and burned as the spreading rash on his skin raised and filled with pus, which would rupture, leaving pock-marks on his skin, a sign that would forever tell those who looked at him or his truthful portraits that his life had only just been spared. His arms, hands, and fingers swelled. His bowels stopped "evacuating."

That year's cattle plague, whence "we dare not eat milk, butter, beef nor anything from that species," made things worse. Josiah's hunger made him that much more vulnerable to the disease. It would have been so easy, so forgiving, if Josiah had coiled up and turned his back forever on the gray, smoke-filled life that surrounded him: a trying life that kept his brother away from the house; a life that ended for his father before Josiah's ninth birthday. His stomach would have knotted had he shared Thomas's even worse visions, that even if Josiah survived the smallpox he might well face such poverty that he would be sent to the new work-house. Distant politicians flattered themselves into believing that young men would there learn discipline and piety. In truth, of course, such a consignment was atrocious. In some workhouses, the death rate was 100 percent, affirming one philanthropist's damning comment that parish officers who send children to the workhouse "never intend that they should live."

But Mary believed that her strength would help her son. Any thoughts she had about death were rooted in a concern over refreshing the fetid air caused by Josiah's disease rather than submitting to the will of God. For weeks Josiah laid still in bed, fading into delirium, "as the small-pox in him took a confluent form, covering him from head to foot, and leaving him, when absolute danger was past, in a state of deplorable weakness." The rules on observing the symptoms and attempting remedies offered in the popular medical handbook on the smallpox were useful, precisely the sort of thing that Mary would consult.

> That, if with a quick, and strong pulse and great heat of the Body, bad symptoms occur, you must conclude that the pulse is too quick, too strong, and the Heat of the Body too great; and therefore, you must endeavour to abate them. For this purpose, give the Sick plentifully of diluting Liquors, acidulated with the Juice of Lemons, or Oranges, or with a few drops of the Spirit of Vitriol . . .

Alternatively, if the pulse was weak and the "vital heat" not much different than in times of health, but yet "bad symptoms occur,"

> you must conclude that the pulse is too weak, and the vital heat too little, and therefore you must endeavour to raise them. For this end you give the sick Mountain or Sack Whey, with a little Nutmeg, Panada's, Gruels, Caudles, &c made with Wine, and water sweetened with sugar, and warmed . . . but wine and spice must be used more or less, as the weakness of the pulse.

While willing to try anything to save her son, each day brought more thoughts of the everlasting scars and physical effects of the disease. "It turns many into frightful spectacles," wrote one Dissenting preacher, who outspokenly supported "experiments" to cure the smallpox, "and is attended with the most dismal Consequences, Loss of Sight, Lameness, long Confinement, a broken Constitution, Countenances so altered that their nearest Relations hardly know them."

Finally, the fever broke. Josiah's pustules began to form seedlike crusts on his skin, and he began to move. Though he had gained enough strength to emerge from his thin feather bed, he found it difficult to walk. He had survived "a season of severe bodily affliction, owing to a humour that had settled in his leg after the small pox, and which on every slight accident became painful and sore," recalled a later relative and long-term friend. But Josiah was ready to resume his apprenticeship; he limped back into the workshops on a crutch, and "for some half the time of his apprenticeship he sat at his work with his leg upon a stool before him."

However ill the practice of the trade may agree with the health, the ability, or the inclination of an apprentice: whether his mind is directed to prefer the study of another, by a riper understanding, which would render him more competent to excel in it; or whether, by the loss of a limb he is disabled from pursuing the first to which he is placed; by *that and that alone* he must abide: he is, in the one case, as irretrievably fixed in that trade, as if he belonged to one of the Castes of India; in the other he has no alternative; he *must starve!*

It was a sentiment years in the making—the "laws" of apprenticeship were harsh. They were prohibitive of pleasure, exclusive and isolating, and because the positions were competitive, favored only the fittest. Josiah, however, was never going to let his weak leg jeopardize his duties, as impossible as he now found them.

If he was to become a master potter, Josiah had first to master the "art" and "mistery" of throwing. There again, he required strength of hand—and leg—as well as head. His family had always worked at the wheel using both legs: one foot to anchor the body, the other (usually the right) to operate the kick-wheel. The only alternative in the past was to acquire a different kind of hand-spun wheel and hire a laborer to work it. For Josiah, however, disability bred versatility.

New ways of preparing clay and forming pieces were beginning to appear, which saved him the struggle of working the wheel independently while still enriching the family trade. By 1745, potters not only in Burslem but all around Staffordshire had adapted to the production of salt-glazed wares and the newer invention of "cream-coloured earthenware," or creamware, which produced a richer, more varied and polished glaze on the pieces. The better quality of these demanded more work, however. For a start, creamware required two firings, whereas other types of pottery needed only one. During the first, the freshly formed piece was transformed into a hard, plain, porous "biscuit" state. At this point the worker who specialized in glazing, called a dipper or colorer, applied powdered lead to each piece, then fired it again at a lower temperature to produce the finished, glossy-smooth product. The process was not only more labor-intensive, but it was soon linked to the failing health of their workers.

A creative potter in Tunstall, just north of Burslem, tackled this problem. Enoch Booth was well known for manufacturing creamware, and just as Josiah was beginning his apprenticeship, Booth was experimenting with a new method of lead glazing, which was applied in a liquid state, helping to alleviate the problems linked to the use of the toxic powder.

The recent addition of powdered white flint stones created another hazard. When dried and mixed with clay, the flint added strength to the pieces so they could be thinner and safely fired at the crucial higher temperatures. But as with lead, grinding flints caused alarming health problems. "Any person ever so healthful or strong working in this business," announced one concerned engineer named Thomas Benson, "cannot possibly survive above two years, occasioned by the dust sucked into his body." But Benson had a solution, and a decade before Josiah began his apprenticeship had patented his improved mill for grinding flints under water, drowning the loose dust, and saving some from the blood-curdling coughs of "potter's rot"—a lethal lung disease.

This innovation, coupled with the new use of liquid lead glazes, were the marvels of pottery manufacture when Josiah entered his apprenticeship in the 1740s. Word spread fast, and during these years the community of potters was ablaze with ideas that could simultaneously improve the quality of their wares and the health of their workers. It was a delicate line of enquiry: "experiments" were expensive, and often potters could not afford errors in the trials. Josiah's cautious brother preferred following his father's tried-and-tested, if unimaginative, methods.

Others risked it. Long John and cousin Thomas never stopped investing in expansion and building the latest mechanical devices to advance their trade. In 1744, they rented land owned by a gentleman in the nearby parish of Norton "To take, farme, & Rent ye old furnace at Lawton & convert it into a flint Mill at the price of Twenty Guineas a year for the Terme of Seven years certain"—making them one of the earliest known Burslem potters to construct a flint mill. They knew the venture had risks, however, adding in their agreement that they would honor their obligations "in all advantages that shall accrue and also ALL Disappointments or Disadvantages yt shall ensue."

The newly erected mills and special rooms for added stages of production instilled in potters a sense of pride in their advancing craft and engendered a sense of camaraderie in the community. Rivalry judiciously gave way to rallying in support of a new technique or tool that would draw more widespread attention to the kind of quality wares that could be produced in Burslem. Everything seemed especially vital after 1744, when new English porcelain manufacturers were established in Chelsea and

Bow in London, at Derby, and, nearer to Burslem, in Pomona and Longton Hall. Fortunately for the Staffordshire potters, their newly improved
durable wares were still cheaper to produce than the delicate soft-paste
body of English porcelain. But the growing question was whether the customers would favor "pottery" or "porcelain."

Young potters like Josiah might be moderately protected from the
dangers of the "potter's rot" with the new designs, but no one, of course,
could cure smallpox or crippling infections, and these remained Josiah's
personal demons.

Compared to what was going on elsewhere in Burslem, the Churchyard Works looked antiquated. Some of the wares that Josiah worked on
from dawn to dusk were made of clay that was mixed with water to a
semiliquid, creamy state called "slip." Slip could be poured into plaster
molds to produce decorated teapots and tureens (after a thin layer of the
slip dried inside the mold the rest of the liquid clay was poured out to
keep the piece hollow), but it could also be used to make "mottled" or
marbled ware, something his family had done for many years. Different-
colored slip—orange, white, and red, sometimes altered when ingredients
such as iron ore (called "magnus") were added—was poured over the surface of the ware and "combed" or blended to imitate a veined hard stone,
such as agate, with its bands of color. It was simple but creative and produced vibrant pieces that looked like jewelry.

Josiah enjoyed working on those pieces; it enabled him to develop the
"art" of the craft and allowed him, finally, to concentrate less on the mus-
cular and more on the mental discipline involved with the business. By
1749, five years after signing his indenture, Josiah's apprenticeship came
to an end, and he had managed successfully to demonstrate that he had
learned "the art, mistery, and occupation" of the potter. He had come a
long way over the ten years since his father died, when he worked in the
potting sheds with his brother Richard, "seated at two corners of a small
room," throwing and shaping balls of clay. Staying on to work for his
brother in the Churchyard Works, he was now able to earn his own wages
and assume his role of responsibility in paying for food and clothes.

For three years following his apprenticeship Josiah was occupied in
this way, contemplating ways to improve the potter's art, hoping to gain
wider acceptance as an equal in the family business. It would have been
natural for two brothers working together to form a partnership, to divide
their skills and mutually invest in their trade. If Josiah needed external

motivation for working to improve his position he had, of course, the perfect model in Long John and cousin Thomas. They were the children of a youngest son, and Long John himself, like Josiah, was the youngest in his family (of seven), yet they had reached unprecedented standing as tradesmen in Burslem. They were mutually devoted and determined, and were shamelessly successful. So much so, in fact, that in 1750, the year after Josiah finished his apprenticeship, everyone in town was awestruck by the imposing house the brothers had just finished building in the town center, on the corner plot next to the Red Lyon pub. It was three stories high, double-fronted, rustic redbrick with a pedimented porch supported on Doric columns. It also had a tiled roof, making it the first home without a thatched roof in Burslem, which, according to one townsman, "was considered a ridiculous expense" until it was finished, then it "astonished the natives." They brazenly named it "Big House," declaring that theirs was not a business to be overlooked.

Josiah and his brother never formed the kind of close relationship that their cousins enjoyed. Thomas, perhaps thinking that Josiah was too daring and indulgent in "endless illusive projects," was not willing to enter into a partnership with his younger brother. On the other hand, Josiah was dissatisfied with what he considered Thomas's unimaginative approach to the art of pottery, but that didn't change his predicament.

In July 1752, his brother, having lost his wife Isabel in childbirth two years before, married Jane Richards. His son, eight-year-old Thomas, was performing the menial duties that had previously fallen to Josiah when his father died, feeding the large fireplace in the kitchen and assisting in the potworks across the muddy yard. Josiah's mother looked after her granddaughters, three-year-old Sarah and two-year-old Mary.

Josiah had just turned twenty-two years old and he wanted to move on from Churchyard House. It was never going to be easy. "No single handed man can live," a contemporary tradesman had written, reflecting on the importance of relationships, "he must have a whole family at work, because a single-handed man is so badly paid he can scarce provide the necessaries of life." But Josiah was determined—stubborn, just like his father and brother. That summer he collected his few belongings and left. He was moving on, by himself.

5
Discipline and Dissent

Josiah was not traveling far—just down Burslem's gentle hills and into the next town of Stoke, about three miles south. He had found lodging in the home of Daniel Mayer, a successful tradesman who shared the Dissenting religious views of Josiah's own family.

Daniel Mayer ran a bustling trade as a "Tailor, Draper, and Man's Mercer," earning enough to build a house in the middle of town with space not only to house a lodger but also to accommodate his shop in the front rooms along the street. Unlike the home of even Josiah's wealthiest cousins, where the mess of raw materials from the potworks was deliberately separated from the "dwelling house," here the working areas were integrated into the large home. Passing customers entered the front rooms of the house, the workshop rooms, where the tailor was surrounded with cloth, working on orders. Everything was "custom made" in these sorts of trades, all supply on demand, with close interaction between the merchant and customer. Josiah's room was in the back, along with the rest of the "family apartments."

Mayer's house was on the main street running through Stoke, a location that not only served his business well but was convenient enough for Josiah to get to the Cliff Bank potworks, where he found new employment. The man he principally worked with was Thomas Alders, a potter who manufactured the usual lead- and salt-glazed tea sets, mugs, and "blue ware," items that were decorated by women "flowerers," who scratched patterns into the pieces vaguely resembling flora or Chinese pagodas that were dusted with powdered smalt, a blue pigment derived from zaffre. Alders's business had had an infusion of cash from a Newcastle-under-Lyme merchant named John Harrison, and they took on Josiah to improve their production of hand-pressed or molded wares.

Here he continued working on the colorful marbled agate ware that he'd specialized in at the Churchyard Works, and began trying his hand at decorating creamware pieces with new kinds of glazes in imitation of some of the goods appearing from the Big House brothers' manufactory. There was a niche fashion at the time for molded round teapots made to look like fruits and vegetables, the surface emulating a head of cauliflower or a pineapple, for instance. A "modeler" or artist would carve the original specimen with the desired decorative motif and produce a mold of it for future casts using the creamy "slip" clay. When the clay crust had dried and the item was ready, Josiah would mix different kinds of ground metals—copper, manganese, iron, cobalt, and so on—and dust or sponge them onto the piece before applying a clear lead glaze and sending it to be fired.

The effects were sometimes dramatic. A potter down the road on the opposite side of Stoke named Thomas Whieldon had been developing what was known as "Tortoiseshell" ware, named after the mingling of brownish-purple and deep, smoky greens on the final finish. Customers across the country adored it, and their eagerness to buy it was a spur to Whieldon's business, allowing him to recruit new apprentices and laborers to expand his business. The more heads and hands driving the creative process the more likely something new and eye-catching would appear.

Creative potters were always eager to peer into the cooled saggars (the refractory clay containers that held the wares to help prevent blistering) being unloaded from the kilns in which the new batches of wares were placed for firing. No one knew what they might discover. It was no longer just a process of digging for different kinds of clays and altering firing temperatures and times. Fifty years after the Elers brothers first showed the Burslem potters what effect pouring salt into kilns could have on the products, it seemed sensible to some to grind up other sorts of elements and chemicals to see what effect they might have on the pottery.

The crude idea that one should be satisfied with the meager living provided by coal and clay became as outmoded as the feudal dogma that peasants were bound to their subservient rank in life by divine ordinance. If families could move from thatched hovels to big brick houses because they believed that nature hid treasures accessible to anyone who was willing to work hard enough—to dig deep enough—to find the reward, then social progress at last seemed possible.

Not everyone shared this progressive view, but Josiah did. Unlike the swath of migrant laborers, whose principal concern was to find enough food and drink to carry them through the next day, Josiah's ambitions were informed by the religious and political principles preached by his Unitarian minister grandfather. He had been taught to believe that there were resources within nature that could benefit those educated to identify and use them. This line of thought was an extension of the "Dissenting" emphasis on "natural" rather than "revealed" religion—the idea that God's handiwork was best understood through rational enquiry rather than the high churchmen's ecclesiastical tradition that relied on biblical exegesis.

Fearing the subversion of ecclesiastical conformity, gentrified conservative Tory society alienated people like the Reverend Stringer and kept similarly minded men from earning degrees at England's ancient institutions or holding public office. Critics decried the alchemical commitment of radical natural philosophers who searched for the philosopher's stone that would turn dirt into gold. Burslem potters like Josiah, whose workshop tubs stunk of chemicals and mixed, wet metal oxides, were not attracting the kind of attention that the natural philosophers of the Royal Society did (whose presence in the middle of London sometimes aroused much more suspicion), but such experimental practices would prove to have a profound effect on life in the most diverse places.

Even if in the 1750s Staffordshire was not seen as much of a threat to the establishment politically or religiously, there was certainly a reforming zeal amongst Dissenters, prominently so in Josiah's family. They were taught to support the reforming Whig Party—those politicians who were suspicious of the residual political influence of the church on the government—and the men accordingly cast their votes in the elections. But there were other ways to effect change.

While Josiah's mother had once relied on her beliefs in the powers of nature and the rationalization of disease for strength during her son's illness, others in the family were looking to nature to provide a source of power to improve their family position. None of the Wedgwoods pursued their business with a desire to accumulate money for its own sake. They certainly took pride in their success, and they enjoyed the attention earned by their rising eminence, but they set an example of entrepreneurial paternalism that others followed. As George Courtauld, a later Unitarian industrialist, would declare, "the aim of business is to provide for the wants and comforts in the world." That aim could be accomplished—improvements in standards of living and moral worth achieved—through the pursuit of "free enquiry," a belief that bound the thoughts of so many "Dissenting" early industrialists. From a business point of view, any effort to improve the kinds of wares produced by experimenting with nature's ingredients offered a chance to reinvest some wealth in the community.

Josiah's cousin, Long John, had elaborated on the importance of pursuing lines of experimental enquiry to improve the trade. In an "Essay on Pottery" he wrote in 1743, he explained that "Potmaking chiefly depends on a knowledge of ye nature of Earth, Air, Fire, Water, Clays, Marls, & Stones, & some Minerals"—all of the natural elements that had long been the focus of experimental natural philosophers—and pottery should be no different. "Earth," he wrote, as it relates to the "potters Art is to be considered in the light of the Chymist's principles because it undergoes ye operation of fire," and a range of other raw materials such as "Oyls, Salts, Sulpher & Water" had material effects on potters' products. Owing to the diversity of natural resources, it was essential that the potter become a researcher.

"Clays are of various sorts," he continued, "same partaking more of ye earthy nature, others more of ye Marley nature, the fatter & better ye Clay for fine pots ye nearer to a Marly nature for course pots of a poorer sandy or Earthy quality." There were potentially endless varieties of colors and consistencies, "some proper for one kind of ware & some for others, some are of a very soft tough nature others very brittle & hard so as to come near stone, some burn very white in the fire others not so white," and the attempt to regulate these results required a record of analytical trials, "which may be considered how great an improvement might be made in the potter if ye nature of all sorts of Marls were more fully known." The potter's success rested on his knowledge of "nature" and his ability to manipulate it. "In short," Long John concluded, "to try which proportion of each sort will work kindly together, Limestone, Alabaster &c ye natures of them may be tryd by several Experiments in mixing with others, Chalks, red Earth, & other Coloured Earth fullers may be considered."

Long John's essay was a master class in the importance to the potter's craft of natural philosophy, experimental enquiry, and record keeping. His and his brother's success was proof of the merits of his formula. But Long

John also made it clear that the Christian mission of practical service to society, aiming to benefit equally its economic and moral interests, should be encouraged amongst the community: a direct bid of support for the Dissenting cause. In a will drafted in 1755, Long John devised that Josiah's brother Thomas would be responsible for "one Clear Annuity or yearly rent Charge of forty Shillings a year so long as there shall remain a Congregation of Dissenters and shall be preached to at the Dissenting Meeting House at Newcastle under Lyme in the said County of Stafford whereof I am now a Member." The money was to be given in yearly or "equal half yearly payments unto the Minister for the time being of the said Meeting house." His gift would keep alive the congregation where Josiah's grandfather once preached and where a new, radical preacher, the Reverend William Willets, was now installed.

Reverend Willets thought along the same lines as Long John and likewise promoted the view that social improvement and "truths" about God's creation were revealed through experimental practices. He also practiced what he preached, attempting to answer a call from the late "illustrious Sir Isaac Newton" for an improved design of a telescope. Calling himself a man of "good will to Philosophy," he wrote a letter to the secretary of the Royal Society "to lay before them a Project of his" for improved methods of grinding glass for better telescopic lenses. It was a confident move for which he begged the Fellows of the Royal Society forgiveness for the "Presumption of a Stranger" in writing; but when they replied stating their opinion of the shortcomings of his design, he didn't give up. He wrote back boldly asking if their objections were "assured by experiment (to which all conjectures must yield)" and stressing that he had faith that "our ingenious mechanicks" could produce what he planned. He clearly lived by his adage, "Invention without Experiment signifys very little."

This was a philosophy that twenty-four-year-old Josiah was beginning to absorb, due in no small part not only to the example of his successful cousins, but to Reverend Willets himself, who in 1754 had married Catherine, Josiah's sister. While Josiah thought of himself as standing "on the lowest rung of the ladder" in his trade, he gained much support for his experiments from Willets, that "truly good man," as Josiah called him. Josiah's own "service to Philosophy" was developing at the same time that his local community was beginning to witness the widespread benefits of such work. Apprehending the "great philosophic fact" that "the sources of truth and knowledge are limitless," Josiah began to borrow books on chemistry from his brother-in-law Willets and copy passages into his notebook. He was discovering many facets of business life that were much more stimulating than anything he had encountered at the Churchyard Works.

What neither Willets nor cousin Long John had written about was how to find the right partner with whom to develop a successful business. And whether it was because Harrison and Alders frowned upon the expense of Josiah's trials or because Josiah preferred the kind of activities he discovered were going on in other potworks, he didn't stay with them for very long. In fact, it was a potter on the other side of Stoke whom Josiah became most interested in. In 1754, he joined in a partnership with Thomas Whieldon, the experimentally minded "Tortoiseshell" man, who was interested in the "secrets" that he knew Josiah alone possessed.

Just a few minutes' walk along the road heading south from Stoke was Thomas Whieldon's cluster of "Pot ovens, houses, Buildings, Ware houses, Work houses, Throwing houses," and strips of mowed lawn. These were well organized and well managed—Whieldon had only been in his new works a few years, having outgrown his other potwork, which he still controlled, about a mile away across the wild meadows. His new premises outstripped all the previous potworks Josiah had worked in, not only in the number of buildings but in the number and quality of people who worked for Whieldon.

Whieldon was thirty-five years old in 1754, and he had an impressive command of his business. "He was shrewd enough to guard his trade secrets carefully, even going to the extent of burying shards to prevent them being imitated by competitors. He had excellent trade connections, especially with the Birmingham metal mounters and silversmiths, whom he supplied with considerable quantities of snuff and other boxes, buttons, and vanity items which when mounted found a popular market." He was skilled at delegating tasks to people responsible for maintaining the premises, looking after the affairs of the second pottery, and supervising the daily work of his teams, which were each responsible for a specific aspect of the works and "from whom he exacted scrupulous obedience, respectful behavior, and strict punctuality." It clearly paid off. Where he had leased his potworks in the 1740s he now bought them outright, and he had just purchased Fenton Hall, closer to Stoke, which he rented out (either in part or the whole of the roomy home) as a £106 annual supplement to his income. He lived with his wife, Sarah, about a mile away in Penkhull, but had also just bought land and was building a new stately home which he called "The Grove" where he could oversee the activities of the potworks.

The teams of workers at Whieldon's manufactory found their employer's rigor and discipline trying at times, amounting to a judgment that he was "not a very likeable character." He needed to be stern and imposing with his standards—London aristocrats who were now receiving crates of his wares were discerning customers—but Josiah admired both the way Whieldon marshaled respect and the way he looked after his workers, paying them well, on an "incentive scale," pay proportionate to productivity. Knowing the importance of having skilled firemen monitoring the kilns and throwers working the wheel, he paid each of his own an above-market price of eight shillings a week. He was also generous with his apprentices, and—above all—he was likely the first to buy "6 tenements or dwghoues" and "two other Cottages or Tenements" within walking distance of the potworks which he let to his workers.

Housing his workers was Whieldon's solution to a problem that had been a matter of national debate, let alone local concern, since that controversial Act of Toleration was passed fifty years earlier (1698). While the act allowed Josiah's family to pursue their liberal, Dissenting brand of faith, it also created apathy amongst the provincial poor. Parochial clergy were alarmed to report in their "Visitation returns" a plummet in church attendance, and commentators charged that the church had lost its authority over the moral and religious behavior of parishioners. Many believed that those boozing, brawling punters who wasted their last pennies in local alehouses were the result of a new breed of "toleration."

Some had argued that this was the result of a waning coherency of the Dissenters, who had "lost that good character for strictness in religion, which had gained them their credit" back in the days when Josiah's grandfather was preaching. Now, there was such ill discipline in the community that "from a delicacy of taste," gentlemen and rich patrons "were ashamed to continue amongst so unpolish'd a people." This damaging allegation about the conduct of "free thinkers" was challenged by one outspoken Dissenter, Philip Doddridge: "I think an honest mechanick, or day-labourer, who attends the Meeting from a religious principle . . . is a much more honourable and generous creature than such a gentleman" as may turn his back on these people, "destitute of the ornaments of education, or splendid circumstances in life."

This was the sentiment shared by Josiah's cousin Long John, and an important rationale behind Long John's patronage of the local Dissenting congregations. "I can imagine nothing more imprudent," Doddridge declared, "than a neglect of the populace (by which I mean all plain people of low education and vulgar taste, who are strangers to the refinements of learning and politeness)," and here he was describing those who *did* attend the congregation meetings. More work to improve the condition of uned-ucated poor was clearly needed; but not through the abstract or "haughty reasonings" of the high church, but by "speaking *plainly* to them" and showing them how useful, and morally valuable, their education can be.

It was bad for business that the "day-labourers" were shunning educa-tion—religious education was the only kind they would ever receive—not only because the consequent lack of "polish" alienated the Dissenting community from their custom, the gentlemen and gentlewomen who were beginning to buy expensive pottery, but because the laborers made for difficult employees in manufactories that relied on their work. This was an economic concern expressed by the politician Sir Francis Brewster, who at the beginning of the century wrote of a looming national disaster. "The neglect of the Poor seems the greatest mistake in our government," he appealed, "to have so many Thousand Poor, who might by their Labours Earn, and so eat our Provisions, and instead of sending them out, as export Manufactures." The poor, he claimed, were a "secret weapon" in the battle for improved trade.

This neglect gripped the attention of Sir Humphrey Mackworth, a conservative member of Parliament, who devised a radical plan to instill discipline and harness untapped labor for commercial reward. The able-bodied poor should not merely earn their own maintenance, as the Eliza-bethan legislators of the Poor Law had suggested, but they should be put to work in state-owned "parish manufactories" where they could turn a profit for the state. In 1704, Sir Humphrey read out a bill to the House of Commons explaining that overseers could "raise a convenient stock" of raw materials "for the Imploying or setting to Work the poor who are able to Work." It would be lawful, he said, "for the Overseers to take one or more house or houses, with their Appurtenances, for the more convenient imploying and setting the Poor to Work; and also one or more Ware house or Ware houses, for the safe keeping of such Goods and Merchandizes to be Manufactured as aforesaid, until the same can be sold to the advantage." Children, both boys and girls, would be given appropriate apprenticeships, supported from "a perpetual fund or stock, for the binding out poor Children Apprentices to Trades and Manual Occupations, whereby much advantage may accrue to the Common-Wealth."

Not everyone thought this was a good idea. The ever politically active Daniel Defoe attacked the idea of turning "Parishes into Ware-houses." Naturally, he admitted, "Multitudes of People make Trade, Trade makes Wealth, Wealth builds Cities, Cities Enrich the Land round them, Land Enrich'd rises in Value, and the Value of Lands Enriches the Government"; but the proposed system was one of "Oppression and Tyranny of the Poor," and this quashes the freedom of market forces, especially in determining the value of labor. "Trade, like all Nature," he concluded—in a spirit of rationalism that would chime in the ears of later industrialists—"most obsequiously obeys the great Law of Cause and Consequence," and "even all the greatest Articles of Trade follow, and as it were pay Homage to this seemingly Minute and Inconsiderable Thing: *The poor Man's Labour*."

Sir Humphrey's bill did not pass, but Defoe's optimism in the natural laws of trade was no more immediately successful. The "crowd of clamouring, unimploy'd, unprovided for Poor People, who make the Nation uneasie, burthen the Rich, clog our Parishes, and make themselves worthy of Laws, and peculiar Management" were still there.

But just after Josiah began working with Thomas Whieldon, Admiral Edward Vernon—a national hero following his victory over the Spanish at Porto Bello, Panama, in 1739—had successfully lobbied for the establishment of a local governing body to set up a "House of Industry" in southern Suffolk, on the other side of England. Its mission was "to administer proper comfort and assistance to the sick, infirm and aged, introduce sobriety and virtue among them, and in an especial manner to render their children useful to society by acquainting them with their duty towards God and man." In 1758, Vernon lent £1,000 (charging 3.5 percent interest) to build the institution, and when it was finished, it was declared that now "many children are rendered useful who otherwise would have figured nowhere but in a landscape of Gainsborough's, the spawn of gipsies, lying upon a sunny bank half naked, with their bundles of stolen wood by their sides."

As it happened, Whieldon and Josiah knew of Admiral Vernon. They had even been examining his body and face for blemishes in their slip casts of him produced to celebrate the Porto Bello Victory. But although they were familiar with his accomplishments in expanding the British Empire, it is less likely that they knew of the experimental "House of Industry" he spearheaded in Suffolk. Instead, entrepreneurial potters like Josiah's cousins Long John and Thomas, or his new partner Whieldon, were discussing their own solutions to the problem of a flagging workforce that hindered the growth of their businesses. Whieldon's small-scale scheme to provide nearby housing for his workers was the most innovative in Staffordshire. Just as experiments with nature presented new kinds of wares for the trade, Whieldon's experiment with social organization yielded a new form of loyalty and commitment from his workers; both forms of experimentation would prove successful.

❧

When "Siah," as Whieldon called Josiah, joined the team, Whieldon spotted in him the traits of ambition and creativity that had already been a boon to his trade. He also realized that Josiah would be a good complement to the others on the team, some of whom had trained with Whieldon as apprentices. One of those former apprentices whose creative energies had earned Whieldon's respect was another Josiah, twenty-one-year-old Josiah Spode, now a journeyman whose weekly pay of 7s 6d matched "the highest wages then given" in the region for someone just coming out of an apprenticeship. Trained to be just like his master, Spode was "a Man of Energy, Promptitude, Decision and great Aptitude for Business," traits that were beginning to shine through in Josiah.

Compared to Josiah, Spode (three years his junior) came from a very poor family—his father had been buried in a pauper's grave when Spode was six—but he and Josiah shared an ambition to prove to others that they were capable of producing the most admired and innovative pieces of pottery. Right now, both young men wanted to impress Whieldon; this was natural for a maturing apprentice and a new partner who wanted to show rewards for the faith Whieldon had showed in them. But both Spode and Josiah struggled with a deeper desire to prove their worth to the man who was not only sedulously devoted to improving his business but bestowed new levels of responsibility on them at a time in each of their lives when they needed a boost up the next "rung of the ladder," as Josiah said. As Whieldon passed through the workshops on routine supervision, Josiah was desperate that he would leave feeling proud of him. He had never had this kind of paternal respect. Neither had Spode. They both worked twice as hard because of it, making sure each piece of pottery they produced would gain the kind of admiration they had lacked as children.

This suited Whieldon. From his perspective, he demanded consistency in the high standards he set for each piece of pottery and he needed new, creative ideas. He agreed to a partnership with Josiah precisely because he needed fresh hands and an experimentally inclined mind to liven up his trade. He thought the kind of work Josiah was doing across town at Harrison and Alders' showed real promise, and Josiah was grateful for the encouragement. "I had already made an imitation of Agat which was esteem'd very beautiful, and a considerable improvement," Josiah remembered, reflecting on his early days with Whieldon, when he was finally able to pursue a wider range of possibilities for creating new kinds of pottery.

> At this time, our Manufacture was in a very unimprov'd state, & the demand for it decreasing, so that the trade was universally complain'd of as being bad, & in a declining condition. White stoneware was the staple Article of our Manufacture, but this had been made a long time, & the prices were now so low that the Potters could not afford to make it as good in any respect, or finish it so high as the ware would otherwise admit of, & with respect to elegance of form, that was a subject very little attended to.

Josiah then noted something that must have disturbed Whieldon personally, which was that even "the next staple Article in the pottery" that had once gained Whieldon such a prominent reputation, "an imitation of Tortis-shell," was also failing to sell. It was no mystery why: "as there had been no improvement in this branch for several years past, the Country was grown very weary of it, & though the price was lower'd from time to time, in order to increase the sales, the expedient did not succeed & something new was wanted to give a little spirit to the business."

Whieldon's hopes that Josiah would provide that "little spirit" were quickly realized. Josiah recognized that "the Country had been surfeited with variegated colors as a sort of blue & green had already been mixed with the Tortis-shell, & this induced me to try for self colour'd Glaze." This was also something that Spode was interested in (eventually he would become famous for perfecting blue underglaze printing on the bone china for which Spode is still known today), but he and Josiah did not work together for very long. Shortly after Josiah had joined Whieldon, Spode decided that it was time to start up his own business as an "Earth Potter" (with some financial help from his new wife, Ellen, eight years his senior). But there were other creative hands who could help.

These included an eighteen-year-old modeler, or "block maker," named William Greatbatch, whom Josiah and Whieldon paid around 2s 6d a week to make and trim the molds that were used in slip casting for the mass production of elaborately shaped items, whether figurines or teapots (shaped like fruits or anything else). Greatbatch was a highly skilled modeler, thought of as an "ingenious young man" even to those who harbored jealousy toward him, and was clearly someone for whom Josiah had much respect, as their enduring professional relationship would show. The friendly acknowledgment of Greatbatch's talents served the boy's confidence well, which was important, since he was filling in the place of one of the Wood brothers, who were widely acknowledged to be the best modelers in the area. Aaron Wood had left Whieldon's employment a few years before Josiah arrived, and his brother Ralph was employed by Long John and cousin Thomas. It was therefore a relief to Whieldon's competitive spirit that Greatbatch turned out to be an adept replacement.

Greatbatch was challenged to come up with new shapes and designs for the wares, and "he seems to have given birth," thought one of Josiah's relatives, later on, to the "STILE ornament to the art of modelling," which struck Josiah as exactly the kind of approach that could prove beneficial to the business, including "new green earthenware in forms of leaves, plates, molded fruits, agate snuff boxes, &c."

Over the next five years, the team at Josiah and Whieldon's manufactory was busy. Each week the ovens rendered another batch of "redware," salt glaze, "solid-agate," and black ware, and a wide range of particular items were packed into crates and shipped off. A large strip of land out the back of the pottery became the graveyard to imperfect and experimental pieces:

"solid-agate" teapot lids, a fragment of a massive redware punch pot with applied grape and vine-leaf decoration, green glazed wares, toys (both redware and tortoiseshell), press-moulded "biscuit" plates with raised fruit decoration, cauliflower lids, creamwares ("biscuit" and glost) a black glazed teapot on tripod feet, tortoiseshell plates, a "solid-agate" mustard pot and a cauliflower cream-jug, two varieties of tureen-cover in the typical green, yellow and brown colouring, much kiln-furniture (earthenware and stoneware), a grape "block" mould, rabbit finials for teapot lids, a tortoiseshell button, "solid-agate" taws and a cube.

It was frantic work, requiring assiduous attention, but over time Josiah noticed that Whieldon was gradually relaxing his attitude toward the business. In 1758, following the death of Sarah, his first wife, Whieldon remarried. He was thirty-nine years old and "The Grove," his elaborate home, was becoming more comfortable than the potworks that he could see from his windows. Whieldon's contentment struck twenty-eight-year-old Josiah as odd. He feared that it wouldn't be long before "the Country" would once again grow weary of their latest molded and salt-glazed productions, pineapple mugs and cauliflower teapots. "The age," Samuel Johnson declared, "is running mad after innovation," and without new products business itself was doomed for the graveyard.

This was no time to take a break. At Chelsea and Bow, the first English porcelain figures were entering the market; in Liverpool, manufacturers of English "Delft" ware were producing two hundred printed wall tiles an hour, using a newly invented process of transfer printing. In 1757, the Dean of Gloucester, Josiah Tucker, observed with bemusement while traveling around England how prominent mechanical, labor-saving devices were becoming. "Few countries are equal, perhaps none excel, the English in the number of contrivances of their Machines to abridge labour," he said. "Yet all these, curious as they may seem, are little more than Preparations or Introductions for further Operations. Therefore, when we still consider that at Birmingham, Wolverhampton, Sheffield and other manufacturing Places, almost every Master Manufacturer hath a new Invention of his own, and is daily improving on those of others; we may aver with some confidence that those parts of England in which these things are seen exhibit a specimen of practical mechanics scarce to be paralleled in any part of the world." Gradually the force of these inventions, which became the tools of the "industrial revolution," disturbed this same commentator, who later bemoaned the unsettling, republican tendencies of those behind "practical mechanics" who were united, he would agree, by "dissent, that religion of trade and manufacturers, the cradle of Philistinism."

As Whieldon eased into a life of retired complacency, Josiah's efforts crystallized with confidence. He had just moved into some comfortable rooms at Fenton Hall, Whieldon's estate up the road nearer Stoke. He spent his evenings jotting down lists of possibilities "for the improvement of our manufacture of earthenware." "These considerations induced me to try for some more solid improvements as well in the Body as the Glazes, the Colours, and the Forms of that articles of our manufacture," Josiah noted. Glaze provided both a functional and a decorative finish to the ware. All articles made from natural clay remain porous in their "biscuit" (once-fired) state, and need a coat of glaze to make them impervious for culinary or domestic uses. Simple glaze was added by dusting the piece with powdered lead ore contained in a parcel of coarse muslin; during the second firing of the piece, the powdered lead ore is gradually roasted to lead oxide, which, in its turn, melts and dissolves the outer skin of the clay vessel. But Josiah had long been interested in applying more complex glazes, which used a mixture of different chemicals—soda and boracic acid, for instance—to alter the color and texture of the wares and to breathe life into his business.

So he converted his kitchen into a small laboratory and turned to a fresh page in his notebook: "Experiment Notebook I." "This suite of experiments was begun at Fenton Hall in the parish of Stoke-on-Trent," he wrote. Page one: "Feb 13—1759." Experiment number one.

Josiah began by mixing different proportions of chemicals and applying the resulting glaze to small sample pieces of plain biscuit earthenware (swatchlike samples), carefully taking notes on each. He was systematic, altering slightly the quantity and kind of his ingredients on each sample. Every week he eagerly laid out a new piece from that oven's batch of his experiments, hoping to identify the one color that surpassed anything else he had seen. It was a time-consuming process because it was impossible to tell what the applied glaze would look like until it came out of the kiln. Like all processes involved with firing, this was part of the hidden "mistery" of the potter's craft. Josiah, however, became a master.

"23 March 1759. Experiment No 7": Josiah was very excited. He jotted in the margin of his notebook, next to the recipe, "A green glaze, to be laid upon Common white (or cream color) Biscuit ware." This moment, this feeling, was what he was hoping for. "This is the result of many experiments, which I made in order to introduce a new species of color'd ware to be fired along with the Tortis-shell and Agat ware in our common Gloss Ovens to be of an even self-color, & laid upon the ware in the form of a color'd glaze."

The next day he went to the workshop, placed a cream-colored earthenware tea canister in front of him, and began to apply his new brilliant translucent green glaze to it, which "should completely cover the piece as evenly as possible," he noted to himself. He then turned it upside down and on an unwitting impulse incised "JW" on its base. That proud, if simple, act of labeling his wares would prove to be one of the most important of his career.

When the piece came out of the oven, he sighed with relief. It was an elegant green glaze that surpassed anyone else's, even that of Long John and cousin Thomas, who had long worked, to little effect, on their own version of green glaze.

Josiah's first innovation had produced a distinctive, unique look to the wares. Rather frustratingly, Whieldon seemed less than captivated by his partner's progress. Josiah wondered whether or not Whieldon's apathy would matter to their business. If he himself continued to work at improving it, perhaps not. But in that case, why split the profits?

Josiah felt more confident than ever. He was now sure he could do better for himself if he had total control over the kinds of wares he wanted to produce. He tucked his experimental notebook into "Willy's" sack (Willy was his new horse, and first big purchase), rode past the workers' cottages, and headed up to Burslem. He had a meeting with Long John and cousin Thomas scheduled, and a proposition for them that he had rehearsed over and over again. Once again, Josiah wanted to go at it alone.

6

"Dues & Demands"

Donning a new jacket and light brown wig (he was meticulous about his appearance), Josiah approached Long John and cousin Thomas's Big House without a hint of trepidation. He would have walked with long, strong strides had his right leg not continued to give him grief. Even fourteen years after his bout of smallpox he was still bothered by a numbness in his knee and a fatigue of the muscles he used to compensate when walking; it was the only thing that distracted him from his work.

He was long past the point of being daunted by the elaborate home that fronted his cousins' extensive potworks—they now had five large bottleneck ovens adjacent to the Red Lyon Inn turning out a steady range of wares every week—but he nonetheless admired the elegance of the new architectural design. In the "house place," an old way of referring to the front hall, was a grand oak staircase with three turned balusters to each step, and the walls had fine paneling. It was certainly more stylish than the rooms he rented at Fenton Hall.

Josiah's timing was rather unfortunate. Only recently on a Friday morning Long John's wife, Mary—whom the long-standing bachelor had married the previous summer, in 1758—had given birth to a stillborn girl. It would have been their first child. But fifty-four-year-old Long John was too fixed in his business ways to miss a meeting, and he greeted Josiah cordially, happy to see that his young cousin, "Thomas's boy," was doing so well.

Josiah was honored to have gained the respect of one of the two most prized potters in Burslem, and he knew that the other, his cousin Thomas (who still spent all his time in the potworks, while Long John now took care of the accounts), felt the same about him. Josiah couldn't imagine cousin Thomas and Long John disagreeing about anything, being as close as they were. Even though Long John was married, they still lived in the same house together, and Thomas had begun courting a cousin, hoping for his own marriage one day.

The last time Josiah had had the chance to present himself to Long John was three years earlier, at the funeral of his rich, eccentric aunt Katherine. She had outlived her third husband by ten years and died childless at Overhouse Estate aged seventy-three. Even though she stipulated in her will that "there may not be above Sixty persons invited to my funeral," it was a lavish affair. Along with the Wedgwood clan who lived in and around Burslem came Long John and cousin Thomas's brother Richard—the now wealthy cheese factor from the leafy, peaceful village of Spen Green, twenty miles away. "Failure" was apparently not in the vocabulary of that family. But "beauty" was.

Josiah had not seen his cousin Sarah since her grandfather's funeral thirteen years earlier, when he was twelve and she was nine. She was now twenty-two, with deep, dark, radiant eyes, fair, fine hair, and creamy-white skin. As cousins they shared some physical traits—they both had thin lips and a curved nose—but "Sally," as she preferred to be called, had high cheekbones and a narrow chin, unlike Josiah's round face and fleshy jowls. From that point on Josiah was besotted.

Everyone in town was talking about Aunt Katherine. Even the poor peered through the brown furze bushes to see her friends and family gathered around the churchyard, all dressed to her specification ("the women to have gloves and the men hatbands and gloves," she instructed). The poor were amongst the many beneficiaries of her will—after the funeral, £3 was to be divided up and distributed amongst them as part of a total of £1,000 in cash legacies bequeathed to the town, servants, and family. Hers was a life of "genteel competence." She was extraordinary in her ability to manage her extensive properties, bankroll charitable societies, and generally conduct herself in what was considered a gentleman's skills, setting an example that far outperformed the landed aristocrat, whose talents lay "with gambling, duelling, sporting and sexual prowess."

Her death changed many people's lives, especially that of Josiah's brother, Thomas. He inherited a substantial share of Aunt Katherine's property, nearly 200 acres in all, including Overhouse Estate, where he had been working in the potworks for the past twelve years. Ownership of the estate had passed out of Josiah's side of the family two generations back, bypassing his father, but once again a Thomas Wedgwood owned the old prestigious home, in addition to the Churchyard House and Works. After almost two decades of struggling to keep his small trade going and a family growing, Josiah's brother Thomas now had the privilege to call himself a "Gentleman."

Not that this brought instant wealth. In fact, it did very little to help him out of the massive debt he had fallen into. Josiah and his other brothers and sisters were still waiting for the twenty-pound inheritance their father wanted to leave them. Some consolation came from Aunt Katherine, though. Nobody was left out of her will—every cousin and kinswoman from distant laboring bricklayers to the Big House brothers received something. Sally, the jewel in Josiah's eye, was remembered with £5. Aunt Katherine thought Josiah needed a bit more, leaving him £10. (Her long-serving maid and friend, Sarah Marsh, received £60.)

A few years on, Josiah had not touched a penny of that £10, and he even managed to save a bit more since he and Whieldon had been doing respectable business. He needed Long John to know this, as they sat and talked in the Big House. It was a point he wanted to stress since it was testimony not only to his industry but to his attitude toward financial responsibility. It wasn't much, he granted—it was no secret that he wasn't given a helping hand in life from his brother, who was endlessly worried about his own son Thomas, now an apprenticed potter. Josiah preferred not to talk about that; it was why he was at Long John's rather than meeting with his "Gentleman" brother.

Josiah then came to the point. His goal was to start up a business by himself. He knew he had the talent and energy, and he saw what fruits could be had if he applied himself the way Whieldon had done when he was Josiah's age. He had been out of his apprenticeship for ten years, he had gained experience working with two different manufacturers, and had looked over the labor of people ranging from prominent modelers to children who were hired to "tread the wheel" (Whieldon's throwing wheels were not self-powered, allowing Josiah to work them occasionally without using his sore leg). He had learned, too, how to manage a sizable potwork, how to keep accounts, and where to look to employ suppliers of goods.

He also, of course, had the skill to help ensure his batches of pottery would not go to waste and cost him an ounce of profit—and he certainly wouldn't be found whittling away hours at the alehouse. He knew that if the clay he molded was too damp, it would immediately crack when fired. He could estimate what temperature his wares needed to be heated to for appropriate hardening, though he wasn't as precise as Long John. He knew how to judge the change of colors while firing and understood that the resultant hue depended on chemical compositions: if air was introduced to a clay containing iron oxide, it would turn the wares red, for example, but if air was excluded by heating it in glowing charcoal, it would turn the pieces blackish-gray. He knew that one must have "all the appearances of a most extensive Laboratory and the machinery of an Experimentalist." Above all, Josiah had proof of his endeavors. He had the new green-glazed ware to show Long John, and promised that in his secret notebook there were more interesting trials he was pursuing.

What Josiah lacked, he explained, was an opportunity to break off on his own. With insufficient funds to buy his own potworks and all the equipment it would need, and with no bank to turn to (and had there been one, he would have fallen into that class of workers that even a century later was condemned to be "manifestly ineligible" to borrow), he could only look to the family for support. He had his £10 to put toward a beginning, and the confidence that he could turn a profit and pay his debt. He needed Long John's help to get started.

Long John no doubt recognized something of himself in young Josiah: the youngest, without family privileges, who resolutely persists where so many others would retreat. He also had to acknowledge that Josiah possessed something that few others in his family had—actual talent at the family craft. These qualities were good enough for Long John, and he had just the thing in mind for Josiah.

One of the properties Long John and cousin Thomas had bought as an investment over the years was a potworks a stone's throw from the Big House, around the corner on Shoe Lane, toward the central square of Burslem. It was a modest size—two ovens (one for lead-glazed wares, the other for "red wares"), with well-built, tile-covered worksheds and rooms, and a small ivy-clad dwelling facing the road. It was called Ivy House Works, and for Josiah it was a dream come true.

Long John demonstrated considerable confidence in his young cousin when he offered to rent Josiah the Ivy House Works, all the more so since the cousins had just witnessed the spectacular failure of their brother-in-law's attempt to succeed in the trade.

Long John and cousin Thomas's older sister Sara fell in love with the "yeoman" son of a local baker named Jonah Malkin. They married in 1740, just as her brothers were first branching out to operate a potworks independent of their father. Jonah did not have much money to begin with and had been working on raising money in dribs and drabs for at least a year, borrowing up to £5 from local Burslem potters who accepted his IOUs on trust. This was not a concern to the Wedgwood family—after all, they had run their share of risks in order to settle themselves in the trade—and with the optimistic vision of their future it was easy to offer moral support. But after his marriage to Sara, Jonah raised the stakes in his attempts to secure enough capital to establish his own potworks.

He entered into a series of bonds for larger amounts—£40, £50, even £60 plus interest—with a number of people, including local potters. These bonds, which were a common way to raise capital for business endeavors on small scale, soon exceeded even the debts through mortgages and bonds that Josiah's brother needed to enter to make ends meet during the same period. Despite borrowing to build up this base, Jonah proved to be an inept potter. Soon he was working with the hope simply of paying off the interest on his loans, for which he turned to his new family for support. "His father lent him £40, his wife £40, the Reverend Jonah Malkin of Wirksworth £25, his sister Margaret £40, his mother's annuity of £70 came his way, his brother-in-law Richard Wedgwood loaned him £111, and John Wedgwood £32." It was a staggering amount, accumulated by hiding existing debts, sliding new loans toward old ones, and rapidly but humbly asking for help. He was never going to recover—his efforts to manage his debts soon surpassed any attempt to turn a profit in his small pottery.

In 1749, just at the time when his brothers-in-law Long John and Thomas were drawing up plans to build the Big House, Jonah and Sara were forced to sell their household effects in a desperate attempt to mollify the hunger of creditors. He took the stack of bonds and bills from his mahogany desk, which was sold with their other belongings. When the sale was over, they managed to raise a paltry £36, enough to cover but one of the bonds. Next went the farming stock. On his way back from paying off one debt with the money raised, he had a bill worth £13 in change. It went straight to Long John, who scribbled on the back: "J.W. has taken to his Account."

That was four days before Christmas. By 24 January 1751, a warrant was issued for Jonah's arrest, including a writ declaring that he had gone into hiding. After £4 of Crown expenses, including a ten-shilling fee for the "Bailiffs for endeavour to arrest Defendant" and a sixteen-shilling journey to the Newcastle jail, Jonah was incarcerated.

Long John had to balance sympathy and support for his sister with skepticism and caution toward his brother-in-law when he agreed to offer what assistance he could. The first thing he did was instruct his Newcastle-under-Lyme lawyer Samuel Boyer to meet with Jonah to determine the depth of the debt. "It is more money considerably than I Imagin'd it would amount to," Boyer delicately wrote to Long John a month later. It was more than probably anyone could have imagined. The list of creditors was the length of an arm, which Boyer tried to represent in a kind light since "I really believe," as he said to Long John, "he has taken the time to think of every body," but it revealed that Jonah owed upward of £1,000, and was owing around £80 in growing interest alone. A plea in *Aris's Birmingham Gazette* showed the gravity of the situation:

> April 8, 1751. To be sold. A messuage with a set of potworks at the Hammill near Burslem, in the County of Stafford, late in the possession on Jonah Malkin, and also several fields of pasture land and meadow ground thereto belonging, being freehold, wherein are five several mines of coals and a great quantity of clay for the potters use. For further particulars enquire of the said Jonah Malkin at Burslem aforesaid or of Mr Boyer at Newcastle-under-Line [*sic*], Staffordshire.

The failed business had to go, along with the remaining pieces of land Jonah owned on the eastern slope of Burslem, as well as "ALL and Singular my Goods Cattle, Chattells, and personall Estate whatsoever or of what nature or kind Soever the same does consist (the Wearing Apparrell of myself & wife only excepted and foreprized)."

A few months later, all they were left with was the clothes on their backs. On the eve of Jonah being sent off to debtors prison, a letter to

Long John arrived from Boyer advising that the sale of the buildings and lands had been unsuccessful. Long John once again stepped in. He offered £950 cash "for his Estate at the Hammell with everything within & without Doors whatsoever with all Mines," with which Jonah was required "to Pay all Dues & Demands." The price was not generous; the estates could potentially have sold for more under less trying circumstances, and Jonah was still left with residual debt, which he borrowed from his sister, containing the lingering problems within the immediate family—the best solution available. Long John didn't want or need this land, part of which Jonah received as an inheritance and part of which he bought with Sara's dowry. But it did earn rent money, just not nearly enough to service Jonah's debts. Long John allowed the present tenant who was renting the lands to remain, but the family relationship with their brother-in-law cooled dramatically. Long John was willing to help his young cousin Josiah, but with the implication that he should expect no special favors.

As Josiah rode back to tell Whieldon that he was ready to move on, Jonah was out plowing Long John's fields on a laborer's daily wages, continuing a withdrawn life. He and Sara never had children.

Jonah was not the only one to go bankrupt, nor was he the last. He was, however, the most recent, which was an unhappy reminder of the perils of venturing into business. But Josiah was eager to take the risk. When he told Whieldon that he was ready to move on, excited about the new glaze he developed, he allegedly declared, "I saw the field was spacious, and the soil so good, as to promise an ample recompense to any who should labor diligently in its cultivation." With Jonah's debacle a warning, he now knew how difficult it could be to cultivate one's sprouting ambitions in the field.

7

The Racehorse

The Ivy House was not large, but Josiah rattled around in it by himself as if it were a mansion. The ivy climbed up the front of the seventeenth-century building, framing its five sets of thin, iron-mullioned windows—two on the ground floor, next to the wooden front door, and three upstairs. He had two small fireplaces, one each side of the house, with a steep wooden staircase right in the middle, acting as a partition between the two living rooms downstairs and two chambers above.

Out at the back across a small, hard earth courtyard were the split-level workshops and his two ovens, with their rounded, hollow bases and tall brick necks one on each side. The workshops, too, were small, but efficiently designed—a miniature of what he found at Whieldon's—nothing like the old Churchyard Works. And as it was in the middle of town, the works were also busier and noisier than any place he had been before. The sounds of grunting sows gave way to masters' shouts and smashing shards. His yard was contiguous with his neighbors': the potter Ralph Wood behind him, the Turk's Head alehouse to the left, and Ruffley's, another potworks, to the right.

Ivy House itself was separated from Shoe Lane by a small front garden enclosed by a waist-high brick wall that kept the convoy of horses and carts at bay by little more than two paces. The road was much busier than when Josiah last lived in Burslem, partly due to the creeping growth in population but also to the activity in the town center where work was afoot to create a market square. The townspeople had removed the maypole and were finally filling in the hazardous pools created after years of men digging for clay. The people of Burslem also began work on their first Town Hall, next to which the open-air meat and vegetable market was soon to be held every Monday and Saturday.

As Long John had made clear, they weren't going to give Josiah an easy ride, and accordingly the Ivy House Works didn't come cheap. Josiah and Long John agreed upon an annual rent for the house and workhouses of £15, beginning May Day 1759. In addition, Josiah had to purchase the wheel from them at £1 8s and other materials for just under another £1, making his first year's bill £17 6s. Josiah was to pay quarterly, and the sole concession he eventually received from his cousins was a £2 reduction after he argued that some of the workhouses needed work.

These weren't Josiah's only expenses. In fact, his largest expense came in the form of the wages he needed to pay the journeyman (skilled artisan) who had just commenced his services, yet another cousin named Thomas Wedgwood. The sixth son of Uncle Aaron, Thomas was four years younger than Josiah, had served his apprenticeship, and was lately employed as a journeyman at a manufactory in Worcester, where he learned how to make a form of porcelain recently developed by his old master. For a "potter ambitious to improve and refine creamware," as Josiah certainly was, his new employee would prove most useful. So much so, in fact, that Josiah came to dub him "Useful Tom," a sobriquet that stuck.

However, Useful Tom came at a high price: £22 a year, slightly above the average for a skilled craftsman, but akin to the respectable wages Whieldon had paid his prized employee, Josiah Spode. Among the lessons Josiah learned from Whieldon was that good labor was worth every pound and he recognized that offering rewards commanded respect amongst the more highly trained workers. For the less skilled—the many who were hired to do routine, manual tasks—high wages were never going to be the answer, as Josiah would later make clear, and he continued to lament the problem of undisciplined labor. Whieldon's scheme of housing his workers close to the manufactory was extraordinary, and far beyond Josiah's reach, at least at the moment. For now, he would have to suffer the "idle, slovenly, irregular habits" of the itinerant men who still needed to be "enlightened" and whose souls religious types were trying to save.

In the eyes of some, Burslem was in desperate need of the spread of God's word. A year after Josiah had settled in the Ivy House Works, John Wesley came to town and faced, with similar success, the insolent men whom Josiah hoped to transform into a disciplined workforce.

For some twenty years Wesley had been on his mission to proselytize the Western world, particularly America and England, to Methodism, his new brand of Dissenting belief. He traveled thousands of miles every year, making his way from village to village, preaching in the open air to curious congregations about how important it was for their souls to feel and acknowledge their sins, to see and love God every moment, and pray, rejoice, and give thanks evermore. In early March 1760, he discovered Burslem.

Upon arriving in what he described as "a scattered town on the top of a hill, inhabited almost entirely by potters," Wesley found a central spot, put down his soap box, and began preaching to "a multitude." "Deep attention sat on every face, though as yet accompanied with deep ignorance," he recorded in his journal. "But if the heart be toward God, He will, in due time, enlighten the understanding."

He soon had an inkling that it was going to take some considerable time. The next evening, Sunday, he returned to his spot at five o'clock, hoping for a good gathering on the day of rest. As he preached, there were disturbances from the back—"five or six were laughing and talking till I had near done," at which point one of the lads lobbed a clod of clay, "which struck me on the side of the head," but he managed to maintain his composure.

It was not the first time Wesley had been hit by the first thing a local "prophet of evil" (one of Wesley's more forgiving characterizations) could find to hurl at him. Farmers at least once threw turnips at him, and his brother Charles, who worked in tandem with John, had his own notable experiences when visiting the area. Some years earlier, when Charles was preaching in South Staffordshire, he described how the street became "full of fierce Ephesian beasts (the principal men setting them on), who roared and shouted, and threw stones incessantly." Charles breathlessly concluded his sermon, hoping he had weathered the brutality, but "a stream of ruffians was suffered to beat me down from the steps, I rose, and having given the blessing, was beat down again, and so a third time."

This was not the normal reception townsfolk gave to visiting preachers. However, Wesley's Methodism was looked upon with extreme skepticism by those who believed that he was attempting to dupe them into giving up money under the threat that their souls would otherwise be condemned to Hell. Only recently, some angry townspeople near Burslem where the Wesley brothers preached proclaimed that they had identified a devious pattern to these visits. First Charles Wesley arrived and, "preaching publicly in the streets and fields," announced that he was going to "reform the colliers, and other illiterate and ignorant Persons," and intimations were given that "a Charity School was designed to be built and endow'd" to teach children Christian principles at no cost to the community; then, as he left, Charles gave a gift of one guinea each to the poor for bread. His brother John soon followed, proposing a subscription among two hundred people for implementing the plan of their charity school—just a bit of money per head, whatever they could afford. Finally a third preacher arrived, a disciple of the Wesleys, who preached about the shortcomings of other faiths, referring to the Church of England clergy as "dumb Dogs" who, when offering Holy Orders, "pretended to be moved by the Holy Ghost, but was all a mere farce"; and then he talked of "eternal damnation" and accused any who rejected his word "of being enemies of his Majesty."

The increasing number of men who preferred to attend the alehouse and indulge in rituals that required singing pub songs rather than hymns were not without opinions and prejudices, and they were not prepared to tolerate threats from traveling preachers peddling new brands of faith. From then on, whenever the Wesleys came near the town, they were attacked by people "flinging Stones and Dirt at them" and smashing the windows of anyone who put up the preachers for the night. By the time John Wesley entered Burslem for his first visit, his reputation had preceded him, and he found himself assaulted by "the beasts of the people" and praying that God, who held "the bridle from above," would restrain them. God had trouble hearing his prayers, and that March in 1760, fifty-seven-year-old Wesley rode off "over the mountains, through furious wind and rain, which was ready to overthrow both man and beast," leaving his work to be finished at another time.

To Josiah's mind, this was a perfect portrait of the problem he himself faced—unruly men who dismissed authority and laughed while doing so. Not that Josiah cared about John Wesley. He thought the preacher's gospel about original sin and the supernatural—Wesley's belief in witchcraft and

Satan—was simply ludicrous. He did, however, find the man's perseverance remarkable. Despite the disruption of clods of clay bouncing off his forehead, Wesley managed to get through to at least a few people each visit, and it was clear that his brand of religion was gaining a substantial following throughout the country. He made sure his visits were not ephemeral. He left behind small gifts, free pamphlets of his prayers, and prodigiously produced cheap abridgments of classics like *Paradise Lost*, "Milton for the masses," as well as grammar books and the immensely popular *Primitive Physick* (1747), a self-help *materia medica* for the poor. Despite the preacher's wayward beliefs, some of his writings would have appealed to Josiah's own taste for "useful" literature, such as the tract Wesley had just finished writing entitled *Electricity made plain and useful*, a summary of Benjamin Franklin's achievements.

Wesley had discovered that the marketplace was an excellent medium to spread his name around. He was a traveling salesman whose ploys did not escape Josiah's notice.

❧

Josiah's strategy to "convert" his workers to a more disciplined life was to work as closely as possible with them. Each morning, Josiah summoned his employees to work by blowing a horn, as did most of the other master potters, just as the postman did to announce his arrival in the town square. This sometimes led to confusion, at least ostensibly, since the workers claimed uncertainty about who was calling whom. Once in, Josiah sat on the workbenches beside them, demonstrating what he required by forming the first models of things he needed his men to imitate. He looked after all the apparatus in his workshops, the "lathes, whirlers, punches, gravers, models, moulds, drying-pans," and other tools; he and Useful Tom shared the jobs of working those ones that required an experienced "knack" to use. At night in the kitchen of the Ivy House, Josiah returned to his chemicals, potions, dyes, and swatches, continuing to record hundreds upon hundreds of experiments in his carefully guarded leather notebook.

At the Ivy House, Josiah wasted no time getting to work on producing the tried and tested, and easily marketable, products such as the familiar agate ware, knife hafts and handles for other sorts of utensils, tiles, tortoiseshell and marble plates finished in a lead glaze—the sort of things he produced with Whieldon. He also produced the stock-in-trade "greengrocery" wares, the teapots and accoutrements shaped like cabbages, cauliflowers, melons, and vegetables, covered with his new trademark "grass green" glaze. It was easy to manufacture such items since they allowed a small degree of error in production—blemishes and "irregularities" didn't matter so much when they were intended to look like oddly shaped fruit and veg. And true to his own expectations, Josiah had developed another unique glaze, this time a yellow-orange one. He thought it would be perfect for a new molded pineapple-shaped teapot, incorporating "grass green" leaves that sprouted from the base of the item. The West Indies fruit was popular with the rich, who thought the matching teapot amusing.

His unique glazes were what, at this time, distinguished Josiah's wares from anything else in the marketplace. There was nothing distinctively "Josiah Wedgwood" about the forms of the pieces themselves. In fact, the decorative bodies of the teapots, canisters, sauce bowls, and the like that were produced by pouring slip into a mold were identical to those issued from Whieldon's and many others' manufactories. In this respect, Josiah still "had other difficulties to encounter arising from the novelty of his works," explained his nephew, Thomas Byerley, later. "Workmanship of the pottery was at this period in a very low state as to its style—The whole country and those in the habit of forming common vessels made in white stone ware enjoyed only three professed modelers—one of these was brought up under Mr Whieldon [during Josiah's] partnership."

The gifted modeler was William Greatbatch, whom Josiah came to know so well while working with Whieldon, and who designed and crafted the models exclusively for Whieldon. However, Josiah had to strike an agreement with his old partner to buy plain "biscuit ware only—for the new work in Burslem where it was sent to be coloured and glazed."

Their partnership helped Josiah enormously, since hiring an artist or modeler—especially with the talent of Greatbatch, or any of the Wood brothers—was expensive and the cost of casting master molds or an original block cutting was, for Josiah's budget, prohibitive. Where Josiah was able subtly to distinguish his wares from others' was in the parts finished by hand. Like all skilled craftsmen, Josiah had a particular touch when forming the knob on a lid, rolling on a handle, or shaping the spout or feet of a piece.

These were not the only local potters to engage in collateral trade with Josiah. He began doing business with Long John and cousin Thomas, as well as others around Burslem, such as the Meir family, potters from Lane Delph, where Josiah had regular dealings with Sarah Muir, the daughter of the master potter who handled the accounts (and in 1762 became proprietor of the pottery), and haggled over prices with Josiah for the sale of biscuit wares which he would glaze. The arrangement worked well for all. Whieldon for one was happy to supply his young protégé with plain wares to help him along in business, and Greatbatch was looking to build a portfolio of regular accounts since, partly urged on by Josiah's example, he was thinking of going into business for himself. He was even looking at a property to rent in Lower Lane, off the newly improved road running in and out of Stoke. For the moment, Josiah's business relationship with Greatbatch was growing closer. It appears that Greatbatch traveled down to London where he acted, in part, as Josiah's agent, "dealing with customers, orders, and shipments of pottery, such as that left at the Cross Keys," a coaching inn near the major trading center of Cheapside in London, where the Elers brothers had once sold their pottery.

❧

There were two main cities on Josiah's mind as he worked long days at the Ivy House Works. One was London, where his wares were distributed to local customers and markets; the other was Liverpool, where new sorts of decorations were applied to some of his wares and whence much of his merchandise departed for foreign export.

The "new sorts of decorations" Josiah began to have done in Liverpool involved the process of "transfer-printing," developed by John Sadler in 1756, and specialized by the printing firm of Sadler & Green. It involved applying a special metallic-oxide ink to an image engraved on a copper plate, which was transferred to paper and then, while the pigment was still wet, pressed onto the ware, transferring the refined picture. It was an immediate triumph. Only weeks after Sadler had devised the technique, he and his partner signed a sworn affidavit for a patent application stating that they "without the aid or assistance" of anyone did, "within the space of six hours . . . print upwards of twelve hundred earthenware tiles of different patterns," which were "more in number and better and neater, than one hundred skilled pot painters could have painted." It was this feat that had so impressed commentators on England's "mechanical" ingenuity. In ways similar to modeling and block molding, it would simply be cheaper at this stage for Josiah to send out his wares and have them decorated than to commission his own copperplate engravings.

But printing couldn't be done on just any piece of pottery—the surface of typical salt-glazed stonewares was too dimpled for the detail of the printed picture. Happily for Josiah, his diligence and perseverance in experimental trials had again served him well.

He had recorded over 400 experiments, filling 169 pages of his notebook, and was in hot pursuit of a pristine white glaze that would substantially improve cream-colored earthenware, which for all manufacturers still tended toward a dirty cream or yellowish tinge. Back with Experiment number 68, he did stumble upon a recipe that stirred him, the proportions of ingredients scribbled as: "India porcelain $5\frac{1}{2}/8$, London crown glass 7/7, Flint glass 16/6. White enamel 4/67, and White lead 32 1/8/3." But 338 experiments later, writing much more cryptically in a secret code that only he knew how to read, Josiah was on the verge on victory. He recorded the formulae in the left column, quantities above coded ingredients, and the results of the trials:

Expt No:

406   1/16 = 4 grs.
  362   3
          This seems to separate, part is run thin like water, and is
a good color

407   1/16 = 4 grs.
  362   4
          Much the same but less the watery part.

408   1/16 = 4 grs.
  362   5
          Much the same but less still of the exuded watery part.

409   1/16 = 4 grs.
  362   26
          Rather better.

410   $1/16 = 4$ grs.
Fired 362 4—
    Worse color but not separated like the above Nos, is more of an uniform Glass but not clear, is what we call *Scummy* on the surface

411   $1/16 = 4$ grs.
    336   3
        A GOOD WT. GLAZE!
        The best of all these trials—uniform—Transparent and nearly colourless

The "good Wt. glaze" Josiah was thrilled to document produced a uniformly smooth, sugary, ivory cream-color ware, unrivaled in its consistency and perfect for transfer printing. By the end of 1761, he was ready to send batches of his new creamware to Sadler & Green in Liverpool for decorating—"5 doz 18s & 24s Teapots at £1.5.0"—and the final firing.

Josiah's timing was perfect. The detailed pictures and words that could be transferred onto wares were creating a sensation amongst consumers. Pictures of "Pipe and Punch Parties" were printed on punch bowls; fashionably clad women were depicted sipping tea on teapots and canisters; popular satirical prints were reprinted onto mugs. Josiah had Sadler reproduce on one mug "The Triple Plea"—a sardonic print from 1725 satirizing the three professions, with verse that complemented Josiah's dry sense of humor:

Law, Physick, and Divinity;
Contend which shall superior be,
The Lawyer pleads He is your Friend,
And will your Rights and Cause defend,
The Doctor swears deny't who will,
That Life and Health are in his Pill,
The grave Divine with Look demure,
To Patients will Heaven assure.
But mark these Friends of ours & see,
Where ends their great Civility,
Without a Fee, the Lawyers Dumb;
Without a Fee the Doctor—Mum;
His Rev'rence says without his Dues,

You must the joys of Heaven lose,
Then be advis'd: In none confide,
But take sound Reason for your Guide.

There seemed no end to the possibilities of what one could do with print-ing on pottery. Now the piece was virtually incidental to the message or illustration on it—a strange but nonetheless exciting new way to think about his wares. Josiah contemplated the mood of the public. They liked humor, but that had been done. They liked rustic scenes from literature—that too was now available on punch bowls, and the sort. They liked famous people, he realized. That's why figurines sold so well.

"Plates & Drawings! I believe you have not considered this—" sug-gested Sadler. People on plates; the idea was appealing. Much simpler to make than cast figurines.

Britain and its colonies had a new king, for a start. Few of George III's subjects would ever get the chance to hear their king (and if they did, few would probably understand his heavy German accent) and not many would see the king in person, so, following his coronation in 1760, the population became familiar with his presence through pictures. They were, it must be said, often derisory, portraying the monarch as "a blind simpleton." "The bulk of the people in every city, town, and village," noted a somewhat bemused John Wesley, "heartily despise his Majesty, and hate him with a perfect hatred."

"Hate" might have been a strong word to describe Josiah's feelings, but he was certainly no fan, in line with his family's Whiggish political and Dissenting religious suspicions about the usefulness of the monarchy. In fact, he thought this way of most of the aristocracy. He refused to manu-facture "armorial ware," since such personalized trinkets were difficult to work with and generally "very bad things for us to meddle with." Crests were "as useless," he said, "as Crest wearers are."

The king may not have fit the bill for a hero, but there were plenty of other candidates, people Josiah had a genuine interest in—politicians and admirals who, by 1761, had everything to do with Josiah's future.

❦

Since 1756, Britain had been involved in a complex war, which had esca-lated from competing French and British interests in North America and the "newly discovered" West Indies. In part it revolved around British westward expansion on the North American continent. With a population thirty-three times the size of the French colonies, British colonial governors felt it was time to expand over the Appalachians and into vast French territories starting in the Ohio Valley. The conflict grew into an international affair, and the fighting soon spread to the West Indies, India, and Europe. Yet what became known as the Seven Years War was as concerned with territory at sea—its thriving trade route—as it was with territory on land.

London merchants had for some years been anxiously following developments in the New World. In 1742, just before the last war with France, they had petitioned Parliament for information about the number of ships deployed to protect and escort merchant convoys conducting trade with the New World. The Admiralty's reply was calm. "The trade of the West Indies has been so well protected by Vice Admiral [Edward] Vernon, and the ships stationed at the islands, that we hear of no losses in those parts; and even in North America, where it is alleged that ships have been lately taken, the same is not imputed in the petition to a want of cruisers but of proper care in some of your Majesty's commanders stationed in those parts."

Admiral Vernon not only captured territories but secured trade routes—becoming a hero for the merchants of England. Almost twenty years after the admiral's early triumphs, Josiah was following the latest developments closely, since his wares were amongst the nation's stock involved in West Indies and North American trade.

While working busily at the Ivy House Works, the atmosphere black as mud, Josiah's mind was often filled with thoughts of pineapples and sun sparkling off the sea, large ships sailing in and out of port. Many people thought of the New World in this way—especially British America and those "newly found" islands, the West Indies—and like many in England, these images were refreshing because they were harbingers of lucrative trade and potential riches: America was already a land of opportunity. As the growing population of colonials was creating new wealth, more luxuries were being demanded from manufacturers in the mother country.

The colonial gentry did not want their remoteness to deny them the amenities enjoyed by their European kin, so they sought the same goods for themselves. Gentility required the amenities of polite life, as the young Benjamin Franklin discovered one morning when his wife presented his breakfast without the usual "two penny earthen porringer with a pewter spoon." Instead, "I found it in a china bowl, with a spoon of silver. They had been bought without my knowledge by my wife, and had cost her the enormous sum of twenty-three shillings, for which she had no other excuse or apology to make but that she thought *her* husband deserved a silver spoon and china bowl as well as any of his neighbours." Over the next ten years, Franklin noted, "as our wealth increased," so too did the appearance of improved china and pottery.

The young entrepreneur was not alone in indulging in what some colonials thought were improvident expenditures. Colonial Americans couldn't get enough. "Our importation of dry goods from England is so vastly great," commented one journalist in New York at the time, "that we are obliged to betake ourselves to all possible arts to make remittances to the British merchants." In Josiah's early years at the Ivy House Works, America was witnessing its first "consumer revolution," and to ride the crest of this profitable wave he packed as many crates as possible and sent them off to Liverpool for ships bound for the New World. Once his and other English manufacturers' crates were unloaded, the vessel was restocked with "cotton from St Thomas's and Surinam; lime-juice and Nicaragua wood from Curacoa; and logwood from the bay"—all part of the transatlantic trade; "and yet," the journalist exclaimed, the cost of imports "drains us of all the silver and gold we can collect." Pre-revolutionary Americans, it has been said, "were more English than they had been in the past since the first years of the colonies."

Thankfully for Josiah, their "Englishness" included a love of tea and a new preference for eating off fine "china" (English-manufactured pottery). "Our people, both in town and country," continued the journalist, "are shamefully gone into the habit of tea-drinking," and where tea drinking abounded, so did accoutrements. So much so that a gentleman traveling through the American countryside reported that even in a simple cottage, a family had stocked up with "superfluous things which showed an inclination to finery," including pewter spoons, a mirror, and "a set of stone tea dishes, and a tea pot." In the New World, Puritan entrepreneurs and independent farmers alike "sought English manufactured goods and in other ways acted as agents of capitalism," especially as their opportunities to manufacture their own wares were not yet available. Not until after the Revolution were potters in America able to manufacture teapots and saucers that were capable of holding such hot liquid, let alone matching the aesthetic quality pioneered in Josiah's hometown. In the years leading up to the Revolution, "colonists set their tables with steadily finer dinnerware. Among the poor, pottery replaced handmade wooden plates. Among the better-off colonists, crude pottery was replaced by finer pottery, much of which was imported."

By the 1760s, the colonial American and West Indies market for English goods was exploding. "Already," observed one European traveler in the early 1750s, "it is really possible to obtain all the things one can get in Europe in Pennsylvania, since so many merchant ships arrive there every year." After each wave of merchant ships that arrived, a flurry of notices appeared in the local press advertising what the captivated and eager consumers could expect next. As early as 1754, the *Boston Gazette* was advertising "new fashioned Turtle-shell tereens," "Tortoise Shell Teapots," and other colored glazed wares that Wedgwood had been busy making since his days with Whieldon. The *Boston News Letter* announced shipments of the "new Cream color printed, printed & guilt, & plain enamelled, double & single Rose" wares, but still advertised "Agate, Tortoise, Mellon, Colly flower, and Pine-apple wares."

In the year that Josiah set up his business, 1759, all eyes were on the English secretary of state, William Pitt the Elder, who was working with the largest budget approved in British history—£13 million for the year—to see who would come out on top of the latest war with France over the new territories. Josiah, while "no politician," as he self-deprecatingly confessed, had faith in him.

As the London literati debated the finer points of Pitt's character (an "absolute master" of the House, thought Horace Walpole), Josiah kept his head down and his hands dirty, relieved and happy that the habit of drinking tea had caught on in the New World. He was just finishing off an order which was being packed into oak crates, ready to be sent off to the *Racehorse*, a vessel owned by a Liverpool trader called William Reid, bound for British America.

Anxious to see what further business he could drum up in Liverpool, Josiah left Burslem with his wares.

8

By the Docks

Liverpool was the premier port for America, a bustling trade center that had grown steadily throughout the past century. It was the most convenient port for the Lancashire textile industry, and therefore attracted the greatest number of ships from the New World delivering raw materials, with a surplus of ships ready to return to America offering freight transport at competitive rates.

Josiah was impressed with the town, one of the "cleanest and best-built," according to the indefatigable traveler John Wesley. Josiah was taken with its size, its damp, salty smell, and even the color of its bricks, which he was unused to. He thoroughly enjoyed indulging in the local cuisine, particularly the oysters, not least since "for 10 pence, a man dines elegantly at an ordinary consisting of a dozen dishes," and he even sipped the extraordinary "West Indies rum punch"—a local specialty. It was certainly all very different from what he humbly referred to as the "rugged Pot-making spot of earth," otherwise known as Burslem.

Thousands of stone and brick houses lined a grid of flat, cobblestoned streets. They were large and well built. "The dwelling house was frequently elevated with the first storey elevated considerably above the level of the street, with high flights of steps, in order to obtain large vaults for the storage of merchandise. In the back part of the house there were often offices under the same roof, and a warehouse erected in the yard." Liverpool housed about thirty thousand people at the time, but it was growing fast. As trade developed with the Americas and the West Indies, Liverpool grew in importence. Merchandise—whether Cheshire salt,

Lancashire coal and textiles, Birmingham metal goods, or Staffordshire pottery—passed through the port going out, while sugar, spices, molasses, and plantain crops arrived from the colonies. The "Old Dock" had opened at the beginning of the century, but the new "Salthouse Dock" (1753) pushed the shipbuilding and repairing businesses a bit further downriver.

All of the shipping activity, stacking of crates, and crying of seagulls filled Josiah with immense excitement about the future. He visited the artists he was doing business with, wanting to double-check that they were not breaking their agreement to print images exclusively on his new "cream ware." Such was the state of competition that any new look had a slight edge in the marketplace, but only so long as his associates remained loyal. "You may rest assured," Sadler told him, "that we never printed a Piece for any Person but yourself." His trips to Liverpool also allowed Josiah to check the quality of the pieces as they came out of the final firing after transfer printing before being loaded onto ships and sent off to America.

"I have had a good deal of talk with Mr Sadler," Josiah later reported, and as always "find him very willing to do anything to improve his patterns." They always talked about coming up with different designs—Sadler trying to push some of his newly etched copperplate engravings—but Jonah decided whether they were tasteful enough. "He has just completed a sett of Landskips for the inside of dishes &c with childish, scrawling sprigs of flowers for the rims, all of which he thinks very clever, but they will not do for us." Josiah was never shy to express his judgment. "I am afraid of trusting too much to their taste, but they have promis'd to offtrace & copy any prints I shall send them without attempting to *mend* or alter them."

After his meetings, Josiah went down to the docks to watch the ships sail out, leaning against the fortifications that had been rapidly built along the banks of the river the previous year when the town was alarmed by the scene of an approaching French naval expedition, soon destroyed in a battle close to the Irish coast. The fortifications stood as a reminder of the perils of war, a particularly acute concern to such an important trading town. Only a few minutes' walk away were the coffeehouses where the merchants and traders liked to meet and where Josiah listened to them haggle over business deals. It was here that he met William Reid.

Besides the trade for which Liverpool was famous, it also boasted "two glass factories, salt, iron, and copper works, eight sugar houses, thirty-six breweries, twenty-seven windmills, fifteen roperies, and a stocking manufactory"; but above all, "Earthen ware manufacture is more extensively carried on [here] than in any other Town of the Kingdom," a statement that referred not only to the hundred or so potters who made wares in midcentury but to a whole range of families, merchants, and artists, "all of whom were connected to the potteries." This made Josiah's trips to Liverpool all the more engaging—he was anxious to find out what exactly this community, his competition, was up to. To his mind, they had all the advantages. Liverpool received vast amounts of clay from Ireland— some of it bound for Bristol potters, but much of the 700 annual tons remained, and they didn't need to worry about inland transport difficulties. They also had interests in developing their businesses, and Josiah, who needed connections to help his own business along, found himself in the right place at the right time.

William Reid was a housepainter by trade, whose father was a local merchant. He was energetic, clever, ambitious, and confident, and he discovered that if he talked to enough people, especially the kind that flooded into Liverpool looking to do business, he would find someone with shared interests to start up a collaborative business endeavor. In the mid-1750s, this is just what Reid had done, when he found partners who were willing to invest in a "Liverpool China Manufactory," which would "sell all kind of blue and white china ware, not inferior to any make in England, both wholesale and retail."

Reid & Co., as the outfit was called, opened their warehouse in Castle Street, just off Dale Street, which led to the market. They also rented about a third of an acre of land off Brownlow Hill—out of town, in the fields on the east side—and built a potworks. Reid wasn't too interested in the technical aspects of the potters' craft; if anything, he would oversee some of the pot-painting that they carried out in house. He hired some potters who formed basic cups and saucers and others who enameled them, and he placed a few notices in the *Liverpool Advertiser*, calling for "any young persons with capacities for drawing and painting" to decorate the wares as close to the current style as possible.

Reid's main interest was in producing as much pottery as possible to load up on the ships and sell to the foreign markets. He knew this was where the real money lay, and before long he had found a few more partners with whom to buy a ship and began acting as an agent for other potters who desired to get their goods to the New World. This was what captured Josiah's attention.

Josiah knew of Reid's warehouse—he would pass it on his way to the docks or the market—and when he had the chance to meet him, Josiah was impressed to learn that his interests extended to the export business. At the time, Reid was in the coffeehouse, haggling with a group of men— the investors in his Liverpool China Manufactory—over insurance rates on cargo he was planning to ship to America (business of this sort was always done in the coffeehouse: Lloyds of London was once Lloyds Coffee House). Reid owed them money stemming from their original invest- ment in his business; he devised a scheme to repay them by giving them each, as underwriters of the insurance policies, a merchant's cost to cover their individual cargo, usually about 2 or 3 percent of the value of the goods, rising to anywhere between 6 and 10 percent during wartime. They knew there was potential to make attractive profits in these deals. Insurers offered a range of coverage:

> All perils of the seas, men of war, fire, enemies, pirates, rovers, thieves, jettisons, letters of mart and counter mart, surprisals, takings at sea, arrests, restraints and detainments of all Kings, Princes, and people, of what nation, condition or quality soever; barratry [breach of duty] of the master and mariners, and all other perils, losses and misfortunes, that have or shall come to the hurt, detriment, or dam- age of the said goods and merchandises, and ship, or any part thereof.

Of course there were risks in being underwriters, that was the name of the game—but it was big business, especially in Liverpool. The premiums in part corresponded to the known "skill, ability, and knowledge" of the captain; but the currently high wartime premiums attracted many to the market.

Anyone could be an insurer, "however unable he might be, from poverty, to make up the losses insured against, provided the merchant was weak enough to trust to such a security." In a market that could yield huge profits to insurers, Reid didn't have trouble getting them to agree, but only after he conceded his cut as "broker."

Following his negotiations, Reid turned his attention to Josiah, and explained what he could offer. For a transportation fee and the cost of insurance, Josiah could have his wares put on board the ship of which Reid was part owner; Reid, as "husband," or manager, of the ship, was obliged to "provide a vessel tight and staunch, and furnished with all tackle and apparel necessary for the intended voyage" and to proceed according to schedule and "without delay."

Josiah would have agreed with one traveler's passing comment that Liverpool "merchants are hospitable, nay friendly, to strangers." Reid was not only friendly but persuasive—he had connections, and all the appearances of a person with the perfect kind of knowledge for a potter, such as Josiah, wanting to enter the foreign export market. But Josiah did not need much persuading. He looked around and saw haggling and trading everywhere; he saw crate after crate of pottery loaded up and shipped off. He wanted to see his there as well.

They did a deal immediately, and when Josiah returned home after that particular trip, he demanded all hands get to work on that shipment; just before his latest trip to Liverpool, he had sent the crates forward to be loaded onto. Reid's ship, the *Racehorse*.

Somewhere in the middle of the Atlantic Ocean were some crates of his wares bound for the colonists who, spending well over £3 per capita annually on imported goods, seemed to have an insatiable appetite. But for now his business in Liverpool was over. Finding more merchants like Reid to take his wares away could wait until his next trip. It all seemed like smooth sailing to Josiah; his new export trade promised to bring in lots of money. But when he returned to Burslem, the euphoric vision dissolved as he stared at the letter before him. The *Racehorse* had been captured by French privateers and its cargo confiscated as war booty.

England's commercial prosperity in the eighteenth century made numerous French commentators irritable. "The territory of Great Britain is only about a third of France and her lands do not compare with ours in goodness," protested a treatise published in 1760. So how could it be that "she has a very rich agriculture, more than twice our trade, and immense shipping"? It was a concern that grew decade to decade, and was highlighted in times of war, when French speculators were convinced that England aimed at monopolizing world trade and, especially, at destroying the trade of France. "France would become dependent on England," French foreign secretaries had been warning for years; "in this case, our manufactures and our navigation will die out and England will become formidable."

Ever since Voltaire made the observation that foreign "trade, which has made richer the citizens of England, has helped to make them free," French critics had kept a close eye on what they saw as the double threat to their own security, freedom, and prosperity: England's manufacturing ingenuity and the rigor with which it traded throughout the world. "Everything is speculation, enterprise, or manufacture," a worried marquis de Biencourt reported. "The Englishmen are sensible enough to manufacture for the people much more than for the rich," allowing them "to sell a great deal regularly." Another French official summed it up: in England, "everybody is seaman or mechanic."

The combination of rapidly improving internal manufacturing and a growing accessible international market was to the French deadly, and people like Josiah—or any of the other manufacturers who concentrated on making this part of their business—were the embodiment of that threat. When England went to war with France, particularly when it was over territories in the New World full of precious raw materials and resources, ships with valuable cargo often became the focus of attack.

During such times, when conducting seafaring trade was dangerous and expensive to insure, French merchants faced less opportunity for profit, further weakening their confidence in their economic prospects. Consequently, *armateurs* financed privateering instead, hoping to benefit from war booty—it was the best chance of making money. When war was declared in 1756, the Bayonne Chamber of Commerce cheered, declaring that the southern French port would be the first to send privateers to sea, and from there to Dunkirk hundreds of ships and thousands of armed men sailed out in search of British merchant ships. Heading out empty, with large crews to handle the sails and rigging more quickly than the sparsely manned merchantman, they were more well equipped not only to outmaneuver and capture the vessels but to recover their cargo, frantically dumped in attempts to escape and save the ship. Few British merchant ships tried to resist; if they did, "the prize was usually taken by fierce hand-to-hand combat."

Despite the advantages of maneuverability and the sanguine tales of rich booty and prizes—British trade *was* larger and more varied than any of its rivals'—it remained the case that most (just over half) of the French privateers who went out in search of a capture returned empty-handed. The British Admiralty had responded to merchants' concerns by providing what it could by way of protection, organizing a profusion of convoys and sailing to more accurate timetables; but with a war to fight and vast space to cover, merchants and insurers often had to trade at their own risks. William Reid knew this, and even though French privateers were spotted in the Irish Sea a year before he sailed, causing the alarm in Liverpool, most ships that sailed from there avoided capture. The *Racehorse* was unlucky. And since resistance probably meant death, Reid, on board as the "husband" of the ship, along with the captain, must have thought it best to surrender, saving their own and their crew's lives.

Josiah personally lost a few hundred pounds' weight of pottery when the *Racehorse* was captured. A number of the crates contained some one thousand wares, worth a substantial amount and part of the cargo which Reid had insured for £3,050. But Reid himself had lost much more.

Not being particularly talented or dedicated to producing quality pottery, Reid's own potworks barely turned a profit, and he relied heavily on the income made from his shipping endeavors. When the cargo from the *Racehorse* was captured, he lost his last chance to raise enough money to keep bills and creditors at bay. Allowed to return from France in 1761, he went to the Liverpool magistrates and declared bankruptcy. This act generated a strange legal challenge to Reid's estate, which consequently threatened to bankrupt Josiah.

The men who agreed to underwrite the *Racehorse*'s cargo felt cheated. They had agreed to insure the vessel, confidently (if riskily) expecting to pocket the £250 in premiums they received. Much of that was in lieu of a portion of the debt Reid already owed them. Now they were responsible for paying out an additional £2,800, while Reid threw up his hands and declared bankruptcy, offering them no way to recoup the further losses they had incurred in Reid's failed enterprise. But the insurers devised a scheme.

They reasoned that since Reid owed them money to begin with, and since he was now declared bankrupt, they would withhold money from the *Racehorse* insurance policies under his name and claim it as compensation from his estate. As they said to the magistrate, they "refuse to pay their said subscriptions alleging that the said William Reid the Bankrupt was indebted on his own private and separate account to them." The money they owed in the policies taken out under Reid's name "was sufficient fully to pay their respective portions" of the debt he owed them. Unfortunately for Josiah, it was under Reid's name that his own merchandise was covered. It seemed that because "William Reid the Bankrupt" owed the six underwriters money (ranging from £100 to £300 each), Josiah would not be compensated for his lost cargo.

Josiah was not the only one to be confused about how this could happen, nor was he the only one to lose money in this debacle. The Liverpool merchant John Dobson was another, and he and Josiah submitted a lawsuit to recover their losses. The court heard that not everyone had lost money. The insurers had in fact paid out £1,800 to Reid's partners, who were neither indebted to them nor bankrupt. But the insurers argued that they had a right to retain Reid's share of the ship, £1,000, toward "settling off mutual debts," the sum covered in policies taken out "in the name of God amen Mr William Reid"—Josiah Wedgwood or John Dobson were not mentioned in any insurance policy. It was a technicality. When deals are done in coffeehouses, with few legal guidelines, problems are bound to arise.

However, the court also learned that "It is the usual custom amongst merchants when any of the partners live out of the town of Liverpool, for someone resident there to transact all the business which Reid the Bankrupt did." Josiah's lawyers argued that it could not "be pretended that the policies of insurance are made in the sole name of Reid," and that they "plainly declare that such policies were made for the two other persons besides Reid." There was "£1,000 owing from owners of the Ship *Racehorse* to different tradesmen for the cargo and outfit . . . and such tradesmen demand their respective debts." Fortunately for Josiah and John Dobson, the other petitioner, the Lord High Chancellor of Great Britain agreed that "an order be had for the Creditors of the *Racehorse* be immediately paid their Debts."

It would not be that easy. The underwriters were themselves merchants in Liverpool, and appeared unable to come up with another £1,000 for Josiah and John Dobson, but had taken possession of "Reid the Bankrupt's" property and were raising money by selling off tea ware and the remaining stock. Then went the premises. Following the petition to the court, however, the creditors assigned their ownership of Reid's property over to the petitioners, Josiah and Dobson, who placed an advertisement in the Liverpool paper:

> To be sold by public auction on the 5th January next [1762] at 6 o'clock. All these new erected buildings now used as a China Manufactory, with the Colour mill and premises appurtenant thereto, situ-

ated on Brownlow Hill, near Liverpool and lately occupied by Reid & Co. of Liverpool, held by lease under the Corporation of Liverpool. Any person desirous to view the premises may apply to Mr Wedgwood at Burslem in Staffordshire, or to Mr John Dobson in Liverpool.

It was the Jonah Malkin story all over again—a hopeful entrepreneur gone bust, whose property and premises were laid bare to the public for the best price they could get.

The auction saved Josiah. He was able to recoup his losses from the capture of the *Racehorse* and rescue his own business. However, the whole episode of the lost cargo cost him valuable income, and he was unable to pay his rent to Long John and cousin Thomas. He was only able to stay afloat because they agreed to take his wares in lieu of cash for payment. This didn't make things any easier for Josiah. It was akin to borrowing money to pay existing debts—spending his time producing goods that would not return any money. He was churning out clay to keep from getting buried.

In 1761 and 1762, Josiah redoubled his efforts to produce wares, sending crate after crate to a well-known dealer in London named James Maidmont, and trying to convince his old friend William Greatbatch to set himself up in Lower Lane near Stoke to provide molded wares.

"Having considered what you and I were talking about," Greatbatch wrote to Josiah, just after the auction of Reid's property, I "am come to the Resolution to proceed and have hired men, taken a place . . . and am preparing things in readiness. I intend to come over to Burslem as soon as opportunity offers. In the interim shou'd be glad to have your proposals what you can afford to give per dozen for Round Teapots all sizes together, Likewise oval, &c." This was good news. Greatbatch now had an exclusive supply of molded wares which Josiah could bake, then dispatch to his decorators in Liverpool, and send off for export.

"I have four men pressing constantly," Greatbatch assured Josiah, "and will push forwards as fast as possible. There will be I expect 60 Doz in about a fortnight time ready and 120 Doz. more in 3 weeks after that, in the meantime shall be glad to have your advice in the form of plates if you have an opportunity." Josiah was also developing plans to expand his business in new directions, and ordered an "apparatus for Tile" from Sadler to begin manufacture of tiles worth about £6 each crate.

Sternly complaining that his suppliers, including Greatbatch, were earning more profit per piece than he could, he began to test the waters to edge up his own profits. He also worked out further arrangements to pay for Sadler & Green's services with wares, which was soon adding up to £30 a month in a monopoly whereby Josiah supplied Sadler with all the wares he wanted for resale as long as Sadler prioritized Josiah's printing orders *and* printed exclusive images for his creamware. But unlike cash, the wares that Josiah was sending as "payment" for Sadler's services sometimes broke in transit, and Sadler had to absorb the loss.

Sadler complained. "Consider the discount we allow you—and the Carriage we pay, the Expence of [engraving] Plates, fire, wages, & the Loss we have by the crack'd and second[-quality] ware you send us, not with your Knowledge I believe, but thro' haste in sorting!"

Josiah decided to take another trip to Liverpool to address these problems; but once again, the trip promised to raise more problems than it solved.

9

Paradise Street

I n the same period that buildings were becoming more durable, their owners began to furnish them with objects increasingly fragile. Unlike wood, brass, or pewter pieces, pottery and glassware were prone to breakage even before they were delivered to the owner. At the Ivy House Works, the cratemen stuffed as much straw and hay as possible into the oak boxes to pad the interior for the delicate tea sets and snuff boxes, but the long journey to America was often treacherous, and no amount of attention in packing would prevent pieces from breaking as crates toppled off carriages or were smashed when rough-handled by "wharfmen," or stevedores, loading them onto the ship.

On many occasions Sadler received a crate of Josiah's wares—containing about 130 items, such as "large oblong dishes, 9 inch plates, fluted tea pots, mosaic teapots," adding up to 250 pounds in weight with a value usually between £7 and £8 only to find that the pieces were cracked or, more often, soaking wet. The latter affected the printing process since "the ware getting wet," Sadler explained to Josiah, resulted in "some of the Tea pots flying all to shivers in firing." Josiah then had to explain this to his workers, imploring them to be careful, pointing out that "our common Bisket ware by long exposure to damp Air acquires a certain quality which will not permit it to Glaze kindly."

Given the state of the roads merely leading in and out of Burslem, it was amazing that any of the potters' goods survived more than the first few miles of the adventure. They were so notoriously bad that travelers were lost for words. "I know not, in the whole range of language, terms sufficiently expressive to describe this infernal road," complained a twenty-seven-year-old Arthur Young, conducting a tour of England to inspect the "condition" of the country. "To look over a map, and perceive that it is a principal one, not only to some towns, but even whole counties, one would naturally conclude it to be at least decent." But the roads were far from decent. They were narrow, twisted, and uneven, often muddy, and worst of all, gashed with ruts worn from the wheels of farm carts. Then there were the holes pitted along the sides, dug to collect clay, causing horses to trip and carriages to jolt.

While he was traveling through the country compiling statistics about the development of agriculture and manufactures, Arthur Young's carriage tilted to the side and ground to a halt just outside Burslem. As he climbed out, his leather boots sunk deep into the mud and he saw a group of men contemplating "a cart of goods overthrown and almost buried." He bent down and slid a stick into the rut; it was four feet deep. "I actually passed three carts broken down in these [last] eighteen miles" on the way from Liverpool and Burslem, he noted. This time, though, the lane was too narrow for his cart to maneuver around another toppled cart in front of them. "I was forced to hire two men at one place to support my chaise from overthrowing" while they forced it up the bank and around, jolting the carriage "in the most intolerable manner." This was clearly not good for businesses that relied on the delivery of often fragile goods. As Young said, "agriculture, manufactures, and commerce must suffer in such a track."

The manufacturers were aware of this. Long John and cousin Thomas were already supporting plans to improve the turnpikes—following the example of the improved road that led south out of Stoke—and investing in schemes to build canals for navigation from the Trent River (on which Stoke was built) to the Mersey, which flowed from the Pennines to the port of Liverpool. Since 1755, preparatory surveys had been conducted to consider how canals might create a network between these rivers and the Thames and Severn rivers, and three years later an ingenious engineer named James Brindley was working on detailed surveys of the actual route.

Brindley was well known around Burslem. He was a cheerful-looking fellow, with large round cheeks and wide eyes, who loved to stop and talk to all the manufacturers about his ideas to improve their practical routines. In 1756, he had become the first person anyone from Burslem knew to build a Newcomen steam engine, which he did for a colliery at Fenton Vivian, near Whieldon's works. The steaming, grunting machine stimulated much discussion between Whieldon and Josiah. Two years later, Long John and cousin Thomas commissioned Brindley to build them a large windmill for grinding flints on their land on the top of Burslem Hill, which stood as a proud monument to Brindley's industry for many years.

But engineering a canal of the sort that would improve trade by carrying goods on calm water from Burslem to Liverpool or London was a major challenge. Cutting across valleys required a range of complicated features, such as tunnels, embankments, and aqueducts. It would take time before any ground would be cut—if at all. Not only were engineering skills an issue, but so too were the cost and political negotiations involved—this meant cutting through many landed gentries' property, and patronage from the right people was necessary before any of the manufacturers would stand to benefit. For the time being, Burslem remained the most difficult place to get access to of all the towns in England, and travelers continued to be warned about the hazards.

"Here let me pause," Arthur Young calmly wrote, attempting to conclude his previous diatribe. "I must in general advise all who travel on any business but absolute necessity, to avoid any journey further north than Newcastle-under-Lyme," indeed, "to avoid it as they would the devil." And if his instructions were not followed, "a thousand to one but they break their necks or their limbs by overthrows or breakdowns."

Josiah certainly was not comfortable with traveling to Liverpool, but it was for business and therefore an "absolute necessity." He was going to be busy there—besides meeting with Sadler and Green to discuss particulars of transfer printing, he needed to meet with other merchants and those with whom he'd arranged to have his wares shipped off to America. Liverpool was becoming an increasingly important place to Josiah; correspondence to and from there occupied much of his time, and his business connections were multiplying.

Just as he was considering his schedule—hands with white knuckles gripping the reins as his horse shuffled along the side of the path while carts edged narrowly by—Young's prophecy proved true. On a horrible road near Warrington, outside Liverpool (a "most infamously bad" road, insisted Young), Josiah's horse stumbled on a rut and toppled. Josiah crashed down, landing on his weak leg.

He continued the journey in anguish. His leg throbbed and each mile closer to his destination it grew more inflamed. His condition can only have been made worse by the discovery that Liverpool was in flames. As he approached the town, Josiah noticed the sky was blacker than usual, with a red glow just above the buildings. People were frantically scrambling with children and sacks of belongings. A quarter of the town was ablaze, but there was hope that the "great conflagration" was being contained. With relief Josiah found that it did not appear to threaten the side of town he was heading for. When he finally reached his lodgings at the Golden Lion in Dale Street, he was assisted up the stairs and collapsed into bed.

The anxious landlady at the Golden Lane called the local surgeon to treat Josiah. The surgeon, Matthew Turner, turned out to be a most intriguing man. Like Josiah he was in his thirties, as well as a Dissenter (who eventually openly declared his atheism) and a staunch Whig in politics. He was also "a good surgeon, a skilful anatomist, a practiced chemist, a draughtsman, a classical scholar, and a ready wit." "Very clever indeed," according to those who knew him.

For obvious reasons, he was guarded in conversation with strangers he had to examine, and he concentrated initially on a diagnosis for Josiah's leg. There was likely a slight fracture in the shin bone, but the general weakness of the leg worried the surgeon. Josiah had told him about the infection he suffered as a child, and that it had always given him problems, so that he was increasingly relying on a cane. Josiah had always known there was something to worry about; he knew that the bad humors in the leg could spread. This was exactly Mr. Turner's concern, but the only option was to amputate, and until there were significant signs of the humors causing more widespread problems, rather than the difficulties of a bruised and fractured bone, the surgeon decided it was worth waiting to see whether the leg improved.

Mr. Turner asked Josiah where the accident happened. He knew the spot that Josiah described well, and explained that he was about to start teaching "anatomy and the theory of forms," as well as chemistry, very near the treacherous spot, at the recently founded Warrington Academy, set up for the education of Dissenters and "young laymen of the like persuasion."

Josiah was fascinated. Suddenly, discussion of the leg was dispensed with and Josiah quizzed his new acquaintance about his scientific experiments. Matthew Turner's investigations, it happened, were widespread. He was interested in all aspects of chemistry—medicinal, culinary, and artistic. He experimented with "varnishes, fumigations, bronze powders, and other chemical appliances," which Josiah was registering as useful topics for himself, and emphasized the importance of "some of the principal Experiments in the Elements of Chemistry" when teaching students. It was clear that Josiah was deeply taken with Mr. Turner's plans. He asked about the scope of the course Turner was to present to the students. "As near as I can guess," Turner replied, "it may be finished in twenty Lectures."

Josiah thought back to all the discussions he'd had with Whieldon about establishing a program for educating the lads of Burslem, and his own family's support for the local Dissenting congregations. What Turner described sounded like a model institution for people who shared their beliefs in promoting "useful," practical education. Apparently, the Academy had been established five years earlier by a committee who made "arrangements for obtaining suitable accommodations for the several tutors, and a public hall, library and class room, with a view to the commencement of the first session, early in the autumn" of 1757. "Accordingly," as one student later recollected, "a range of buildings at the north-west end of the bridge [over the Mersey] was engaged, to which was attached a considerable extent of garden ground, and a handsome terrace-walk, on the banks of the Mersey; possessing, altogether, a respectable collegiate appearance." In fact, at the very moment Turner and Josiah were discussing the Academy, its instructors were moving into the new buildings, where "a room was properly fitted up, and useful apparatus provided for the cultivation of this most valuable branch of natural knowledge." The patrons of the Academy invested handsomely—the scientific instruments alone cost £100.

Josiah could not have made a more appropriate contact, even if it was by accident. He did not know it at the time, but, in the words of the trustees of the Warrington Academy, Turner was "a gentleman deservedly esteemed for his abilities as a Chemist" and a skilled lecturer in "practical and commercial Chemistry"—a teacher "very much to the satisfaction of all who attended him."

The surgeon in turn recognized that his patient was clearly no average pottery merchant passing through Liverpool looking for a quick sale, and was equally absorbed in Josiah's description of his own chemical investigations and ideas about the improvement of pottery. Josiah described his potworks in Burslem and his interest in promoting the education of the local men, along the same lines of "rational dissent" that Warrington Academy had established. To their bemusement, they also discovered that they had mutual acquaintances: Turner knew, at least by name, Dr. Harwood, the Dissenting minister at Congleton, and the Reverend William Willets, Josiah's brother-in-law at Newcastle-under-Lyme. There were people in Liverpool that Turner was sure Josiah would enjoy meeting, and vice versa. There would be plenty of opportunity for that, Turner assured his patient, since his convalescence was going to take a couple of weeks at least.

That was not news that delighted Josiah. He had a business to run, workers to supervise, orders to fill, crates to pack, money to make, and a stack of bills to pay. He was forced to rely entirely on "Useful Tom," which concerned him, not because he lacked faith in his cousin, but because now was not the time to rely on anyone other than himself. His only comfort was that he could engage in regular correspondence with his cousin and he was reassured when he received prompt replies to his anxious queries through the post. A few letters to his mother put her at ease about his condition; there was one other person who was relieved, even elated, to hear from Josiah. They had kept in touch after Aunt Katherine's funeral, and nervously revealed more about their feelings toward each other in every letter. It was Josiah's "dear girl," his "loving Sally"—the only one other than his mother who still called him "Joss."

Josiah was not left in isolation for any long stretch of time. On one of Mr. Turner's early visits to ascertain his patient's progress, he brought along a friend he wanted Josiah to meet. His name was Thomas Bentley.

❧

Bentley was a man of weighty presence: "courtly" was the preferred description by his friends. He was heavily set, with strong but friendly features. His head seemed unusually large, even though he was bald, save the wrap of brown hair at the base of his skull, from ear to ear.

He was just a few months older than Josiah (he was born in Scropton, Derbyshire, on New Year's Day, 1730), but he came from a much more

privileged background. His father was a minor country gentleman, a successful farmer who owned lands in Dovedale, on the borders of Staffordshire and Derbyshire. His parents were Dissenters, and they sent their
only son to the nearby Presbyterian Collegiate Academy, where Bentley
had the luxury of studying for six years. He had the benefit of a broad-
based education: he studied the classics in Greek and Latin, he learned
French and Italian, and he practiced composition and mathematics. It was
the kind of well-rounded education that later, as a financier of Warrington Academy, he would help ensure that other youths would receive.

Bentley had a well-trained mind for trade and commerce. When he
finished school at sixteen, his father indentured him to a wool and cotton
manufacturer in Manchester, where he served a seven-year apprenticeship and "underwent a training in accounts and acquired an insight into
the ways of business." Completing that, as well as a Grand Tour through
France and Italy when he was twenty-three, Bentley moved to Liverpool
and rented an office on King Street, where he first worked as a shipping
agent for cotton manufacturers and then opened up a woollen warehouse
in partnership with James Boardman, a like-minded man who was interested in promoting plans "for a charity school among Protestant Dissenters in Liverpool," something that had begun back in 1739.

Bentley had a magnetic personality, and, as Turner had anticipated,
Josiah and he talked effortlessly for hours. Frequenting Josiah's room
overlooking Dale Street, Bentley pulled up a chair and they discussed
ships, pottery, literature, education, religion, and politics. Bentley, Josiah
discovered, was eminently liberal in his views, and struggled with the fact
that some of his merchant business was linked to the nefarious slave trade.
They pondered the principles that governed the sometimes beastly nature
of business, which had the force to strip humanity of its dignity and
shackle unwilling people to a violent life in a strange new world. Josiah
learned that Bentley had tried to "persuade the merchants and masters of
vessels trading to Africa to promote a trade in ivory, palm oil, woods, and
other produce of the country," but to no avail. "Sinews bought and sold"
afforded better profit, "and the bells of Saint Nicolas's Church rang their
merry peals on the periodical returns of the ships from their diabolical
voyages." Each was left to a period of silent reflection.

But each of them also had hope that a rational analysis of how to
enhance education and opportunity for people would lead to a better
society. Josiah admired Bentley's passion for "improvement." He learned

about Bentley's ambitious plans for Liverpool, and how he used London's cultural institutions as a model of development. Within the last decade the much-celebrated British Museum had been established, as well as the Society for the Encouragement of Arts, Manufactures and Commerce; the Society of Antiquaries in London's Chancery Lane had just received its royal charter. It was all happening there, and Bentley wanted to see these things happen in Liverpool. Thankfully his friends, such as Matthew Turner, were happy to offer him all the support and encouragement he needed.

Everyone had faith in Bentley's endeavors, especially since he had already succeeded in doing so much. He was one of the most active founders of the new Liverpool Public Library and he had orchestrated the founding of an Octagon Chapel in Temple Court in the town center for independent services that was in the process of being built. His latest ideas involved establishing a Liverpool Society of Arts, and he was calling his friends around to discuss his plans.

It dawned on Bentley that he had seen Josiah's name before—he recalled the advertisement in the local press about the auction of Reid & Co.'s manufactory. Suddenly Josiah's trip to Liverpool became all the more worthwhile, despite the inconvenience of being incapacitated. Bentley volunteered to offer some assistance; after all, he was rather more successful than Reid at organizing foreign trade, and he knew a host of people in Liverpool that Josiah should meet. The tutors and learned gentlemen connected to Warrington Academy often gathered at his spacious home on Paradise Street, in the fashionable part of town; as soon as Josiah was back on his feet, albeit gingerly, he was added to the guest list.

❧

The house was handsome—elegantly furnished and well looked after by Elizabeth Oates, Bentley's sister-in-law. His wife, Hannah, had died three years earlier in childbirth, and Elizabeth, Hannah's older, unmarried sister, agreed to move from her home in Chesterfield "to take charge of his household." Josiah was fond of her; she was "bright, clever, amiable, and interesting," apparently just as her sister had been.

Soon they were joined by a chattering crowd, and Josiah was introduced to a number of people who would become fast friends: the young lecturer in languages and belles lettres Joseph Priestley; the tutor in divinity John Aikin; the chief minister of Warrington Academy John Seddon; and some of Bentley's other friends, including his neighbor, the skilled "mechanist" and watchmaker John Wyke (the first watch manufacturer in Liverpool).

Josiah was honored to be invited to such an event. He felt it was more than a polite gesture to a wounded stranger marooned in town. He could see that this was a close group of friends. "The tutors at Warrington have sufficient society amongst themselves," explained Priestley, that "we had not much acquaintance out of the Academy." He, like the others, knew where to go for entertainment in the evenings. "I was always received by Mr Bentley," said Priestley. It was a relief to Josiah to be so readily accepted in their "society."

Everyone shared a common interest in what Priestley declared was "the serious pursuit of truth," and the discussions that emerged from their lectures at Warrington, which "often had the air of friendly conversations," spilled over to their evening soirées. Everyone was encouraged "to make whatever remarks we pleased, and we did it with the greatest, but without any offensive, freedom." Josiah found it enthralling.

Each remark seemed intimately related to his everyday concerns, but he was not surprised. After all, he was surrounded by people who had devised a five-year plan of study on all subjects "intended for a life of Business and Commerce." They were subjects designed to appeal to people like Josiah, who was further interested to learn that the Academy trained people like Hugh Mulligan, "an engraver for the potters, as well as a painter of porcelain"—maybe Josiah would hire him, his new friends added, jovially. Josiah would not forget the suggestion.

Amidst all the exciting conversations about art, politics, and the future of Liverpool, Josiah and Priestley settled in a corner and talked science. Priestley, a Unitarian and political liberal like the others, was three years younger than Josiah, but taller and thinner. He was a man who was curious about everything but who had given deep thought to all his beliefs, and who would contemplate philosophical problems at great length. He had a mature intellect and was demonstrably erudite—even at the age of four he could repeat all 107 questions and answers of the Shorter Westminster Catechism "without missing a word." He grew up in a strictly Dissenting Calvinist community and studied Hebrew, Latin, and Greek under the direction of a local minister.

Yet despite all his abilities, Priestley sometimes appeared to lack confidence. He spoke with a stammer which, when combined with his growing reputation as a "furious freethinker," prejudiced potential employers' faith in his ability to lecture. Frustrated, he had even announced his intention to open his own school, "but," observed a biographer, "not a single pupil came to him." His friends at Warrington, however, were not at all bothered. On the contrary, "I greatly admire Mr. Priestley," said Mr. Turner, "and am certain that any school must flourish that has such teachers in it." Priestley returned the compliment, and, sharing Josiah's keen interest in philosophical experiments, praised those conducted by Turner, whom he called "a considerable artist this way." "I attended a course of chemical lectures" by the "ingenious" Turner, said Priestley. "I was one who assisted" him, thus whetting his appetite for the science that he had decided to dedicate so much of his life to. Those lectures at Warrington Academy proved to be the beginning not only of an intense passion for science and philosophy but of new discussions—often debates—about social inequality, money, education, and religion.

The discussion at Bentley's went on late into the night, and Josiah was sorry the evening had come to an end. Besides being a great host, Bentley was, as Priestley said, "a man of great taste, improved understanding, and good disposition." Josiah agreed, and as he was traveling back to Burslem— almost a month after his accident—he felt that this was the beginning of a powerful and profitable relationship. He was right.

10

"Improveable Subjects"

When Josiah returned to Burslem, he was eager to pen a letter to his new "much esteemed Friend," hoping Bentley "will not think the address too free," but declaring that "I shall not care how Quakerish or otherwise antique it may sound, as it perfectly corresponds with the sentiments I have & wish to continue towards you." Josiah had been profoundly touched by the "many kind offices I receiv'd in my confinement at your hospitable town. My good Doctor & you in particular have my warmest gratitude for the share you *both* had in promoting my recovery."

It was the first of thousands of letters in their profitable correspondence. What began as a fortuitous introduction evolved into a friendship intent on promoting each other's desire to better themselves in life. (Josiah jokingly referred to himself and friends as "his Majesty's improveable subjects," conscientious that Dissenters were often condemned for their "inferior"—even threatening—beliefs about "divine rights" of rule.) While not as stimulated by natural philosophy as Josiah, Bentley nevertheless appreciated the values of experimental science as a route to expanding knowledge of nature, and was eager to discuss various ways they might offer mutual support for their business ventures.

In fact, Josiah had grown so restless in his sickbed "confinement" and so inspired by the conversations he had with the Warrington Academy circle that he already "found time to make an experiment or two upon the Aether," mentioning to Bentley that he had also written to Turner seeking his input on other experiments on "crucible making" as well as "the nature of clays." He had new ideas about improving glazes, colors, and materials which now involved applying more technical chemical principles to the processes. For this, he welcomed help.

According to Priestley, scientific discussions were "likely to provide the principal basis of friendship." Such enlightened intercourse was encouraging, engaging, philosophical—and productive. As he told Josiah, he valued having acquaintances to whom he could voice his opinions and elaborate his ideas; it made sense to listen to each other, he thought, "for the pleasure of communicating our discoveries is one great means of engaging us to enter upon and pursue such laborious investigations."

Josiah agreed. "I have told you what a troublesome correspondent you may have of me," he playfully warned Bentley soon after his return to Burslem; "you may think more for your ease to drop than continue the correspondence." Knowing he wouldn't, he, like Priestley, relished the thought of having a sounding board for his ideas, someone he could call on for advice: "at other times I may call upon you for assistance to settle an opinion—or to help me form a probable conjecture of things beyond our ken and sometimes I may want that valuable and most difficult office of friendship, reproof." Rarely would he finish a letter to one of his new acquaintances without relaying some information about his scientific research. This was true even in letters to old family friends whom Josiah encouraged to conduct research for their own benefit.

Besides beginning a new stream of correspondence with Bentley, Josiah started to spend more time in thoughtful discussions about literature with two people closer to him whom he had much respect for: his sister Catherine and her husband, the learned Reverend William Willets. When Josiah returned from Liverpool, he formed part of a small reading group with the two of them, taking recommendations on what books to read from trusted friends, with Bentley now a heavy influence, or from reviews in journals such as the popular *Gentleman's Magazine* (which began monthly publication in 1731), the *Monthly Review* (1749), or the *Critical Review* (1756). Unimpressed with that week's reading, the Swiss poet Salomon Gessner's *The Death of Abel* (Collyer's English translation from the German was just published), Josiah volunteered some alternative reading to a family friend. "I have lately purchased some chymicall books," he put in a letter he co-wrote with his sister Catherine, "which, amongst a variety of other things, treat a good deal about metals, their affinities, mixtures, &c and the result of their various combinations. If you think these would be of any use to you," Josiah offered, "I will with pleasure lend them to you."

Josiah's reading group exchanged ideas and impressions on a wide range of literature in ways typical amongst literate, "improving" men and women. "Critical and curious" minds contrasted and collected "data" (a word Josiah used in referring to any "given fact" derived through research) with such fervent ambition that a demand even emerged for the compilation of encyclopedias—new publishing ventures at this time (the first volume of Diderot's *Encyclopédie* was published in 1751; the *Encyclopaedia Britannica* was still six years away)—to impose some order on the torrent of new knowledge, *scientia*. Monthly magazines moved from one page to the next discussing new books that overlapped the subjects of science, politics, history, travel, literature, and religion just as swiftly as Josiah turned from his sister's comments on Gessner's popular epic poem to tracts on chemical affinity. Dipping in and out of genres provided hours of evening entertainment and stimulation. While some pious readers preferred the Bible—always the bestseller—with its deep-seated truths about the world, others, like Josiah and his circle of friends and family, were enthralled by what secrets might be unveiled within the thousands of pages sailing through printing presses every day.

"Secrets," or informed whispers, about the government were high on Josiah's list of worthy revelations. A surfeit of antiministerial pamphlets published at this time were promising sources for him, and an irritating phenomenon to government spokesmen. Writers of political pamphlets attacking the government were "more numerous" than ever before, complained a contributor to the Tory-loving *Critical Review*, "as well as more indecent, more shallow, and more incorrect because," he claimed; "the bulk of them write only for the profit of their publications" rather than on matters of principle.

Josiah would disagree. Bentley, well educated, well traveled, and well read, opened Josiah's mind to critical perspectives on a whole range of social issues, from current affairs to historical conditions of governmental rule. From their start in 1762, the letters between Josiah and Bentley cautiously examined and elaborated their views on what they considered legitimate reasons to criticize the government. Urged to explore social commentary expressed in newspapers and periodicals, Josiah quickly found his voice. One fiery issue particularly alarming to Whig politicians and their constituency was that young King George III was determined to exercise in full his constitutional prerogatives in bestowing royal patronage to break up the political regimes of Sir Robert Walpole and the Pelhams, a powerful force until 1760. Worse, the costly war over territory in the New World had raged into its sixth year. Spain had recently declared itself an ally with France to challenge Britain for a colonial empire, prompting British attacks on Havana, Dominica, and Martinique, and causing further disruption to trade in the West Indies.

Amongst all the political events that stimulated discussion in Josiah's circle, the war, unsurprisingly, was often the leading topic, since it directly affected their trade. This was why Josiah laid aside discussion of German literature and volunteered the donation of his "chymicall books" to their friends, two brothers who lived in Walshall, near Birmingham, who confessed to Josiah that their "business is so much affected by our war with Spain." Praising their "joynt industry, and you must not think I flatter if I add ingenuity too," Josiah was quick to serve up science as a possible remedy for their ailing business. This was fast becoming Josiah's golden rule of business: reading chemistry served mercantile interests since it had the potential to provide creative impetus to productivity, especially in trying times.

However high science was in Josiah's ranking of worthwhile literature, he needed to confront the challenges others waged against the concept of "self-improvement" by developing an appetite for reading. Although to some the events of the 1760s invited reflection and informed commentary, other self-promoting "guardians of culture" believed the decade was becoming one of publishing decadence. The commercialization of reading—driven in part by profit-seeking booksellers, "those pimps of literature," according to another conservative critic in the *Critical Review*—was reducing a respectable intellectual exercise to a hedonistic and indiscriminate pursuit. "Novel *manufactories*" were peddling romance rather than religion; learning to read, Anglican academics argued, no longer equated with learning how to behave properly. Curiously, even the "enlightened" program of extending education to the poorer of His Majesty's subjects by founding charity schools—something Josiah's sister was directly involved with—was blamed for the corruption of conduct.

It came down to a prejudice reinforcing the hierarchy of education within society: charity schools were so concerned with enhancing reading skills they neglected to encourage manual "labour and industry" amongst the poor. What good was it to "improve" one's head when it was only through the use of one's hands that a livelihood would be earned? Josiah, along with friends and family linked to his reading group, were developing their own response to such a question.

Encouraged by Bentley, Josiah spent long evenings thinking about the values of learning to read and write, and the importance of articulating points of view clearly and effectively, as well as the opportunities to exchange these ideas. Pamphleteering gave a voice, a presence, to Dissenters and other marginalized groups who had long suffered from political subjugation. Of course, as Josiah had experienced at Bentley's house in Liverpool, like-minded individuals had the chance to exchange views on any subject in the privacy of their homes and to a lesser—more guarded— degree through their correspondence. But the soaring phenomenon of cheap mass printing provided a persuasive force for propagating views, whether discontented or prescriptive.

Publish! was Josiah's advice to Bentley, whom he spared "a tedious acct of acids, alcalies, precipitation, saturation, etc," instead encouraging Bentley to make public his "excellent piece upon *female education*." Josiah was not the first to receive Bentley's attention and guidance in developing a "life of the mind." Bentley believed in promoting education for all, stressing the importance of education amongst children, and of establishing non-denominational chapels to cater for these needs. One of Bentley's current philanthropic endeavors was the founding of an independent and self-governing chapel at Temple Court in Liverpool, named "The Octagon" from its shape. Similar to the Octagon Chapel built by Unitarians in Norwich in 1756, the shape of the building symbolized the congregation's responsibility to recognize diversity in worship. As part of what Josiah called Bentley's "instinctive goodness," and his commitment to promote "the finest feelings of the improved human mind," Bentley had sketched out a plan for extending greater education to women, a manuscript which Josiah read while laid up in Liverpool. While Josiah among others commended the piece, Bentley continued to mull over it.

"Why will not the benevolent author be prevail'd upon to publish a thing which would benefit thousands without hurting one!" Josiah demanded to know, somewhat surprised about Bentley's reservations when he was otherwise so encouraging of open conversation.

"It is not perfect," replied Bentley, revealing a modesty and caution, rather than arrogance, that would come to irk the more impulsive Josiah.

"It is perfect enough to do a great deal of good," retorted Josiah, "therefore on behalf of myself & many others . . . male [as well] as female, who are daily lamenting the want of a proper education, & would gladly make use of such a help as you have prepared, I say in behalf of myself and 10,000 fellow sufferers, I do now call upon you to publish the above mentioned book." Forget what "a few hypercriticks (for such only, I think, you have to fear)" will say, advised Josiah, and reflect on "how soon our young folks nowadays grow up to be men & women & enter into the busy world; I cannot help regretting that unless you get the better of your scruples soon, one generation at least must lose the benefit they might otherwise receive from your generous labours."

For five months Josiah had been encouraging Bentley to put "the finishing hand to his valuable MS" and send it to the printers, but for five months Bentley remained "a *talent buried*" in his study. During the same period, Josiah and the Willets continued their reading group, expanding their reading list, perusing polemical and theoretical tracts which provoked more thoughtful discussion than Josiah had ever experienced.

"I am about to furnish a shelf or two of a book-case," a newly intellectualized Josiah told Bentley; "if you would assist me with your advice in the furniture, I should esteem it a particular favour." Apropos recent discussions and just translated into English was Rousseau's *Emile, or, On Education* (1762), which, if Bentley gave the nod, Josiah was ready to devour.

Through all the literature Josiah was consuming with Bentley's advice—in the areas of politics, science, history, and philosophy—he was beginning to question whether the capacity for moral and mental improvement was determined by "instinct" or was a product of "charity." He pondered whether self-improvement, especially in the "younger part of our species," was attainable as a result of human determination and instruction, or whether those ranked ignorant and poor as distinguished from the educated and privileged were destined ever to remain so.

Josiah started to think even more broadly about the concepts of equality and inequality in society, and about what "improvement" could mean to the children of artisan laborers, such as himself. While some literati proclaimed that "Mr Locke's excellent Treatise of Education is known to every Body"—a presumptuous if almost forgivable comment since it had gone through twenty-five English editions after publication in 1693—Josiah was just beginning to discover Enlightenment philosophy.

Bentley was the most educated person Josiah had befriended, and he enthusiastically embraced all the guidance he offered. Each letter from Bentley was a gift. "You cannot think how happy you make me with these Good, long affectionate & instructing letters," Josiah would write. "They inspire me with taste, emulation & everything that is necessary for the production of fine things." Bentley gave Josiah the confidence to believe that he too could be as capable of digesting the "new philosophy" being espoused by *philosophes* and elaborated by his new friends. Josiah said that Bentley's letters acted as "my Magazines, Reviews, Chronicles, & I had allmost said my Bible." He laughed, reflecting on the irony.

Josiah had gained new insights into the views long expressed by Dissenting preachers, including his brother-in-law William Willets, about the corruption of traditional education in society. The Anglican Church denied those who disagreed with some of its tenets the privilege of receiving degrees at the two English universities that existed, Oxford and Cambridge. Furthermore, authorities quashed the efforts of churchmen to print their own prayer books to "instruct the ignorant," due to, as Josiah complained, "motives that do no honor to the cloth." The corrupt politics of education and self-improvement were hidden under the cloak of "providential design"—that God created all in the place they were most useful to serve. To the discomfort of those who upheld the traditional pillars of society—Anglican religion and the authority of the Crown—the secret, dishonorable "motives" of subjugation were being more openly challenged.

Josiah worried over this in a letter to Bentley on 26 October 1762, the day after the second anniversary of George III's accession to the throne— a day when Anglican preachers across the country read from the Book of Common Prayer, when echoing throughout chapels was praise for "our most gracious Sovereign Lord King George," whom God was beseeched to grant "health and wealth long to live, strengthen him that he may vanquish and overcome all his enemies." This was the time when the established church preached that the authority of government was decreed by Scripture and all Christians were obliged to submit to it. "Submit yourself to every ordinance of man for the Lord's sake," read the First Epistle General of St. Peter, which taught one to guard against doubting the faith, "whether it be to the King as supreme; or unto governors." Do not, it continued, use "your liberty for a cloke of maliciousness," but act "as the servants of God."

The uncomfortable juxtaposition of one's "liberty" against required servitude was what troubled Josiah and his friends. Their skepticism about the motives of the church's—and the state's—commitment to educate and improve the poor was borne from witnessing the way Dissenters' freedom to disagree with authority was blindly condemned as malicious. Anyone who "altered to his own liking" the message in prayer books (which William Willets had just written an "excellent little essay" about, according to Josiah and Bentley), was not, as Josiah sarcastically declared, showing "ample effusion of such a truly Christian spirit amongst all professed teachers of the religion of the benevolent Jesus."

No one had an easy time defining, let alone defending, the concept of individual "liberty" in the eighteenth century, though many people proffered their views. To some Tory historians writing in the Restoration period, liberties were regulated by laws, and the laws of England originated in the sovereign power of the king. There were no "inalienable rights," argued Robert Brady, author of the *Complete History of England*, published in 1685. "There is a clear demonstration, that all *Liberties* and *Privileges* the people can pretend to, were the *Grants* and *Concessions* of the Kings of this Nation and derived from the Crown." This was an influential argument, which the Tory politicians of the 1760s relished but which Whig modernizers and Dissenters found insufferable.

Bentley, though, found a refreshing rebuttal in his favorite author, James Thomson, famous for the epic nature poem *The Seasons* (1726–30) and the words to "Rule, Britannia," written in 1740. It was in Thomson's poem *Liberty* (1735–36) that his "Goddess of Liberty" traveled to ancient lands, concluding on her return to Britain:

> On Virtue can alone my Kingdom stand,
> On public virtue, every Virtue join'd.
> For, lost this social cement of mankind,
> The Greatest Empires, by scarce felt Degrees,
> Will moulder soft away; till, tottering loose,
> They prone at last to total Ruin rush.
> Unblest by Virtue, Government a league,
> Becomes a circling Junto of the Great.
> To rob by Law; Religion mild a Yoke
> To tame the stooping soul, a Trick of State . . .

When Josiah read Thomson's "fine poem on Liberty" after listening to Bentley's encomiums, he was duly impressed, saying it had "more than answered my expectations." Josiah detected the author's "goodness of heart" and "zeal" for his subject. "Happy would it be for this island," thought Josiah, "were his three virtues the foundation of British liberty: independent life, integrity in office, & a passion for the common weal more strictly adhered amongst us."

Of the three, he knew too well that there was no "common weal" amongst the people, particularly regarding their educational welfare. So philosophers were challenging fundamental models of education by promoting freedom of enquiry and, as a result, their works were being banned. Rousseau's *Emile* was condemned by the Archbishop of Paris for its dismissal of the Bible as a source of education, and publicly burned. This piqued Josiah's interest even more, "notwithstanding his Holiness has forbid its entrance into his domains," as he said defiantly. Rousseau soon became a favorite amongst Josiah's friends, who would talk about how they "formed a strong desire to educate" their children "according to the system of Rousseau," where natural sciences, such as astronomy or chemistry, could serve their independence. While Josiah's Liverpool friends such as Matthew Turner and Joseph Priestley were helping him to see new ways that experimental science could contribute to the improvement of business by enhancing the quality and novelty of his products, he was now beginning to see ways that empirical philosophy reached out to the improvement of people.

Like John Locke before him, whose empirical approach to education appealed to the experimentalist in Josiah and his friends (and who espoused the idea that nine out of ten people were "good or evil, useful or not, by their education"), Rousseau's prescription for an education directed by the exploration of nature, whereby, he said, "we make scientific instruments of ourselves," saw "value" as both moral and economic. Business, enlightened entrepreneurs were beginning to see, was a moral enterprise. The idea that "improvement" of minds and manufacturing processes were *both* driven by the pursuit of experimental philosophy—which was also held responsible for posing a challenge to the king's divine right to rule—would rest heavily in Josiah's mind when he contemplated how quickly "our young folks . . . enter the busy world."

Life was far more complicated when engaged in Enlightenment philosophy, not least because of the many paradoxes it revealed within contemporary society relating to ideas of freedom and justifications for servitude. These issues would reverberate in Josiah's ears and enrage discontented citizens who suffered inequalities in society. Josiah would long struggle with these problems, addressed by many but articulated so poignantly by one of the first he read, Rousseau, in the opening to his *Social Contract*, published nearly simultaneously with *Emile*, in a phrase that would remain famous for centuries: "Man is born free, and everywhere he is in chains."

11

"O Grief of Griefs"

Notwithstanding Josiah's belief that fireside discussions of current affairs and forays into philosophy had the potential to improve further his business and his mind, he never ceased the conventional grind of producing as many crates of marginally profitable stock-in-trade wares like butter cups and saucers as possible. Whatever the potential for improvement, he still needed to pay rent to Long John and cousin Thomas—once again he was running months late—and wages to his workers. The war posed an endless challenge to transatlantic trade, and mopping up the domestic demand for common pieces and supplying simple agate, enameled salt glaze, and redware, the "pretty but not expensive" items, in the words of one retailer, was all Josiah could do in attempt to keep on top of his finances.

Each day he supervised his team of around fifteen workmen and children—the throwers and turners, the painters, glazers, and flowerers, the fireman, and the packers, who were under strict instructions to place nearly a hundred pieces of pottery per crate in such a way as to keep them dry and safe during delivery. No one found this easy, and no one more than Josiah knew that the deplorable condition of the local roads was the main culprit damaging the goods. It was a geographical oddity that Burslem, "this rugged Pot-making spot of earth," as Josiah called it, was the center of production of pottery, yet remained thoroughly inaccessible for lack of decent roads. The local economy relied on travel. Josiah himself needed to travel to see his agents and understandably dreaded it. He decided that something had to be done.

One day in 1762, Josiah—now thirty-two—arranged to meet with a few other potters in the area, who all agreed that living at the end of a muddy, miry trail served no one's interest. Despite John Wesley's disparaging remark a couple of years earlier that the potters lived in "a scattered town on the top of a hill," Burslem was in fact, as they pointed out, home to "near one hundred and fifty separate Potteries," which found "constant employment and support for near seven thousand people," working in teams around a forest of new brick bottleneck ovens. It was a busy hill. The two-year-old open-air market in the city center, next to the new Town Hall, bustled every Saturday and Monday with merchants selling meat and vegetables, fish and linen. The potters were making money. "The Trade flourishes," Josiah and the others observed, "so much as to have increased Two-thirds within the last fourteen years." As they spoke, whether they knew it for certain or not, the earthenware and china potteries in their region of North Staffordshire were the largest in the country, employing on average more people than potteries in Manchester, Liverpool, or London. Yet no roads led to Burslem.

Josiah declared they needed to start a campaign, and that they should petition Parliament for a turnpike between Burslem and the county of Cheshire, at the least. To make clear the benefits to everyone and marshal support for the scheme, Josiah gingerly stepped onto a stage at Newcastle-under-Lyme Town Hall, rested on a crutch, and spoke to the gathered audience. It was his first public speech—and a tough audience. The gentlemen of Newcastle objected to the proposed turnpike, fearing that the new "bypass" road would affect the tolls paid for access to the road currently leading through their town. Josiah rose to the occasion, pleading "impartiality" and arguing the advantages and importance of Burslem working together with its neighbors.

"It might be asked," Josiah said, "from whence does Newcastle derive its principal advantages, as a market & a trading town? Is it not from the populous villages & manufactories in her neighbourhood?" Thousands of tons of raw materials yearly passed by the road, "which puttith bread into the mouths & findeth employment for many thousands of poor people. . . . And you know what sort of road it is!" The great necessity of mending it, argued Josiah, was to "enable us to bring our goods to *foreign markets* as cheap as the manufactories setting up in other parts (which are endeavouring to rival us & thereby deprive us of a trade so advantageous to these parts). . . ." It was the first time he had publicly pointed out the threat that rivals "in other parts" posed to their economy and the importance of servicing the "foreign markets." Josiah had never felt so engaged with politics as when he nodded at the applause for his speech and was helped off stage.

The petition they eventually sent to Parliament reiterated the points, stressing that clay, flint stones, and salt needed to be brought to Burslem from across Britain by land carriage, and that "the ware in these Potteries is exported in vast quantities from London, Bristol, Liverpool, Hull, and other seaports, to our several colonies in America and the West Indies, as well as to almost every port in Europe." Their businesses linked together a long chain of employment: "The manufactures, sailors, bargemen, carriers, colliers, men employed in the salt-works, and others who are supported by the pot-trade, amount to a great many thousand people." Surely, the petition humbly added, they were "not unworthy of the attention of Parliament."

Bentley no doubt urged Josiah along in his activities and encouraged him to visit London, one of Bentley's favorite cities, in person if he was to send political petitions to Parliament. Westminster was remarkably accessible to electors, and in the radically spirited season of 1763, rowdy merchants and pot-wallopers (or "pot-wabblers," as certain borough householders were called from "having boiled their pots therein" as residents) regularly turned out in large numbers for political rallies waving their copies of John Wilkes's *The North Briton*, a weekly rag that alleged government and royal corruption. It was an interesting time to visit the capital, especially for merchants with as heavy an interest in foreign affairs as Josiah. In February 1763, the Treaty of Paris was signed, finally ending the Seven Years War, and inaugurating a new period of controversy in internal British politics.

By the end of March, Josiah was willing to make the journey, which he thought could serve different ends. Other than his political interests, it was time he see firsthand the new products that were selling at merchant stalls in Cheapside, around the corner from St. Paul's, where his friend and former agent William Greatbatch (now fully set up on his own as Josiah's supplier of slip casts) formerly delivered Josiah's wares to retailers. Items of all sorts from manufactories across Britain were sold here, which made it a good place to spot emerging trends and pinch new ideas for the trade. A few shillings spent on what he could use as a prototype teapot or china plate might yield a tidy profit once he trained his workers to copy the product. However creative Josiah strove to be in the chemical enhancement of clay or his glazes, the reality of the business remained that the potter's craft was one of imitation and reproduction. Remembering that fact would eventually prove immensely rewarding for Josiah.

In London, one could fade away into the bland gray of the fog and the simple dress of the city dwellers, and Josiah's reaction was equally bland. Besides his dealings with the trade, he had long heard stories about life in London from his older brother John, who had moved there from Burslem before their father died in 1739, and had eventually become a successful merchant with his firm Wedgwood & Bliss on Cateaton Street. Josiah had been in regular contact with John lately, having persuaded him to act as his London agent now that Greatbatch had gone off on his own. It seemed a good arrangement, and it was not far from John's warehouse that Josiah took up lodgings at the Swan with Two Necks on Lad Lane, a large, two-story coaching inn with a balustrade gallery overlooking a square dirt yard with stables and storage rooms.

Josiah's general feeling was that London was too sprawling, busy, and anonymous for any comfort, but from a business perspective it was a valuable entrepôt. It was, of course, unrivaled for its plethora of shops. From quality upholsterers, gold- and silversmiths, instrument makers, perfumiers, jewelers, and drapers to corner coffeeshops, stationers, chemists, and florists, London had it all. In the early spring of 1763, Josiah shopped for shirts for himself and as gifts for his sister's children, otherwise "sister Willet's [*sic*] little lasses will go to bed without their nightcaps," he joked to his brother. But even the spectrum of shops seemed to be fading into the stonework. The previous year an ordinance had been passed prohibiting hanging trade signs, which were being made larger as aggressive shopkeepers vied for the air space above crowded streets. But as they swung above the heads of passersby, gusts of wind sometimes tore them off the facades of the jerrybuilt Georgian terraces, killing off prospective customers.

Remarkably, the streets of London seemed in no better shape than those in Burslem. Even as King George traveled from St. James's Palace to Westminster to open Parliament, where a decision would eventually be made as to whether to build the potters' desired turnpike, faggots had to be laid down in rutted lanes to assist the passage of the royal carriage. But when Josiah arrived at the Palace of Westminster, boots caked in mud, to listen to parliamentary debates, the problem of the roads temporarily evaporated from his mind.

"This day I had the mortification to hear the royal assent given to the odious Cyder Bill," he wrote to Bentley from his room the evening of 31

March. "The City of London petitioned the House of Lords against it, but to no purpose. Lord Bute harangued a long time in favour of the Bill & his own administration."

The Earl of Bute was the main subject of Wilkes's invective in *The North Briton*, which criticized the king's decision to appoint him the previous year as prime minister. In the outspoken opinion of Wilkes and other members of Parliament, Lord Bute was not only incompetent but a crony of the king's, who was appointed to help quash the power of the Whigs. This was already enough to make the man distasteful to Josiah and his friends (those "with candour equal to" Bentley's), but his "lofty strain" of support for the Cider Bill was taken as a further blow against the interests of the mercantile community.

The fact was that the war had cost the country dearly. The national debt had risen from £70 million at the beginning of the war in 1756 to £150 million in 1763. Among emerging arguments within government that the colonies should be made to pay for some of the cost of the war—perhaps in the form of a stamp duty on legal documents and newspapers, for instance—Lord Bute proposed to tax cider (among other things, including wine) at four shillings a hogshead, an act that would extend the powers of excise officers who collected excise under an oppressive system of household inspection without the need of warrants, prying into people's lives in ways unprecedented before the introduction of income tax.

The passage of the bill, Josiah reported, "gives universal disgust here & is the general topic of every political club in town." The problem, as Josiah saw it, lay not in the type of commodity being taxed, but in the disputes that would arise "betwixt the importer & the Custom House officers" regarding the classification of goods for certain rates of taxation. Josiah mentioned the problems of distinguishing between "grease" and "Irish butter" when Parliament debated the passage of the so-called Grease Bill the following week. Not only did these bills complicate trade, creating hindrances that no one who relied on exports and imports wanted to see, but they provided alarming new powers of authority for customs and excise officers, who would now increase in number and extend the tentacles of a covetous government. "The extension of the excise laws," as Josiah wrote to Bentley, "are most certainly calculated in their very nature to abridge the liberty of the subject."

Ironically, it was the potters' proclamation of how much annual duty they paid to the government—purportedly amounting to £5,000, about as much as the country would gain through Bute's additional taxes—that might indeed have made them "worthy the attention of Parliament," which promptly passed the bill for building their turnpike road, marking the first improvement in the landscape to help the potters' trade. But this was no compensation for the risks to free trade.

Bentley, to Josiah's surprise, did not react as bitterly as Josiah and his "friends of liberty" to these measures, which, they feared, might not be tethered to any legitimate principles. "I do my dear friend," Josiah confessed to Bentley, "for the first time differ somewhat from you in my sentiments on that subject." But the issues were too weighty to deal with in a few sentences scrawled in late-night letters; their differences would have to wait until Josiah arrived in Liverpool on his way back to Burslem from London.

The trip had been trying, with little to see in the state of the economy that would offer comfort to an ambitious small businessman. London manufactories at the heart of Josiah's interests were ailing. The Bow porcelain factory had just been declared bankrupt, and Nicholas Sprimont, who sold figures and decorative vases for the higher end of the market, was chronically ill, leaving the future of his Chelsea factory in doubt.

Josiah, nevertheless, had reason to be confident. Not only were his efforts to improve the local roads prominent within his community and recognized with their success, but his dedicated work at the Ivy House over the past year had yielded surprising results. His personal trade was performing well, supplying as much as he was capable of producing to both the domestic and West Indies markets, and just before he left for London had saved enough money to sign a lease for a second potworks.

For £21 a year, Josiah expanded into the Brick House, a pottery inherited by William Adams, a minor to whom Josiah paid rent through the boy's legal guardian, John Shrigley.

The Brick House was one of three potteries owned by the Adams family in Burslem. It was an early seventeenth-century house, unique for being built of brick when timber was customary, which sat on a sizable plot of land down a southwest-bending road leading away from the market square. It lacked the picturesque charm of little Ivy House, but with its end gables, attic dormers, and transomed windows had its own elegance. Most important, it was proven by the successful Adams family to be a productive pottery. This was going to be Useful Tom's new residence, where he would personally manage what Josiah would refer to as his "useful wares," the everyday, staple products that were so reliable, though not spectacular, in sales. Meanwhile, to help him at the Ivy House, Josiah brought back from London another family member who needed work, his nephew Tom Byerley.

Byerley was one of his eldest sister Margaret's three children. Margaret, a widow, with the help of her brothers and Reverend William Willets, had opened up a drapery shop in nearby Newcastle-under-Lyme and paid to send young Tom to school. He was fifteen when Josiah agreed to take him away from London, where he had worked for some years with Josiah's brother John in Cheapside. Tom was not the most dedicated shop assistant. It seemed he had other things on his mind. When they arrived in Burslem, Byerley's "trunk came down with all his papers, &c.," Josiah told Bentley; "these unraveled a part of his history we were strangers to." The boy wanted to be a writer, but Josiah thought he lacked talent, and stuffed a few sample pages into the parcel which he sent to Bentley. "What can be done with so young a subject of authorism so terribly infected with the cacoethes scribendi [a "writing disease"] as to take possession of a garret at fifteen!" cried Josiah, feeling an odd sense of avuncular responsibility. "What we shall now do with a lad of his turn of mind I cannot tell."

Perhaps all was not lost, Josiah reasoned. After all, the boy clearly had a creative flare and was not ignorant, just a touch eccentric. Being bookish, Byerley was put to work on the business accounts, and was encouraged to learn French so he could translate foreign works for Josiah. Perhaps he would provide a valuable perspective in the reading group. He was, as Josiah told Bentley, "a very good boy & I hope will make a usefull member of Society."

Byerley's main job was to help ease the daily management of the firm and allow Josiah to focus his attention on that which had been warming his heart for years. It was something that churned his stomach and crept into his mind at night, but that had nothing to do with either politics or pottery.

❧

The admonition in the First Epistle General of St. Peter to "abstain from fleshy lusts, which war against the soul," and instead engage in "good conversation" was not meant to encourage conversation *about* fleshy lusts, but that didn't stop Josiah and Bentley from having late-night port-fueled têtes-à-têtes about such erotic pleasures. It would have, however, offered them a chance to laugh that, for once, they were following the Book of Common Prayer at its word.

Hidden somewhere in the depths of Bentley's study was no doubt a sampling of "lascivious erudition," an amorous repository churned out by those "pimps of literature" that enjoyed so much popularity. It could easily have reflected the experiences Bentley gained from his days as a Grand Tourist (if he was anything like the debauched youth he traveled with) and which now, in his premature widowhood, provided a sinful source of tales with which to regale the less worldly Josiah. Even coming from the rather straitlaced and dutiful upbringing of the rationally minded Dissenting community, it was difficult to overlook the flood of Georgian sex advice manuals that dispensed with the Augustinian notion that erotic pleasures were driven by mere lust and insisted instead that they be treated seriously. Discussions relating to emotions and sexual conduct surfaced in tracts of all kinds—in pamphlets, magazine articles, satirical prints, or leather-bound books.

The moment's sensation was the scandalous publication just produced by Josiah's new political hero, John Wilkes. His poem, *An Essay on Woman*, was one of the first parodies of Alexander Pope's *Essay on Man*, which Wilkes wrote with a pornographic twist. Where Pope pondered,

> Say first, of God above, or Man below,
> What can we reason, but from what we know?

Wilkes preferred to ask,

> Say first, of Woman's latent charms below,
> What can we reason, but from what we know?

Later, Pope's

> Presumptuous Man! the reason wouldst thou find,
> Why form'd so weak, so little and so blind?

was turned into

> Presumptuous Prick! the reason wouldst thou find,
> Why formed so weak, so little and so blind?

Wilkes's concluding moral:

> Since Life can little more supply
> Than just a few good fucks, and then we die.

The bawdy poem, which likely gave Josiah and Bentley a good laugh, did no favors for Wilkes's political career, which was swiftly ended when he was charged with seditious libel after alleging in *The North Briton* that Lord Bute only became prime minister following an affair with the king's mother.

A more conventional and immensely popular tract at hand that was widely distributed and discussed was *Aristotle's Master-Piece* (1710). This was an anonymous compilation of folklore and medical ideas about sex and reproduction, first published in Britain in 1684 and often reprinted in various editions and versions. Read by young men and women, even given to new brides as a gift from discerning relatives, it offered instruction on how to make sex enjoyable and efficient. When a couple is ready, it read, "and if their imaginations were charmed with sweet and melodious airs, and care and thought of business drowned in a glass of racy wine, that their spirits may be raised to the highest pitch of ardour and joy, it would not be amiss." But all the advice on sex was proffered to married couples, and was sure to instruct men that real pleasure was found only after the vows, offering a glimpse of postmarital bliss:

> Now, my fair bride, new will I storm the mint
> Of love and joy, and rifle all that's in't;
> Now shall my infranchis'd hand, on ev'ry side,
> Shall o'er thy naked polish'd ivory slide.
> Freely shall now my longing eyes behold
> Thy bared snow, and thy undrained gold;
> No curtain now tho' of transparent lawn,
> Shall be before thy virgin treasure drawn,
> I will enjoy thee now, my fairest, come,
> And fly with me to love's Elysium.

Bentley knew that his good friend longed to have "infranchis'd hands," and took the opportunity to rib him about the prospect of marriage. "His head is turned," Bentley would say, he's going to be "noosed." "I suppose," Josiah responded, those "are synomims with you wicked Batchelors & Widowers.... The case you suppose your head being Corrupted is a very possible one, it is a kind of Original Sin of which you are not thoro'ly clear." However jovial or risqué the literature and conversation, there was also sincerity. When Josiah lowered the tone and asked Bentley, "Are your *last* & *first* thoughts ever employ'd on these subjects?" the air of frivolity and innuendo cleared as Bentley's thoughts turned to the memory of his wife, who had died three years earlier, after only two years of marriage, along with their only child during complications giving birth. She was dear to his heart, and he was thankful to have her caring sister to form a Platonic family. He hoped Josiah would find the courage to seek out the one he loved.

At thirty-three, Josiah was not unique in being a bachelor. For those raised with strong craft or mercantile interests, late marriages were usual within the family, though his older brother Thomas, feeling secure with the knowledge that he at least had a home and a workshop if not much money, proved the rule. But for Josiah, as for many other younger siblings in laboring families, a life of thrift and asceticism was encouraged, leading to rationalized celibacy. Remaining single was good for business. Along with pleasure—if that is what one was after, for the aristocracy was more often interested in creating economic unions—marriage brought babies, and Josiah had long known the economic implications of familial growth. There was, however, another reason that might have played on Josiah's mind and reined in his marriage plans: the love of his life, his cousin Sally, was not in the same station of life as him. She was rich.

Sally's widowed father, Richard, possessed the same entrepreneurial energy as his brothers—Long John and cousin Thomas—and divided his time between overseeing his business as a prosperous cheese factor and making respectable sums of money as a local banker. In 1763, his income was up to £1,800 a year, enough to make him comfortable living the life of a "Squire Western." Josiah, while distant kin, would remain—at least in Richard's eyes—someone who belonged in a potter's shed rather than a parlor room. This mattered to Josiah, as much as it mattered to men of his position across class-conscious Britain. The vast majority of agricultural laborers, husbandmen, and artisans married women of similar standing from their own village. It was practically unheard of for them to marry a wealthier woman who lived over twenty miles away; yet that was what Josiah wanted to do.

As he donned one of his new shirts from London and fixed the light brown wig on his head, he attempted to calm his nerves: As he saw it, Sally's father, Richard Wedgwood Esquire, had reason to be satisfied with his accomplishments. He had the good professional relationship with Richard's "Big House" brothers (exchanging numerous orders a year with them), and had endured the trials of working as an assistant in a muddy hovel to become the proprietor of two potworks. He even had a hand in getting Parliament to build a new road between Burslem and Richard's backyard—Sally could visit her home with ease.

Richard, alas, saw things differently. Twenty-nine-year-old Sally was his only daughter, a living memory of his wife, and with only one other sibling—her older brother Jack—she stood to inherit a considerable fortune, in the region of £20,000 (upwards of $2 million today). Richard was simply not enamored of the idea that she would marry a mere potter. He was willing, however, to give Sally a say. For years she and Josiah had flirted with each other, and every other Sunday Josiah rode the twenty-odd miles to see Sally on her cantankerous father's 75-acre estate. Josiah was captivated by her wit and sensitivity, and she was attracted to his naive charm and bright-eyed visions of the future. Perhaps she saw in him the kind of warmhearted dedication and commitment that had served her own uncles so well. Whatever it was, she had faith in Josiah and an attachment she wished not to lose.

Richard, a tall man, with a fondness for velvet and bookkeeping, deliberated what to do with the couple. He would allow them to marry, he declared, but only when, or if, Josiah could offer him £4,000 jointure money. Josiah was devastated. It did not take him long to double-check and recount: his early savings of about £20, half of which was gained by an additional inheritance from a cousin, had been reinvested in his business and was a sliver of the demanded sum.

Josiah turned frantically to his account books. Every possibility of raising, borrowing, or promising the money had to be explored. One possibility lay in the lingering debacle of the *Racehorse* scandal. He was still administering the estate of "Reid the Bankrupt," and the insurance money was still outstanding, though hundreds of pounds were being raised through china sold at auction and the collection of bills owed.

More so than for Josiah, however, the complications were running Reid and his family into uncomfortable depths of humiliation, which tugged at Josiah's heartstrings. He received a letter from Reid pleading for some humanitarian aid. "Consider my case," Reid begged; "it's [a] most melancholy thing that I, my wife & children must be most miserable if I cannot have my liberty in going about my affairs which would tend to the good of the creditors. . . ." Pleading for a certificate that would allow him to resume his trade, Reid wrote that it was never his intention to mislead anyone. "I know my owners insurance," he said, "& despise the authors who" refused to honor their policies. Josiah and the co-executor, Mr. Dobson, assisted Reid with some money and a public collection, but it could never be enough. "God knows what a melancholy tryall I have gone through," cried Reid; but he was not the only one to have fallen on hard times.

Josiah had tried to stretch out his lines of credit by following a conventional, if also ethically questionable, business practice of delaying payment for services until income from his own sales was realized. The person this now affected was his friend William Greatbatch. Typically, Greatbatch would visit Josiah in Burslem to deliver models and slip casts, take new orders, and pick up monies owed; but Greatbatch had his own problems. "I intended to come over to Burslam on Friday next," wrote Greatbatch in late May 1763, "but my little boy is so very ill that I am doubtful." A week later he reminded Josiah about his bills; "Desire you'l Remit what cash is Convenient for you . . . I could not possible come over myself for my Dear wife was taken so ill this morning." The next day, Josiah received another letter. "Desire you'l Remit me some cash by the bearer on the present occasion, for the Lord has been pleased to take my Dear Boy this morning." Josiah paid the bills. It seemed that for every stride forward—for every black entry in his account book—something pressing intervened to set him back a yard.

As the year drew to an end, he was obsessed with what bills he could collect on and what improvements he might make to satisfy Richard. Scribbling as if in a daydream on the back of a list of debts owed to him, he wrote the word "glazing" some twenty times on the paper, and in the middle of the page the word "Love." Finally, he approached Sally's father again, in one last act of desperation. He offered a compromise, a mixture of promises of future income, a commitment to engage in business with Richard and the Big House brothers, and some loans. It was not exactly what the merciless Richard wanted, but Josiah held his breath.

Days passed in uncertain silence as he waited anxiously to hear from Richard. It was the most emotionally unsettling Christmas he had experi-

enced since the winter following his father's death in 1739. Even a seasonal missive from Bentley lay unanswered on his desk. "I [would have]
acknowledg'd your very kind letter before now," Josiah finally wrote, lan-
guidly, early in the new year, "but hoped by waiting a post or two to be able
either to tell you of my happiness or at least the time I expected to be
made so." But he had nothing to report.

"O *grief of griefs*," he stressed, "that pleasure is still denied me & I cannot bear to keep my friend in suspense any longer, though I own myself
somewhat asham'd & greatly mortify'd to be still kept at bay from those
exalted pleasures you have often told me (& I am very willing to believe)
attend the Married state." Thoughts of "virgin treasure" and "bared snow"
in "love's Elysium" flooded through his veins. "If you know my temper &
sentiments on these affairs you will be sensible how I am mortify'd when
I tell you I have gone through a long series of bargain making of settlements, reversions, provisions, &c, &c." It was like no other business
arrangement he had been engaged with.

"Gone through it, did I say! Would to Hymen I had—No, I am still in
the Attorney's hands, from which I hope it is no harm to pray '*good Ld
deliver me.*' " If it was not for the insidious "marriage marketplace" but left
to the young lovers' hearts, they would already be celebrating. Josiah
despised the fact that love was being reduced to numbers like a chemical
formula, that it was being transformed into a business practice. Did
Richard think Josiah could "improve" himself the way a product is
improved, with a new glaze? "Miss W and I are perfectly agreed & could
settle the whole affair in three lines & so many minutes," complained
Josiah. "But our Pappa, over carefull of his daughter's interest would by
some demands which I cannot comply with, go near to separate us, if we
were not better determin'd."

After another meeting of "great form" and three weeks of negotiation
between Josiah, "Mr W," and each of their attorneys, warm jubilation was
allowed to thaw the gloom of the January frost. "All things being amicably
settled betwixt my Pappa elect & myself I yesterday prevail'd upon my
dear girl to name the day, the blissful day!" His heart was pounding when
he announced to Bentley about the prospect that "Wednesday next" held
for him, "When she will reward all my faithful services & take me to her
arms! To her Nuptial Bed! To pleasures which I am yet ignorant of, and
you my dear friend can much better conceive than I shall ever be able to
express. . . ." Bentley no doubt followed Josiah's recommendation that "on

that auspicious day, think it no sin, to wash your philosophic evening pipe with a glass or two extraordinary, to hail your friend & wish him good speed into the realms of matrimony." Josiah then prepared himself for one of the very few weeks in his life when "no business may intrude on my pleasures."

PART II
History
1764–1769

12
Recipe for Success

Josiah and Sally solemnized their marriage in the ancient and pictur-esque parish of Astbury, in Cheshire, on 25 January 1764. The occa-sion must have been blissful. Josiah wished "to hear, see, feel or understand nothing" but Sally "for a handful of the first months after Matrimony." It allowed him for the first time to experience the intimate sensations of another's flesh, an opportunity much in the minds of his impertinent "Gossiping friends." Some couples were fortunate enough to "bundle," a courting custom whereby the two spent the night together in bed while retaining an "essential part of [their] dress," sometimes sepa-rated by a wooden board for good measure. That was not part of Josiah's courtship. Nor, of course, would he ever have been tempted to turn to prostitution, as prominent as it was in London and Liverpool, not only for risk of disease but because he was a romantic, not a rake, and could see no rationale for anonymous liaisons.

For most of his life his own flesh, marked with the traces of his child-hood disease, was driven from his consciousness. His own limb, from his right knee down, was a sore encumbrance. The most personal touch he experienced from anyone was therapeutic—his mother's hand on his hot forehead, the cursory squeeze of a physician's fingers on his calf. His phys-iology was so adapted to feeling pain that cosseting sensual pleasures was undoubtedly, as he said, more "than I shall ever be able to express."

Sally and Josiah moved into the Brick House since it was larger than the Ivy House and offered them the potential to grow as a family. While the house clearly could not match the grandeur of her father's or uncles' homes, Sally was as anxious to settle in as Josiah had once been to establish himself in his own affairs. There were no surprises awaiting her: she knew the adjoining potworks would be messy, not like the green lawn outside her previous chambers, and that she would be woken up by the foul blast of a horn before Josiah met his team of artisans in the workshops. She was, after all, raised a Wedgwood. As Josiah beamed to Bentley, already they were "two married lovers as happy as this world can make them."

Josiah was beside himself with pride. He had enormous respect for Sally, who in captivating ways reminded him of his own sister, Catherine. Beyond being well educated and exhibiting a reasoned temperament, she had a fiery intellect and incisive interests. All were qualities that Josiah knew well in his sister, who never shied away from presenting her thoughts in the smoky evening debates with the men. It was no surprise, therefore, that Sally and Catherine fast became close as sisters.

Besides devouring the impassioned political discussions that formed the principal diet each time she and Josiah met with the Willets or Bentley, Sally was also committed to being part of her husband's professional life. Neither she nor Josiah ever saw their marriage merely as convenient for companionship. It was a partnership from the beginning, and she was dedicated to doing what she could to help Josiah by learning the intricacies of his craft. Josiah considered this invaluable.

Like many other struggling young men who would prove successful, Josiah had benefited throughout his life from the support of the women who surrounded him. Being fatherless since the age of nine, Josiah received from his mother Mary a physical and intellectual nurturing that few others had the occasion or inclination to offer. When he was young, she was committed to bestowing in "Joss" sound, rational principles which she believed would help him deal with any of life's knocks. Though she was unable to give Josiah any money—that went to his older brother Thomas in return for her provisions and lodging—what she offered proved an invaluable gift. He had always remained close to her.

The beneficent aunt Katherine, who contributed so substantially to charity and poor relief (even spending £200 on a new house for the rector), gave Josiah a crucial start for his own career, also throwing a lifeline to his older brother when he found himself floundering to keep the family fed. His sister Catherine Willets's home always provided a most enjoyable retreat for Josiah and Sally. She offered her younger brother emotional support when he ventured out on his own, and invited him to be part of her life with her husband, and though it was William from whom Josiah learned fundamentals of chemistry and experimental philosophy, Catherine had helped stimulate Josiah's creative and critical thoughts in their reading group discussions.

In an era when an emerging capitalist order was so outspokenly "fraternal" in form, and when women were considered legally and politically as property, rather than possessing property and supporting business, it is worth noting examples of the pivotal role women could play—in public and private—in promoting family business (and not solely as laborers). Because of the property laws, which naturally extended to financial marriage settlements, men could benefit by marrying into wealth and so boosting their own enterprise. The Birmingham iron master Matthew Boulton, soon to be a friendly rival of Josiah's, gained the initial bulk of the wealth necessary to invest in his manufactory by marrying two sisters sequentially. Less well known in history, but crucial when examining the mechanisms of capital investment in the eighteenth century, are the examples of women *as* investors. The fact that "they made up 20 per cent of loan capital traded in late eighteenth-century towns" and that their wealth often supported the joint stock companies behind municipal utilities, shows how lucky many entrepreneurs were to have such support. Josiah was one of these. Upon marrying Sally, he now had what three generations of his cousins had been denied by birth—what he was likewise denied by being born last—and what he so desperately sought to obtain through "improvement" of himself and his business: wealth.

"What forlorn Animals the best of us are," Josiah once said to Bentley, whose sister-in-law was away, "when destitute of a Female head of a Family." Josiah would soon grow more dependent on Sally than he could have imagined, especially as she offered him more than money to help his work. In the evenings, from a well-worn habit, he withdrew to his own special workshop, opened up his coveted notebook, and resumed a course of chemical experiments with which he endlessly hoped to improve the quality and colors of the glaze applied to his wares. For years he had done this alone, working in silence. Now Sally would join him, and under candlelight would sit at the notebook and record what chemical combinations failed and what looked a promising result. Perched on the bench, positioned to ease the weight of the baby inside her, she never complained about the stench of fused alkalis or smoking arsenic that was a feature of laboratory life.

It was a valued collaboration. "Sally is my chief helpmate," he proudly wrote to his brother John in London, informing him that he was on the verge of success in obtaining a purer white-glazed finish. "She hath learnt my characters, at least to write them, but can scarcely read them at present," referring to the secret code he used to record each chemical experiment. The price of certain metallic ores that could add variety remained expensive and the local clay had a dirty and frustratingly unalterable tinge. It was therefore easy for local potters to rely on the customary "grass-green" and brownish yellow glazes to make tortoiseshell plates and earthenware vessels in the shape of fruits, such as pineapples, which had enjoyed a revival in interest as national attention turned to the exotic islands of the West Indies and South Pacific. But any discovery of a new color or unique preparation of the raw materials was valuable knowledge and would likely result in bribed workers sniffing around rooms of the pottery they were not invited to visit. One of Josiah's treasured secrets was the formula that had yielded the "good White glaze" in 1761 and had so improved his creamware. Not that he was satisfied; he never stopped experimenting with it.

But this was all part of the business which Josiah and Sally now worked at together. Sharing secret codes, writing recipes for potential success, moving between different rooms to monitor the progression of a product from conception to preparation to kiln firing: it was satisfying, even exciting. "I often think if you could but once enter into the *spirit* of it," Josiah wrote to his brother John, it "would be the prettiest employment for you imaginable." The knowledge that everyone in Burslem was covered in clay dust and flint grime—it was why he left for London in the first place—left John unconvinced, but Sally understood what Josiah meant.

❧

While Josiah praised the efforts of his "chief helpmate," Sally's wealth also played no small role in enhancing the quality of the pottery. Or, until he died, her father's wealth. Soon after their marriage, Richard Wedgwood began giving Josiah hundreds of pounds of cash, which—whether following the "negotiations" of the marriage settlement or on his own initiative—Josiah funneled straight into the improvement of his potworks.

One of the changes he made was architectural and instrumental to creating a new kind of discipline amongst his workers. He had a bell rigged to a turret amidst his workshops, and every morning at quarter to six he rang it to tell his employees it was time to work. Not every potter in Burslem worked on the same schedule, but every one of them (and even the postman) sounded a horn to summon their workers. It apparently took a dedicated ear to distinguish each tone, so Josiah eliminated possible confusion, or entreaties thereof, by establishing his own sound. From then on, the Brick House Works was also known as the "Bell Works," and Josiah was beginning to call attention to himself as a distinctive master potter by ringing his bell.

Installing the bell was Josiah's first management innovation. For a long time he had known the importance of disciplining the workforce, especially when it came to regulating working hours and distracting dilatory workers from the allure of the alehouses. The day had to begin and end for the team in unison, or time and productivity would be lost. Gone were the days when the rise and fall of the sun directed people's work habits; now it was up to Josiah's sense of timing. He could shorten lunch breaks and prolong the working day. "Time wasted is existence, used is life!" was the adage of Bentley's neighbor, John Wyke—the watchmaker who attended the evening soirées with the rest of the Warrington circle. He would etch his maxims on the back of his watches—well out of the range of affordability for Josiah's workers—including "O time! Than gold more sacred." Josiah, who got along well with Wyke, knew more than ever now that time was money. He had barely caught his breath from making as much of it as quickly as possible so he could marry Sally.

Other improvements were on their way. He had recently purchased "an excellent book" by Charles Plumier published in Paris called *L'Art de Tourner* (*The Art of the Turner*), which promised to teach one how "to make all works of the turn to perfection." The "turn" referred to engine turning, or working with a lathe.

Conventional lathes, "parallel lathes," were first introduced in Burslem by those innovative Dutchmen, the Elers brothers, at the end of the seventeenth century. A pot or vase, usually "Tea & Coffee Ware," was turned on the lathe (by "lathe-treaders," usually children) and the steady, skilled hand of a turner would use a series of sharp instruments to thin, shape, and incise uniform patterns—ridges and stripes, for instance— onto the rotating object. They were extremely useful, and celebrated for rendering precise, regular cuts in the pieces. But more recently, certain mechanical alterations had been made—notably by a Birmingham "mechanik" named John Taylor and an engineer named William Cox—which inverted the process, enabling the creation of more complicated patterns. Now the cutting tool was fixed, stationary, and various shafts altered the motion of the rotating object, making it "eccentric," so that geometric, fluted, and roselike patterns could be repetitively inscribed on the pottery piece.

Josiah had spotted one of these new engine lathes while passing through Birmingham in 1763, and stretched to make the investment to obtain one. Now, with some ideas proposed in Plumier's book, which contained a number of illustrations showing how further mechanical changes in the machine's design could produce more elaborate and detailed patterns, he was anxious to make improvements on his "hobby horse," his nickname for the engine. "This branch hath cost me a great deal of time & thought & must cost me more," said Josiah, "& am afraid that some of my best friends will hardly escape." He had already paid nearly £4 to a mechanic for work on his lathe—"forming a big hoop," which would pull a rope to spin the shaft to which the piece of pottery was fixed. But now the main obstacle was that he could not read French. So he sent a chapter of the book to Bentley, "which if you can get translated for me it will oblige me much, & will thankfully pay any expense attending it." This was why he was having Byerley learn French, but the boy had a long way to go, and Josiah could not "wait his time."

Meanwhile, he and Sally continued to work in the laboratory, where they had "just begun a course of experiments for a white body & glaze which promiseth well." He hoped to make his cream ware whiter with more consistency, so that it would take sharper images in Sadler & Green's transfer-printing process. The results were especially important as he had just received a prestigious order from a client whom he wanted to impress: Sir William Meredith.

Meredith was elected a Whig MP for Liverpool in 1761, had recently been made a Lord of the Admiralty, and resided principally in London. He had done some banking business with Richard Wedgwood, who provided Meredith with a substantial £1,900 loan, and had learned of the promising career of Richard's new son-in-law. Meredith was also a patron of the arts, a collector of prints, vases, and antique artifacts. In late 1764, he had the idea of commissioning a set of tableware embossed with his family coat of arms, and he approached Josiah's London agent, his brother John, to place the order.

In response to the reduced foreign trade of wartime, Josiah had been busy "in sorting out my 2nd red-ware" and packing crates of pottery seconds. These were the blemished items that stacked up before Josiah perfected one of his improvements—mistakes he could not afford to smash and throw into shard piles. Right now he had lots of pieces he and his turners had tried to produce with the novel lathe, and he was sending them to London, hoping to get for them whatever he could. "I have no orders for them," he told his nephew, Tom Byerley, who had grown restless in Burslem and was back in London, "but hope they'll suit the Gentlemen named on each crate & believe they will find them cheaper than any they can buy as the faults of most of them are small." Essentially, Byerley was to travel door to door, showing the ware to former customers "& wait upon the Gentln to know their sentiments." It was, Josiah conceded, a rather inelegant way to create a market for his goods, if also risky since direct sales in this manner violated the agreements Josiah had with his London retailers.

"You must not mention them to such shops as Lambden & Woods, Veres &c," Josiah warned Byerley, knowing this was bad practice, but as they were "lowering value so fast," he had no choice. "If any of them refuse having the crates now sent then you must try elsewhere for they must be sold, but remember," he added, "some of these pots are unavoidably much worse than others, so they must not be sold on return, they may open the crate before they buy them if they insist upon it, but they must take or leave 'em altogether." Reversing this rule of sale would later gain Josiah much admiration amongst his customers.

Meredith's order, however, marked the beginning of a rapid turnaround in Josiah's business, which came at a time when foreign trade was happily regaining lost ground. "If you can spare Tom I should be glad you wd send him down [to Burslem] immediately," Josiah wrote to John. "Our London orders & some foreign ones just come to hand and are very large, & require my constant attention in ordering & seeing got up &c &c, for that reason I shall send no more 2nd Eng[ine]d T pots to be dispos'd of by him." Byerley was wanted in Burslem particularly to deal with mounting paperwork and accounts. "I am confined more to writeing than is anyway consistent with my interests," complained Josiah, now especially wanting to focus his energy on Meredith's order.

It was not often, if at all up to this point, that Josiah received an order from the titled, such as Meredith, a baronet. Those had usually gone to Long John and cousin Thomas, still by far the wealthiest potters in Burslem, whose £800 sales in 1765 hit a career peak, with the titled and nobility amongst their regular customers. Josiah was thrilled to receive such patronage, writing to Sir William "with my humble thanks for the honour of your two last Letters & your obliging offers." True to his ambition and pride, he had high hopes for the quality of the service Meredith ordered. "I wish Sir William would give me a copper plate with his Arms suitable for Table plates & a Crest (if he would like it) to fill up one of the compartments in the dish rims," he said to John, confidently adding that "it would then be in my power to present him with one of the completest services of Staffordshire Ware, ever got up in the County." Josiah was determined to outshine all others.

He was almost ready to provide "the completest" as well as most attractive service of earthenware ever produced in Staffordshire, or in the world for that matter. He and his turners were becoming well practiced in the use of the engine lathe, adding accuracy and consistency of design, and the creamware was looking whiter and better than ever. It was no small accolade that Enoch Booth, who had made the first innovations in creamware in the 1740s, was now placing orders by the dozen of Josiah's "Cream Colour teapots," often urging him to be prompt as "we aut to foyer this week & must have them to do foyering as it will disappoint us of filling 2 orders if not." Josiah's wares were beginning to look distinctive, at least to the trained eye of potters and retailers who handled them every day.

Despite all the daily work Josiah put into enhancing his wares, they were not yet obviously in a class of their own in the eyes of the public. This became painfully clear when Tom Byerley confused some pieces of one of Josiah's competitors—a potter named Baddeley—with their own. Was Tom "trying a trick upon us?" asked a shocked Josiah, when he saw a crate of goods bound for London mixed with the two. "These are the worst I have seen," he commented, holding one of Baddeley's teapots. "If Tom does not know the difference betwixt Mr Somebody's T Pots & mine, he is upon par with Mr Whites customers"—referring to one of his London retailers. What was uncomfortable for Josiah, who decided that this incident was worth telling John about, was that customers were not easily spotting the hard won improvements in his products. To many, "pottery" more often than not meant an unremarkable vessel from which to pour tea and serve biscuits. This indifferent perspective needed to be changed. Josiah, "every night forming schemes" to impress the customers, wanted John to pitch the wares more aggressively, to *educate* the London consumer about why his wares were the best.

Ironically, the endeavor to promote Josiah's wares had recently fallen to a consumer, Sir William Meredith, who had, to Josiah's amazement, ordered another "small service of printed dishes &c &d," and was "promising to recommend them" to his company in London. It was Josiah's reward for devoting his resources to getting the first order out in so timely a manner, and it humbled the potter to be so honored. "You have heaped your favours on me so abundantly," Josiah wrote to Meredith,

> that though my heart is overflowing with sentiments of gratitude & thankfulness I am at a loss where to begin my acknowledgements.
>
> Your goodness is leading me into improvements of the manufacture I am engaged in & patronizing those improvements you have encouraged me to attempt, demand my utmost attention. With such inducements to industry in my calling, if I do not outstrip my fellows, it must be oweing either to great want of Genius, or application.

How valuable it was, he thought, to have such a prestigious and influential patron. He did not know the half of it.

13
Fit for a King and Queen

"Sukey is a fine sprightly lass," Josiah informed his brother John, doting on the arrival of his first child, Susanna, at the beginning of 1765. As soon as her uncle could break away from London and join them, wrote Josiah, he would find that Sukey "will bear a good deal of dandleing & you can sing—lulaby Baby—whilst I rock the Cradle."

Josiah was enchanted with the baby girl, gazing at her soft, rosy cheeks and blooming smile. "The finest Girl!" he cried. "So like her father!" On a Thursday evening in late January, Josiah and Sally were joined by the Willets, Josiah's mother Mary, and "my Daddy," Richard Wedgwood, for a lobster dinner celebration. It was Sukey's baptism; but since "the weather is too bad to carry her to our Abby at present," she would be christened at home, "*privately* Churched," said Josiah, satisfied with the domestic arrangements.

In front of a roaring fire at the Brick House, the family dined elegantly and drank the finest port from Richard's cellar. The "extremely good" lobsters were an unexpected gift from John, which pleasantly satisfied Richard's demanding tastes. "Tell John Wedgwood," rumbled the "old Gentleman," "that I drink to his health & thank him for the Lobsters, they are very fine & a creature that I like." This broke the ice on the occasion, and during the three days that Richard lodged with his son-in-law and daughter, he was, Josiah was relieved to report, "unusual very merry & very good company." With scarcely enough time to digest the food and absorb the moment, Josiah was out the door, "mounted upon my hobbyhorse again," to address pressing issues of business. "I shall hardly find time for nursing," he admitted, as he had another debate which threatened their "scheme of navigation."

For generations, potters in North Staffordshire had relied on three river navigations for their trade. Clay from Cornwall and Devon, notable for being whiter than the local, reddish clay, was shipped along the coast to the Mersey, at Liverpool, and continued its journey up the Weaver River to Winsford, in Cheshire, about thirty miles from Burslem. Wagons and packhorses completed the trip, were then loaded with crates of finished products for the return journey, bound for the Liverpool ports. Almost thirty miles in the other direction, just south of Derby, was Willington, on the Trent, made navigable in the seventeenth century, from which wares were shipped to London and flint stones from the northeast coast were brought to the Midlands. Some forty miles southwest was Bridgnorth, just west of Birmingham on the Severn River, where one contemporary noted "about eight tons of pot ware to be conveyed to Bristol," with return deliveries of "white clay for Burslem."

Water trade routes spilling in from the coasts dried up within this thirty-mile or so radius of Burslem, and the potters now schemed to extend them in order to make the movement of their goods and supplies easier than any road would allow. As Josiah said, their inspired aim was "the Uniting of Seas & distant country." Given Josiah's experience with the turnpike scheme a few years earlier, he was a natural choice for the potters representative. But unlike the turnpike debates, where only Newcastle innkeepers challenged the plans for an improved road to Cheshire, this project had much knottier and more powerful interests at stake.

Ten years earlier, when Liverpool merchants and local landowners had been involved with a grand project to build a network of canals for dependable navigation, they'd commissioned a survey to explore the possibility of connecting the Mersey to the Trent. The rough, contorted landscape made this no easy task, and the Liverpool interest died away, focusing instead on a less ambitious, localized plan. Three years later, through the initiative of a Staffordshire landowner, Granville Leveson-Gower (the first Earl Gower), and master potters including Thomas Whieldon and the Big House brothers, the ingenious engineer James "the Schemer" Brindley, known around Burslem for building landmark flint mills, was hired to survey the land to build a canal between Stoke and the Trent. The next year, 1759, a separate canal project was inaugurated by the twenty-two-year-old Duke of Bridgewater (whose brother-in-law was

Lord Gower). His project, which had obtained parliamentary approval, would connect the coal mines on his estate in Worsley, in the northern county of Lancashire, to Manchester, eight miles south.

To public fascination, the canal—which included Brindley's spectacular aqueduct, with 63-foot-tall stone arches carrying the canal 40 feet above a river it had to traverse—was completed in 1761. Despite a rugged landscape and competing political interests, it was now clear that canals could work, and by the end of 1764 Josiah and his fellow potters, once again including his old boss Thomas Whieldon and the Big House brothers, prepared the way to build the so-called Grand Trunk Canal to connect the Trent and Mersey rivers.

It would, however, be a hugely expensive endeavor. Josiah conservatively estimated that it would cost £80,000, money which had to be raised by subscription. On a Friday evening in early March 1765, Josiah met Brindley for dinner and drinks at the Leopold Hotel, a new public house run by a distant cousin of Josiah's, Ellen Wedgwood. "Our Gentlemen seem very warm in setting this matter on foot again," he noted, "& I could scarcely withstand the pressing solicitations I had from all present to undertake a journey or two for that purpose." His job was to tour the area to drum up support for the navigation scheme and to meet with those who, fearing potential damage to their own interests, might object to the canal being built. Josiah did not need much persuading, believing that the project "is undoubtedly the best thing that could possibly be planned for this country"; and so, learning as much as he could from Brindley about canal digging, he set off to canvas support. If the subscribers offered what money they could, they'd own a share of what was sure to be a profitable venture.

First, he went to Birmingham, to meet "with one Mr. Loyd in the Banking business" (Lloyds Bank opened this year), who, it seemed, "is one of the Proprietors in the Burton Navigation which will be injured by our intended Canal," but who, he hoped, would see the overall benefit to business in Birmingham if their canal was built. "We made it appear pretty evident to the Gentlemen of Birmingham that £10,000 per annum would be immediately sav'd to them in the Article of Land Carriage to and from the River Trent, so soon as the Canal was brought to their Town," offering great advantage especially to the merchants who shipped iron and flax to Russia.

One merchant who became particularly interested in Josiah's ideas was Samuel Garbett, an accomplished chemist and later chairman of the Birmingham Commercial Committee. Garbett owned a manufactory servicing the iron industry and, convinced of the benefits that such a navigation system could bring, had already been in communication with an agent of Lord Gower's to inquire about the Duke of Bridgewater's canal system. He offered some advice to Josiah, recommending that to guarantee the success of their project, they needed to obtain the patronage of the wealthiest landowners they could. Lord Gower, he suggested, might be a good person to start with.

Josiah, no fan of the aristocracy, did not look forward to prostrating himself in front of the leisured class to beg for support, but he recognized that Garbett, who seemed "a very intelligent Gentleman," was right. After writing a carefully crafted letter of introduction on behalf of "freeholders, tradesmen, & principal inhabitants of Burslem and the parts adjacent," Josiah "had the honour of waiting upon Ld Gower with a plan &c &c and a petition from the Pottery praying his Ld Ship to take the intended navigation under his protection & patronage." In the grandiose environ of Gower's estate, Josiah presented their proposal. To his relief, if also mild surprise, it was "very graciously received." Lord Gower was sensible of the utility of the scheme and, Josiah was assured, willing to promote its execution. It seemed everything had gone as well as could be imagined, "so far as the mind of a *great Man* can be known by its Countenance & professions," said Josiah.

The praise was sarcastic, repeating what he had read—biting his lip—from Samuel Garbett. Garbett informed Josiah that Lord Gower's "*Countenance* is of extreme consequence," more so, he implied, than Josiah could ever recognize, and that "if He engages the Duke of Bridgewater, I don't see any alarming opposition, for all the Arguments from common Landholders are no more than general arguments against all inland navigation, and will be laughed at unless supported by a few such as Lord Gower & the Duke of Bridgewater, who have great ministerial weight." There was, Garbett concluding, only one thing that could serve the cause better: "if the King should patronize us, as I hope, there will not be any great Men warmly against us whose interest is not injured by it."

Having a royal patron would undoubtedly be most beneficial, but, it seemed, out of Josiah's hands. The young Duke of Bridgewater, however, was worth making the trip to see. "I have been waiting upon his Grace, the Duke of Bridgewater with plans &c respecting Inland Navigation," Josiah told his brother, John, with a nonchalance that tried to hide the hauteur of the occasion. Bridgewater's estate was only fifty miles north of Burslem, but Josiah had come a long way from being an unknown, unrecognized, unassuming potter. Now he was walking and talking with dukes, spending "about 8 hours in his Grace's company." After saying that he would offer his patronage, Bridgewater surprised Josiah by giving him an order "for the completest Service of Table service in the Cream Colour that I could make." It seems the duke had other interests besides building canals and selling coal, and thought that the potter might be interested in some of the collection of antiquities he'd acquired on the Grand Tour of Europe, as well as some curiosities discovered closer to home. He "shewed us a Roman Urn 1500 years old at least, made of red china, & found by his workmen in Castlefield near Manchester," Josiah told his brother. Then the day ended elegantly, "sailing in his Gondola nine miles along his Canal, through a most delightful vale to Manchester."

If Josiah had ever doubted either, he had every reason now to be confident in his own "Genius & industry." Others also seemed impressed by his exploits, which identified him as yet another Wedgwood on the ascendancy. This was probably why Mr. Smallwood, an acquaintance of Josiah's from Newcastle, unexpectedly stopped by the Bell Works, willing to interrupt the day's routine work for a chance to see Josiah's reaction to a letter he delivered.

⌀

Josiah was cursing the hot July weather that made Sukey uncomfortable and all of his employees languid. The heat from the kilns in the workshops was intense, made worse by the heavy steam from the arks (a well in the floor), where a blanket of wet clay was being warmed to eliminate excess moisture. Still, it was better than London.

Josiah was worried about his brother John, who for months had been struggling with an unremitting illness. Back in the spring, Josiah had encouraged John to take a break, "for I do not think that that close, smoky place will ever agree with your constitution, & I do very earnestly intreat you to come & take the benefit of your native, salutary, country Air." John claimed that he was too busy, but Josiah was insistent, knowing that business was useful to serve human interests, not the other way around. If "you have not set the finishing hand to your affairs there, you may leave an agent to do it for you," he advised. "Whatever inconvenience you may suffer by doing so, it cannot be put into competition with that invaluable blessing—Health!" Eventually, John agreed, but thought France might be more salubrious than Staffordshire. Josiah had to concede that much, and wished his brother *bon voyage*, until Mr. Smallwood appeared at the workshop door.

The letter that Josiah promptly read drove him from his bench on a hasty retreat to his office, shouting for his "post boy" to follow at once and leaving Smallwood to find his own way out. Josiah quickly penned a letter to John about a change of plans.

"Dear Brother," he wrote, getting right to the point, "I do not believe I can spare you out of London this summer, if business comes in for you at this rate, for instance—An order from St James's for a service of Staffordshire ware." It was an open invitation, issued from a Miss Deborah Chetwynd, "Seamstress and Laundress to the Queen" and daughter of the Master of the Mint, for potters to offer designs in a competition to provide a "compleat sett of tea things, with a gold ground & raised flowers upon it in green," for use by the queen herself. It was a large order: a dozen teacups and saucers, the same number of coffee cups, six pairs of candlesticks, and an assortment of matching cream pots, sugar dishes, and fruit bowls. Josiah leapt at the chance to compete for the order, and straightaway needed his brother to procure some "gold powder" from a shop in Soho, so he could begin experimenting with it.

Just as he was about to seal and hand the letter to his post boy, a flood of other concerns came to mind. He unfolded the letter and added a postscript. He needed to know whether Chetwynd would

> Expect the gold to be burnt in, as it is upon the Chelsea china, or secured with a varnish only, like the Birmingham waiters & other Japan ware. If the saucers must have a gold ground both inside and out, & what colour the cups & other articles must be within, if a fine cream colour will do, whether the flowers upon the cups &c must be in also relievs or bass relieve, if the former, whether that will not be very inconvenient for the saucers, it will be extremely difficult to execute. What size will be most agreeable too for tea cups, & Tea pots, & if there should not be a cream jug & Jarrs. If the hand candlesticks & Melons must have gold ground to match the Tea Things, or what sort of colour they must be.

Josiah wanted "to ask a hundred questions," and fortunately he could trust John to ask them on his behalf. He knew his brother was unwell, but this was urgent. "Pray put on *the best suit of cloathes you ever had in your life* & take the first opportunity of going to Court," he begged. John dutifully followed his instructions.

The enthusiasm at the supper table that night must have been brimming over. The letter delivered by Mr. Smallwood could change everything. Josiah was given the chance to do what, he imagined, "nobody else would undertake." Perhaps no other potter in Staffordshire had enough self-assurance and ambition to do so. Perhaps no one else was crazy enough. It *was* a huge gamble: it would be expensive, but more poignantly, one ran the risk of offering something to the queen that might be judged inadequate. Nevertheless, true to form, Josiah met the challenge with headstrong determination.

In the sweltering London heat, John piled on the layers of clothes that a gentleman would wear to court, from the bag-wig with rolls of curls on his head to his stockings. After his appointment with Miss Chetwynd, he sat at Windsor Lodge and wrote all the answers to Josiah's questions, ending with a note from Miss Chetwynd, hoping that Josiah would be able to accommodate the queen's wishes. This was the line Josiah was waiting for: his brother's research had won him the chance to provide the queen with her tableware. Now it was up to him to manufacture it. "You may be sure," Josiah wrote back, "my best endeavours will not be wanting to make the articles she orders as complete & elegant as possible," adding, "I shall be very proud of the honour of sending a box of patterns to the Queen" for her enjoyment. And for an additional gift—already playing the patronage game like a politician—"I intend sending two sets of Vases, Creamcolour engine turn'd, & printed." As an afterthought, he remembered what John must have gone through to have this meeting, confessing that "the pleasure of your letter was more than ballanc'd with the fear I had, least the heat of the weather, the bustle of the Company & situation you were in should be too much for you." Indeed, John was feeling worse than ever, but he was proud that his visit to Miss Chetwynd had the potential result of procuring a patron beyond all expectations.

A service for the queen. This would make more pressing than ever Josiah's whole approach to the production of his wares, especially in his attention to detail. Every item would be testimony to his abilities. He wanted to show Her Royal Highness a sample of his new cream color glaze, of the fine craftsmanship yielded with the use of his engine lathe, and new designs he had drawn up so that each item of the set would "appear to be made for each other, & intended for Royalty."

Josiah planned to spare no effort or expense. He sketched out some patterns and sent them to John to be transferred to a copper engraving so he could have elegant pictures printed of his proposed products. Meanwhile, a hurried Josiah spent "night & day" in his workshop, "preparing sprigs, handles, spouts, shapes, making experimts in burning gold &c &c for the tea service. . . ." Once engaged with the project, his nerves began to show. Of course he would ensure that his "best endeavours" would be given to provide an excellent service, "but suppose we fail in burning the gold on, must we in that case stove it on. . . . Must the saucers & other articles be gilt any farther on the outside than from the top edge to the foot?"

There was no time to relax—no time to read the paper or raise support for the canals or play with Sukey. Sally had even become his amanuensis to help speed through correspondence. What made things especially trying was that July saw the arrival of the infamous Burslem "wakes," the festival allegedly linked to the Feast of St. Peter, but which had become a tradition of gaming, drinking, and decadence. At least that's how Josiah saw it this year when he loudly cursed "the foolish wakes," which above all were costly to his business. The workers received no wages during their revelry, of course, since they were paid either by the day (the more skilled artisans) or by the number of pieces produced, *good* pieces. But each day they spent at play was a day's less production for Josiah and all the other master potters. No manufacturer liked this holiday, or any holiday for that matter. It made no "trade sense," which was a point made some sixty years earlier when a barrister named Sir Henry Pollexfen estimated that "2 Millions of Working People at 6*d.* per day comes to 50,000*l.*," which translates into so much revenue lost to the nation "by every Holyday that is kept."

"I am just teased of my life with dilatory, drunken, Idle, worthless workmen which prevents my proceeding with the tea service," Josiah complained, "to which more sorts of workmen are necessary than one would imagine." It was no use grumbling while he sweated away in his workshop, burning more inches of candles faster than ever before as he prepared samples and patterns for the queen's review. "You cannot think how busy all these things together make me," he sighed to his brother, who needed promptly to advise "what patterns I shall send to Court."

Adding to the pressure was the arrival of another letter informing him "that the Queen was impatient," being anxious to have the special service for a dinner that she had planned. Yet there were practical problems with the production of the service that were slowing progress.

It was no good looking for ways to cut corners to save time. "From experience I can tell you, that the sooner" they are fired, "the more imperfect they will be." He was not finished experimenting with detail on the "sprigs in green & gold ground" and was "mortifyd to find it does not look so well as I expected. . . . Powdered gold wld do the best for me if I knew how to polish it after it was burnt"; but Josiah lacked the knowledge. It was—as a formula on paper—simple enough. Josiah's useful handbook, Robert Dossie's *Handmaid to the Arts* (1758), instructed one to "take any quantity of leaf gold, and grind it with virgin honey, on a stone, till the texture be perfectly broken," then "put it into a china basin with water and stir it so that the honey be melted." The steps then got more complicated, involving a concoction of "gum animi," "asphaltum," "red Lead," and "litharge of gold," mixed, boiled, and strained through a flannel, at which point Josiah—skilled chemist as he was—had no grasp of the tacit knowledge required to apply the substance to the pottery.

He decided someone must know how to decorate with gold the way the queen wanted it, and he urged John to snoop around the Chelsea works or the Bow china works searching for someone who will "perhaps tell you how it is polished for a little money." Despite Josiah's lack of skill, "I believe it is neither a secret or a very curious art for women only are employ'd in it at Chelsea." If only, he sighed, some of those women— whose employment in manufactories across Britain was increasing, and who helped to double the incomes of Staffordshire potters with their specialized skills in "flowering" and painting items—were working for him. Failing that, he turned to his chemical library, being advised that some European chemist had worked on the problem of combining different substances, but he could not, "find any French book on Chymical affinitys," as he spat with frustration.

For the first time, Josiah became noticeably despondent about the task at hand. "For some tryals I made today I hope to be able *in time* to accomplish it, but not I fear in time for the Merry Meal," he confessed to John. "If you should see Miss Chetwynd again, pray do not say anything more that may lend to raise her expectations of the T. service, as that may help disappoint her." After three more days and nights split between his laboratory and workshop, Josiah needed yet more gold powder sent up from London, "as a great deal of it is gone in experiments." Literally burning through gold in an effort to perfect the queen's service was costing him dearly, but he was prepared—not for the last time—to sacrifice a profit on one order for the sake of honoring such a prestigious patron. Thankfully he now felt optimistic that "I will forward the Creamcolour services as desired I hope the next week."

By the end of August, after nearly two months of exhaustive and costly work, Josiah was able to catch his breath and tell Bentley with relief that "I sent a crate of patterns off for the Queen last Saturday & desire your best wishes for their success." Now he had only to wait for the verdict.

14

The Vexed and the Virtuosi

The creamware service he sent to St. James's Palace was a remarkable achievement. Its ivory-white, smoothly glazed surface created a decorative effect that was strikingly different from the common brown or rust-colored wares locally produced. The tureens, compotiers, sauce bowls, and coffee cups had unusual but elegant curves; the conventional "scroll handle" (S-shaped) on coffeepots and mugs was adapted to more ornamental "crossover" (two intertwined straps) handles. The plain plates introduced a new design—the round rim subtly altered to the shape of a flower's petals—which became known as the "Royal Pattern."

Before the queen had the chance to comment on the delivery of Josiah's service, rumors had spread that an innovative manufacturer was supplying quality "cream ware" pottery that even the king had expressed admiration for. It marked the end of the search for a form of pottery that could compete with porcelain. Nothing excited aristocrats more than the early hint of a new trend, and pampered dining rooms were soon filled with the chatter of new orders.

"Dr Swan dined with Ld Gower this week," Josiah had heard on the grapevine, and "after dinner your Brot Josiah's potworks were the subject of conversation for some time, the Cream Coloured table services in particular, I believe it was his Lordship who said that nothing of the sort could exceed them for a fine glaze &c &c." The idea that a small manufacturer from the provincial hills of the Midlands could receive such high praise from people of such "great ministerial weight" was bemusing to Josiah, and received mild skepticism from well-heeled gentlemen who combed

Europe for the finest items of commerce. Some wondered whether Josiah Wedgwood's pottery matched, for instance, the quality of the wares produced by the French manufactory at Sèvres, owned for the last twelve years by Louis XV. Samples, of course, were to be found in the finest collections of England's landed gentry. "His Ld Ship said that the late Ld Bolingbroke collected all the curious modeled earthen ware he could in France which were brought over to England & that it would be worth my while to go to London on purpose to see it." Josiah took this less as a challenge than as an intriguing opportunity to collect more ideas about what to copy when manufacturing his own wares. After all, the sources of inspiration at Cheapside were drying up.

Before Josiah had the chance to pursue any fresh ideas, he was amazed one Wednesday morning in August—as were, no doubt, his neighbors on the withered hill of Burslem—when a chain of carriages pulled up in front of the Brick House carrying the Duke of Marlborough, Lord Gower, Lord Spencer, "& others," to see Josiah's works. These were among the richest gentlemen in the kingdom, Lord Spencer alone owning 100,000 acres of land stretching over 27 different counties. Now they were at Josiah's pottery, walking across a dirt yard past squawking, flailing chickens to the dusty workshops where the much-discussed "cream ware" originated. Josiah's home had become a national curiosity, an attraction for the aristocracy, who had a "madness to gaze at trifles" in the new manufactories. Not entirely sure what to make of the visit, Josiah mentioned to his brother that "they have bought some things & seem'd much entertain'd & pleas'd."

For every new order that went out following the delivery of the queen's service, twice as many seemed to come in. "I sent a parcel to you which I hope is come to hand," Josiah wrote to John, who was still struggling to regain his health and longing for a little relief, but "I cannot promise you that it shall be the last of that sort." On his desk, Josiah had orders "from the Duke of Grafton & Richard Hopkins, Esq, for services of Cream colour the same as Sr Charles Cootes, in a former letter from Sr Wm [Meredith] are ords for the same to General Honeywood—Mr Stevens & another Gentln in all with which I recd from him in Town eight services amount of the whole about £60. . . . Lady Broughton had a desert service . . ." It was an effort to stay on top of all the orders, not only filling them in a timely manner but organizing the accounts, the invoices, and payments.

Josiah had an idea. He drafted a template for orders and a template for bills, leaving blank lines for filling in variable pieces of information, such as the quantity ordered, the customer's details, and the date. He wanted John to have the forms engraved, so that numerous copies could be printed off on demand "to distribute as occasion serves," which would save John or Tom Byerley time and effort. He also had a new strategy for receiving monies owed.

Traditionally, orders, normally being small and relatively inexpensive, were delivered to retailers or customers on credit, often on the exchange of promissory notes or "trade tokens." But now, business was booming—"I have this year sent goods to amount of about £1,000 to London all of which is owing for," Josiah told his brother, "& I shall not care how soon I was counting some of the money." Each order had its own price, varying in part as to whether it was for export, shops, or a private family. For exports, Josiah added 5 percent discount on orders "for ready money," the goods "being paid for here at the time of packing." Shops still dealt on credit, but aristocrats were notoriously bad at paying bills, and Josiah's first and continuing patron, Sir William Meredith, offered some frank advice. "You had best get your Brother to take the bills and receive the money on delivery."

"This advice," said Josiah, "I think is too wholesome to be slighted & indeed I do not want these great folks to know that the Potters ever do give any credit at all. A word to the wise is enough." Reviewing his accounts, he discovered one more problem. Since his services "have been mentioned at St James's," he'd noticed that certain services he had used— some engraving and delivery work, in particular—had suddenly become expensive. "I am very suspicious," wrote Josiah, of certain people "over charging [their] work especially in the spoon moulds," and desired John "therefore to know his charge before you pay him." Celebrity, it was becoming clear, had hidden and unexpected expenses. Everyone, he'd began to realize, struggled to steal profit, and Josiah had to find new ways of protecting his interests—on all fronts.

The "profit motive" was exactly what got the Duke of Bridgewater's agent, John Gilbert, and his brother, Thomas Gilbert—MP for Newcastle-under-Lyme and agent for Lord Gower—directly involved with the proposals to build the Trent & Mersey Canal. Thomas Gilbert initiated his own scheme to "Unite Seas & countrys," sensing a profit that he felt should be placed in the pocket of the aristocracy, not manufacturers.

When Josiah heard about this, he was "astonish'd, Confounded & vexed." For months, he had scarcely "thought of anything at all but Pottmaking & Navigating," being conscientious not to let the many new orders take him entirely away from the long-term plan of connecting the Potteries to the rest of the world. Thomas Gilbert, who Josiah had learned was the principal author of the opposing plan, was full of "dark, mysterious & ungenerous" ideas that would undermine the dedication of "the Persons who had hitherto lent their heads, hands & purses in planning & forwarding our scheme of Navigation." Josiah was not going to let such a travesty occur, and, with boldness and bravado that he never knew he possessed, he rushed to Lichfield with James Brindley to see Lord Gower. They "intruded unasked upon a junto" with Thomas Gilbert and none other than Samuel Garbett, the Birmingham manufacturer, who received him with frozen glares, making it clear that "they did not want my company."

He would not be deterred from upsetting their "chimerical plan," holding his ground by declaring that "I had thought more on this subject than most of our people had," and they had therefore "placed me in the forefront of the battle." Josiah faced up for a "skirmish" with the selfish MP, who with political legerdemain "did not choose to answer *point blank* to some questions which I had prepared for him." Samuel Garbett then piped up with an argument which Josiah patiently listened to before counterattacking. "The consequence of which was that in 10 minutes time he found his *baseless Fabrick* tumbling down to the ground & deserted it immediately." Josiah was relishing his conquests.

In the midst of their debates, "we were called to sup with Ld Gower." Never before had Josiah dined in the company of such dignitaries, nor had he ever been permitted to discourse on equal terms with, and in the company of, politicians, which Lord Gower invited him to do when desirous that both parties' plans be explained to him. He was touched by the civility of his host, and surprised that such an influential man, a "*great Man*"—former MP and Lord of the Admiralty, and now Lord Chamberlain of the Royal Household—could be so "*sensible & Humane.*"

As Gilbert—who naturally spoke first—presented his ideas on behalf of the Duke of Bridgewater, Josiah could easily have lost his nerve, intimidated by his surroundings. But his eyes and mind never drifted, and he listened steadfastly to the speech. "Think my friend how I was delighted to find that he had not one argument, inference, or flourish to make in the whole harangue," he told Bentley. Each point "I *felt* myself able with the greatest clearness to confute." He emphasized his emotional state. "My *heart* was ingaged in the cause, & that I believe made my thoughts & expressions obedient to my wish."

When he was called upon to make his reply, Josiah was direct, bluntly posing a question to his lordship. "When a set of men had employed their time, talents & their purses for ten years together in the execution of a design by which the Public would gain 300%... what is their reward? Would it not be very cruel," he asked, exposing Gilbert's plan of creating a monopoly, if "a new sett of Masters are raised up to controul both them & their works?"

"Gilbert," Lord Gower said, after a moment's reflection on Josiah's statements, "I do not think their plan can be rejected by Parliament." Josiah had clashed with titans and won. He rode away feeling he had entered a new station in life. "I scarcely know without a good deal of recollection whether I am a Landed Gentleman, an Engineer or a Potter," a dazed Josiah told Bentley, "for indeed I am all three & many other characters by turns." Nor would his elevation stop there: He had just learned that he was about to meet the queen, a rendezvous that would make dinner with Lord Gower pale by comparison.

Even after the flair Josiah demonstrated for sparring against those with "ministerial weight," it is easy to understand the nervousness he felt the morning he secured a brand-new light brown dress wig, buttoned up his scarlet lace waistcoat, eased into his blue velvet jacket, and strapped on his new sword, a proud gift to himself from Great Newport Street in London. It was a nice stylish touch—a decorative accessory he knew was requisite when visiting the most fashionable people in the country. He had an expensive shave, and, feeling primed and confident, he climbed into a coach and called for Buckingham House at St. James's Park, otherwise known as the "Queen's House," London's richest residence.

Josiah had been told that the queen was much impressed with the service he had worked on so frantically. The pieces were finished in his unique cream color, with green and gold decorations as requested, but, best of all, the engine-turned cups fitted the saucers and the lid fitted the pot. As promised, it was craftsmanship fit for a queen, and Charlotte was so satisfied with her new service that she bestowed a special privilege on

Josiah. For posterity, he recorded his version of how he earned a special place in history:

> Having already introduced several improvements into this art, as well with respect to the forms and colours of the wares, as the composition of which they are made, [I] invented a new species of earthenware for the table, quite new in its appearance, covered with a rich and brilliant glaze, bearing sudden vicissitudes of heat and cold without injury. . . . To this manufacture the Queen was pleased to give her name and patronage, commanding it to be called Queen's Ware, and honouring the inventor by appointing him Her Majesty's potter.

Queen Charlotte's "command" that Josiah should rename his creamware "Queen's Ware" was, more probably, an assent to an offer he made—the gift of naming the service in her honor, linking its uniqueness and "brilliance" to the image of Her Majesty—in return for using her assent to gain credibility in the marketplace for fashionable goods. It was a formula that Josiah studied as much as the chemistry of his glazes. As he said to Bentley, "if a Royal or Noble introduction be as necessary to the sale of an Article of *Luxury*, as real Elegance & beauty, then the Manufacturer, if he consults his own interests, will bestow as much pains, & expense too, if necessary, in gaining the former of these advantages."

In a stroke of marketing genius, Josiah promptly placed an advertisement in *Aris's Birmingham Gazette*, simply announcing that "Mr Josiah Wedgwood, of Burslem, has had the honor of being appointed Potter to Her Majesty." Not only would it serve Josiah's reputation well, but, as Bentley pointed out, it showed the Tory-loving royalty "to have the success of all our manufactures much at heart, and to understand the importance of them," though "Farmer George" never showed an interest in visiting the workshops of industry.

Josiah had come a long way from the small, thatched cottage with a muddy courtyard and a single bottleneck oven to Her Majesty's drawing room. But he already had thoughts about getting more customers, expressing ambitions to become not only Potter to Her Majesty but "Vase maker General to the Universe."

When Josiah left Buckingham House, he strolled along Pall Mall, passing "large shoals" of ladies endlessly seeking, it seemed to him, fashionable entertainment and objects of attention. If only he could draw their attention, he thought, but *how*? Each visit to London reaffirmed his impression that the new concept of "showrooms" was the key to turning "the dirt under our feet into *Gold*," as he sanguinely promised to Bentley, whom Josiah was trying to persuade to enter into a formal partnership. He first came upon the idea when Lord Gower and the other gentlemen paid a visit to the Bell Works, and possibly frustrated by having to endure the treacherous roads, they wondered why "I have not a Warehouse in London where patterns of all the sorts may be seen."

For months, he had been thinking about expanding his business beyond Burslem to London, with rooms and staff to cater to the whims of his new customers. Having his brother John there as an agent was not enough, since John was too busy with his own warehouse to keep on top of Josiah's trade. "I have often mentioned having a man in London the greatest part of the year shewing patterns, taking orders, settling accts &c &c," he told John, "& as I increase my work, & throw it still more into the ornamental way, I shall have the greater need of such assistance." He sought his brother's advice about how much this was likely to cost: "would £50 a year keep such a Person in London & pay rent for 2 rooms"?

While scouting for new premises, Josiah ducked into a coffeehouse to pen a progress report to Bentley. He was not having the best of luck. "What I have seen is too small & not the most convenient situation," he sighed. But roaming through London while he "set out upon a large plan in writing to you," one thing was becoming clear to him: Pall Mall—with its Restoration buildings and regal residents—"is the best situation in London. It is convenient for the Whole of this Great Town, the avenues to it open, & everybody comes there some time or another." It was of this wide street, with its colonnades and clubs (Almack's, Boodle's, and the Carlton among them), that the poet John Gay wrote in his *Trivia; or the Art of Walking the Streets of London* (1716):

> Shops breathe perfumes, thro' sashes ribbons glow
> The mutual arms of ladies and the beaux

It was the perfect place to set up shop.

While describing one of the rooms he had visited, Josiah told Bentley about his meeting with the owners, "a very good old Gentleman [who] has a young wife, & to her I am making my Court." Josiah was always looking for a sale, and a chance personal meeting with a young, wealthy woman of the house could turn into a potential order if he could shrewdly advertise his wares while explaining why he was interested in the rooms. He was especially hopeful since, he observed, "they are both of the Virtu species," meaning they were amongst the "virtuosi"—also known as the "Dilettanti"—the eighteenth-century collectors of ancient antiques. It was a rather new "species" to appear amongst the less than noble ranks of society, though the virtuosi had enough wealth to collect anything that was in fashion, most of it gathered whilst gallivanting around Europe on their Grand Tours. Josiah told them about his wares and about being "Potter to Her Majesty." His interest and kindness piqued, the old gentleman invited Josiah to take a look at his personal cabinet of antiquities, "a fine Collection of Raphael, Etruscan, & other very Curious Earthen wares." It was a curious collection indeed—crude, dirty, cracked pieces of ancient pottery, typical of the sort of thing now being brought back crate after crate from the shores of the Mediterranean.

What eccentric, and infectious, interests the leisured class had, Josiah thought, as he sat in the coffeehouse writing to Bentley. He took the last sip from his saucer, put the folded letter into his pocket, and set off exploring once again.

Some time later, he stopped to rest in St. James's Park, and watched the ladies and gentlemen of quality take their airings. Each one, he thought, was a potential customer, if only he could get them to walk through a room stocking his wares. But teacups and snuff boxes, however well crafted, were as wearisome to the fashionable as wool. He remembered well his experiences when working with Whieldon: tastes change quickly, and it was important to plan the next innovation in time to ride the changing tide. A year after he delivered the service to the queen, he was shocked that "the demand for this said *Creamcolour*, Alias, *Queen's Ware*, Alias, *Ivory*, still increases. It is really amazing," he told Bentley, "how rapidly the use of it has spread almost over the whole Globe, & how universally it is liked." Happily for Josiah, the spreading popularity of his tea services corresponded to the exponential growth in the distribution of tea. In 1765, over 7 million kilograms of tea were exported to Europe, double the amount shipped twenty years earlier. But he entertained no hopes that it would last long.

Josiah wanted to capitalize on the sales to America as quickly as possible. Even he was growing wearisome of the "green and gold" imitation of the Queen's ware. "I am quite clearing my Wareho of Colour'd ware," he said, adding that he was "heartily sick of the commodity & have been so long but durst not venture to quit it 'till I had got something better in hand."

He needed something new to show—and to sell—to the fashionable people parading along Pall Mall, and, remembering a recent conversation, it dawned on him that he might just have something that would catch their attention. It had to do with a bit of history he'd learned from his "virtuoso" friend, a story that stretched back to the beginning of civilization.

15
"Exquisite Models"

Everyone knew it was a catastrophe, but as Goethe would say, it "yielded so much pleasure to the rest of humanity." On a hot August afternoon in A.D. 79, Mount Vesuvius erupted, burying the local towns of Campania, a waterside resort for wealthy Romans. A witness to the event from across the trembling Bay of Naples was Pliny the Younger, who wrote letters to the historian Tacitus describing the blackened, burnt bits of pumice showering into the sea; dust permeating the air, emitting a sulphur stench; and rocky debris blocking the escape of Vesuvius' victims, including his uncle, Pliny the Elder. Those who perished, imagined Pliny, thought that the world was perishing with them.

When it was over, the towns were buried under seventy-five feet of ash and mud. Shocked survivors stared at the distant smoldering, molten mass. "The mind shudders to remember," confessed Pliny. Over time, with the exception of his succinct account, much was forgotten. Centuries elapsed; the Roman Empire collapsed; new towns were built along the bay; new vineyards established new roots.

Nearly seventeen hundred years later, a peasant digging in a well surfaced with building fragments and pieces of marble. The new rulers of the region, the Bourbon dynasty, descended on this find with enthusiasm. In 1738, the Campanian town of Herculaneum was uncovered; a decade later, workers reached a second town, Pompeii. Bronzes, statues, jewels, and even paintings were unearthed. Tourists as well as residents were fascinated; connoisseurs were captivated—if also intrusive. "There might certainly be collected great light from this reservoir of antiquities," huffed

Horace Walpole, "if a man of learning had the inspection of it," referring to men such as himself. Travelers to the ancient lands and "Enlightened" scholars argued in their publications and clubs that their artistic and archeological researches were crucial to understanding the historical development of society in general. "While the antiquary investigates the origins of the Arts," explained the historical painter and drawing instructor Thomas Burgess, "he is led back to the first dawnings of civil life, and the progressive rise of political institutions. It is obvious, therefore, how wide a compass of human learning is subject to the researches of the Antiquarian." But he was echoing popular sentiment; already there was no chance of keeping people away. The public imagination was enraptured. While Josiah's workers were digging up clay and forming it into tableware, the plundering of buried cities had begun.

British Grand Tourists were especially enchanted with excavation. In their homeland, antiquarians such as William Stukeley were combing parish grounds, uncovering ancient landscapes and studying sacred ruins. But a different kind of history was emerging in Italy. What lay before them was a uniquely preserved scene from the past. And the story was growing more complex. Evidence suggested that art and culture had been influenced by both the Greeks and the Etruscans—that mysterious ancient people who once thrived just north of Rome. History was beginning to reveal more about classical heritage than ever before, and these were lessons classically educated Europeans were eager to learn.

Attention turned north, to the Tuscan mountains, a landscape that hid even older secrets. This was also familiar ground to Grand Tourists, who annually passed through it on their way to Rome and Naples. The ancient Etruscans, known mainly through the writings of Livy and Virgil, had been a formidable people—fighting off the Greeks for domination of the Mediterranean, then the Romans, who eventually conquered and subjugated them. But they remained enigmatic. No one knew how their home—Etruria—originated. No one could understand their language. What one could see was their grave. Etruscan nobility had been buried in splendor, in chambers covered by mounds of earth or set into hillsides, the vaulted roofs decorated with colored murals of dancing, banqueting, hunting, fishing, and horse racing. Renaissance artists such as Michelangelo are thought to have occasionally copied the few Etruscan frescoes then known, but the real impulse to penetrate the vaults of antiquity came with the Age of Enlightenment. Inscriptions and carved or painted images had begun to reveal a richer narrative of the past than widely read literary legends. Just as excavation was spreading in the Neapolitan South, uncovering remnants of life in Pompeii and Herculaneum, the tombs of *their* ancestors were being pried open in the North, with equal excitement and anticipation.

Under the brilliant blue skies of Tuscany, along roads hedged by broad-leafed pollarded poplars, travelers passed excavation sites being etched into the landscape, veiled from hundreds of peasants digging deeper into the "cities of the dead" (*necropoleis*) by a thin haze of dust. By the mid-eighteenth century, a host of British artists were permanently resident in the region with papal permission to superintend their own excavations. In 1748, the Scottish artist Gavin Hamilton arrived on the scene, first earning a living by painting portraits of touring patricians, then acting as a dealer in the trade in Etruscan antiquities.

A party of Grand Tourists gathered on horses and mules and followed Hamilton to see the digging at the ancient tombs and temples. Gazing down from a sandy ridge, they glimpsed pediments protruding from the tiered ground, while workers emerged from tunnels hauling decorative bas-reliefs, funerary steles, and, most enticingly, ornamental vases. They spied artists sketching the artifacts in situ but witnessed the dealers carefully protecting their sites from prying eyes, ignoring any notion of the sanctity of the location but concerned to smuggle their finds into the unofficial art market. And indeed, the enthusiastic visitors hurriedly made Hamilton offers on the latest discoveries. One client not only possessed wealth and the desire to collect, but had also the political clout and the friendship of the King of Naples. This was William Hamilton, no relation to his dealer, but British envoy to Naples, who was perfectly placed to link together an alliance of artists, agents, and connoisseurs in a profitable trade in antiquities. He was also preparing a publication illustrating his personal collection that would help establish "neo-classicism" as the eighteenth century's greatest fashion and, by chance, provide a blueprint for an unlikely empire in the making created by a little-known entrepreneur in Burslem.

Soon after his arrival as ambassador in 1767, William Hamilton's home, on a steep hill with spectacular views of the Bay of Naples, was already gaining a reputation as *the* gathering place for vivacious assemblies. The sprawling Palazzo Sessa, formerly a monastic building, was a main attraction for local worthies as well as passing tourists. "It is the custom," explained one British visitor to Naples in 1768, "when neither the Opera, nor any particular engagement prevent [us] to meet at his house, where we amuse ourselves as we are disposed, either at cards, the billiard-table, or his little concert; some form themselves into small parties of conversation, and as the members of this society are often Ambassadors, Nuncios, Monsignoris, Envoys, Residents, and the first quality of Naples, you will conceive it to be instructive as well as honourable." The leader of the Neapolitan quality was the king himself, who added that even he enjoyed visiting Hamilton's house because that was where "an interesting group of lovely women, literati, and artists were assembled."

Hamilton also had a home two miles from the base of Mount Vesuvius, named Villa Angelica. It was equally picturesque, surrounded by a fertile vineyard with lava-baked paths heading up the mountain. Here, Hamilton and his wife, Catherine, entertained guests more intimately than at Palazzo Sessa. One guest was Charles Burney, father of the future novelist, who was then traveling through Naples collecting information for his *General History of Music,* and was invited to the villa with his friend, Captain Forbes.

The visitors arrived on a crisp autumn Friday afternoon and immediately found the household convivial, indulging in one meal after another, washed down with copious amounts of fine Neapolitan wine, punctuated with concerts performed by two of Hamilton's pages, "who play very well one on the fiddle and the other on the violoncello." Late afternoon was siesta time, when the Hamiltons courteously set up a "field bed" for Captain Forbes, who, originally planning to bow out, "was easily prevailed upon to pig in the same room with me," said Burney. The party awoke after sunset for more musical entertainment and stories of Burney's research, "musical talk," as he called it.

All talk stopped when they heard a loud explosion coming from the "very busy" volcano. They ran to the veranda while Hamilton fumbled with "glasses of all sorts" with which to focus on the mountain—his own passionate subject of research. But even without any apparatus everyone clearly saw "showers of immense red hot stones" raining down on the mountain; "we were certain that they mounted near 1000 feet above the summit." The rumble was deeper than thunder, wrote an astounded Burney, and the sight "very awful and beautiful, resembling in great the most ingenious and fine fireworks I ever saw." "It was," confirmed Catherine, who was by no means unfamiliar with the volcano's activities, "an astonishing sight."

The turbulent mountain kept Burney awake much of the night, but he was anxious to rise early and follow one of the paths up the side of Vesuvius to take a closer look. Alas, Hamilton advised that it was too daring while such "quantities of sulphurous smoke" emanated and uncertainty remained as to "where the stones will drop." So Burney decided to take the chaise and "visit the lava of former eruptions and to coast round the foot of Vesuvius as far as we could with safety by keeping always to the windward." Burney came prepared. He put on his flannel waistcoat, leather stockings, "old good-for-nothing shoes," and a greatcoat—ready to climb ("sometimes on all fours") over the rugged lava, cinders, and ashes, feeling sorry for Captain Forbes, who emerged for a second time from his makeshift field bed ready to go with only the previous day's elegant silk suit to wear.

It was a privilege to go with a guide as knowledgeable and enthusiastic as William Hamilton, who was once spotted in a back street of Naples in full court dress carrying home, with the help of a local Peasant, some recently excavated dusty vases he had just purchased. That was why Burney was willing to crawl on all fours around the mountain—he knew the blanket of ash and debris hid potential treasures.

Hamilton easily spotted a kindred spirit, and suggested to Burney's delight that if he wanted to see some of these treasures, he should come to look at the collection at Palazzo Sessa.

According to one visitor, it was no secret that "the Neapolitans are more suspicious and jealous" of Hamilton than anyone else for having amassed such a collection—more than two thousand antique objects, including over seven hundred ancient vases and six hundred bronzes, alongside a separate collection of over six thousand coins. But in Britain his efforts to promote the study of the classical past were celebrated. In the second half of the eighteenth century, Grand Tourists had returned to Britain on the rising tide of neoclassical interest, leading to the founding of the Society of Dilettanti in 1734, formed, as one contemporary explained, by some of the gilded youth "who had travelled in Italy and were desirous of encouraging, at home, a Taste for those objects which had contributed so much to their entertainment abroad." The Dilettanti worked to achieve their ostensible goals by putting themselves forward as exemplary artistic patrons; they zealously collected and encouraged others to follow suit, supporting publications that sought "less to dazzle than instruct" future students of classical antiquity. Charles Burney was one such "student." When he returned to London, he was welcomed by the Dilettanti, who supported Burney's nomination to the Royal Academy of Art, the new institution opened by George III, at their urging, in 1768. Burney was a perfect candidate. In the view of Sir Joseph Banks, the president of the eminently prestigious Royal Society—he was "one of the most learned men we have among us."

Their numbers were growing, and Burney's friend, William Hamilton, was fast becoming the doyen of fine taste. The artist and president of the Academy, Sir Joshua Reynolds, dubbed him "head of the Virtuosi" upon Hamilton's inauguration into the Society of the Dilettanti. Six members gathered around Hamilton, who sat at a table with an Etruscan vase from his collection placed in front of him. Reynolds faced them, sketching the scene for a group portrait. The society's president, Sir Watkin Williams Wynn, had just downed a glass of red wine in a toast to Hamilton's health, and gestured toward the vase. It was a gesture to acknowledge Hamilton's promotion of the Enlightenment ideals they celebrated—to advance the science of "taste" by example through rational instruction. He was now part of the eighteenth-century "cult of connoisseurship," though it was a culture that worried the tutors of some of the more flamboyant patricians, who recklessly frittered away their wealth in buying expensive antiques in attempts to improve their "Tastes." Some critics, like Horace Walpole, dismissed the club. While he agreed in principle that there was virtue in antiquarian study, he doubted whether the Dilettanti would set a good example. After all, he jested, "the nominal qualification for membership is having been in Italy, the real one, being drunk." But it was the society's financial support for the publication of others' antiquarian researches that would earn its members recognition. Their latest member, Hamilton, was well aware of this.

His own enormous collection had received widespread admiration since, between 1766 and 1767, he had published four sumptuous folio volumes illustrating his collection, offering "exquisite Models" that would aid future artists in the development of their observation and drawing skills.

Sir Joshua Reynolds was among the first to offer praise, writing a warmhearted letter saying how much he admired the work, and how confident he was that it "will tend to the advancement of the Arts, as adding more materials for Genius to work upon." Hamilton appreciated the comment. "Good models," he affirmed, thinking of the elaborate engravings in his publication, "give birth to ideas by exciting the imagination. . . ."

Aspiring to fulfill the Dilettanti dream, his elaborate production was not intended to provide "merely the objects of fruitless admiration" but rather to "revive an ancient Art." He could not have foreseen what a master potter from the Midlands with a bountiful imagination and mountains of determination would do when he encountered those illustrations.

16

The Creators of Beauty

"I have now bought the Estate," Josiah eagerly told Bentley in 1766, confident that his offer of £3,000 would be accepted by Mrs. Ashenhurst, the aging proprietress of Ridge House and its land on the ridge of a valley west of Burslem. He anticipated that the deal would be completed the next spring, and quickly set upon surveying the land for a suitable place to build his and Sally's new home, a welcome prospect now that Sally had given birth to their second child, John. The land would also accommodate the grand factory he had visions of constructing. He was hoping that Bentley would take a break from his duties and visit their "dirty spot of Earth," as it was candidly described by the "elevated mind" of their mutual friend Ralph Griffiths, the editor of the *Monthly Review*.

Josiah was particularly keen to have him visit since they had just "increased their connections." Bentley had agreed to open his Liverpool warehouse to Josiah's goods and "be a Pot merchant," acting as an import and export agent and managing the sale and stock of the wares at his discretion. Whatever goods Josiah bought from other suppliers for export, he and Bentley would split the profits "evenly betwixt us." If Josiah sent him "goods of my own manufacture, I allow you a 10% commission as before." Bentley had in the past sold items for Josiah and arranged for their shipment abroad at a commission, but this move marked the beginning of a closer professional partnership between them, one that Josiah hoped would grow even stronger.

"My Sally says your *fat sides* require a good deal of shaking & would recommend a journey on *horseback*, not in the Coach, to Burslem," he joked.

What's more, "she will not fix upon a spot for either house or Gardens no nor even the Stables 'till you have viewed & given your opinion of the premises." Josiah countered the jibe about his widowed friend's portly shape by flattering him that he should think of himself as "Capability Brown," the famous landscape gardener. "Ten Guineas if I remember is the price of a single call, with or without the advantage of his direction, to make a lawn & piece of Water here—Cut down that wood & plant it there, level that rising ground, & raise yonder valley &c &c." Why would they need to hire a Brown, Josiah asked, when Bentley had "a hundred times the genius," and at the expense of a mere fifty-mile ride, so much more could be accomplished? "As our connections are to become extensive in the Potting business," Josiah said, with a glimmer in his eye, "it is absolutely necessary you should visit the Manufacture, see what is going forward there, make your bargains accordingly, & lend your assistance towards its farther improvement."

Bentley's visit to Burslem started a discussion with Josiah and Sally about plans for the house and factory that would weave through their correspondence for months. They also considered increasing the sales of pottery to America and the West Indies, hoping that the postwar political unrest would not interfere yet again with their lucrative trade. For months past Josiah had been clearing out the recesses of his warehouse, sending "Cargoes of Creamcolour & perhaps a little green and Gold for hot climates," asking Bentley to organize a shipment to the capital of British West Florida, to "sell all the green and gold for Pensacola, [and] the new discover'd Islands," adding that "Green desert ware is often wanted, *in reality* for the West India Islands."

Hoping to benefit from colonial admiration for the Whig prime minister William Pitt the Elder (Earl of Chatham), Josiah was also stimulated by a comment Lord Gower recently made when he returned for another tour of the potworks with his family. He "asked me if I had not sent Mr Pitt over in shoals to America." They had done a portrait plate almost a decade earlier when Admiral Vernon became a national hero, so why not Pitt? he wondered. "What do you think about sending Mr Pitt upon Crockery ware to America? A Quantity might certainly be sold there now & some advantage made of the American prejudice in favour of the great man."

This time, Josiah was not being sarcastic when referring to such an influential statesman as a "great man." Josiah and Bentley, as well as so many other merchants involved in the foreign market, cheered Pitt's campaign to protect national trade by criticizing government proposals that threatened it, such as the Stamp Act. "It is my opinion," Pitt had declared to Parliament, "that this kingdom has no right to lay a tax on the colonies. . . . Trade is your object with them and taxing was ill advised. If you do not make suitable laws for them, they will make laws for you, my Lords." In the face of fierce American resistance to the Stamp Act, and following another impassioned speech by Pitt in January 1766, the act was repealed.

But before Josiah and Bentley had a chance to execute the design for Pitt's portrait on a plate, a shadow was cast by a looming cloud that once again threatened their colonial trade. "The American business is in a critical condition," a gravely concerned Josiah wrote, a year after Pitt's speech, "& I do not know what to determine upon without you, for you will be concern'd in the event as well as myself."

Pitt had fallen ill, and his nemesis, George Grenville, a protégé of Lord Bute (and Pitt's brother-in-law), was once again arguing that "the troops to be kept up in America shou'd be Paid by the Colonies" through new taxes. The chancellor of the exchequer, Charles Townshend, agreed, and began drafting an "American Import Duties Bill" to raise revenue. Of particular concern to Josiah was article VII of what became known as the Townshend Act, which discontinued "the drawbacks payable on china earthenware exported to America," eliminating the refund on the duty manufacturers such as Josiah were liable to pay. This meant more money out of Josiah's pocket, and more limitations on trade.

Ever since Grenville's first speeches as prime minister in 1763 which led to the passing of the Stamp Act, and his persecution of Wilkes for publishing *The North Briton*, Josiah and Bentley, as well as most others looking out for mercantile interests, had cultivated a hatred for Grenville. In December 1766, when debates between Pitt and Grenville on the quartering of troops and new taxes were inflamed, Bentley had even written an anonymous article (as was customary) in the *Monthly Review*, attacking a book on trade and finances by Grenville's former secretary to the Treasury, Thomas Whately.

"Tho' the subject of commerce has been frequently investigated, it is far from being so well and universally understood as to render the illustrations of future Writers unnecessary," wrote Bentley. "Indeed many of our commercial laws are so extremely absurd, as to injure those manufactures and branches of trade which they were intended to encourage, to retard improvements, and prohibit invention; so that they stand in great need of general *Review.*" The book, Bentley bluntly put it, was full of "circumstantial enumerations" and "written in favour of a party"—the Tories. "It must be confessed," he continued, hoping anonymity would permit particular vehemence, "this noble work would require a knowledge of facts, a clearness of understanding, an impartiality of judgement, a love of the public welfare; and a *portion of undisturbed leisure for deliberation*, which rarely fall to the lot of any man; and never to one of our bustling financiers, or Ministers of State."

Josiah unwittingly read his friend's diatribe while reading the *Monthly Review* out loud to Sally one evening for "Deary's amusement." "Why Joss!" Sally shouted out, shrewdly recognizing their friend's brand of argument and manner of writing, "one would think thou wast reading one of Bentley's letters," which suddenly struck Josiah as being "very certain." "I shall not wonder to hear," Josiah then joked to Bentley, "that George Grenville has sent to inquire of the Publisher, who it was that wrote that letter." It was Bentley's intrepid determination to "set our *Great* & *Little* folk right" that Josiah and Sally admired so much in their friend.

The debates over taxation and colonial unrest which had such a bearing on trade gripped Josiah's attention every evening as he read the papers. They reawakened an anxiety that had haunted him for years. At the beginning of 1765, in the midst of debates affecting colonial trade, a concerned Josiah had written to the only politician he then had contact with, Sir William Meredith. "The bulk of our particular manufacture you know is exported to foreign markets," explained Josiah, "for our home consumption is very trifleing in comparison to what is sent abroad, & the principal of these markets are the Continent & islands of N. America. . . . This trade to our Colonies," he continued, "we are apprehensive of losing in a few years," if not from strangling trade regulations, then because the colonists "have set on foot some Potwork there" to compete with the mother country's manufacturers.

Josiah was especially alarmed to learn that a master potter from Staffordshire named Bartham had emigrated to America and set about "hireing a number of our hands for establishing new Pottworks in South Carolina." As the "necessaries of life & consequently the price of labour" were "daily advancing," making the management of a manufactory more expensive and stressful, Josiah thought it "highly probable"—no, he changed his mind categorically—"I make no question but more will fol-low them & join their Brother Artists & Manufacturers of every class who are from all quarters takeing a rapid flight." By impressing "the evil" of "these emigrations" upon Sir William, a great patron "of the arts & Com-merce of your Country," he hoped something might be done.

But two years later, the continuing turmoil offered no relief. "Mr Grenville & his party seem determin'd to *Conquer England in America*," reported Josiah during a visit to London in 1767, echoing Pitt's own proclamation when he added that "the Americans will then make Laws for themselves & if we continue our Policy—for us too in a very short time." Bartham's example, Josiah teased, might yet prevail. "If we must all be driven to America you & I shall do very well amongst the Cherokees."

In fact, Josiah was far from prepared to give up his ground, and a pos-sible resolution to his immediate concerns came from an unlikely source: an order for wares from Lady Grenville. "Would you think it," he sarcasti-cally exclaimed to Bentley, "I am this morning going by Command to visit your old friend George Grenville. You may make yourself easy about America, we will settle their affairs whilst his Lady is giving her order for Crockery ware." Josiah had in the past overcome personal aversions for the sake of a sale or promoting his own interests, and this curious encounter was no exception. This was also true when, in a further attempt to enrich his manufactory and draw on the potential that America had to offer in these trying times, Josiah contemplated contacting none other than Charles Townshend.

The idea came up during a discussion with the Duke of Bridgewater, when Josiah inquired about the prospects of obtaining a patent granting him exclusive rights to the import of "Cherokee" clay, also known as kaolin, from America. He had lately been conducting routine experiments on different kinds of clay he bought from clay merchants—which included "a lump" from South Carolina, "which surprised me a good deal." It had some unusual qualities: it was whiter than most clay, and remained so after firing at high temperatures, when it took on a translu-cent glossy quality. After consulting his chemical friends, including Priest-ley and a new acquaintance, the engineer James Watt, he learned that "kaolin will come out of the fire perfectly white" because it lacked "phlo-giston," which (according to contemporary theory) allowed substances to burn. This might, Josiah thought, be the secret ingredient he needed to make real Chinese porcelain—such a sought-after commodity that it would be like being able to "turn dirt into *Gold*."

Josiah immediately asked Bentley to inquire about importing more of it; but it "must be got as clean from soil or any heterogenius matter, as if it was to be eat & put into Casks or Boxes," which recorded exactly the place, and depth, from which it was mined. Later, he bought a map of North America by the traveler, cartographer, and geologist John Mitchell, who Josiah also personally visited to talk about clay deposits. He even "kept incognito" at a meeting with "three Gentlemen who had resided long in South Carolina, one of whom gave me a small sample of the Cherok earth, by way of Curiosity, not knowing who, or what I was." He discovered information about its location—the main source was three hundred miles inland from Charles Town—and some practical detail about how to transport it abroad. What he requested of Charles Townshend was no less than a monopoly on kaolin's use in Britain.

The Duke of Bridgewater was skeptical of Josiah's plan. "The Chancellor of the Exchequer might be applyd to grant it to me Duty free, & to lay a duty upon all imported by others"; but, explained the duke, as it would need to be a parliamentary affair and "very probably would not pass, but would inevitably lay the whole affair open." Drawing attention to his scheme would especially work against Josiah's wishes, the duke continued, with a wink, since "Mr Townshend and Ld Shelbourne" were friends with none other than Samuel Garbett, the scheming Birmingham merchant who had interfered with the plans for the Trent & Mersey Canal, and who, he intimated, "is sure to be advised of it."

Given the political climate, created not least by Townshend, it would certainly have been a coup d'état if Josiah had had his way. Facing likely rejection, Josiah settled upon the duke's prudent advice that he "send a Person over immediately without applying for a grant, a Patent or anything else."

Josiah thought hard about who he could send to America as an agent. One possibility was Thomas Griffiths, the brother of his literary friend Ralph, who, Josiah learned, "hath resided many years in N.A. & is seasoned to the S.C. Climate by a severe fever he underwent at Charles Town & has had many connections with the Indians." Thomas had bought into a share of 3,000 acres of land with two partners with a plan to make sugar from maple, "which secret he had learned from the native Indians," but was frustrated in his scheme for lack of money. He offered his services to Josiah, who worried mildly that the entrepreneur might "take it into his head to redeem, with my money, his share of the improvements his partners have made on their grant of land." Though he came from a respectable and friendly family, "I have known such instances of Persons changing their sentiments & principles with the Climate." In the end, Josiah concluded that it was worth the risk. One way or another, Josiah wanted that special clay, and Thomas Griffiths packed his bags.

The other side of Josiah's interests offered him little relief from apprehension about his "downright serious business" plans. As friendly and cooperative as Bentley was, he still resisted Josiah's inducements to enter into a more formal, and committed, partnership, which would require his removal to Burslem from Liverpool. Bentley meditated on the difficulties of the move, which Josiah picked apart one by one.

"I have total ignorance of the business," claimed Bentley. "That I deny," was Josiah's riposte. "You have taste, the best foundation for our intended concern, & which must be our *Primum Mobile*, for without that, all will stand still. . . ." Bentley emphasized that he did not know the practical side of the craft, which Josiah assured him "will soon be learned by so apt a scholar. The very air of this Country will soon inspire you with the more Mechanical part of our trade."

Bentley foresaw all the difficulties in quitting his current position and ending his prospering partnership with Samuel Boardman, which they had only just established in 1764. Josiah agreed that it was a risk, a "matter of Calculation, in which there is no data to proceed upon, but probabilities of future contingencies, which we cannot investigate." However, Josiah was emphatic that it was a risk worth taking. "I have, it's true, a great opinion of the design answering our most sanguine expectations with respect to profit," he said. But one concern of Bentley's "staggers my hopes more than anything else": leaving his friends and pleasures of Liverpool.

Josiah trod cautiously. "Can you part from your Octagon, & enlightened Octagonian brethren, to join the diminutive & weak society of a Country Chapel? Can you give up the rational & elevated enjoyment of your Philosophical Club, for the puerile tete a tete of a Country fireside?"

Could he pry himself away from his evening soirées with all those "learned & ingenious friends" in town "to employ yourself amongst Mechanicks, dirt & smoke?"

Josiah paused. However true, perhaps that wasn't the most attractive way to put it—There was no Gainsborough elegance in this portrait of provincial, manufacturing life. But there was a deeper sense of satisfaction to be derived from it. "I have some hopes," said Josiah, that if you "fall in love with & make a Mistress of this new business, as I have done in mine, I should have little or no doubt of our success." Josiah implored Bentley to think of the power one had as a manufacturer, who with "raw Materials, the infinite ductility of the Clay," can be "the Creator as it were of beauty, rather than merely be the vehicle, or medium to convey it from one hand to another."

Knowing how slowly things were progressing with the purchase of Ridge House Estate and construction of the works, he begged Bentley to take time to think it over. Part of the anticipated delay was at the hands of the Derbyshire architect Joseph Pickford, who was hired to develop plans for the new houses and factory. Josiah had been introduced to Pickford through mutual friends of Bentley's, but after one quick look at his first drawings, "Sally and I pronounce'd its doom," as did Bentley, who by the time these plans were passed around was flattering Josiah by listening more closely to ideas about the proposed partnership.

Josiah wanted everything to be just right, and "proposed to Mr Pickford an alteration or two" on what he was now calling Bentley's new home. He enlarged the rooms here and there, so that Bentley could "sup in *comfortably*." He liked some of the exterior details, but thought "three outside doors are too many for your small house, & would render it very windy, cold, & uncomfortable." The brew house was "abominable." But these were "trifling alterations," which he and Bentley worked on during one of their meetings regarding the new premises, which Josiah named "Etruria."

Nothing was quite as easy as they hoped. "This building of houses my Friend so far as we have hitherto gone is very near akin to *Building Castles in the Air*," exclaimed Josiah in desperation. "The old Mansions are all swept clean away! & you see a totally new one erected in their stead," all of which, of course, was being hashed out at considerable cost—the whole project stretching above a staggering £10,000 ($1 million). "So help me—Bentley," cried Josiah, "to create new Vases for the payment of my Architect." Thankfully, the "new mansion" that Josiah preferred to Pickford's original Palladian plan was "5 to £700 less than the former," and was designed to be "more in the Modern, & I think *true* taste."

As if all this was not enough, Josiah received the unsettling news that old Mrs. Ashenhurst was not satisfied with his £3,000 offer for her estate, and was angling to accept a competing offer. "Indeed," he wrote to Bentley, hoping to assuage his friend's anxieties about the whole affair, "I am not in possession of the land you know to build you either a House or Works, but am with the Old Ladys Steward & you have furnished me with a very strong inducement to comply with almost any terms they shall propose." That, alas, would take yet more time.

Wishing to progress from frustrated plans to future prosperity, Josiah traveled to London in the hope of finding a shop to rent, where he envisioned "setts of Vases should decorate the Walls & both these articles may, every few days, be so altered, revers'd & transform'd as to render the whole a new scene," a showroom strategy where "business & amusement can be made to go hand in hand." He also continued the more pleasant conversation he had earlier begun with Bentley about "anything curious in the Pottery branch" relating to "antiquities."

When he returned to Burslem at the beginning of June 1767, he felt rejuvenated, with "a heart perfectly at ease & rejoicing with my family & friends at our meeting together again in health and safety." He excitedly wrote to Bentley, telling him of all the "designs, Models, Moulds, Clays, Colours &c &c for the Vasework by which means we shall be able to do business *effectually* 12 months sooner than we could without those preparatory steps. . . ." But no sooner had the cheerful letter for Bentley been sent than one from William Hodgson, a merchant in London and friend of his brother John's, arrived that would once again upset his spirits.

17
An Afflicted Heart

I t took Josiah a day to gain enough strength to inform Bentley of the melancholy news that "Your friend & My poor Brother is Dead." John was forty-six years old, nearly ten years older than Josiah, yet it was only recently, when John agreed to help his younger brother engage with the London marketplace, that the two had become very close. John had been entirely dedicated to Josiah's welfare, squarely confronting his responsibilities as they grew more burdensome despite suffering from bouts of severe illness throughout the years. Whether it was attending court or knocking on doors to collect outstanding bills, he never failed Josiah, who was in disbelief that John "is no more, is no longer the warm & benevolent friend, affectionate Brother, or chearfull Companion, but is now a lifeless, insensible Clod of Earth. A sad reverse."

What made the shock all the more severe were the mysterious circumstances surrounding his brother's death as pieced together by his friends. On the ill-fated night four evenings earlier, John went to watch fireworks at Ranelagh, the public gardens on the banks of the Thames in Chelsea, where fashionable crowds frequented concerts, balls, and masquerades. Afterwards, he went to the White Swan Inn, at Westminster Bridge, "where we used to dine & get a little refreshment," until about midnight. He asked for a room, "but unfortunately they were unable to accommodate him, so that he was obliged to go seek for one elsewhere, & in passing the River side, tis supposed he slipped in." His body was found floating in the Thames at 5 a.m. the next morning.

Those were all the particulars that Mr. Hodgson could relay, and "it is

indeed too much for me," Josiah confessed. "I can scarcely think at all."
But his mind kept coming back to retrace the last hours of John's life.
"Many things if you were here I should ask you," he told Hodgson, "& yet
I am afraid to know them." Josiah couldn't shake the feeling that there
was some foul play or devious cause at work. "I know you will do everything in your power to preserve the memory of your Deceased friend
from censure," he continued, but "I shall be very unhappy till I know
some further particulars...." A brief report in a local London newspaper
might have fueled Josiah's suspicions:

> Monday evening a man threw himself into the River near the
> White Swan at Chelsea and was drowned, and yesterday his body was
> thrown on shore by the tide near that place; the cause of his commit-
> ting this action is said to be a disappointment in a love affair.

Whatever else, if anything, Josiah or his brother's friends learned about
John's death appears to have been buried with the past.

At the same time, Josiah was relieved that John had a good friend to
"perform the last offices of humanity," and who could advise "what is to be
done on this melancholy occasion." He asked Hodgson to retrieve "a little
box" from a desk at the warehouse that Josiah used "in which I put the
notes he had for his money, & other papers" and to think about "my late
Brothers Connections & who to invite to the funeral." His older brother
Thomas was preparing to travel from Burslem to London, but Josiah
needed to stay at home. Sally was on the verge of delivering their third
child and could not be left alone.

Josiah was the executor of his brother's will, and ensured that fond
impressions would be left of his brother. "Everything is to be done in a
handsome manner, he has left enough behind him to do it with," he
announced. John would have been honored. "As a small Testimony of the
Esteem my poor Brother had for you," he informed Bentley, "he hath left
you five Guineas to buy a mourning ring. I know he always wished to be
remembered by you." Now more than ever Josiah was thankful to have a
friend that so many held in such high regard.

> I know you will sympathise with me in my distress, & I need not
> tell you how doubly welcome a few lines will be at this time from a
> real, affectionate, & sensible friend, such a one as you have ever been

to me since I had the happiness of being known to you. Let us now be dearer to each other if possible than other, let me adopt you for my Brother & fill up the chasm this cruel accident has made in my afflicted heart.—Excuse me, my dear friend, the subject is too much for me. I am your miserable friend.

A month passed and Josiah remained "in distress," rereading letters through "a Valley of Tears" from friends that were "a Cordial to my afflicted heart." "The loss of a Brother, a sensible, Benevolent, & truly affectionate Brother," tore a breach in "a heart rather too susceptible of grief." This was the longest period of time since Josiah's leg injury in Liverpool in 1762 that he spent convalescing rather than working.

But business, he knew, must go on or he and his family would face further distress. He became alert to his lethargy when Bentley traveled to London for pressing issues connected to his own affairs. He had spent time there on behalf of the Corporation of Liverpool to address debates connected with new legislation on bankruptcy, and in late July 1767 was there to support a friend in a court case. When Bentley's friend lost his case, which appeared to have some residual effects on Bentley's own business affairs, Josiah was quick to console. "Besides all pecuniary considerations" in this "unlucky turn in your affairs," he wrote, "you have too much Philosophy . . . to be deeply, or too long affected by a mere accident." Bentley should turn to his friend, and "infuse into his bosom a portion of that cheerfulness & flow of good spirits, you are so largely possessed of" and remember to "look forward & be happy."

After writing this, Josiah seemed to follow his own advice. He recognized the need to return to work, and had begun a course of experiments to refocus his mind. "Labour I will not call it," he said, preferring to use the term "entertainment." To collect materials for his experiments, Josiah traveled to local mines, where he obtained different fusible substances which he mixed with clay and analyzed for chemical constituents that might be used for new glazes. But what lifted his spirits even more was that Sally was now suckling the newest arrival to their family, Richard—or "Dicky." Almost two months after John's death, Josiah was able to inform Bentley with joy that "Mrs Wedgwood & her Wedgwoodikin are both well."

"I am now sunk over head & ears into business again, & have now, at this present time of writing, a Warehouse full of Gentlemen & Ladys," Josiah reported to Bentley a month after Dicky's birth. Whether it was to make up for lost time or to discharge the pent-up anxieties about work, he was busier than he could ever remember, experimenting, traveling, selling, and sketching. "Why you never knew so busy a Mortal as I am," he exclaimed. "Highways—surveying Ridge House Estate—Experiments for Porcelain, or at least a new Earthenware, fill up every moment almost of my time & would take a good deal more if I had it."

He had a catalogue of orders at hand and a range of products that were flying out of his warehouse in crates. "Creamcolor Tyles are much wanted," he noted, "& the consumption will be great for Dairys, Baths, Summer Houses, *Temples* &c &c." This was the sort of stock-in-trade ware that always provided the bedrock of Josiah's business. His experimental triumphs, such as cream—alias Queen's—ware, provided a welcome windfall, but as always Josiah was anticipating a change in consumer taste; "every rarity soon grows stale," he said, which was why he still longed to disappear into his laboratory at night. "Many of my experiments turn out to my wishes, & convince me more and more, of the extensive capability of our Manufacture for further improvements," he assured Bentley, encouraging him to share his dream about future success. "It is at present (comparatively) in a rude, uncultivated state, & may easily be polish'd & brought to much greater perfection. Such a revolution, I believe, is at hand, & you must assist in, & profit by it."

Josiah believed that the "revolution" was not only linked to the production of new kinds of products but to the way people shopped. He'd spotted the new phenomenon of conspicuous consumption and believed he had "a mode of introducing this article amongst that sort of Customers who can afford to pay for anything they like, though the price is a little too high for People in the middle station." It was, Josiah felt, time for change.

"We will," he proclaimed, "COMMAND SUCCESS . . . if you can make this branch of business worth your pursuit." "I have some tryals that will do you good to look at," he pleaded, which will "make you an Etruscan" yet! "Leave off trimming your old skiff, come & assist in putting a new one upon the Stocks."

Ironically, it was the present boom in business that kept him one breath away from entering this new world. "My present business is too good to be neglected for uncertainties," an unusually cautious Josiah determined, "& I must, so long as that is the case, be content without arriving at those improvements in my Manufacture, which a little application would bring within my reach." However, he added, drawing attention to a step forward which he thought might whet Bentley's appetite, "I have improved bodys enough for Vases & ornaments are really an inexhaustible field for us to range in." The "field," Josiah believed, of "ornaments"— decorative rather than "useful" wares—was where they would find their first hidden treasure. His next visit to London convinced him of this.

Since his chance meeting with the "virtuosi" couple in London over a year earlier, where he had first seen Etruscan vases in the old gentleman's cabinet of curiosities, Josiah had been searching avidly for information about ancient antiquities, particularly the decorative, "ornamental" vases that Grand Tourists proudly displayed as trophies of travel.

He naturally turned to Bentley to enquire about "a volume or two" he could read that "may be of use to me in the Antiquities," wanting to study everything from colors and textures to design. "Who knows what you may hit upon, or what we may strike out betwixt us?" he wrote, but "you may depend on an ample share of the profits arising from any such discoveries." Bentley's best advice was for Josiah to visit the British Museum, where over the decade since its founding curiosities and literature of that sort had increasingly stocked the shelves. As Josiah was preparing for his London trip, he dashed off a letter to Bentley, asking for *written instructions what books I am to buy, & what Books I am to see at the Museum &c &c.*"

Just before his brother's death, Josiah had rented a two-bedroom flat from a shoemaker in Charles Street, very near to fashionable Grosvenor Square, where he stayed on his trip to London. It was cramped and cluttered with his wares, which were essentially sitting in storage, wanting "nothing but arrangement to sell them." He still dreamed of a larger place, which would

> enable me to shew various Table and desert services, completely set out on two ranges of Tables, six or eight at least; such services are absolutely necessary to be shewn, in order to *do the needful* with the Ladys in the neatest, genteelest and best method. The same, or indeed a much greater variety of setts of vases should decorate the

Walls, and both these articles may, every few days, be so alter'd, rever-s'd & transform'd as to render the whole a new scene, even to the same Company, every time they shall bring their friends to visit us.

Besides scouring museums and bookstores, Josiah took the opportunity to search for new staff, and he spent his days talking to modelers, "enamellers," "carvers," and other artists to work on his new ideas for ornamental pottery. After one particularly stimulating day, he was eager to update Bentley on new developments.

"One of the objects" of the day "was seeking after a house, or rather Warehouse in which I have at last succeeded to my wishes, & quite beyond my most sanguine expectations." It was a large new house on Great Newport Street in Soho, around the corner from Charing Cross Road, and, better yet, he had reached an agreement with an enameler named David Rhodes who was to move in and begin working on new patterns. He "work'd several years at a China work" and "is a perfect master of the Antique stile in ornaments, Vases &c." It was a happy coincidence, for just that day Josiah had been discussing details of the "Antique stile" with new acquaintances, a certain Sir William Schaw and Lady Jane Cathcart.

Lord Cathcart had recently been appointed the British ambassador to St. Petersburg and was at the moment preparing for his commission, which included a request for an order of dinner and dessert service marked with his crest. Lord and Lady Cathcart were members of what Josiah recognized as "the Virtu species"—Lady Jane's brother happened to be William Hamilton, the envoy in Naples—and Josiah acted as swiftly as ever to promote his services. It worked. They spent "several hours" together that Thursday, according to Josiah, and Lord and Lady Cathcart were clearly intrigued by his enthusiasm for and commitment to his craft, as well as the fact that the queen topped an impressive list of clients. Lord Cathcart always kept a diplomatic eye on others to gauge the possible rewards that might be gained in future relationships, and he left Josiah's company confident that he had just met someone worth knowing. Josiah felt the same, telling Bentley that "we are to do great things for each other."

It was an enticing way to end his letter; his name-dropping let Bentley know that he was beginning to assemble valuable contacts around the world. It was a suggestion of yet more future success, and so a further inducement to recruit Bentley, who, Josiah felt, was on the verge of agreeing to their partnership.

Fig 1. Portrait of Josiah Wedgwood approaching his fiftieth birthday, by
George Stubbs. This portrait was completed in 1780 and
painted on Wedgwood earthenware.

Fig 2. Collection of early Staffordshire wares, salt-glazed stoneware, typical of production *ca* 1750s.

Fig 3. The Churchyard Works, the family potworks built by Josiah's great-grandfather along Church Lane on the southern edge of Burslem, where Josiah was born. St. John's Church is behind the house. From a nineteenth-century engraving.

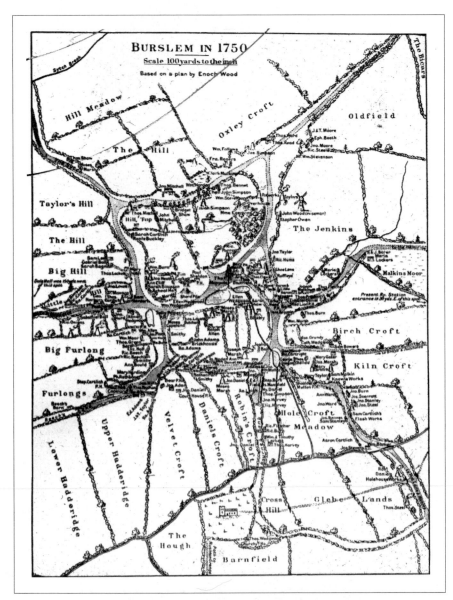

Fig 4. Plan of the town of Burslem, *ca* 1750, showing St. John's Church to the south. Overhouse Estate is to the north, while the site of Big House, next to the Red Lion Inn, is at the junction to the right of the maypole.

Fig 5. Portrait of Thomas Whieldon, artist unknown. Josiah was taken into partnership with Whieldon in 1754 and began a series of chemical experiments that would revolutionize pottery.

Fig 6. Cauliflower teapot, *ca* 1763, so popular and widely produced during Josiah's Whieldon years.

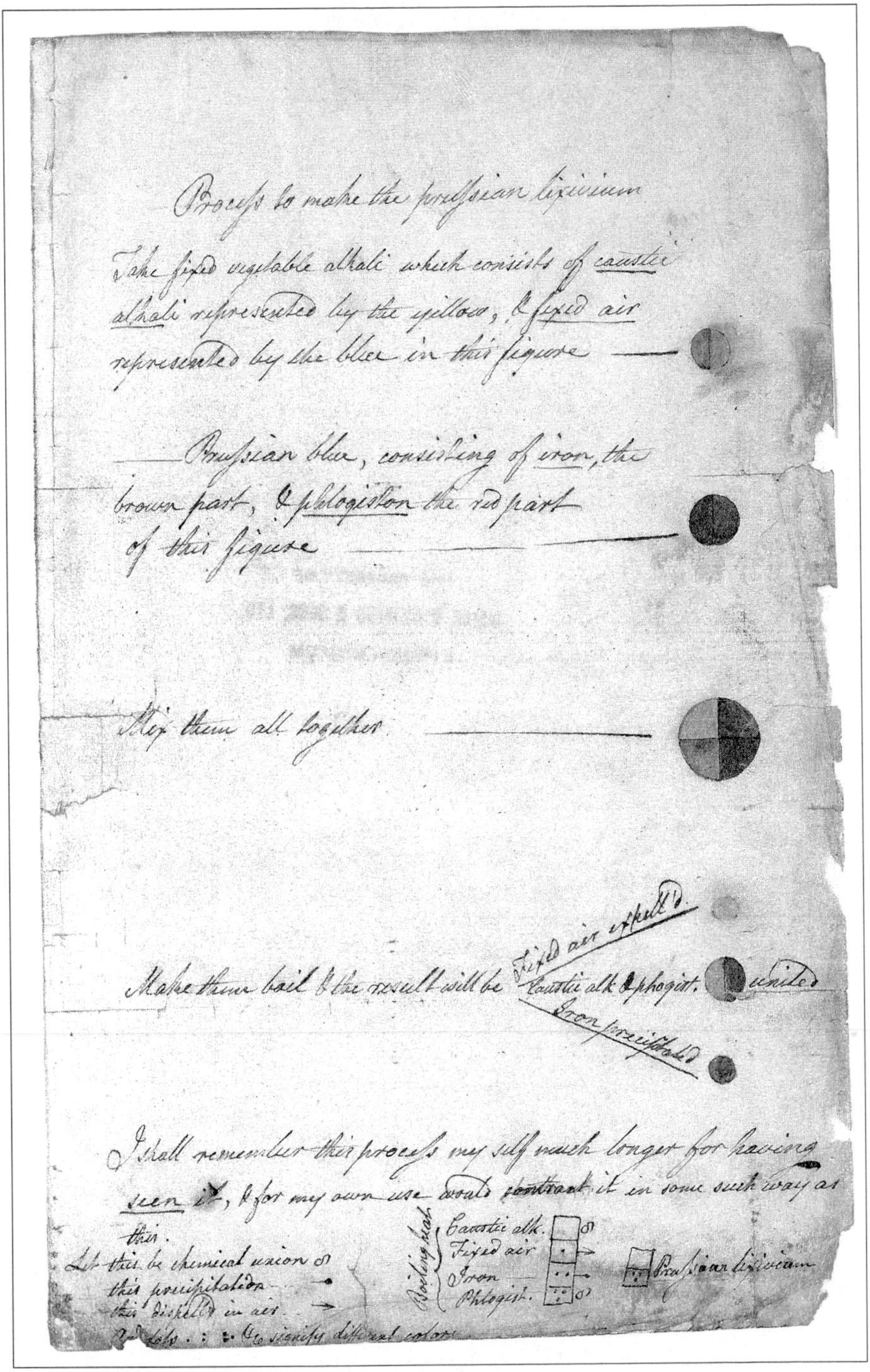
Process to make the prussian lixivium

Take fixed vegetable alkali which consists of caustic alkali represented by the yellow, & fixed air represented by the blue in this figure ——

—— Prussian blue, consisting of iron, the brown part, & phlogiston the red part of this figure ——

Mix them all together ——

Make them boil & the result will be Fixed air expelled
Caustic alk & phlogist. united
Iron precipitated

I shall remember this process my self much longer for having seen it, & for my own use would contract it in some such way as this.

Let this be chemical union
this precipitation
this dispelled in air
& dots : ∴ &c signify different colors

Boiling heat
Caustic alk.
Fixed air
Iron
Phlogist.
Prussian lixivium

Fig 7. A page from Josiah's guarded "Experiment Book" (begun in 1759), where he recorded chemical formulas for new glazes in secret code to defend against espionage.

Fig 8. The Ivy House Works, Josiah's first independent potworks, which he leased from his relatives "Long John" and cousin Thomas in 1759 for £15 a year. From a drawing by a descendant *ca* 1864.

Fig 9. Thomas Bentley, Josiah's close friend from their meeting in Liverpool in 1762, who later joined as partner and managed the London showrooms (1769–1780). Attributed to Joseph Wright.

Fig 10. Joseph Priestley, radical chemist and Dissenting philosopher. Priestley shared his experimental findings with Josiah, who in turn equipped Priestley's laboratory with ceramic apparatus.

Fig 11. The Brick House Works, known as the "Bell Works" after Josiah installed a bell to call his laborers to work, was Josiah's second independent potworks, which he leased from the Adams family in 1763. It was here that his wife, Sally, would join him after their marriage the following year.

Fig 12. Dr. Erasmus Darwin, great-grandfather of Charles and close family friend and physician to the Wedgwoods. Darwin and Wedgwood met at the Lunar Society—whose members gathered during the full moon to discuss philosophy and politics—at the industrialist Matthew Boulton's house in Soho, near Birmingham.

Fig 13. Sarah Wedgwood, who preferred to be called Sally, in a portrait by Sir Joshua Reynolds in 1782, when she was forty-eight.

Fig 14. Selection of "Queen's Ware"—creamware—pieces so named after Josiah impressed Queen Charlotte with the quality of the dinner service she ordered in 1765. Its ivory-white glaze was unique at the time, the fruit of Josiah's tireless chemical experimentation.

Fig 15. A "Queen's Ware" teapot manufactured by Josiah *ca* 1770—one of many pieces of pottery with transfer printing by the Liverpool firm Sadler & Green that depicted a political or commemorative scene. The pot shows the likeness of John Wilkes, whom the Wedgwoods and Bentley admired for his support of parliamentary reform in Britain and the liberties of the American colonies.

Fig 16. A portrait medallion of Josiah's patroness Queen Charlotte (white cameo on blue jasperware), part of a series depicting "Heads of Illustrious Moderns," which Josiah and Bentley produced after Josiah's invention of jasper (unique for its colors and porcelainlike translucence) in 1778.

Fig 17. The virtuosi—aficionados of the antique—shopping for ancient vases in Naples, Italy, from which Josiah not only fashioned his reproductions of "Etruscan" vases but gleaned ideas about displaying his own wares in his London show-rooms. Sir William Hamilton is the tall, thin gentleman third from the right of the picture.

Fig 18. Lady Jane Cathcart, wife of the British envoy to St. Petersburg Lord Cathcart and sister of Sir William Hamilton. She inspired Josiah to imitate the ancient vases her brother collected in Italy, and introduced his wares to the aristocracy in Russia: Catherine the Great placed two extensive orders with Wedgwood.

Fig 19. One of six "First Day Vases" Josiah threw to mark the official opening of the
Etruria Factory, near Burslem in Staffordshire, on 13 June 1769. The vases were made of black
basalt, with classical figures painted in red encaustic enamel.

VIEW OF ETRURIA WORK.

Fig 20. Etching of Etruria Factory, conveniently built along the Trent & Mersey Canal.
Josiah campaigned aggressively to have the canal dug. Completed in 1777, it added a critical trunk
to the inland navigation system in Britain and eased the transportation of
raw materials and finished products.

Fig 21. Etching of a throwing room in Etruria, where throwers formed pieces on the potter's wheel. This was one of many rooms in the factory—among modeling, glazing, molding, flowering, and finishing rooms—where work was highly specialized. Wedgwood was careful to prevent anyone—even his employees—from being able to understand, and so steal, his methods.

Fig 22. Matthew Boulton, the Birmingham "buckle maker"—a friendly rival industrialist to Wedgwood and Bentley. Boulton organized the Lunar Society meetings at his home next to his Soho metal factory.

Fig 23. The "Portland Vase," a 10-inch-high exact replica of the ancient vase sold to the Duchess of Portland by Sir William Hamilton in 1784, and copied in limited numbers by Josiah in black and white jasper in 1790. This vase, rare for not being discarded for its imperfections, was blistered because of a slight miscalculation in its firing temperature—a common frustration for Josiah before he perfected the firing process.

Fig 24. A wood engraving depicting a one-legged Josiah as conceived by a Japanese artist, *ca* 1880. While Josiah's leg was amputated in 1768 following an infection related to a childhood disease, he had specially manufactured prostheses formed in the shape of a normal leg and never had himself represented with a straight peg leg.

Fig 25. Portrait of the Wedgwood family on the grounds of Etruria Hall, by George Stubbs, 1780. *Left to right*: Mary Anne, Sarah, Thomas, Catherine, Susannah ("Sukey"), Josiah II ("Joss"), John ("Jack"), and Sally and Josiah. A discerning eye might detect a small puff of smoke in the distance over Josiah's left shoulder—the only allusion to the industrial basis of the family's new wealth.

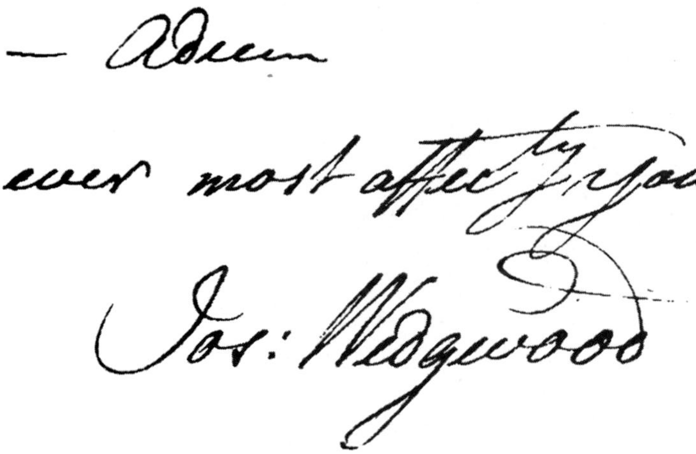

Fig 26. Josiah's final words, in his distinctive handwriting,
in one of more than a thousand letters to Bentley.

At the same time, Lord Cathcart was adding up the diplomatic rewards he could gain for himself by presenting Catherine the Great with the kind of gift that the King and Queen of England themselves enjoyed, perhaps a tea set or some dinnerware. Perhaps—even better—his new friend could design a unique set especially for the Russian empress. Both parties would benefit: Catherine would be honored by Lord Cathcart's diplomatic gift, and Josiah Wedgwood's reputation would flourish. This Burslem potter would become the world's first mass-market export manufacturer. In fact, the commission would fulfill an ambition that Josiah had declared to Lord Cathcart, a plan to manufacture a novel product he hoped would "surprise *the World* with wonders."

The surprise was the production of those ornamental vases he was now obsessed with, which "almost overwhelm my patience," and which delighted the virtuosi, including Lord and Lady Cathcart. Josiah had explained to them that he was thinking of producing something that was not necessarily functional, or "useful," but rather an item purchased specifically for display; something that would take pride of place on a mantelpiece or in a cabinet.

Josiah was no Grand Tourist, but Lord and Lady Cathcart understood exactly what the potter was talking about, knowing well the market for such fashionable items. Lady Cathcart, it so happened, was then reading about ornamental vases in a book her brother Hamilton was about to have published. It immediately struck her that one of the first "great things" they could do for Josiah would be to lend him some of the lavish plates from Hamilton's illustrated volumes, showing in the finest detail ever to be printed the richness of Etruscan art. She packaged it up and prepared to send it to Burslem.

❧

When Josiah returned from London, he took no time to rest before juggling endless duties. A few months earlier, Sally was excited to observe Josiah "leaving home in a great hurry" to "*finally* settle the plan" on the design of Etruria with the architect Mr. Pickford and later, with equal relief, to finalize the purchase of the land. The troublesome Mrs. Ashenhurst had died suddenly in the midst of rejecting Josiah's offer, leaving her executor a quick sale, and appeasing everyone now involved.

His days were spent with "about 50 people"—builders, workers, visitors, and family. "We were making sagars at Etruria, building the steps,

Glazeing the Windows, & getting forward as fast as possible; your house"—for Bentley had finally agreed to join Josiah as a partner in the new works—"is tiled and the sash frames come." He had also taken on a new apprentice "with good fingers," as a modeler, since "we shall want many festoons & other ornaments upon Vases," and laborers were stopping by the Bell Works, attracted by all the construction they heard was coming down the valley, wanting "to know when they must begin" work there. He stayed up late at night working on new patterns for "Root flowerpots . . . Essence pots . . . Vases & ornaments . . . Toilet furniture . . . Elegant teachests" and "Ten thousand other *substantial forms.*" Under a dim candlelight in his workshop, with "hands so cold I can scarcely hold the pen," he found the time to update Bentley on his progress. He saw little of Sally or his children. Dicky was "a Charming boy . . . his Mother tells me," he said. It was all becoming too much.

Months of inclement weather over the past year had led Josiah to complain about "the hazardous state of my health." "This return of my Complaint sunk my spirits, & dishearten'd me greatly in the prosecution of my schemes," he wrote, but "I have now begun a course of Exercise which I intend to continue, & consists in riding on Horseback for 10 to 20 miles a day, & by way of food & Physick, I take whey & yolks of Eggs in abundance, with a mixture of Rhubarb & soap." Despite these attempts at improving his regimen, the frantic months of extensive traveling and long days supervising the works at the pottery—frequently ascending and descending ladders and stairs to various workshops and offices—had inflamed a "bilious complaint"; further, he had, as he told one of his employees, "over-walk'd & over-work'd my knee lately."

The pain in his knee was acute, and Dr. James Bent, a local physician, prescribed an emetic to cause vomiting—on the theory that it might release some of the rotten bile irritating his leg. This offered temporary relief, but, Josiah complained, "the pain had no soon left my knee than I was very ill in other respects, attended with great heat & difficulty of Breathing," leading him to feel perversely relieved when the pain returned to his knee and the other symptoms ceased. After a brief consultation Josiah knew there was only one solution: It was time to remove the leg.

No one had any doubts about the dangers of the surgery, and none more than the patient, who was sharply aware of the fact that there was no way to deaden the pain. A few drops of laudanum might help calm the nerves, but it required phenomenal fortitude to survive what was nothing less than torture that began the moment the saw scraped the skin. Some patients chose to have their vision obscured from the operation, but Josiah was one to confront an ordeal face on.

Josiah sat in a chair at the Brick House; with him were two surgeons (one to saw, the other to stitch); a physician of whom Josiah was growing increasingly fond, Dr. Erasmus Darwin; and his close friend Thomas Bentley, who was there temporarily to look after the business and whose "brotherly love & affection" would help soothe Sally's nerves.

It was not long after the door closed for the procedure on that Saturday afternoon, 28 May 1768, when Sally, anxiously sitting in another room with Sukey, little John, and their newborn, ten-month-old Dicky, received the reassuring news that all had passed without alarm. That same day, Josiah's new in-house bookkeeper, Peter Swift, though occupied writing an invoice of goods for the London showroom, took a brief moment to relay the news.

> Sir,
> Your favour of the 26th is just come to hand, but can make no reply to the contents. Mr. Wedgwood has this day had his leg taken off, & is as well as can be expected after such an execution. The Revd Mr. Horne's goods are packed, and one Crate for the ware-house, the particulars of which I shall insert at foot, or as much as time will permit. . . .

Peter's commitment to getting on with business would have made his employer proud.

But Josiah could barely think about his wares. For the next week he lay in an opium-induced oblivion, cared for by Sally, who changed his bandages and administered his medicine. It was the most silent week of his career; for Sally, it was, conceivably, the most physically and emotionally consuming.

While Josiah slept in his recovery room, Dicky was "violently seized with a Complaint in his Bowls" and falling gravely ill. Sally was engulfed with fear, sorrow, and her own silence. She was hesitant to worry her debilitated husband. "I think Mrs. Wedgwood has had severe tryals of late," remarked Peter Swift, in his typically understated manner.

Like his older sister and brother a year before, Dicky had been given a smallpox inoculation, on the advice of Erasmus Darwin, who was sure of the benefits of the procedure to keep at bay the disease which "walketh in darkness." "One grain of variolous matter, inserted by inoculation," Darwin later succinctly stated, "shall in about seven days stimulate the system into unnatural action; which in about seven days more produces ten thousand times the quantity of a similar material thrown out on the skin in postules!"

Josiah and Sally, trained as they were to appreciate such prescriptions for the rational management of health, were quick to sign their children up for the treatment. Josiah, of course, was especially committed to try the wonders of "the experiment" if it promised to save his children from "that terrible disease" which had given him so much trouble. It was a controversial decision—many Anglicans and Catholics condemned the procedure, accusing doctors of playing God, "that it is bringing a Distemper upon ourselves, and thereby usurping the sacred Prerogative of God, who kills and makes alive, who wounds and heals, as he pleases." This was dismissed as pandering to superstition by that outspoken Dissenter Philip Doddridge in his *Case for Receiving the Small-Pox by Inoculation*. If everything was God's will, he wrote, "It were as rational to conclude, that our Lives should be preserv'd without eating and drinking, and that we shall be delivered from Danger without a prudent care for our own Safety." With no "Divine oracle" to consult, "Observation and Experiment must guide us." This was and had long been Josiah's sentiment: "Everything derives from experiment." Science and medicine should be embraced, used to promote the improvement of humanity. Experiments, Josiah was convinced, were risks worth taking.

After some "Convulsions at the first appearance of the eruption" and a period of becoming "so very Ill that I confess I repented what we had done," all the children recovered. But once again, five months after his inoculation, Dicky had fallen violently ill.

Five days after Josiah's operation, the surgeons returned to remove his bandages and inspect the wound for any sign of infection. "Wedgwood continues in a good way," Peter was relieved to inform his London associates; "his Leg was opened on Thursday for the first time, & both the Surgeons said it could not possibly be better, & he has every good Symptom, so that we have the greatest hopes of a perfect cure." The bright outlook was rapidly clouded with grief. On that same day, Josiah looked into Sally's mournful eyes and knew: God had received their ten-month-old baby.

18
The Arts Reborn

Within a month of his operation, Josiah was up and returning to business, having "left off my laudanum & do better without it," visiting the workshops and taking therapeutic "airings" in a chaise. He wrote to Bentley to say that the skin on the upper part of his wound was healed, and to ask him to send Sally's "love & respects" for Bentley's support and kind words about her strength of character. "Mrs. Wedgwood says you are a sad flattering Mortal," he teased. "Give over Joss!" Sally finally yelled, frustrated that her patient was overworking again, "and tell our friend Bentley that I command it." It was one of the few times since his operation that he managed to take pen in hand and compose his own correspondence, which was a job that Sally had performed on his behalf, being not only Josiah's nurse but also his amanuensis, as involved as ever in business tasks.

From this day on, Josiah was once again squared up to the chores of business, dealing with the architect of his new factory and a growing team of employees, both in Burslem and at the London showroom on Great Newport Street. "Now I am recover'd so far as to be able to write, I find myself head & ears in debt in that way, & every post is increasing the heavy load," he complained. "It is this which confines me to the house, & retards my perfect recovery more than anything else, & though I put as much of this business off me, as I decently can, yet I have very many letters which, *when I am able to, & at home*, must be wrote by my own hand, or they wo'd give offence." With typical philosophical curiosity, Josiah, even when trying to get on with business, found himself occupied in studying his altered limb. "My leg is almost healed," he observed, commenting that his wound was now precisely two inches by one and a half. "I measured it with the compasses this morning when I dress'd it—yes, *when I dress'd it*, for I have turned my surgeon adrift & Sally & I are sole managers now."

As part of his rapid recovery, and with the aid of a peg leg, Josiah went rambling in Cheshire a few weeks later and happened to meet "another artist." "He is a Mathematical instrument maker," he noted, adding that he was considering hiring him "in making & repairing Engine Lathes, punches & tools of Various sorts." A talented "mechanic" was always a welcome contact, especially when Josiah spotted that his new acquaintance wore a wooden leg and had turned his woodworking skills to being "a wooden-leg maker." "His name is Brown," said Josiah, and before he knew it, this Jack of all trades was "at present making me some legs." Josiah would spare no cost and required a prosthesis carefully crafted to look as much like his previous leg as possible, not only capable of wearing his stocking and shoe but also mechanically jointed so that the foot could move. It was an ingenious design—often worked on and improved by later instrument makers who also maintained the mechanical equipment in the factory. Rarely it seems did Josiah rely on his simple "peg leg," and with one or two later exceptions, all portraits and statues show him with a fully formed right leg.

In the midst of catching up with correspondence, Josiah remembered that "a long time ago" he'd requested William Cox, whom in 1765 Josiah had made the manager of his London premises then at Charles Street, to "ask Ld or Lady Cathcart if I should return the prints I had from them & so learn how I could be supplyd with the three volumes of them which are publishing abroad." He had been much impressed with Lady Cathcart's generosity in lending him a few of the drawings of vases from her brother, William Hamilton's, work. Now he wanted Cox to pay his respects to Lord and Lady Cathcart, since, in his words, "I shall be very glad to see the fine Etruscans you have set my mouth a watering after."

His wishes were soon answered. Lady Cathcart had sent him a carefully wrapped parcel with bundles of engraved illustrations. Casting his eyes over its contents, he was as excited and overwhelmed with inspiration as when Mr. Smallwood had delivered that letter from Miss Chetwynd on behalf of the queen three years previously. He pored over the illustrations and, flooded with ideas, eagerly drew up some sketches for his own designs and sent them to Bentley, hoping he could find time to "dip into them." Josiah was keen that his friend grasp the full effect of reproducing objects that were sought after for the cabinets of the virtuosi. He wrote about "the colours of the Earthen Vases, the paintings, the substances used by the Ancient Potters, with their methods of working, burning, &c."—all details that were relevant if one was to gain appreciation and respect amongst the cult of connoisseurs it was so important to impress.

The virtuosi, such as Hamilton, believed their illustrations and collections would aid future artists to (in Hamilton's words) "revive the arts" in Britain. When classicists, historians, artists, and art patrons studied the antiquities, they believed they could learn the academic principles upon which "modern" art—their own neoclassical productions—should be established. As the French *philosophe* Montesquieu remarked in his *Voyage d'Italie*, "there are some statues which the connoisseurs have established as examples and rules . . . it is from them that the Moderns have built up their system of proportions, and it is they which have virtually given us the arts."

With Lady Cathcart's invaluable support, Josiah hoped that by imitating the "chaste simplicity" of ancient antiquities, he could elevate the craft of pottery to an art form. The highest forms of art for the select few who earned membership in the newly founded Royal Academy of Arts, however, were drawing historical and landscape scenes and plaster models from live nudes. To them, pottery was not an art but a useful craft, akin to the work of engravers—a group who were also, to their frustration, excluded from membership to the Academy. But Josiah was refashioning himself—trying to shake off the bigotry with which high-minded artists regarded artisans and to promote metropolitan respect for the marginalized provincial potter. This was no easy goal, for the divide between the two worlds was as wide as the gulf between Pall Mall and Gin Lane. Josiah, though, was committed to fashioning an identity somewhere in between, and when he joined a group of acquaintances at the home of the literary editor Ralph Griffiths to meet "as a Society of Artists" (just after the Academy was founded in December 1798), he was on the way to doing just that. "You will easily perceive the use we may make of such an institution," he said to Bentley.

The early praise Josiah received for his creamware surprised some aristocratic collectors, who wondered if his wares could be more attractive than those produced at, for instance, Sèvres. It was hard for them to imagine that what was commonly conceived of as a muddy hovel in the Midlands could compete with Louis XV's famous manufactory in France.

Josiah knew it was a tall order for his hometown to be ranked (in terms of reproducing "taste") with cities where the rich resided. It was difficult enough to convince his good friend Bentley to give up his cultural connections at Liverpool to live in this "dirty, smoky place," and near impossible to get artists swanning around London to take up employment in Burslem. The originality of his vision kept his hopes afloat; no one had ever tried to apply the potter's skills to the modeling of antiquity as he was planning to do. It was true that a decade earlier some Staffordshire potters had attempted to produce salt-glazed figurines modeled after Spinario, for instance, but these were crude products, never praised for their beauty. His planned replica vases would, he hoped, be a different story.

After a year of business, personal, and physical trials, Josiah was once again enthused with the prospect before him. Undaunted by the Royal Academy, he believed the potter's craft was perfectly suited to serve those sentimental about history, the attitude currently elevating art to its privileged status. The raw material of the earth created an intimate bond with the past, hiding ancient treasures once formed of the very soil to which they returned, only to be dug up again by curious collectors amazed at their beauty. Now Josiah and Bentley had enrolled history on their side by resurrecting "Etruria" to rework the raw materials and encourage potters to aspire toward recapturing "universal beauty." Bentley, who had formally signed a partnership agreement with Josiah "in making ornamental Earthenware," in November 1767, reiterated that it was "in the original works of the ancients, to which our artists can have access, that they must expect to find just and beautiful ideas," and it was in Hamilton's own collection "that they must search for hidden treasure."

The decision to name his new premises and estate "Etruria" offered more than an exotic place name. It fashioned a new identity for Josiah's wares and represented the learned quest to recapture the ancient principles of "grace" and beauty. He called his employees his "Etruscans." Going one step further to prove his dedication to Hamilton's call for a "revival" of the ancient arts, Josiah began experimenting with techniques and materials that would re-create what it was like to be an ancient potter, claiming that he now breathed what he euphemistically referred to as "Etruscan air" (dropping references to this "smokey place" in favor of dreaming about Tuscany's blue skies and gentle breezes). The raw materials used by the ancients, he thought, had a distinctive quality to them. "I apprehend the Etruscan body owes its lightness to a mixture, either natural or artificial, of volcanic ashes." Attempting to replicate the substance, he took "a good red clay" and would "mix with it as much ground charcoal as can be conveniently worked in." He also asked his chemically minded friends how the different climates of Italy and England might affect the product, since different gases—the subject of Priestley's investigations—in the atmosphere might alter the color of the wares during firing. It was a fantastically innovative way of using experimental science to understand history, predating the scientific methods of excavation and analysis developed in nineteenth-century archeology.

Time was once again of the essence, especially as Josiah was alert to the fact that other manufacturers were already planning to steal his idea. In August 1768, he had been told by a reliable source that a London china merchant was sending Humphrey Palmer, a potter near Burslem, copies of "all my patterns as they arrive at my rooms in London." He wanted William Cox to be vigilant when receiving goods and displaying the new items.

> You must try if you can recollect any particular Persons repeatedly buying a few pairs, or single articles of yr new patterns as they arrive, very probably it may be some sham Gentleman or Lady equipped for the purpose with their footman or maid to carry them home to prevent discovery. That they do get my patterns from you in some such way I am certain, but the further particulars you must endeavour to discover.

Even if the designs of the "Etruscan" wares were not yet discovered, Josiah learned that other craftsmen were expanding their business to include "ornamental" objects such as vases.

"What do you think of that!" he exclaimed to Bentley when he met one potential competitor in London, adding—in a playfully condescending tone: "Do you not tremble for our Embryotick Manufacture?" At least this particular competitor was a "Stone Manufacture," and unlikely to tread on their Etruscan toes. But a gathering group of rivals were bound to be close behind. He might have even learned that other manufacturers were, at that precise moment, doing what he most feared by producing their own imitations of ancient figures. The Sèvres factory had produced its first batch of biscuit statuettes after the antique, but was struggling with the initiative. More alarming, given the swarms of British Grand Tourists there, was the fact that the Capodimonte "china" factory in

Naples had been known to produce a porcelain figure of Laocoon being strangled by green snakes as in the description in Virgil's *Aeneid*. Josiah's worries were only assuaged by the thought that no one in Britain was as yet on his heels. His ambition to reach his goal before anyone else left him restless on many nights, stirred by dreams of the profits almost within his grasp.

"I have had many *Visions* since you left us"—he reported to Bentley at the end of 1768, finishing a series of experiments trying to improve the quality of his Etruscan ware while overseeing the completion of the factory and the new homes—"some of which are so *strange & fore-boding*, that I have even been so weak as to write them in a book." Details were proving to be the bane of progress. He was producing the pieces by the crate, but the colors were off, the proportions wrong, and there were other irritating imperfections. He was not even sure what to call the pieces: were they urns or vases? A semantic detail, perhaps, but integral to a promotion where authenticity was vital.

Josiah attempted to remain appropriately philosophical, reminding himself and his partner that "in the manufacturing of these delicate compositions, & the disappointments you must expect to meet with when you become a Potter so that if you can be picking up a little patience & storeing it against a time of need, there may be no sort of harm in it." Yet such calm considerations were again punctuated by bouts of excited anticipation and restless, anxious nights. "I have lately had a vision by night of some new Vases, Tablets &c with which Articles we shall certainly serve the *whole World* . . . We are far enough before our rivals, & when ever we apprehend they are *treading too near our heals*, we can at any time manage them. . . ." Confidence was crucial, especially as money was running low and only the official opening of the new factory could rescue his finances.

Inclement weather over the summer months of 1768 was a major hindrance to the progress in building the new houses and factory that would come to be Etruria. The house foundations were all down, but the buildings stood at "plinth height" because the workers were unable to make bricks amidst all the rain. Whatever frustrations and problems the delay would cause, Josiah was worried that the architect, Mr. Pickford, was coming down too hard on the workmen. He "does not seem to consider their having any feelings at all," said Josiah.

"I have seen a great many instances of it & may perhaps sometime or other find a mode of conveying a lecture to him upon a proper treatment of our inferiours & to prove that our humble friends, as somebody beautifully calls them, have like passions with ourselves & are capable of feeling pain or pleasure nearly in the same manner as their Masters—but this must be done obliquely."

While building work was frozen, Josiah and Bentley continued developing details for the factory, on which the ground was not yet even broken. One of Josiah's central concerns was to make sure that it was built in just the right spot to take full advantage of the Trent & Mersey Canal, the exact route of which was now being carefully plotted by the engineer Hugh Henshall. Some six hundred men were busy at work in a northern segment of it, where ten miles had already been dug out, and it would not be long before the workers would make their way down by Burslem. Josiah, of course, knew that the canal would pass through the land he'd so eagerly bought as part of the old Ridge House Estate since its lower elevation—essentially on the base of the large ridge of moorland that led to Burslem—provided the natural geography for the canal's path; but he now needed exact plans. As soon as Henshall surveyed the land, Josiah obtained a copy of his drawings and sketched the relative position of his factory.

Josiah showed Bentley the sketch. Along a thick black line running north to south, at the corner where the canal intersected the road leading southwest to Newcastle-under-Lyme, was Josiah's picture of his perfectly positioned "Vase works." It was to be a long (150-yard), rectangular building, with numerous rooms built around two courtyards, and eight "hovels," or kilns. Each room and yard would have a different function. The building was architecturally anchored by a round, domed room, "for plates and dishes only"—probably intended as a drying and storage room.

There were three covered buildings in all, separated by two walled-in, two-story courtyards. The first building was a warehouse; the adjacent walled courtyard was for storing coal, with a section for "clay & rubbish, that nothing may be seen or exposed on the outside of the building"; the higher, three-story, central building, between the two symmetrical courtyards, housed the main rooms for the production of every sort of "useful ware," the stock-in-trade plates and pots that his cousin Useful Tom had proven so valuable at managing for the Ivy House; through the second courtyard, where more clay was stored and rejected items were buried, was "the ornamental work," where the revolutionary "Etruscan vases" were to be manufactured. Everything was contained within these protective walls, and all aspects of the production of the wares would take place in separate rooms, reflecting the increasingly specialized division of labor, working around precision machines such as the engine lathe, finely balanced throwing wheels, and large mills for mixing clay. Josiah had drawn up plans for the largest and most specialized potworks ever designed, and arguably the most efficient, well-situated, and (as he said) "modern" factory in the world.

As plans progressed, however, some of Josiah's "brethren," the other Staffordshire potters, grew suspicious of his intimacy with the engineers of the canal and the grand plans for his new factory—funded in large part from his wife's wealth. Josiah's hard work to raise subscriptions and canvass political support for the canal was at first rewarded with praise and with his non-stipendiary appointment as treasurer of the company established to build the canal; but now it seemed he had always intended to use inside knowledge of the canal project to unfair advantage. After all, while Josiah was the most outspoken regarding the advantages of the canal to the "*country's* trade," all the Staffordshire potters owned a stake in the project, raising £20,000 amongst themselves for its construction (£6,000 from the Wedgwood clan itself, including Long John and cousin Thomas, a figure that still paled in comparison to the more than £140,000 contributed by local gentry).

"Some of my good Neighbours have taken it into their heads to think I shall have too pleasant & valuable a situation by the side of the Canal as it is plan'd & executing thro' my Estate," Josiah had reported to Bentley. "This has raised a little envy in their breasts, & as they are Proprietors they have represented to the Committee that the Canal ought to be made along the Meadows, as that is the shortest, & most natural course for it. That it will receive more water & retain better what it does receive as the upper course is over sloping banks & sandbeds." A committee was set up, and Josiah, feeling he "was a match for them all," once again prepared a forceful argument defending his integrity and enrolled the support of the canal engineers to give a "true state of the case."

Needless to say, Josiah's interests won, and he continued to press on with aggressive plans to buy more land around the estate as extra elbow room, keeping competitors clear of his view. "I believe you will think me almost out of my senses for thinking of buying more land," he wrote to Bentley, "& indeed it is not because I shall have money to spare that I would make this purchase . . ." But, as he explained, "it is full of limestone which I shall unavoidably lay dry in guttering for my own." It would allow him the potential to expand in the future, and, above all, "if I do not buy it for those purposes somebody else will who may be very disagreeable neighbours." Sensibly, given the recent local reaction to his development plans, he noted that "my application is at present a secret."

Josiah's concern about not having "spare money" to risk was rising; throughout the summer of 1768, his business finances were dwindling. His wife's capital was most likely the source of payment for the first stage of building work (approximately £2,000), but Pickford's bills were piling high. One unexpected, and rather spectacular, expense was a bill for over £600 incurred on his suddenly receiving six tons of "Cherokee" clay which Thomas Griffiths had procured and shipped from America. Josiah was shocked by the bill, though he had yet to learn of the extraordinary circumstances under which the clay came to him.

To compound the problem, the person who should be knocking on doors to collect debts, Tom Byerley, was yet again struck with wanderlust and was this time off to Philadelphia in search of stardom. It was terrible timing for Josiah, who, having a soft spot for his nephew, nevertheless did what he could do pay Byerley's way to America, advancing him £70 for the trip. "He promises to be very good," he told Bentley, "& I hope for his own sake, as well as his friends, that he will perform his promises." But there was no time to worry about it. Attention turned to his accounts, and Josiah saw that once again his customers were delinquent on their payments. He had to rely on William Cox in London, whom he implored to *make hay whilst the sun shines*" and collect the outstanding debts. While he was at it, Josiah asked Cox to take along with him examples of his new wares, the first pieces produced in the "antique" style. The ploy was to show possible customers what was soon to be available if they paid up promptly. As a result of Cox's door-to-door visits, interest was soon spreading throughout London.

"Mr Cox is as mad as a march Hare for Etruscan Vases," Josiah enthusiastically wrote to Bentley from London in November 1768, on his first trip since his amputation. "Pray get a quantity made or we shall disgust our good customers by disappointing them in their expectations. But raise no dust at home though about them, for that will make our antagonists open all their eyes & ears too & push them forwarder than they would perhaps move at their own natural rate." Josiah followed up with visits to all the noblemen he could, and was advised by one, Sir Henry Chairs, that "they are vastly admired (the Vases) but the Ladies think them dear" at Josiah's suggested price of between seven and nine shillings each; "however he says *they will sell.*"

Coins ringing in his ears, Josiah was now sure that his idea of reproducing Etruscan vases was the consumer "revolution" he'd promised his partner he would create. His samples, though still "rude" in his opinion, since he still lacked the ability to replicate with consistency the ancient "grace," were proving the perfect prelude to the grand opening of Etruria.

Having whetted the appetite of the aristocracy, Josiah now wanted to push the boundaries of their budgets for ornamental pottery. He was sure that as word spread amongst the rich, he could encourage them to buy even more expensive vases by making the items appear limited and exclusive. Josiah prepared four "serpent handled antique vases, part of which have the handles twisted & are finished in a more elegant manner than the others." Josiah's Burslem bookkeeper, Peter Swift, sent these to Cox in London with instructions that they "not let be seen till the others are all sold, & then raise the price of them 1/ each for being higher finished." At the last minute Josiah amended the instructions, bumping up the price. "Those charg'd 9/ must be 10/6, and those 7/6 be 9/, never mind their being thought dear," Josiah instructed Cox; "do not keep them open in the rooms, shew them only to People of Fashion." Josiah was betting that once word was out that a limited number of new vases were available to the privileged, deemed "ingenious" in their composition and elegant—indeed, even artistic—in their design by a few prominent patrons, then the price would simply reflect the idea that only people of status had real taste. It was a principle of consumerism that Josiah himself helped define: Deny the majority the ability to purchase art, then use their lack of means as proof of inadequate taste.

Meanwhile, more anxious than ever to stockpile models unearthed from ancient lands, Josiah continued scouring London for more ideas. "I am collecting some figures (antique) to be made in Etruscan earth," he reported, adding that the Dilettanti Sir William Chambers "& many others have a high opinion of them to mix with the Vases, by both these articles I hope we shall make a revolution in the chimney pieces & strip them of their present gaudy furniture of patch'd & painted figures." Before long, Josiah was happily informing Sally that "new cabinets are opening to me every day," and he had just received an invitation to visit with Sir Watkin Williams Wynn at his home in St. James's Square "to shew me some things for the *improvement of Vases* he has brought home from his Travels," which was one of the finest collections made in the eighteenth century.

Josiah reckoned that since so much interest was being drummed up by his and Cox's visits to others, they should leave out a catalogue of illustrations of his vases (the modern equivalent to Hamilton's pictures of the antique) in the Great Newport Street showroom, "as they will be looked over by our customers here, & they will often get us orders & be a pretty amusement for the Ladies when they are waiting which is often the case as there are sometimes four of five different companys & I need not tell you"— he added to Bentley—"that it will be our interest to amuse, & divert & please, and astonish, nay & even ravish the Ladies. But who am I writing to!—Not to my wife I hope, no she must wink here, this is all under the rose, to my good friend, Vase maker General to the Universe."

The strategy of visiting nobility, inviting only select "Fashionable" to glimpse at the rare "backroom" pieces, and displaying a catalogue with spectacular colored engravings of a range of vases (to "prevent the *sameness* which must be rather disgusting if we confin'd the shew to one sort only"), paid off. Before Josiah could articulate it, his "revolution" was in full swing. "Etruscan Vases are the run at present," he declared at the beginning of February 1769. "The great demand here may not be baulked. I could sell £50 or £100 worth per day if I had them!" Lord Bessborough, who had traveled in Europe with his wife (who was in fact much more interested in Grand Tourism), paid Josiah the highest respect he could ever receive. The "fine old Gentleman, a very fine old Gentleman," Josiah stressed, who "admires our vases & manufacture prodigiously, says we shall exceed the Antients, that friezes & many other things may be made, that I am a very ingenious man (theres for you now, did I not tell you what a fine old Gentleman he was) & that he will do me every service in his power," starting with an order for three vases.

What was imperative was that the new factory was opened *before* the competition got in on the act. "Pray do exert yourself to get the works at Etruria finished," he urged both Bentley and Useful Tom from London; "in the mean time let all the hands that can be spared & can work at Vases be imployed in them."

Thankfully, things *were* beginning to show progress on the building front. At the end of 1768, Josiah (now back in Burslem) was able to report that the "works are cover'd in, & they are beginning upon the Cellar arches, & the Chamber & ground floors, as soon as these are finish'd I shall order them to be fitted up & put some men into them to make sagars, prepare clay, build ovens, &c &c that we may begin to do something *in earnest* as soon as possible." Throughout the next six months, a large blanket of land was transformed into a grand building site. Josiah and Sally's modest manor house, Etruria Hall, was taking its symmetrical Georgian form on the east hill overlooking the site of the works down the slope to the west. What was planned to be Bentley's house, called the Bank House, was being built on the land further south. There was a barn, offices, the ornamental and useful works, an inn, and forty-two houses next to an orchard which would be rented out to the workers. Josiah called it "Etruria Village," a model community which was his improvement on his old partner Thomas Whieldon's commitment to provide affordable and convenient housing for his employees.

In April 1769, Josiah assured Bentley that "I am getting things forward at Etruria as fast as possible."

> The slip kiln is nearly finish'd upon our friend Mr Whitehurst's plan, the Sagars are got ready to fire, & I have sent some fired ones from hence to support the new ones in the oven. Two mills are nearly fin-sh'd, & your house is going on as fast as the Works. The Joyners have left mine to finish yours, which Mr Pickford assures me shall be completed in seven weeks at farthest.

At long last, Josiah and Bentley had decided on a date for a ceremony to mark the official opening of Etruria. While the works were still under construction, they built a platform on which a hand-turned potter's wheel was placed with a tub of prepared clay. The hot sun on that Tuesday, 13 June 1769, dried out the muddy fields of the seven-acre construction site.

A crowed gathered, the workers and potters relieved to have a half day off. Sally, who was eight months pregnant with what would soon be their next son, Joss, along with Sukey and little John, stood next to Richard Wedgwood and Sally's brother, John. Long John and cousin Thomas, with their children, arrived, as did the Brindleys, the Henshalls, and the Whieldons. One conspicuous family absence was Byerley, who in his wild enjoyment of America had run out of money and had been thrown in jail. Josiah was frustrated with his nephew, and felt sorrier for his sister, but he "dare not acquaint her with this last instance of his incurable madness. Nothing more can be done for him & he must take the consequences of his own misconduct."

At the ceremony, Josiah gave a brief speech, and then he and Bentley put on a show that would become legendary. Josiah donned the potter's "slops," the leather apron and cap, and formed one mound of clay after another into elegant Etruscan vases, while Bentley cranked the shaft to spin the wheel. Josiah threw six vases in black basalts, fashioned after Hamilton's *Etruscan Antiquities*, which his artist David Rhodes painted with red figures depicting "Hercules in the Garden of the Hesperides," with the inscription:

> June XIII M.DCC LXIX
> One of the First Day's Productions
> at
> Etruria Staffordshire
> by
> Wedgwood & Bentley
> Artes Etruriae Renascuntur

The last line of the inscription said it all: "The arts of Etruria are reborn."

PART III
Rebirth
1769–1776

19

Ingenious Working People
and Formidable Opponents

Amid the hoary Ruins Sculpture first,
Deep-digging, from the cavern dark and damp,
Their Grave for Ages, bad her marble Race
Spring to new Light. Joy sparkled in her Eyes . . .
                                    —James Thomson, *Liberty*

The symbolism of the moment would not be lost on Josiah or on Bentley, whose favorite author, James Thomson, had provided the script in the poem the partners mutually praised, *Liberty*. Wedgwood & Bentley's (as the firm was now officially called) Etruria factory was being built as a proud monument to the pursuit of freedom—to trade, to earn money, and to create a new future from a buried past.

The landscape and status of the industry had attained a new level. The world now looked at Staffordshire as the source of a manufacturing revolution. "In general," commented Arthur Young, who in 1770 published a survey of industrial and agricultural experiments across the country, "we owe the possession of this most flourishing manufacture to the inventive genius of Mr Wedgwood, who not only originally introduced the present cream coloured ware, but has since been the inventor of every improvement, the other manufactures being little better than mere imitators." Recognizing Bentley's valued role, Young added that Wedgwood "has lately entered into a partnership with a man of sense and spirit, who will have taste enough to continue in the inventive plan . . . in case of accidents," acknowledging everyone's precarious grasp on health and the risks to life, especially in the workshops of industry, that all laborers—and "Masters"—faced. This was a primary reason that entrepreneurs were eager to engage in partnerships; if something happened to one of them, it should "not suffer the manufacture to decline."

What was notable about Wedgwood & Bentley's, as well as other firms being forged at just this time, was that the partnership was between two unrelated people. Looking outside the family for partnership was, until now, extremely rare, mainly because hitherto it was practically impossible for a family to build up its own wealth if a large share of the business was owned by another family. The change, represented in Wedgwood and Bentley's partnership, reflected the phenomenal growth in revenue and assets generated by modern processes of industrialization, which involved bringing in the best talent, "sense and spirit," whoever it meant.

Josiah's own accomplishments did not take centerstage at their inaugural ceremony; instead, every form of clay, the mortar and brick of the rising works, and now over a hundred personal employees who met high standards of craftsmanship and commitment to the "ancient" craft were being celebrated. They shone out amongst a community that had grown immensely since Josiah's childhood. Arthur Young estimated that there were "300 houses, which are calculated to employ on an average of 20 hands each or 6,000 on the whole," but that the total "variety of people" involved with all aspects of the trade "cannot be much short of 10,000 and it is increasing every day."

Once when Josiah wrote to Bentley excited about successful improvements to his engine lathe, which his "ingenious" smith promised to keep secret and "make them for no on else," he suddenly paused and recognized the need to forsake what he called "narrow selfish views" of the benefits to one's own business: "let our improvements take a free cause for the benefits of our *Brethren & Country*." Certainly Josiah was happy to have the head start, but he followed a moral code of conduct preached by his Unitarian "brethren" such as William Willets, or Reverend Stringer, that wealth became "valuable" when it enriched the community, not merely the individual. It was a sentiment succinctly expressed on another occasion when Bentley bantered about Josiah's "doctrines of *money getting*," to which Josiah replied, drawing a breath of sincerity, that "I do not expect my Pupils to divest themselves of Humanity, to make, or amplify a fortune."

He, of course, hoped they would personally benefit from the scientific and mechanical improvements to their business—they banked on it—but the success amounted to nothing if it did not reflect an improvement in the conditions of life for all provincial, disenfranchised manufacturers, whose position in society was—Josiah and Bentley, among thousands of others, believed—wrongly subjugated because of their Dissenting religious and political beliefs. Their accomplishments in designing new materials and products, and the money they made for their products, amounted to nothing if they did not generate broader social change. The principles of mercantile freedoms should extend to social freedoms to create, in essence, a more egalitarian society.

Josiah and Bentley were not alone in their belief in the usefulness of their enterprise; indeed, it was a belief shared by manufacturers across the world. In Britain, the founders of the Society for the Encouragement of Arts, Manufactures and Commerce in 1754 had made explicit links between industrial pursuits and the growth in wealth and power of the state. In self-congratulatory terms, the society associated the innovative work of its rapidly rising membership—it had grown from seventeen members in its first year to over two thousand a decade later—with Britain's coeval military and economic successes. This represented the culmination of centuries of struggle "against foreign despotism and false religion." "No truly benevolent or public spirited Briton can hesitate" to support the society, announced one of its early members, Charles Powell. "It will not only unite in one common Bond all real Patriots, or as I should call them the Patrons of the Nation, but will in time, I hope utterly extirpate all Party distinctions, the Bar of Society and Civil Government."

It was because they purportedly had national, not personal, interests at heart that manufacturers should be "encouraged," and not marginalized in society. Robert Dossie, a founding member of the society, developed the point in his two-volume *Handmaid to the Arts* (1758), which the society sponsored and which Josiah, like many manufacturers, found an essential handbook for practical tips on japanning, gilding, glazing, and the like.

> That the national improvement of skill and taste in the execution of works of design is a matter of great importance to any country... [and] of the commercial advantages resulting from it, will be allowed by all.... The strong disposition that prevails not only in the European countries, but in the respective settlements of their people in Asia and America, for using those decorations and ornaments in dress as well as buildings and furniture... gives at present the foundation of several of the most considerable branches of trade: which are daily

increasing, with the luxury, that seems removing from the East, and spreading itself over these Western countries and their colonies.

New ornamental items and artistic or craft designs, which made even mundane items like snuff boxes or heat screens more appealing, generated wealth for manufacturers; but as Dossie pointed out (and as others including Josiah echoed to politicians), manufacturers faced international competition, and even in something as seemingly straightforward as the skill of varnishing, "there is a rivalship betwixt ourselves and the French, [which] renders the cultivation and propagation of this art of great importance to commerce."

By "cultivation and propagation" of manufacturers' efforts to promote commerce, Dossie meant, among other things, to encourage a more equitable system of taxation. Manufacturers increasingly saw their work as contributing to the strength and power of the nation, but were frustrated that the wealth they generated provided no more equal footing for them relative to the power of the landed peers and aristocrats in "civil government." When Josiah and Bentley celebrated the opening of Etruria's books in 1769, the central government taxes totaled £11 million, of which £1.7 million was gained through local property and assessed taxes, where the aristocracy's (and MPs') capital wealth lay. With no income tax yet, by far the main source of state revenue was through customs and excise, and taxation of raw materials (Staffordshire potters, for instance, paid an annual duty of around £5,000 upon the salt consumed for glazing in the 1760s). With George III's government's penchant for introducing new mercantile taxes (which Bentley had so bitterly attacked in the pages of the *Monthly Review*), the manufacturers clearly felt they were being penalized, not "encouraged," in their efforts to improve the economy. But this, manufacturers across Britain knew, was going to be a long battle. The inequalities in the economic realms of society would in the eighteenth century become symbolized by the spread of Asian silk amongst the fashionable in London while the woollen industry in the North languished.

But societies such as that for the Promotion of Arts, Manufactures and Commerce provided an important collective voice, and both Josiah and Bentley, it is no surprise, were closely involved with it, as were other manufacturers Josiah began to watch carefully. One was Matthew Boulton, who—while sharing the "common Bond" for promoting British industry—soon became Josiah's formidable rival.

In 1759, the year Josiah established his independent Ivy House Works with Long John and cousin Thomas's help, the thirty-one-year-old Birmingham bucklemaker Matthew Boulton inherited his father's metalworks manufactory and was dreaming up plans to expand his business to include other "mechanic inventions, toys and utensils of various kinds in gold, silver, steel, copper, tortoiseshell, enamels, and many vitreous and metallic compositions." He had already started producing "philosophical instruments," including thermometers and scales, and had been voicing his interest in producing electrical machines.

It was this part of his business that attracted the attention of a fifty-two-year-old Philadelphia *philosophe* and representative of the Pennsylvania Assembly, Benjamin Franklin, who was sent "Home to England" to petition the Crown for more equitable treatment regarding matters of taxation. But Franklin also took advantage of his foreign residence—his third out of a total of eight trips to England during his life—to tour the manufacturing regions of the Midlands, whence his ancestors came, and where he found a band of "industrious, ingenious working people [who] think themselves vastly happy that they live in dear old England." He set about collecting linen, snuff boxes, "something from all the China Works in England," and other items, which he sent home "to show the Difference of Workmanship" between the different crafts.

One of his stops in 1758 was at Boulton's Birmingham manufactory, where Franklin not only picked up some buckles but was introduced to some of Boulton's new friends, such as the robust, highly innovative, free-thinking radical physician Erasmus Darwin, who had recently set up his medical practice in nearby Lichfield. For Franklin, unaware that he would return to England on several other occasions for a lengthy residence, this was only a shopping spree. But the friendships he forged during this trip provided the foundation for a long-lasting association with Midlands manufacturers and innovators, which soon came to include Josiah, with whom Franklin shared a transatlantic vision of industrial progress and profitable trade between England and America. One of their common complaints, of course, was the British government's policy on colonial affairs, against which Franklin and his friends were beginning actively to voice their dissenting opinions.

Besides sharing general thoughts about the potential progress of colonial trade, Boulton pursued his own vision of what he wanted to accomplish as a world-leading manufacturer, but he was facing a problem that would take the better part of the next decade to solve. Much of his manufactory, like so many others in the "age of invention" (as Samuel Johnson marveled), relied on machine production—mechanically operated engines performing tasks such as turning lathes and stamping sheet metal. His engines were driven by a water mill, only the source of the water was always running dry, either from drought or diversion to the demanding Birmingham Canal. Boulton called on Darwin and Franklin to help find a solution to this problem by attempting to make practical a primitive design of Boulton's to create an engine powered by steam. To this end, a barrage of questions needed to be answered, from the chemically oriented, such as determining the temperature at which evaporation was most effective (prompting Darwin to engage in a series of experiments on sulphurous and saline "vapours"—"Food for Fire-Engines!" he called it), to questions of craftsmanship ("Query. Which of the steam valves do you like best?" Boulton asked Franklin at one point).

One day, years later, another visitor arrived at Boulton's "Soho" works—the factory he finished building outside Birmingham in 1766 with finances gained through two successive marriages (the first to Mary Robinson, then upon her death to her younger sister, Anne, who were worth £14,000 each). Boulton had heard of James Watt, and knew that he was working on his own design for a steam engine under the employment of an owner of an ironworks in Glasgow. In fact, Watt was already preparing drawings of his unique steam engine for a patent application, but was frustrated with "the villainous bad workmanship" he had to contend with in the actual production of his engine. Boulton's workshops were a stark contrast, having a well-ordered, disciplined, and highly skilled workforce. If they worked together to build the steam engine, then they would resolve both Boulton's problem and Watt's dissatisfaction. But perhaps even more could be accomplished.

Boulton began thinking. "My idea was to settle a manufactory near my own, by the side of our canal, where I would erect all the conveniences necessary for the completion of engines, and from which manufactory we would serve all the world with engines of all sizes," he said grandiosely. Why be modest? After all, he was convinced that he and his new partner had a technology that would revolutionize industry by turning fire and steam into mechanical muscle. Forget buckles. In the future when people such as James Boswell would ask him what business he was in, he had a proud answer, which would later (to the present day) be emblazoned on the walls of museums of science and industry: "I sell here, Sir, what all the world desires to have—POWER."

Boulton's achievements, and the well-timed collaborative efforts that went into making them, passed within particular notice of other ambitious industrialists, not least the partners of Wedgwood & Bentley. Josiah had begun thinking about his own source of power after he first met Boulton while in Birmingham en route to London in 1767. They met through the introduction of a mutual friend, Erasmus Darwin, and he toured the new Soho factory. First he was taken with a well-crafted lathe, which operated a "crown" motion he had never encountered. "I intend to ask him if he would like to part with" his lathe, Josiah cheekily told Bentley. But with the factory's 500-plus employees, which (Boulton claimed) gave him an annual turnover of £30,000 (compared at this time with Josiah's dozens of employees and an annual turnover of perhaps £5,000–£6,000), Josiah was clearly impressed and not a little envious. "He is I believe the first—or most complete manufacturer in England, in metal. He is very ingenious, Philosophical & Agreeable." It was this trip, combined with the inspiring idea he was soon to have in London relating to ancient vases, that provided Josiah with a new blueprint for the future.

Long before Boulton and Watt's steam engine found its place at Etruria, Josiah was able to benefit from befriending Boulton. In March 1768, he went to Birmingham, where he spent a whole weekend with Boulton talking shop and hammering out mutually beneficial deals. It was decided that Josiah would supply ornamental vases, which Boulton would finish by applying colorful gold and purple works of metal to the plain piece. Boulton declared that he was going to "supplant the French in the gilt business," and Josiah was seduced by his confidence. By the end of the weekend he was able to assure Bentley that they had "laid the foundations for improving our Manufacture, & extending the sale of it to every corner of Europe." It seemed a promising collaboration, making them "Patrons of the Nation," joining forces to quash the foreign competition that appeared to be threatening. "Mr Boulton tells me I should be surprised to

know what a trade has lately been made out of Vases at Paris," Josiah
wrote.

> The Artists have even come over to London, picked up all the old
> whimsically ugly things they could meet with, carried them to Paris
> where they have mounted & ornamented them with metal, & sold
> them to the Virtuosi of every Nation, & Particularly to Millords
> d'Anglise, for the greatest raritys, & if you remember we saw many
> such things at Ld Bolingbrokes which he brought over with him from
> France.

Plans had cooled when Josiah fell ill and took time to convalesce following
his amputation, when he received a friendly, but brief, visit from Boulton,
who looked around the Brick House Works with Bentley. But later in the
year, in November 1768, as Etruria was beginning to come together under
its various roofs, Josiah ran into Boulton again, this time in London.

"Mr. Boulton is picking up Vases, & going to make them in Bronze,"
Josiah informed Bentley, who was in Burslem overseeing the construction. Again, Boulton "proposes an alliance betwixt the Pottery & Metal
branches, Viz., that we shall make such things as will be suitable for
mounting, & not have a *Pott* look, & he will finish them with the mounts.
What do you think of it?" Josiah wondered, guessing that Bentley would
probably think it best if left alone.

"Very true," preempted Josiah, "but he will be doing [it], so that the
question is whether we shall refuse having anything to do with him, and
thereby affront him, & set him off doing them himself, or employing his
friend Garbett. If we join with him in this scheme, I apprehend we can
always bind him to us by making him such things as nobody else can, &
thereby make it his interest to be good." Before long, Josiah began to learn
more about Boulton's character, his business strategy, and his confidence.
"Mr Boulton has not sent any of his things to St James's," Josiah commented, thinking it odd not to offer gifts to the royal household in hopes
of receiving more orders. "He soars higher, & is scheming to be sent for by
his Majesty!" Josiah had to admire his audaciousness. "I wish him success,"
he said generously; "he has a fine spirit, & I think by going hand in hand,
we may in many respects be useful to each other."

But however enticing the idea that innovation might be nurtured by
collaboration, they also knew (and Bentley appeared to be acutely aware)

that capital expansion was driven by competition. So while it was clear that Josiah and Boulton were capable of helping each other, it was not long before each was investing everything in stealing markets from his arch-entrepreneurial rival.

Boulton started the skirmish by doing some quick calculations. Since he was planning to expand his business, and he liked the idea of putting ornamental detail on plain pottery vases, then why go to an external source for the base product? Boulton imagined that he would profit more if he collaborated with Josiah on specialized pieces—such as setting Wedgwood's cameos and intáglios (carved designs) in cut-steel mountings. But vases he could manufacture himself. It did not take long for Boulton to convince himself, especially as Wedgwood and Bentley were dragging their feet, and he soon made his intentions known.

Josiah was philosophical about what he immediately saw as impersonal but nevertheless ruthless competition. Needing to think things through, he dispatched a long letter to his partner, echoing Bentley's sentiment that resolution on reflection is real courage. "If Etruria cannot stand its ground, but must give way to Soho, & fall before her, let us not sell the victorie too cheap but maintain our ground like men, & endeavour, even in our defeat to share the laurels with our Conquerors." He would need to rise to the challenge to spar with so formidable an opponent as Boulton, but he felt capable.

Once again, he calmed himself by writing a letter to Bentley, reflecting on the latest challenge to his ambition. He took pride in competing with someone he admired as much as Boulton. "It doubles my courage to have the first Manufacturer in England to encounter with," Josiah declared. A noteworthy tribute, conferring not simply a preferential rank by dint of the fact that Boulton beat him to the mark in building a factory, but an honorable status by acknowledging Boulton possessed rare qualifications. "I like the man, I like his spirit," he said. "He will not be a mere snivelling Copyist like the antagonists I have hitherto had, but will venture to step out of the lines upon occasion, & afford us some diversion in the combat."

It was a competition to capture the market; the victor would have to create consumer demand for unique wares that would fashion taste and establish the vogue. Josiah had high hopes for his Etruscan vases, but was nevertheless concerned about the competition on his heels. "I have got the start of my Brethren in the article of Vases farther than I ever did in anything else, & it is by much the most profitable branch I ever launched into," he wrote to Bentley; " 'tis a pity to lose it soon—there is no danger—

true, not of losing the business, but the prices may be lower'd by a competition, & if the imitations are tolerable, the demand from us may be diminish'd, for all our buyers are not, though many of them are, qualified to discern nice differences in forms & ornament." The last remark was a stinging criticism of the discriminating "taste" which the aristocracy believed was its province alone. Just as he began to worry about rivals clumsily intruding on his scheme, Josiah had received news that would propel him and Bentley into the next stage of their careers. His sister, Margaret Byerley, had returned to Burslem from London, where she had visited the new showrooms in Great Newport Street. "No getting to the door for coaches," she said, "nor into the room for ladies & Gentn & Vases. . . . Vases was all the cry." Josiah knew that the Etruscans had provided him with the success he needed.

But he had no time to rest on his Etruscan laurels. There was much to do. He was tired, concerned, and needed to prepare for battle.

Boulton had a lean labor force of hundreds who followed a disciplined regimen in the sixty specialized workshops and vast warehouses of his new Soho factory. And it was growing fast. Feeling confident, Boulton sent an agent, a man named Wendler, on a mission to Italy to scout the local market for fashionable art. The agent was given a wide remit, encouraged to purchase anything that would help Boulton "to know the taste, the fashions, the toys, both useful and ornamental, the implements, vessels &c. that prevail in different parts of Europe, as I should be glad to work for all Europe in all things that they may have occasion for." Indeed he would. Before long, Boulton found himself in the happy situation of selling to the Europeans, in territory that Wedgwood & Bentley had hoped to make their own.

20

French Frippery and Russian Husks

Lord and Lady Cathcart assumed residence in St. Petersburg in 1768, where Lord Cathcart was British envoy to the court of the Empress Catherine II. Before they departed London, however, Josiah took advantage of one last opportunity to meet with his patron. "I have waited upon Ld Cathcart," Josiah informed Boulton, when they still intended on collaboration, "to bring about the plan we settled of introducing my manufacture at the Court of Russia." Once again they proved invaluable patrons, and Josiah reported that "the Ambassador, but particularly his Lady, came into my measures with the utmost readiness." They had officially ordered "a large service" of crested dinnerware which they wanted delivered to Russia.

Using traveling diplomats' homes as foreign showrooms was a wonderful opportunity to gain exposure in distant markets, a strategy Josiah learned a few years earlier when by chance "an East Indian Captain & another Gentleman & Lady from those parts" ordered "a Good deal of my Ware, some of it *Printed & Gilt*, to take with them for presents to their friends, & for their own use. They told me it was already much in use there, & in much higher estimation than the finest Porcellain, the Captain said he had dined off a very complete service just before he left India." Now Josiah had reason to hope that, through the example of Lord and Lady Cathcart's dinner parties, the Russians would also acquire a high estimation of his wares.

One practical problem that concerned Josiah was the cost of delivering the goods abroad. He already had problems collecting debts from his wealthy customers as close as London. A possible solution which he'd considered at home was to offer free delivery if the goods were purchased cash-on-delivery. But while that paid the bills, "I cannot raise the prices in proportion," he determined, "& if I pay the Carriage without altering the prices it will make near £500 per annum difference in my profits. Besides some of my customers (if I sell goods at deliver'd prices at all) will want them deliver'd at all lengths from 20 to 300 miles." Eventually Josiah needed to compromise according to his customers' demands; he offered free carriage for cash-on-delivery orders in London and implemented a policy of replacing any item that was damaged in transit anywhere.

Delivering goods to the rest of the world was more difficult. For his American market, he employed third-party retail agents to deal with the particular issues of selling goods to colonists, and the risk was the less from Josiah's perspective since the principal market there was for his reject pieces. It was all that consumers in America and the West Indies could afford, since Josiah's seconds and even thirds were the cost that most Staffordshire potters charged for their primary pieces. Exploiting his reputation as much as possible, he was now charging up to three times as much for his wares (even "stock-in-trade" useful wares) as anyone else.

But in Europe, Wedgwood & Bentley would receive orders direct from nobility, and had to find ways of insuring the goods for delivery and receiving payment. Lady Cathcart offered a suggestion: "If the Bills are sent to me with all the charges of packaging, shipping, & exchange of money included, address'd to any Merchant here, as soon as the goods are Delivered I will take care that the same be duly honor'd." She added that there was really no other way. "I have no commd of money in London, & can do no otherwise." Josiah then asked Bentley to find a Russian merchant through whom they could do business. It would be a headache, but Lady Cathcart promised it was worth it. She even followed up her letter with another, assuring Josiah that "anything of Gildin & shew is liked best at St Petersburg."

Encouraging as it was to develop business abroad, the other practical problem that faced Wedgwood & Bentley was that the demand for their ornamental wares was adding immense pressures at the potworks. With the new factory not yet operational, Josiah found himself complaining to Bentley that he was receiving orders he could not fill: "We have a large ordr from yr house for abot 50 crates all of thirds, but cannot possibly complete it. It is all for Jamaica." He was also having problems filling the orders of his primary clientele, the London elite. "Ld Barrington is angry with me for neglecting to send a table service he ordered a long time since at my Rooms in Town," he said; "he has had a great deal of Company & nothing to eat off."

Josiah was desperate for more help. Useful Tom was proving as valuable as ever, redoubling his efforts to manage the "useful works" since Byerley's voyage to America, and Bentley was now in London managing the showroom. He had gently advised Josiah that even the new estate of Etruria, where his new home, Bank House, was still being built, was not the best place to employ his talents. He needed the metropolis, and it made more sense that his education and connections were put to use by engaging with the fashionable customers in London, where he could also scout for artists to work on the wares. By the end of 1769, Bentley had moved into a house with a large garden in Chelsea, and oversaw the finishing stages of the decoration of the ornamental vases and showroom displays.

With the London side of business in Bentley's capable hands, Josiah summoned William Cox to "take a little of the weight of business off my shoulders" in Burslem, allowing Josiah to concentrate on "a list of the workmen" employed in nearby potteries, from which he "intend[ed] hiring such as will suit us at Etruria."

As the bricklayers set up the walls of all the buildings on the sprawling factory grounds, local laborers were attracted by the possibilities of dramatically improved conditions. Needing to build up his own army of workers, Josiah was less concerned with scrutinizing their abilities than getting them on the books. "I shall hire all the Men that offer & I think likely to do us any good," he said. Once under his command, Josiah was sure that he could train them to perform to his standards. The workers' "Village" was now under construction, and the homes—as well as the plan to provide education, training, and even health care for the workers— made it especially appealing to those who were concerned about being cared for after their retirement. (A full-blown retirement scheme, whereby a fraction of workers' salary was withheld, was later introduced in a plan devised by Josiah's friend Joseph Priestley.)

"A Porter has offer'd himself who I think is likely, he is abt 50, can write, is a stern morose or rather resolute Character, & wants a fix'd situation for the remainder of his days," Josiah told Bentley. "The worker in metal I mention'd to you in my last has try'd various schemes but never could succeed *as a Master*, he is pretty well stricken in years & will now be content with a place that will procure him food and raiment for life." When these men saw what kinds of amenities were being constructed at Etruria, they thought it perfect. It pleased Josiah no end that his investment in Etruria might solve the problem of the "Lazy & fickle & not likely to stay long in any one place" labor force that so frustrated him. Now, he was able to hire the most talented people available, who "several others would fain to hire" but who "chose to come to me."

While the staff and the factory continued to grow, Josiah returned to the issue of providing Lord and Lady Cathcart with their large dinner service, and thought of sending them some additional, unsolicited patterns which he hoped would be received with the implicit understanding that Lady Cathcart might display them for her visitors. Not sure how he could convey this clearly—without offense to her—he consulted Bentley. "They must not be *presented*, & we must not pretend to charge for them, so that they must neither be *given* nor *sold*,—but we must borrow a pair of her Ladyships chimney pieces to shew them upon . . . May not you give Ld Cathcart a hint that we are preparing to paint the Etruscan Vases after Mr Hamilton's Book," thereby suggesting reciprocity in free publicity.

Lady Cathcart was far more astute than Josiah seemed to give her credit for, and as soon as she began to receive his wares, she immediately engaged the interest of her Russian acquaintances. "I am on the spot to be of Service," she told Josiah, and true to her desire to promote trade between England and Russia, Josiah immediately received orders from Russian gentlemen. All too predictably, he also immediately encountered the practical difficulties in delivering and protecting his orders. In one instance, there was lack of communication about the cost and conditions of insuring a service about to be sent to Russia. "I was not order'd to insure," Josiah explained, "& I know the risque is the gentleman's who order'd the Goods," but he anticipated that "if they do not *receive* the goods, they will not pay for them." If only *"gentlemen* were *Merchants*, & *knew the rules of trade*," life would be much simpler. In this instance, Josiah was forced to insure the order at his own cost.

To Josiah and Bentley, these were minor frustrations. They were thankful for their connections in assisting their entry into a new market, and optimistic that their foreign trade would flourish. Bentley particularly, in a reversal of roles from the pre-partnership days when Josiah was so boastful about their future profits, felt confident of their situation, and assured Josiah in no uncertain terms that they would outperform any competitors. It was a belief that comforted Josiah, who had just learned of Matthew Boulton's intentions to drop the idea of collaboration and treat them as rivals.

Sukey was now four, little John three, and their "bantling," little Joss, one month old. The older two missed their father, but for both Sally and Josiah, there was no time for weekend relaxation and family play. Josiah dined virtually every night of the week at the potworks. "Saturday is the busiest of my busy days," he complained to Bentley, to whom he spent hours writing on Sunday mornings, children tugging as his elbows, to catch up on the week's developments, "if these Bratts will let me," he sardonically continued. On the last Sunday of September 1769, he had much to report on the nature of the competition.

On his way up to Burslem, William Cox stopped by Boulton's in Birmingham "to look at their Manufacture." It was intended as a cordial visit, and Boulton took his guest on a tour, showing him how to make buttons, watch chains, and toys, "but would not permit him to see their Vase work." Cox inquired why. "I find," Josiah told Bentley, "they are affronted at my not complying with their orders for the Vases to be mounted," and that subsequently, "they had been offer'd the Vases for mounting by several Potters, but were now determined to make the black Vases (Earthenware Vases, they took care to tell him) themselves, & were building works for that purpose!" Josiah was rather stunned at the news since the idea of a metalworker suddenly deciding to become a pottery manufacturer was akin to saddling a sheep for a ride in the country. Josiah joked that he expected them to start recruiting his laborers for the princely sum of £200 or £300 a year to manage their new works; but Cox—who was rather reserved and somewhat shy—seemed more concerned about Boulton's behavior. "They talked to him in the stile & manner of Rivals to us," Josiah said, "big in their own conceits, with some mighty blow their uplifted hands were prepared to let fall upon us. So stand firm my friend," Josiah sarcastically commanded Bentley, "& let us support this threatened attack like Veterans prepar'd for every shock or change of fortune that can befall us."

Bentley had, in fact, already anticipated Boulton's maneuver and assured Josiah that they were capable of capturing the foreign markets, especially the French market, which Boulton had earlier made such a fuss about. "Do you really think that we may make a *complete conquest* of France," Josiah asked.

Conquer France in Burslem?—My blood moves quicker. I feel my strength increase for the contest—Assist me my friend, & the victorie is our own. We will make them (now I must say *Potts* & how vulgar it sounds) I won't though, I say we will fashn our Porcelain after their own hearts, & captivate them with the Elegance & simplicity of the Ancients. But do they love simplicity? Are you certain the French nation will be pleased with simplicity in their Vessels? Either I have been greatly deceive'd, or a wonderful reformation has taken place amongst them—*French* & *Frippery* have jingled together so long in my ideas that I scarcely know how to separate them, & much of their work which I have seen *cover'd over with ornament*, had confirmed me in the opinion.

Bentley diligently answered Josiah's questions, providing a list of reasons "for the *Virtuosi* of France being fond of *Elegant Simplicity*," which further convinced Josiah of the brilliance of his own idea to imitate the ancient arts, anticipating the rejection of rococo in favor of neoclassicism. What he did not anticipate was that the taste for his wares in general would catch on further afield, particularly in Russia.

"The field is vast indeed!" exclaimed Josiah. Amongst ideas Josiah was throwing out regarding capturing markets in Ireland, Germany, Holland, and even China, another "Avenue into the Russian Empire" had opened up. In 1770, Catherine the Great, who so eagerly bought Western productions, considering "foreigners as a kind of superior beings, in regard to the arts and sciences," had commissioned a Queen's ware dinner service that was decorated with a border of continuous wheat husks painted in purple. The "Russian Service," as Josiah referred to it, was painted by artists under Bentley's supervision at the Chelsea Decorating Studio, one of the backrooms of their Great Newport Street showroom.

Once the empress acquired her creamware "Husk" service, the Russian aristocracy, as had the British aristocracy upon Queen Charlotte's commission, became eager to acquire Wedgwood services of their own. Josiah received letters from Lady Cathcart that promised more "Ords from Russia this Spring [that] may do great things."

"What is good will sell here," she told him, "what is new will be greedily sought after, & more bespoke. . . . If you send good Merchandise, I think the Sale is certain." She advised Josiah of an English merchant resident in Russia, who spoke the language, was "remarkably sensible," and in her estimation likely to be the best person to act as an agent for Josiah's trade to that country. "I flatter myself I can be of great use" forwarding among the Russians' knowledge of Josiah's wares; but she sternly advised Josiah not to rashly inflate his prices, "for that has often destroyed our trade. I hope you won't lose the opportunity of this spring as your ware is now in fashion. . . . And with the confidence that what is offered is as Cheap as it ought to be I shall speak of it to all my acquaintance without fear or reserve."

"What shall I say to this good Lady," Josiah longed to know. "Her Goodness to us beggars all thanks." With Useful Tom working to supplement the labor to manufacture the Etruscan vases, which he told Bentley were "the run" at the moment, they had been sluggish in selling useful wares, and Josiah had begun to worry that the demand for the stock-in-trade wares was slowing down. Therefore,

> the Russian trade comes very opportunely for the useful ware, & may prevent me lowering prices here.
>
> The *General trade* seems to be going to ruin on the Gallop—large stocks on hand both in London & the Country, & little demand. The Potters seem sensible of their situation, & are quite in a pannick for their trade, & indeed I think with great reason, for *low prices* must beget *low quality* in the manufacture, which will beget *contempt*, which will beget *neglect* & *disuse*, and there is an end of the trade.

While the ornamental wares remained a huge success (in 1770, Josiah's accounts showed profits upwards of £4,000) and new markets were expanding for his useful wares, he had reason to be more comfortable weathering the ups and downs of consumer demand. He was, after all, many paces ahead of his "brethren." "How many Lords and Dukes Visit your rooms, praise your beauties, thin your shelves, & fill your purses," Josiah playfully asked Bentley in 1771, "& if you will take the trouble to acquaint us with the daily ravages made in your stores, we will endeavour to replenish them." His monthly trade with his Liverpool printers Sadler & Green reached £650, a huge increase over the £30 a month of a decade earlier. Wedgwood & Bentley's strength was such that Bentley flattered Josiah by dubbing him the "Generalissimo" of trade, which Josiah humbly thought "over rates my powers in War."

The formidable Boulton soon cast a shadow on his prospects for Russian sales, however. About the same time as Lady Cathcart arranged for Josiah's spring sales, Boulton packed up a collection of his ormolu vases—decorated with gold and other metals in the manner he'd earlier discussed with Josiah—and sent it to Russia for the attention of Lord Cathcart. It was a strategy straight out of the pages of Wedgwood's book—perhaps freely given in friendlier moments—and it worked. Lord and Lady Cathcart, being interested solely in promoting commerce while providing the empress with unique products from the West (from any of England's entrepreneurs), showed them to Empress Catherine who, declaring them "superior in every respect to the French," bought the lot. For Boulton, it was a *coup d'éat*.

But victory celebrations at Soho as well as Wedgwood and Bentley efforts to regain lost ground were soon halted by news that saddened all and reminded them of the humanity that tied their interests together as "Patrons of the Nation": in September 1771, Lady Cathcart died in St. Petersburg. Lord Cathcart prepared to return to Britain alone.

21
Wanting Air for Sally

For Josiah, time to spend with the family seemed to be diminishing, especially since the few hours he did spend at home were often used writing more letters to Bentley, albeit with "Sukey & Jack at my elbows" ("little Jos says ta ta," he added when signing one letter). While it is clear that Josiah talked at length to Sally regarding business developments and relied on her judgment in many matters of "taste" in the decoration of their wares, she had other concerns that occupied her time.

As the factory grew, so did their family, and while they were always anxious about what Josiah seemed to see as evaporating cash reserves (mainly due to heavy reinvestment in the business, recruiting labor, and modernizing the tools of the trade), their standard of living was in fact rising fast. Sally took on the task of managing their personal affairs, not only overseeing the education and health of their children but "my sister's children as well. Two of Catherine and William's girls, Kitty and Jenny, were near in age to Sukey, and were very close friends, made more so by the Willets' later move into the vacant Bank House. As close as the two families were, Josiah and Sally agreed to pay for the education of all the children, continuing the family tradition of ensuring the "improvement" of future generations.

Sally also became closely involved with helping the employees settle into their new environment. They hired many men as well as women artists, sometimes married couples, from all over England. Sally took a personal interest in getting to know them. It was important, she felt, to understand their characters and concerns in order for the business to succeed and for the employees to show dedication and commitment to the job.

Josiah, though more concerned with the workers' technical skills, also believed in the principle of creating as agreeable an environment as possible. It was this philosophy that had led him to build houses for his workers, attempt improvements in their physical working conditions and health, and, eventually, engage in an insurance scheme to protect their welfare.

As complementary and distinguished as both Sally and Josiah's efforts to manage their (and others') lives were, Sally occasionally grew restless being confined predominantly to Burslem and the Brick House Works. She, like Josiah, longed to settle in their new home, Etruria Hall, which she designed and furnished; but unlike Josiah, she didn't have much opportunity to get out and travel about. He was frequently on the road—increasingly spending time in London, sometimes stopping at Lichfield or Birmingham en route to visit Darwin or Boulton—but Sally wanted the closest thing she could get to a holiday. Passionate as she was about politics, at the end of 1768 she seized the opportunity to travel to London.

In November 1768, Josiah and Sally, accompanied by Catherine Willets and a maidservant, set off. William remained in Newcastle to watch over his children, while Bentley went to Burslem to look after the Wedgwoods' children and to oversee the construction of Etruria. With Josiah bound to be on the commercial ramble in London, Sally and Catherine would be left to their own devices. It suited them fine; "we have all things in common," said Sally, and this was *their* trip.

They were going to stay at their rooms above the showroom at the new premises in Great Newport Street, Soho. The rooms were not large, and they were simple, with some select pieces of tasteful furniture to make a comfortable stay for Josiah when his presence was required in London. The main chamber room had a four-poster bed and a mahogany night table. There was a large mahogany dining table which one suspects was more often covered with bills, books, and catalogues than chinaware, and twelve hair-bottom mahogany chairs. Another room had a simple feather bed and a walnut bureau. The inventory which William Cox drew up of the rooms before his move to new premises in Chelsea otherwise noted only a "glass frame" for the dining room, a kettle, and four pair of blankets.

In preparation for Sally and Catherine's arrival for their month-long vacation, Josiah decided to spruce up the simple, guest-quarter feel to the rooms for more comfort. "New grates are put up in some of the rooms; new beds and fenders are bought; a glass bookcase is set up in the drawing room; and a wealth of comfortable bedding comes up by wagon from Staffordshire." Sally and Catherine appreciated their fireside comfort when the cold, rainy weather dampened their plans to see the city.

"We have a variety of weather," Sally informed Bentley, to whom she regularly wrote with news of their trip and to acknowledge Bentley's assurance that the children were doing well. "Wet mornings & fine afternoons which makes the Streets so dirty it prevents our rambling so much as we wish either by Moon or by Sun however we omit very few Oppertunitys, & I can assure you are right busy on Saturday night." They headed for Drury Lane "& were very much entertained" at the theater. They dined with Mr. and Mrs. Hodgson, who had looked after the final arrangements for brother John's funeral the year before, and met with Ralph Griffiths, where the group debated politics. Sally stressed that they *debated*; "it is," she declared, "nothing uncommon for Gentlemen & Ladies to differ in their Politicks."

John Wilkes had just returned to London from Paris, where he had fled when facing prosecution for libel after the publication in 1763 of his *North Briton*, in which he notoriously attacked the king and prime minister. Wilkes, the son of a malt distiller and champion of middle-class and Dissenting desires to reform Parliament, stood as a candidate for Middlesex, a relatively poor borough north of London, in the April 1768 election. Wilkes hoped his candidacy would generate enough publicity and support amongst his followers to protect him from prosecutors. Indeed, he swept the poll, a pronounced victory in part attributable to the barricades his supporters—including local laborers dissatisfied with their wages and working conditions—erected in roads leading to the polling station in Brentford, allowing through only those who wore Wilkes's colors.

Despite his popularity and success at the polls, he was immediately arrested, sentenced to twenty-two months in prison, fined £1,000, confined to the King's Bench Prison, and expelled from the House of Commons. It was a move that Wilkes, an extraordinary self-propagandist, used to prove to the world that Britain's constitutional principles were being grossly violated by the government.

"If ministers can once usurp the powers of declaring who *shall not* be your representative," he thundered, "the next step is very easy, and will follow speedily. It is that of telling you whom you *shall* send to Parliament, and then the boasted Constitution of England will be entirely torn up by the roots." Radical Protestant reformers and "Rational Dissenters" (especially Josiah and Bentley's close friend, Joseph Priestley) used the opportunity to spread the philosophy of man's "natural rights," to stress personal virtues and "qualities of industry, sobriety, frugality, enterprise," self-improvement and opening careers to people on a meritocratic basis.

Less philosophical protesters took to the streets. A riotous crowd descended on St. George's Fields near the prison in protest at Wilkes's punishment. The magistrate who appeared to read out the Riot Act was struck on the head with a brick, and troops opened fire on the crowd, killing several people. The repercussions of this lasted for months, leading to more riots and demonstrations. Sally was gripped with the news as it unfolded in London. "As I am deeply enter'd into politicks," she told Bentley,

> & you was so kind to encourage me in that most *Laudable* study by enquiring who was next to be murder'd, I could not forbear giving you the earliest intelligence of 14 that have suffer'd Martyrdom for their Countrys good this day at Brentford. This afternoon Mrs Willett & myself have been to hear the debates at the house of Commons. No Male Animals were admitted so my good man cou'd not attend us.

While Sally cheered the crowds who supported Wilkes, Catherine found the debates and riots overwhelming. She shared the beliefs and the political principles of her husband, Sally, Josiah, and their friends; but, as William Cox told Bentley, "the Middlesex Election hath Frightened Mrs Willets so that she wisheth herself at home Again," where, safely removed from the ruckus at "Whitfields Parliament" and Westminster, they could debate without risk of injury. But Sally was energized by the passion of the people.

"Mrs Wedgwood is pushing me off the stool," Cox scribbled to Bentley, his "inch of Time" at the writing desk to pen his daily bulletin over. Sally was eager to update Bentley on another day's political developments. Josiah was somewhere in London collecting ideas, and Sally wished that Bentley could be there to see all that was happening. Alas, she could only "hope to smoak a pipe with you very soon" and discuss the country's affairs.

When they weren't politicking, Catherine was happy to report that "we are hurried to & fro in this great Metropolis," paying "a dozen Visits in the City & bin entertained very agreeably." Bentley wrote to them eliminating any worries they might have had about their children's conduct. Sally heard "such fine things of my Lad [two-year-old John, known as Jack] & I will thank you again for conveying that *Smile* to me. I have seen it ever since & you do not, cannot, know how much good it has done me." Bentley similarly told Catherine that he had been to visit "Mr Willets & the Children," and he commented on the youngest. "Jacks smile Pleased me much," Catherine said to Bentley; "but," she teased, "why did not Polly smile too?"

All the "Ladys' engagements" in London exhausted even Josiah. "I will not trust to writing in the evening any more," he told Bentley, having as much difficulty as William Cox in keeping his seat at the writing desk.

> I find it impracticable, engagements of my own, or the Ladies are always filling up those hours, indeed we are under the necessity of incroaching upon regular bedtime, to have an hours rest, or enjoyment of ourselves in peace & tranquility & notwithstanding every moment is employ'd & we are in a constant bustle, I have for my own part got very little done yet & the Ladies have business enough cut out for them to employ them a month longer . . .

Sally thought Josiah's complaints about how busy they were making his life were unjustified. "My good man is upon the ramble continually," she retorted, "and I am almost afraid he will lay out the price of his estate in Vases [which] he makes nothing of giving 5 or 6 guineas for," but—and this was the rub—"if we do but lay out half the money in ribband or lace there is such an uproar as you never heard."

Their month's stay in London continued its hectic way. At the end of December, Sally was able to send a message to Bentley from Newcastle that they were "just arriv'd, in good health & tolerable spirits" upon "completion of their peregrinations," but "as the chattle of the Bratts seems so ingaging after this long absence, they propose spending the evening here before they come to Burslem." The next day, it was back to business as usual.

❧

A year after their London trip, Josiah was once again on the road and Sally was, as usual, busy holding down the fort in Burslem. But this time, Sally had a surprise for Josiah when he returned. He had suffered a difficult journey back from London, meeting "with several accidents on the road, such as springs snapping, shafts breaking, &c, which delay'd us something in our journeying," taking him three days to make it home. But as his chaise descended the final hill from Newcastle leading to the valley where Etruria was under construction,

> I was rewarded for all the risques & pains I had undergone in a tedious long & dirty journey. . . .
>
> I found my Sally & family at Etruria! Just come there to take possession of the Etruscan plains, & sleep upon them for the first night.—Was not all this very clever now of my own dear Girls contriving. She expected her Joss on the very evening he arriv'd, had got the disagreeable business of removing all over, & I wo'd not have been another night from home for the Indies.

Sally had inaugurated the new lifestyle in their home at Etruria. The design of the house was much admired by all who had seen it—a mutual friend of theirs and Erasmus Darwin's called it "fit for a Prince." It had turned into a substantial country house, three stories high, in a well-proportioned style becoming popular in Georgian architecture. The lofty entry hall met a large staircase. The rooms to either side were large, with multiple windows. It was not perfect—yet. Josiah was unhappy with the pointing on the bricks, a fence needed to be finished, and the garden was a disaster, the pond was a mud pit. But Sally was determined to be in her new home and Josiah was happy to comply. She had also arranged a "company" dinner to be held at Burslem's Town Hall for 120 of their workmen, a prudent gesture in recognition of completion of the first stage of the massive construction job.

Sally's levelheadedness and willingness to engage with so many dimensions of the business proved a great relief to Josiah when he was struck with another illness that made working difficult. He was convinced he was going blind. He saw spots when he looked at the sky or blank paper when he tried to write, and clouds appeared when he looked at any distant objects or landscapes. "They are near, or farther from the Eyes in proportion to the distance of the object I am looking upon," he said. He consulted a doctor who had purportedly cured the Duke of Bedford and the Duchess of Norfolk of a similar disorder, who "hopes he shall be able to set me to rights but says there is always *some danger* in these cases." Josiah was ordered to wash his eyes three times a day with a medicinal cocktail; but after some weeks following this prescription, Josiah's fears only grew worse. "My *life*, as well as my *sight* is at stake," he said, in a fit of hypochondria, since he was told that two "miserable patients" near Burslem had died from the disease, which was "seated near the brain wch is often the case, Vertigoes convulsions &c put a period to life & sight together." In the meantime, "I am often practicing to *see* with my *fingers*, & think I shld make a tolerable proficient in that science for one who begins his studys so late in life, but shall make a wretched walker in the dark with one single leg."

The symptoms subsided and he survived, just in time for Sally to give birth to their fifth child in May 1771. "Little Tom, for so they call him," Josiah informed Bentley. The next day they were visited by both the Willets clan and the Darwins—Erasmus and two of his boys, five-year-old Robert and eleven-year-old Erasmus. Darwin's wife had died a year earlier. Sukey got along with the boys very well, and would grow increasingly fond of Robert.

Throughout the next year, Josiah remained "nailed down here as fast as a rock," suffering "a vast deal of *hard weather* as we call it here." "We poor villagers neither escape a blast or a drop of rain," he concluded, especially as he had no mature trees on the moorland ridge to help break the bracing winds. But early in 1772 he was at long last relieved to be "removing our Wheels, & Lathes, & all our furniture & hands from Burslem to Etruria," to the new factory, "& this makes us very busy."

Back in 1769 he had been given notice to leave the Brick House Works since the owner, William Adams, had come of age. "My Landlord is married and will come to them himself," wrote Josiah then. "Here's a fine piece of work cut out for me!" Sally's initiative in moving into Etruria Hall helped domestic matters, but without the use of the Bell Works there had been added stress on production until now, when the bell from his old works was hung in its new turret and struck for the first time to call workers to their new workshops.

"The sun shines, & the birds sing so finely," an elated Josiah wrote, celebrating the brief relief from the harsh weather they had of late, "that it goes against the grain to be confin'd in a room, when every living creature ought to be in the open Air swelling the chorus of universal praise for the chearing influence of the Sun, & the prospect of a returning Spring." But when he went to drag Sally out of the house to help rejoice, he learned that the severe winter weather had taken a more severe toll on Sally's health than they had realized.

⁊❧

"Mrs Wedgwood is Ill of Rheumatism, quite laid up at present," Josiah told Bentley. She became so weak, she had to be "Carried to & from her bed." For weeks, her health had been fluctuating, and with occasional brief blasts of sunshine, Sally was able to "take an airing on Horseback"; but more often than not Etruria was drenched in a cold rain, which did her no good and worried their friend and physician, Erasmus Darwin.

"He says he is afraid her disorder will be stubborn," said Josiah; "they have bled her twice & are now going to blister her. She is very ill, not the least help for herself. Her wrists, shoulders, neck, Hips, knees, Ancles, & feet are all violently affected, & she is as complete a Cripple as you can imagine." Darwin recommended that Josiah take her to Buxton, in Derbyshire, where she might benefit from the mineral water that flowed tepid from the ground into baths (heated, Darwin explained, from the earth's "central fires"). Here, as elsewhere in spa towns, which gained immense popularity amongst the fashionable in the eighteenth century, patients soaked in tubs and drank from the springs. Such therapy was one of the current medical trends amongst doctors, like Darwin, who believed that the waters had chemical properties (which they were trying to identify) beneficial to weak constitutions. Other doctors disagreed, believing that it merely provided a placebo effect, attributing imagined benefits to the pungent odor and distinctive taste of the waters, without which "patients would have no confidence in their virtues." Still others worried that the present lack of knowledge might lead to dangerous abuses. Buxton water in particular, argued one physician, "is not to be trifled with, for if it be unnecessarily used, it will certainly do Harm."

Josiah and Sally were inclined to place their faith in the "rational," if experimental, system of medical knowledge, especially since they knew that Darwin had been working on the chemical analysis of Derbyshire waters; but Josiah also thought it prudent to seek a second opinion. He contacted Mr. Bent, the surgeon who had amputated his leg, to ask if the Buxton waters were the most beneficial, or whether, for instance, Bath might not be a better place to go.

While Josiah certainly had Sally's interests at heart, he nevertheless could not resist making a trip out of Etruria to serve his business interests as well. For years he had been conscientious of the effect that "the Season" had on commerce in different towns, commenting to Bentley in 1769 that "I believe London will, like Bath, extend her season through the whole year!" Knowing that his fashionable customers spent so much time and money in Bath, he set his sights on opening a shop there as soon as he could afford to. By 1772, the plan was ready to materialize. In March, Bentley had settled on premises he thought acceptable, and had hired a couple, Mr. and Mrs. Ward, to manage the shop. Josiah had Useful Tom working overtime "to prepare a sortment of useful ware, services, &c &c" to stock the new showroom. Since Sally's fever had eased and it appeared she could manage the journey, the thought crept into his mind that he might be present when the showroom opened.

He first approached Sally and "mention'd going to Bath to her, instead of Buxton, & I should be glad to give Mr & Mrs Ward a little assistance at their first opening if possible." It appears she had no objection, so that Josiah then consulted Bent and Darwin. "Mr Bent is on my side," said Josiah, but "Dr Darwin is rather against me." Darwin may have been worried about the length of the trip from Etruria to Bath, and may even have been influenced by the physician William Falconer's treatise (just published) on Bath's waters, with reference to their effects on rheumatism, in which he provided twenty-five pages of contraindications to taking the therapy. Josiah, however, determined he would gently persist with the idea, reckoning that nothing would happen for at least a month, an inconvenience, since time was of the essence. "Pray when does the spring season begin, & end, at Bath," Josiah inquired of Bentley.

A month later, Sally was feeling moderately better. "Mrs. Wedgwood has been well enough to ride out for some days past, but cannot yet dress herself & her Arms are rather worse this morning." She was hoping to gain enough strength over the next ten or twelve days to travel to Manchester, where Sukey and her cousins, Jenny and Kitty Willets, were to be sent to boarding school, but another change in the weather quashed those plans. "Mrs Wedgwood is again confin'd to her bed chamber," Josiah informed Bentley toward the end of April. "We have for some days past had very cold weather, a severe North East Wind, & snow . . . I despair her being able to go abroad [out of town] anywhere without a few weeks of warm weather . . ."

At the beginning of May, amidst enormous confusion at the Etruria factory, "half remov'd, the men all unsettled, both in body & mind, nothing in a finsh'd, settled, state," Josiah was needed to deliver "the little

Lasses" to a Mrs. Holland in Manchester, with whom they lodged while attending school. "I have left them with a very good Woman," he said, "& hope they will be happy, & improved." He also took the opportunity to stop by the town of Bolton on his return, "to look at the school intended for Jack [now six years old] when there is a vacancy for him."

❧

It was like "a man leaving his house on fire"; but despite all the difficulties of settling into Etruria, Josiah was off once again the next month, when Sally experienced another temporary upturn in health and agreed to visit Bath. She was by no means perfectly fit—they estimated that a decent recovery would take roughly three weeks in Bath—but she was feeling well enough to socialize there, drink to their distant friends' health each night, and enjoy the intimacy of the balmy June nights.

In the day, Josiah helped prepare his Bath showroom, and scout the competition in the area. He wasn't very satisfied with the shop Bentley had found for them, since the street was busy with "Coal Carts, Coal horses & Asses—& a great way from the Town & Parades & not very near principal Pump Room." It seemed far from the fashionable city center, near Market Place, where Josiah spotted "a very rich shop" that was selling "a large assortment of Mr. Boulton's Vases." The vases were ornamented with minerals which the shop's proprietor drew to Josiah's attention. He told Josiah "of Mr Boulton's having ingaged at several £1000 expense the only mine in the World" that produced the precious stones, "and that nobody else could have any of that material."

Josiah listened patiently to this "long tale," but then discreetly pulled the gentleman aside and advised him "not to tell that story too often as many Gentlemen who came to Bath had been to Derbyshire, seen the mine, & knew it to be free & open to all the world, on paying a certain known mine rent to the Land owner." The shopkeeper stared at Josiah, and "assur'd me upon his honor" that he had only repeated what Boulton had told him was true.

"Well done Boulton, says I, *inwardly*," Josiah laughed, taken with his rival's cunning sales tactics. He then asked the shopkeeper how well the vases sold. "So so," the gentleman replied. "I am afraid," a satisfied Josiah declared, "they will never answer Mr Boulton's end as a Manufacturer."

After a few weeks of therapy in Bath, Josiah was disappointed to report that "Mrs Wedgwoods lameness continues." He was particularly concerned that her joints were affected, "especially her knees," and worried she might face surgery, or worse. They "make a crackling noise like dryd parchment whenever she bends them." Moreoever, Sally was growing uneasy about being away from Etruria Hall for so long, and was developing "a longing after home & for her Bratts," John, Josiah, and baby Thomas, who was being cared for by a hired nanny and Useful Tom's wife, with their three children. Catherine Willets was due to give birth any day, but wrote to Sally to tell her that "Mr Willets has just been at Etruria to look at your offspring" and all was well. "Tom grows every way very fast, will almost overrun them. . . . Sukey likes Manchester very well & Mrs Holland is very kind to them all." She also had news of a housekeeper that Josiah thought of hiring to ease Sally's burdens. A letter of recommendation advised that the woman "will be an advantage to the children as they will learn none of those evils to which they are subject to in the company with the generality of servants, she is particularly handy & useful about sick persons." She sounded promising; and by the following week, when Sally learned that Catherine was "safely delivered of a very fine girl" and that "Tommy has four teeth," she was desperate to get home.

When they made it back to Etruria, a full month later, Sally was "almost a skeleton, & has not strength to walk 20 yards." Mr. Bent was of the opinion that her health was rapidly deteriorating once more due to a "Breeding disease," since she was again pregnant. "All hopes I had conceiv'd of her speedy recovery are all vanish'd," said Josiah, getting visibly more anxious. "Her sickness & vomiting, with all the unfavorable symptoms are return'd, & as Doctor Darwin, who attended her yesterday, apprehends an inflammation of the Liver, & she is so extremely weak and emaciated I am really alarm'd for her safety, & in great distress." He begged Bentley to refrain from writing about this in his return letters, hoping to disguise his anxieties from Sally. Bentley had plenty of other things to fill his letters with, since Josiah kept sane by flooding him with particular questions about new sorts of wares they were hoping to sell.

A month later, in early September, Sally miscarried "& nothing but the greatest attention in nursing & keeping everything quiet about her can save her life." She was emaciated and pale, "& does not seem to have a drop of blood in her body." Erasmus Darwin was now regularly making the sixty-mile return journey from Lichfield to Etruria, and prescribed "a course of steel, in the form of ten grains of fresh iron fillings mixed with quince marmalade taken twice a day (with four drops of laudanum added to each dose)." Darwin was particularly eager to help such good friends after his own wife's death two years earlier, when, as he said, "the dear Partner of all the Cares and Pleasures of my Life ceased to be ill—and I felt myself alone in the World."

Josiah supplemented the iron shavings with ripe plums and cider, "but I believe I shall not gain much credit in my office amongst the female nurses here," he said. The approaching autumn did not bode well for her health, yet he hoped "to fortify her against winter."

Josiah was in anguish, and not surprisingly, he noticed that he too had "lost a great deal of flesh," prompting Darwin to urge him to eat despite the trying circumstances. To compound his distress, Josiah discovered "a scene of vilany amongst our servants in the House," who, while Sally suffered upstairs, were "robbing us of everything they could carry off." As if carrying on with business, organizing the factory, and doctoring and fearing for Sally's life was not enough, he now had "to sweep the House of every servt we have in it, Male & Female, some from the field Men & others from the works." He was devastated to learn that the staff, whom Sally had tried so hard to befriend and help settle, were "inclin'd to attack their Mistress" when she was vulnerable. He had to keep this from Sally, and was plotting to "complete the revolution" in staff termination and replacement when she left the house to stay with her family in Cheshire.

Only she was not strong enough to travel, and remained bed-bound, early in November "in a very dangerous situation." Winter was once again descending on them like a scourge. "I am almost distracted with my fears for her, & for myself, for I should, in losing her go near to lose myself also, & I fear, though I shudder at writeing it, that she has but a poor chance for recovering her present illness." Their surgeon Mr. Bent "thinks the only thing that can save her wod be going to Italy or the south of France," Josiah told Bentley; but that was an enormous risk. Josiah took her to Lichfield to stay with Darwin for ten days, allowing him to deal with the "revolution in our household" and "hope that the change of place, Air & company will have a good effect."

Sally remained ill. Her "favourite Esculapius" optimistically told Josiah that "if we can preserve her thro' the cold weather to April, she will do very well, & make a perfect recovery in the summer." The winter would be bleak.

22

"All the Gardens in England"

I t would prove to be a difficult year for other parts of Josiah's family as well. His older brother, Thomas, fell gravely ill. He lived at Overhouse Estate with his second wife, Jane, and five children (three from his first marriage) and had never over the last twenty years improved on his properties much; nor had he come to excel as a potter, just as Josiah had predicted when he left to go off on his own.

Thomas struggled for years to recoup the losses incurred as a result of his father's poor management of the potworks. Never, in fact, did he pay the £20 inheritance his father left to Josiah and his siblings—Josiah himself delivered that out of his own pocket after he married Sally. Throughout his life, Thomas slogged at his small potworks—he had eighteen employees, it appears, whom he looked after as best he could (accounts reflect a regular purchase of eighteen coats, which were probably part of his workers' wages)—but they never managed to muster much business. When he fell ill, he had a meager £172 of earthenware stock: simple wares, such as baking dishes, blue and white cups and saucers, mustard plates, and "sortables." His potworks were serviced with four horses, two carts, four lathes, two throwing wheels, and some tools, in all amounting to a mere £130.

Josiah had long had infrequent and rather formal contact with his older brother, who—Josiah noted—"has had vexations & fretting enough for ten years past to have destroyed half a dozen constitutions." Finally in February 1773, Jane, who was a reserved and somewhat mysterious woman, called upon Josiah to visit his brother, who had been confined to the house for several months and whose health, like Sally's, was rapidly deteriorating.

When Josiah arrived at the house, he discovered that the family was "in a deplorable way." Josiah asked Erasmus Darwin to examine Thomas. Josiah told Bentley that his brother was suffering from "Ailments of various kinds, which seem now to have resolv'd themselves into a Dropsy. His Legs & Body swell, his appetite is nearly lost, & he sleeps but little." Equally gloomy was the unsettled state of his personal affairs which, "Having Children by two Wives, one of whom you know is alive, & a sad Rakish Boy for his eldest son," meant that it would not be an easy matter to "bring about a settlement" in the event of his death. He had to act swiftly. Darwin estimated that Thomas had no more than weeks to live.

To confound matters, according to Josiah, the "Rakish" eldest son from Thomas's first marriage, twenty-nine-year-old Thomas, was having a mental breakdown caused by the "extreme narrowness & something rather worse" of his stepmother. For years he had been "ill-treated & almost ruined" by her "black misdeeds," which his sisters had escaped through marriage. At her husband's deathbed, Jane confessed to Josiah "that it was her daily study to set his Father against him, in which, alas, she succeeded too well, that she has wrong'd him every way." Even her younger son, who was in a state of shock at his father's demise, became overwhelmed with "the foolish talk & behaviour of his Mother to him [which] made him for some time quite an Idiot."

Josiah managed to get his brother to write a will just in time. Thomas passed away at the end of February, and the family was left with relatively little. Jane received £50 worth of furniture (one third of the value of all the furniture) and the rental income from six houses they owned as part of his original inheritance, but she had already stolen money and furniture which she stored at a neighbor's house. His four younger children shared legacies totaling £1,100, and his eldest son inherited Overhouse Estate and its potworks. Josiah was kind to young Thomas, and did all he could to include him as part of his family. At times, Josiah was encouraged by the boy's prospects. "The improvement of my Nephew, & his reformation which is daily confirming gives me a very sensible pleasure," he said. But this Thomas was no better than his father or grandfather at business, and he repeatedly needed to borrow money from Josiah. Sadly, he would never do very well, and Josiah found himself financially supporting him, as well as his younger stepbrother, "who is not one remove from an idiot"; and "the vilest wretch that ever lived," the stepmother, who spent the rest of her twelve years "deprived of reason, & overwhelmed with guilt & despair."

Just after Thomas's death, Josiah at long last had something positive to report: "Mrs W has had a good night & is as much better this morning as one could expect from so favourable a circumstance." Spring had sprung and summer was on its way. Thinking of Darwin's prognosis, he was elated to report that Sally had pulled through and was smiling once again.

$\approx$

Spending time at Overhouse Estate with his dying brother was like stepping into the past for Josiah. Indeed, Burslem was beginning to feel like a world apart to him. Etruria was far more sophisticated than anything the community had seen before. Etruria Hall put the Big House to shame, and whether by coincidence or design, it was built just within view from the top of the Big House, so Long John and cousin Thomas could always gaze at his success. With all the family sadness, however—including the death of Long John's one-year-old son from smallpox in 1772—Josiah had no desire to boast.

About the only bright spot in the gloom and worry of 1772 was the unexpected news that Bentley was "upon the verge of the Holy Estate of Matrimony." While working at the London showroom two years earlier, Bentley had met Mary Stamford, the daughter of a Derbyshire merchant. "How," Josiah teased, "can it be possible that you should meet" the "Lady of your choice" at their rooms on Great Newport Street? "Nothing surely can have more the Air of Romance," he concluded. Bentley had kept the marriage plans rather quiet, no doubt finding it difficult to discuss when Josiah's letters were so full of concern over Sally's frail health. Although, said Josiah, "we all wait with great impatience for the remainder of the curious History which the good Lady has promis'd you," he revealed only one slight, but immediate, concern: whether Bentley had any plans for moving from London.

Josiah still had a desire to expand their London showrooms to encourage better sales amongst his fashionable customers. He had heard that the Society for the Encouragement of Arts, Manufacture and Commerce was taking up rooms in a new development along the north, bank of the Thames called the Adelphi, designed by the Adams brothers. The development consisted of twenty-four terraced houses that were finished by some of the best painters and craftsmen available, including Angelica Kauffmann, Giovanni Cipriani, and Antonio Zucchi. Built in 1772, its first tenants included David Garrick and Dr. Johnson's famous friend, the dandy Topham Beauclerk, and later Richard Arkwright. Now Wedgwood & Bentley (for Bentley assured him that he and his new bride would be staying on in London) wanted a presence in it.

With the opportunity to have their rooms custom-built, Josiah and Bentley immersed themselves in the minutiae of the design, putting to paper ideas that they believed would create the perfect suite of offices and showrooms. Different spaces were specifically designed to display different kinds of wares from both the useful and ornamental branches, including a Dessert Room with a "dessert Table" in the middle, a "Vase Room," and a gallery with encaustic plaques and bas-reliefs "suitable for large Halls and Stair Cases." A gently rising main staircase would lead to more rooms of vases, with "cabinet drawers under, down to the floor, for pictures, Gems, Heads, &c." A rear staircase led to offices for keeping accounts and writing, where Josiah imagined an ingenious communication system by which "a Tin pipe may be put to a note upon the Desk below when any particular account &c is wanted above & another convenience of the same sort from the back stairs into the Packing House." Josiah also wanted the largest window they could get for the front of the shop. Not only would this throw much light into the room but, as had never been done before (partly because the science of glassworks could not yet produce such windows), it "should be rather Magnificent on the Outside to render it conspicuous."

The plan to move into the Adelphi never materialized. One reason was that the high rent—£400 annually—was too risky, given the problems inherent in the design of the whole complex (crucially, the Thames Embankment was not built high enough and what would have been Wedgwood & Bentley's warehouses would be prone to flooding). But they had another possible venue: No. 12 Greek Street, south of Soho Square. Portland House, named after the owners of the estate, the Dukes of Portland, was the largest house in the street, having a seven-window frontage at a width of over fifty-four feet. An added bonus was that little work was required to transform it into a showroom space since a previous tenant was a medical man, and had built a large dissecting room. "I like the idea of a dissecting room," said Josiah, thinking that it would be ideal to convert into a gallery. Although Josiah had to sacrifice the idea of one large window in the front, they did implement some of their other imaginative designs, including fitting a network of speaking tubes throughout the building to expedite communication.

The new premises, for which Wedgwood & Bentley paid £300 annually, came at an opportune moment. In 1772, Parliament approved the government's purchase of William Hamilton's collection of antiquities, deeming it "simple, beautiful and varied beyond description," items "far superior to any that have ever been collected," which would now be on public display in the British Museum. Josiah wanted his shop to imitate the museum displays, which, he was sure, would generate new levels of interest in his Etruscan wares. He also suspected that more competitors would move onto his turf. When his "First Day's vases" were thrown at Etruria in 1769, he was the first potter to imitate the ancients by having his artists paint red figures in the antique style on his black basalt vases, and he hoped to remain the only one for as long as possible by patenting the technique of "Encaustic Painting."

The figures on the Etruscan wares were painted by Josiah's artists with an antique-looking matte finish, rather than the familiar glossy enamel. The secret lay in the special formula for Josiah's pigment: a chemical concoction including bronze powder, vitriol of iron, crude antimony, and specific proportions of other chemicals. Josiah hoped his patent would protect not only the specific formula for his special paint but also the concept of imitating ancient wares with it. He was not so lucky.

Immediately after Josiah disclosed his formula as part of his patent, which he obtained in 1769, a London merchant was discovered to be selling "antique" vases with encaustic painting. Josiah traced them back to a potter named Humphrey Palmer, from nearby Hanley (adjacent to Burslem). Josiah sued him for "trespass" but was immediately concerned about his lack of evidence. "The *selling* you can prove easily & clearly," he wrote to Bentley; "the *Making* I cannot prove at all," and further, he couldn't prove that Palmer and the London merchant were partners, which he thought was the crucial link. "That matter is kept a secret," he said, while encouraging Bentley to "have a coffee with Neale, the London merchant selling the encaustic vases, to tell him what he's doing to judge whether 'he sins willfully.' "

Trying to avoid an expensive lawsuit which he might lose anyway, Josiah approached Humphrey Palmer hoping they could settle out of court, using neutral potters and artists as arbitrators. "But in short, after much talk & shuffling . . . he durst not agree . . . & had trifled with me exceedingly in the meantime." So Josiah pursued his case, gathering "evidence" by soliciting expert opinion. He talked to two potters, "& they declare that they are certain whatever the Law may determine the country will universally give the invention of Etruscan painting to me"; and he showed the specification of his formula to two "clever" enamelers (they had read Hogarth's analysis of beauty and Burke on the sublime, he noted), who "declare they do not prepare their colours in the same manner & likewise no one else does."

Josiah succeeded in obtaining an injunction, but the proceeding proved to be a drawn-out affair; eventually, in return for an undisclosed sum payable to Wedgwood & Bentley, Palmer became "a sharer in the patent." Josiah was immensely frustrated and never bothered taking out a patent again. If he did, he would be forced to reveal the secrets of his laborious experimental trials. "There is nothing relating to business," he said, "I so much wish for as being released from these degrading slavish chains, these mean selfish fears of other people copying my works." He therefore relied on a marketing strategy that used the element of surprise to keep him ahead of the competition.

While Bentley encouraged Josiah to produce the different kinds of wares that he had been contemplating to add variety to the showrooms, Josiah thought this was too risky. "If everything we do & produce must be instantly copied by the Artists—our rivals—should we not proceed with some prudent caution, & reserve, & not shew either one, or the other, *too much at once*"? Espousing a philosophy he'd developed years before when working with Whieldon, he suggested that only when the fashionable item "had its day" should they then "surprise the World"—"keep the public attention awake"—by bringing out a new item. He began to flood his correspondents with ideas about possibilities for the next project. Perhaps, he thought, after Etruscan ware grew stale, he would produce figures after Raphael: "in order of time we ought to do so." "Variations," Josiah stated, "will produce business enough for all the hands we can possible get together."

This was his strategy for dealing with the majority of his rivals, all those "sniveling copyists" for whom he had no respect. But dealing with "the Boultons & . . . the great ones of the land," those with their own skills and original ideas, remained a different matter. Josiah was frustrated that Boulton was gaining so much attention by auctioning his ormolu wares. They were fetching amazing prices. "I am not without some little pain for our Nobility & Gentry themselves," Josiah claimed, when wondering why Boulton's "glitter" of ornamental metal was proving attractive. "What heads, or Eyes could stand all this dazzling profusion of riches & ornament if something was not provided for their relief"—such as an ancient simplicity. "I have some hopes for our black, Etruscan, & Grecian vases still," Josiah said.

Clever as his commercial strategies were, it would be an unexpected order through the Russian consul in London, Alexander Baxter, that catapulted Wedgwood to the apex of his fame, and finished off Boulton as a rival in this branch of industry. The order, received early in 1773, was from "my Great Patroness in the North," Catherine the Great, who commissioned an extraordinary dinner service she intended to use at state occasions for up to fifty people at Chesmenski Palace, in an area referred to as La Grenouillière, "the frog marsh." The set amounted to over 950 items, including 680 pieces for dinner and a 264-piece dessert set, with additional tureens, decorative fruit baskets, and ice cream "glaciers." The set was to be prepared "in the Royal pattern," with a painted border upon the rims of the dishes similar to her previous "Husk" service, but this time with a symbolic green frog in the border and with "*every piece having a different subject*" in the middle.

Josiah quailed at the practical difficulties involved in preparing each item, "tolerably done," with a unique view of British landscapes and buildings. "Why all the Gardens in England will scarcely furnish subjects sufficient for this sett," he said. He knew that such an ambitious task had been ordered by the King of Prussia, depicting scenes of his own dominions for his own use, but it was not as large as this, and Josiah shuddered to think of the cost of production.

He thought of all the artists involved, copying pictures from galleries or books. "Do you think the subjects must all be from *real views* & *real Buildings*," he worriedly asked Bentley, "& that it is expected from us to send draftsmen all over the Kingdom to take these views—if so, what time, or what money?" He imagined it would take two or three years to complete. "Suppose the Empress should die," he remarked, "it will be a very expensive business."

He guessed it would cost in the region of £1,000 to £1,500 to produce, which the Russian consul thought a bit steep, asking Wedgwood if he could do it more cheaply. "If his Mistress heard him she would rap his knuckles." Of course they *could* do them more cheaply, Josiah said, as low perhaps as £400 or £500, but it would "not be *fit for an Empress's Table*, or do us any Credit."

Wedgwood & Bentley took the risk and faced up to the challenge. Josiah hired an artist to start with the landscapes around Staffordshire. He equipped him with a *camera obscura* and gave him instructions to "take 100 views upon the road." Josiah judged they could compromise to a degree with the source of their illustrations, which if they were all taken on site, would—the artists estimated—cost upwards of £3,000. Besides, they could use "the paintings in most Noblemans & Gentlemans houses of real views" and "the *publish'd views* & the real Parks & Gardens" to keep costs down. Since they were so willing to let Josiah use their collection of vases as models, he was sure aristocrats would allow his artists to sketch from other parts of their collection, especially when their estates would be depicted for the "first Empress in the World."

Throughout the following year, the artists painted over one thousand two hundred different views, representing, as Bentley said, "all of the centuries and styles, from the Huts of the Hebridean islands to the masterpieces of English architecture." Amongst scenes of St. James's Palace, Kew Gardens, and such splendid estates as Chatsworth, Wedgwood & Bentley also included pictures of industrial progress, such as the Plymouth dockyard, a Bristol colliery, the Bridgewater Canal, and—framed within a large, oval service dish—a sign of industrial achievement itself: Etruria. Nowhere amongst the 950-odd pieces was Wedgwood able to find room for Boulton's Soho works.

The good news was that the excellent team of artists they employed, led by three women landscape painters—Mrs. Wilcox, Miss Glisson, and Miss Pars—finished the job in just over a year, well under the estimated time. The bad news was, the cost of its production well exceeded Josiah's original estimates, amounting to around £2,500. Given all the activity and engagement with the "Noblemans & Gentlemans" they used in its preparation, when the service was nearing completion, Wedgwood & Bentley considered whether it would be beneficial to display the service to the public before it was sent off to Russia. Many of the ladies and gentlemen whose estates were represented were curious to see what their homes looked like on plates. The benefit, Josiah thought, was that "it would bring an immense number of people of fashion into our Rooms— would fully complete our notoriety to the whole Island, & help us greatly, no doubt, in the sale of our goods, both useful & ornamental. It would confirm the consequence we have attain'd, & increase it, by showing that we are employ'd in a much higher scale than other Manufacturers." On the other hand, there was some danger. "Suppose a Gentleman thinks himself neglected, either by the omission of his seat, when his Neighbours is taken, or by putting it upon a small piece, or not flattering it suffi- ciently." They then risked condemnation, "he then becomes our enemy . . . & Damns it with the Russian Ambassador & with every one he is able to." Josiah left the decision to Bentley's prudent judgment.

Bentley decided it was worth the risk, but they fixed upon a tactic of issuing tickets to raise interest by making the display of the Russian ser- vice an exclusive event. One of the ticket holders was the bluestocking Mary Delany, who declared herself "giddy" when looking over the collec- tion. "It consists I believe of as many pieces as there are days of the year, if not hours," she wrote.

> There are three rooms below and two above filled with it, laid out on tables, every thing that can be wanted to serve a dinner; the ground the common ware pale brimstone, the drawings in purple, the borders a wreath of flowers, the middle of each piece a particular view of all the remarkable places in the King's dominions neatly executed. I suppose it will come to a princely price; it is well for the manufacturer, which I am glad of, as his ingenuity and industry deserve encouragement.

However, she was briefly taken aback when she spotted an error on one of the plates, which misattributed the ownership of her niece's home, Ilam House. She promptly pointed it out, ensuring that they "acknowledge its *true master* to her Imperial Majesty." Aristocrats' carriages soon crowded Greek Street to the point of creating a traffic jam, culminating in a per- sonal visit from the queen, who, according to Bentley, expressed "her approbation in pretty strong terms."

As much as this magnificent commission did for Wedgwood & Bent- ley's pride and reputation, it was—to Josiah's annoyance—"tedious busi- ness," conducted for little profit. Catherine, who was proud of the service, keeping it on open display for all visiting dignitaries to view, paid just over

16,000 rubles for it (approximately £2,700), giving Wedgwood & Bentley a meager £200 profit. Also, it was a one-off, which meant that, unlike the original Queen's ware service or his Etruscan vases, it would not generate a flood of orders from those eager to emulate the empress.

Josiah knew he needed to move on to new things. So, wiping his brow after each day of overseeing the production of "Catherine's Ware," he returned to his experiment book. Catherine's service had certainly outdone Boulton's earlier coup in Russia, but Josiah was pursuing another scheme to win the war. If Boulton thought that misleading the Bath merchant about the rarity of the gems he used in his ormolu vases was clever, he was about to learn a lesson in true one-upmanship. Josiah had been experimenting with the five tons of clay that Griffiths had brought back from America a few years earlier and was obtaining some remarkable results. Above all he planned to use the amazing saga of the clay itself to full effect.

23

"Off for the Cherokee Nation"

When Josiah complained that it was going to cost him twenty-five guineas to send Thomas Griffiths from London to Charles Town, South Carolina, he had no idea how high the physical and emotional cost of the journey would be.

Josiah begrudgingly obtained a ticket on the *America* in July 1767, and on the sixteenth, with the ship under the command of Captain Raineer, Griffiths sailed. Disagreeable weather made it a slow journey, but after two months at sea—enjoying the occasional meal of shark and witnessing a young woman in the steerage deliver a baby girl—the vessel finally arrived, at "a miserable hot and sickly time." He rested and acclimatized for two weeks at the port; then, having stocked up on tea and coffee, three quarts of alcohol, and a tomahawk ax "for the journey," Griffiths mounted his rented horse, named March, and "went off for the Cherokee Nation."

He headed out northwest, toward the southern Appalachian region, wandering through fields and forests, over meadows along serpentine trails, through hundreds of miles of "very deep and daingerous Roads." The weather was "very hot and fainty," and at an inn a few days later he observed "the People almost all dying of the ague and feaver." Two nights later, with March exhausted, he "was obliged to sleep under a Tree with my horse, very near the place where five people had been Rob'd and Murder'd but two days before, by the Virginia Crackers and Rebells; a Set of Thieves that were join'd together to rob Travillers and plunder and destroy the poor defensless Inhabitants of the New Settlements."

On the trail the next day Griffiths happened to meet a trader, something of a rarity since travelers often covered twenty or thirty miles without seeing a person or so much as a hut. They joined company, and six miles later, as the sun was setting through the woods, his companion became agitated by the sight of two men ahead. He "pray'd me to give him one of my Pisstolls and keep the other in my hand Ready cock'd." As his companion anticipated, "they soon gallop'd up a Deer Track into our Road, with a 'how do you do Gentlemen, how far have you come this Road? Have you met any horsemen?', and then wished us a good evening." After turning back to ask whether they had heard any news of robbers, "which we anser'd in the Negative," they continued on their path. "It was well we were together and that we had firearms," Griffiths added, "as he had knowledge of one fellow, and believed him to be concerrn'd in the late Murders," which proved accurate, as Griffiths later saw one of the men executed for his crimes.

Griffiths soon parted company with his acquaintance; days later, some 200 miles from Charles Town by his estimation, he arrived at a plantation called Whitehall, where he was asked to accompany an Indian woman, belonging to the Chiefs of the Cherokees, back home. She had been taken and ransomed "by our Indian deputy of the Illinois" and rescued by John Stuart, Superintendent of Indian Affairs (Stuart's life had been saved by the great Cherokee chief, Attakullakulla, at the time of the fall of Fort Loudon). After three nights on the road, Griffiths and the Indian woman arrived at old Fort Prince George, a trading post across the Little Tennessee River from Old Kowes (Keowee), formerly the chief town of the lower Cherokees, just south of the present North Carolina border.

"At this Fort I delivered up my Squaw and Letters" to the commanding officer. Griffiths discovered that the commissaries for Indian affairs were meeting with a number of chiefs, "Great Bear," "the Rising faun," "old woolf," and "attaw kullucllah" himself. "All these met at this Fort to call a Counsell and held a grand talk concerning a peace with the Norward Enemies." Happy to be off the trail and under a tent, Griffiths ate, drank, smoked, and "began to be famileer with these Strainge Copper collourd Gentry," and when the moment was right, he requested permission to travel through their nation, in search of "curiosities," "in particular to speculate in their any White Earth." Accordingly, the commanding officer called over a linguist, who was instructed to be "very particular on the subject" with the chiefs, who, after a long hesitation and several debates amongst themselves, granted him permission.

Two young warriors "seemed to consent with some Reluctance," Griffiths observed, "saying they had been troubled with some young men long before, who made great holes in their Land, took away their fine White Clay, and gave em only promises for it." They were concerned since "they did not know what use the Mountain might be to them, or their Children." However, Griffiths had behaved like a "True Brother" by safely bringing the Indian woman home, and they "did not care to disappoint me for that time." He then departed the fort with great formality, "such as singing and shaking hands; besides making a publick show of their gifts and offerings for Peace."

Heading north along the Savannah River into the valley, he passed small villages of Indians with old men, women, and conjurers, who offered him grapes and apples. The younger men were out hunting. In one village, he visited "my old Consort," the Indian woman he had escorted to Fort Prince George. According to the Indian custom, her imprisonment obliged her to undergo an eight-day confinement in the "Town house," after which she was "to be stripp'd, dipp'd, wellwash'd, and so Conducted home to her husband." He met another old Indian woman who had "undergone that dreadful barbarity, of being shot thro the shoulder, Tomahawked in the breast, and then scalped" by her husband, but lived.

At the end of October 1767, after nearly a month of travel, "in fear of every Leaf that rattled" in the forest, he had passed picturesque waterfalls, brooks, and springs into present-day North Carolina. "In my way I passed the spot where Coll Montgomery was greatly Repulsed by the Indians," he noted, reflecting on the Battle of Echoe, and "the place where Coll Grant gained complete victory over em." He did not stop to gaze at the scenery for long. As November arrived, so too did strong northeast winds "with cold and heavy Rain or Sleet," which poured all day long.

"By that time there was scarce life in either me or my poar horse." He spotted a faint glow of a fire in the distance and stumbled toward a cabin. "Unluckily the master was gone out," he said, "but the poar old Squaw dried my Cloathes as well as she could, and wrapped me up in a blanket and a Bear Skin." The next morning her husband, an Englishman named Mr. Downy, returned, and stewed some fowls, "which made me a Glorious Repast."

Soon Griffiths arrived at "Cowes Town" (Keowee), on the Little Tennessee River near Iotla Creek. "I remained a few days, and furnished myself with a Servant, Tools, Blankets and Bear Skins," and on 3 November they set off on the last leg of the journey, up to "Ayeree Mountain," deep in the Cherokee backcountry. "Here we laboured hard for three Days in clearing away Rubbish out of the old Pitt which could not be less than twelve or fifteen ton." Once the pit was cleared, he picked up a spade of clay and examined it. The Cherokee clay, otherwise called kaolin from the Chinese for Kau-ling ("high ridge"), was pure white, and precious. This was Griffiths's equivalent to a gold mine, the kind of clay necessary to make real porcelain.

As he was admiring his find, the chiefs of the Ayeree Mountain appeared and took him prisoner, "telling me I was a trespasser in these lands," and that they had received private instructions not to consent to any of their clay being dug unless they received 500 pounds of leather for every ton of earth. Griffiths sent for a linguist and argued that there was a misunderstanding with the gentlemen at Fort George; "after a strong talk which lasted for four hours," they settled matters and Griffiths was able to continue his work. To help with negotiations, "I invited em together & treated em with Rum and such Music as I was capable of, which made em dance with great agility; especially when the Bottle had gone about well; which is the only way to make friendship with any Indians, provided they are not made Drunk."

By the time Griffiths was allowed to return to work four days later, the weather had turned, and heavy rains fell throughout the night, creating a torrent that flowed down the mountain with such force that not only did it fill his pit "but melted, stained and spoil'd all I had dug"; adjacent red strata bled into the pure white clay, and a mud slide had destroyed his wigwam, "so that we were nearly perished with wet and cold."

It took Griffiths over a month to redig and dry the clay he intended to take back to England, working frantically to finish before the ground froze. After taking the opportunity to "hunt, fossil & Botanize," he and the packhorses he loaded up began the return journey in mid-December. They had only traveled a few days when his horse stumbled on a narrow, slippery path and rolled over. Griffiths was thrown to the ground and "the poar Beast tumbled into a Creek & was spoiled. . . . This was an unlucky circumstance as I had then several hundred Miles to Travil, besides the loss of a fine young Cherokee horse."

Reaching Fort George on 27 December, when "I could gladly have kissed the soldiers for joy," he loaded five wagons with five tons of clay and set off for the last leg of his journey. On 4 February 1768, Griffiths "arrived once more at dear and long-wished for Charles Town." He was back in Burslem by the end of April to deliver the five tons of white clay to Josiah, along with an account of his journey and a three-page list of expenses totaling £615 19s 3d.

24
Poison and Porcelain

When the clay arrived in April 1768, Josiah had the weight of many other things on his mind, and was shortly to have his leg amputated. What he immediately grasped was its incredible cost to him—which at the time he could not afford—but before long he recognized the value of Griffiths's hazardous journey.

The white clay from America had a fascinating history, which would be part of every piece of pottery he manufactured with it. It was as if the Indian spirits were embodied in the earth—captured in the mound of clay now stored in the covered courtyard of his factory. Just as he had "revived" the ancient arts and re-created an Etruscan legacy, he wanted to use the exoticism of the Cherokee Nation to enhance the uniqueness of his wares. But he knew that the clay was valuable in other ways aside from its history. He knew that kaolin, as a species of clay, was already enriched by its unique composition, which made it—and it alone—the chief ingredient in the production of porcelain.

❧

Porcelain is a thousand-year-old Chinese invention that remained a mystery to Westerners until 1708, when the recipe for it was discovered by Johann Böttger, leading to the prompt establishment of the Royal Saxon Porcelain factory at Dresden (moved to Meissen in 1710). Then, of course, the production of this "white gold" was kept the most closely guarded secret in Europe. The reward for discovering the formula—for hitting upon the potter's version of the philosopher's stone—was the privileged ability to charge patrons exorbitant prices for such prestigious items. That is, if the manufacturer could be consistent.

The first manufacturer of hard-paste porcelain in Britain was William Cookworthy, a Quaker apothecary and chemist from Plymouth, in Devon. In 1745, Andrew Duché, a Huguenot colonist from Virginia, brought him samples of kaolin clay from the site at which Griffiths was later to dig. After studying the qualities of the clay, which Duché demonstrated could be turned into porcelain cups (he is considered America's first porcelain manufacturer), Cookworthy discovered deposits of kaolin near St. Austell in Cornwall.

Experimenting with the kaolin clay and gathering information about the manufacture of porcelain elsewhere, Cookworthy eventually found the secret of producing hard-paste porcelain (kaolin mixed with china stone, petuntse, as opposed to soft-paste porcelain, which uses grit, or "frit," to give it its durability). In 1768, he obtained the first patent for manufacture, which gave him a monopoly on the use of some of the Cornish materials for which he paid certain landowners for mining rights.

At the time, Josiah—and indeed other Staffordshire potters—was not interested in manufacturing hard-paste porcelain. They perceived too many complications in its manufacture and had witnessed some porcelain manufacturers go bankrupt; however, they were interested in the Cornish clay, since its whiteness enhanced the desired cream color of earthenware. Even though in 1767 Josiah had been advised that Parliament would not allow him his own monopoly on the American kaolin, and that the cost of importing it was in any case prohibitive, he had five tons of the clay and turned his attention to producing a rival to the hard-paste porcelain being manufactured in Plymouth. The time was ripe. "I apprehend our customers will not much longer be content with Queens ware," he commented in 1774, "it now being render'd vulgar & common everywhere."

Josiah wanted to remain in a class of his own. His primary customers were the rich—they paid extraordinary prices for exclusive items which covered the initial high costs of production. But once the techniques, materials, molds, and skills were developed well enough for Wedgwood & Bentley to manufacture the products at half the expense, the craze among the rich had died down, allowing them the option to mass-produce and sell at a cheaper price. There was, after all, another market developing, which Josiah spoke of in a famous comment on 23 August 1772, when his ornamental vases were well stocked in aristocrats' homes.

> The Great People have had their Vases in their Palaces long enough for them to be seen & admir'd by the *Middling Class* of People, which Class we know are vastly, I had almost said infinitely, superior in number, to the Great, & though a *great price* was I believe, at first necessary to make the Vases esteemed *Ornaments for Palaces* that reason no longer exists. Their character is established & the middling People would probably buy quantities of them at a reduced price.

Josiah, being part of that new "Middling Class," albeit in its upper divisions, recognized the middle class as a professional class, and respected the level of improvement in education and living conditions it had begun to achieve. But as a class of *consumers*, who wanted to emulate "the Great People," Josiah considered them no better than the "seconds" and "thirds" of his pottery. They simply did not have the spending power to be deemed "legislators in taste," as Josiah called his preferred customers.

"Few Ladies, you know, dare venture at anything out of the common stile till authoriz'd by their betters—by the Ladies of superior spirit who set the ton," Josiah told Bentley. Such was the trend for emulation that the *British Magazine* complained that the "present vogue for imitating the manners of high life hath spread itself so far among the gentle folks of lower life that in a few years we shall probably have no common people at all." Josiah doubted that the "high" and "low" would ever amount to the same class, knowing that the *ton* could buy their exclusiveness while the middling sorts could not. He would exploit their "superior number" but they were never his primary market.

He was especially adamant about this when Mr. Ward, his Bath showroom manager, advertised in the newspaper and delivered handbills at the Pump Room as other shopkeepers did. This was "a mode of advertising I never approv'd of," Josiah angrily wrote. "We have hitherto appeared in a very different light to common shopkeepers, but this step, in my opinion, will sink us exceedingly."

Josiah's worries about "sinking" due to a change in the public perception of the quality of his products suddenly crystallized in 1773, when he discovered that the public were about to be warned that eating off Wedgwood's Queen's ware might be hazardous to their health.

Physicians had long known about the dangers of working with lead. In 1745, an English translation of *Diseases of Tradesmen* (1700), by Bernardino Ramazini, known as the "father of occupational health," placed potters alongside lead miners as workers most at risk. By then, the process of liquid lead glazing on earthenwares was commonplace, tendering the wares waterproof and adding decorative color by using a wide range of metallic pigments.

Lead glaze presented a glossy, clean-looking surface, but preparing the glaze was hazardous. Potters needed first to grind the lead into a dust, then melt it before daubing it onto the piece of pottery, which was then sent to the kiln for its second firing. During this process, as Ramazini noted, potters "receive, by the Mouth and Nostrils, and all the Pores of the Body, all the virulent Parts of the Lead thus melted in water and dissolved, and are by that means frenzied with heavy Disorders." The symptoms were widely remarked. "First of all their hands begin to shake and tremble, soon after they become paralytic, lethargic, splenetic, cachectic, and toothless; and, in fine, we scarcely see a Potter that has not a leaden cadaverous complexion." Lead, it was clear, had "pernicious principles," for which there was no cure (though "mercurial purges" were recommended) but it was commercially a vital material. The glaze had allowed people to eat and drink from the wares. "What a great change would the world be put to," observed Ramazini, if everyone was forced to rely on "pewter and copper vessels."

But in the 1760s, other physicians were wondering if the dangers of lead poisoning were limited to those involved with the production of pottery. In 1767, the physician George Baker studied an endemic outbreak of "Devonshire Colic," when some three hundred people were taken to Exeter hospitals with complaints that, as Benjamin Franklin (whom Baker consulted) observed, resembled symptoms shown by painters who suffered lead poisoning. He also noted that the outbreak—which had been noticed in previous years—coincided with the apple harvest. With these clues, Baker examined Devonshire cider and found traces of lead. He then examined the cider presses and found that, unlike cider presses in other regions, in Devonshire the cisterns were made of lead, which, he concluded, contaminated the apple juice and affected those who drank the cider.

Even though some doctors rejected the idea that a chemical reaction between the fruit's acid and the lead could cause contamination—and facing outright hostility from the cider makers—Baker persisted with his claims, and he published an article that linked the occurrence of "dry stomach-ach" to lead poisoning. When he discovered that there was a colic outbreak in Spain, which some thought was caused by a bad batch of grapes in Madrid wine, Baker offered his own theory. "May it not reasonably be imagined," he remarked, "that some part of this endemic evil may be owing to glazed earthen vessels, which are generally used at Madrid, for almost all culinary purposes?" This was the first time someone had suggested that the common lead-glazed pottery, used everywhere, not just in Madrid, might cause those who ate or drank from it to fall ill.

Baker went on to elaborate his theory by comparing modern pottery to ancient pottery, working under the (false) premise that, unlike modern potters, the ancients did not suffer from colic. "That part of the old earthenware, preserved in the British Museum, supposed to be of Roman manufacture, is not glazed," he noted. "Those vessels, which are called Etruscan, and are supposed to be of greater antiquity than the Roman, have indeed a paint or polish on their surfaces, but that does not appear to resemble our modern saturnine vitrification." Indeed, at this point Josiah had not yet produced his imitation Etruscan vases, or presented to the world his patented. "Encaustic Painting," which was more in the ancient style, and different from the common, shiny lead glaze. Baker was convinced that the so-called modern improvements generated by what he referred to as the "age of chemistry" were in fact responsible for spreading disease amongst consumers. His conclusion was that because "the ancients were ignorant of this art, it seems probable that their ignorance, in this instance, contributed its part toward securing them from the colic."

This argument, which Baker presented to the Royal College of Physicians in 1767, appears to have escaped Josiah's attention, but it prompted other physicians to follow up with their own investigations. One of them was Thomas Percival, the leading Manchester physician, whom Josiah happened to meet while on a trip to the Buxton mineral baths in 1773. Part of Percival's research involved analyzing the mineral content of the waters at Buxton, intending to illuminate the debate over the risks of consuming mineral water. When he met Josiah and learned they had mutual friends, including Joseph Priestley, Percival courteously gave Josiah his manuscript entitled "Observations and Experiments on the poison of Lead," drawing his attention to the section on lead-glazed pottery.

Josiah read the relevant passage and was instantly upset. Percival seemed to have put Josiah himself under the microscope, writing that "The very beautiful polish of the Burslem pottery, commonly called the Queen's Ware, inclined me to suspect that lead, which is easily vitrified with sand and kali, enters into the composition of glazing." To determine whether his conjecture was true, Percival experimented on some of the pottery, discovering that "lead is an ingredient in the glazing of the Queen's Ware," though in a small proportion, which Percival believed was harmless; but he warned against preserving "acid fruits and pickles" in it, which could have the same effect as the Devonshire cider outbreak.

Percival asked Josiah if what he had determined was correct, "& I told him it was," answered Josiah, "& that Lead is likewise an ingredient in Flint & almost every other kind of Glass, at which he express'd his surprise, & I suppose will be trying his experiments upon Glasses before he publishes." He sent a copy of the paper to Bentley in hope that he could find a way to "mend" Percival's account by rewriting it to remove the association to lead poisoning, "for though the Doctor is convinced that he may eat his pudding with perfect safety off our Manufacture, yet when whimsical & ignorant people read account of *Lead & Poison & Queen's Ware* in the same paragraph they may associate the ideas together as we do of Darkness & spirits, & never after see one of our plates without the idea of being poison'd by it."

Bentley immediately saw this as a crucial issue, and felt that he needed to know exactly what Josiah had said to Percival, since he worried that Josiah might have piqued a debate with the doctor about his results. "I did not dispute Dr Percival's conclusion," Josiah explained. "I only urged that Lead was an ingredient in all Glasses & Glazes for culinary uses, & that from examining a plate which had been in use for 5 or 6 years I was very certain a Person might eat every meal of his whole life off Queen's ware without a possibility almost of his taking in a grain of dissolv'd Lead from the Glaze if he lived to the Age of Methusalah." Josiah's frustration was that, while Percival pointed out that he "had taken care to express himself very cautiously"—in fact, he would later coin the phrase "medical ethics"—the doctor seemed to have no sense of the commercial impact of his comments. Josiah hoped that Bentley could convince Percival that he was "likely by publishing that paragraph to deprive some thousands of their daily bread & the nation of one of its capital Manufactures."

Which was the greater danger, asked Josiah, eating off Queen's ware or "the fatal blow to the Manufacture" that such a suggestion might provide?

Percival did not change his paragraph, but by the time his small book was published a year later, in 1774, another physician, Dr. Gouldson, who had fewer scruples than Percival and an apparent (and unexplained) vendetta against potters, published a pamphlet "to shew how pernicious" lead-glazed earthenware was. This was circulating amongst the ladies and gentlemen at Buxton—people already concerned about their health. "I believe," an angry Josiah sarcastically remarked, "we had better publish a pamphlet shewing the pernicious consequences of Lead in our Flint Glass, with some doubts whether it may be perfectly innocent in our Mirrors, Lustres &c &c," in order to jump on the bandwagon.

Not that Josiah lightly dismissed the problems. He embraced every new invention or design that worked to save potters' lives, applauding Thomas Benson's solution to the problem of inhaling flint dust by designing an engine to grind flint stones under water (patented in 1713), which had proved so beneficial to the potters' craft. As Benson had said, due to the high death rates among workers responsible for grinding flint, "it is now very difficult to find persons who will engage in the business to the great detriment and obstruction of said trade." Even though flint grinding subsequently carried fewer risks, workshop labor remained difficult to recruit due to the prominence of other diseases, such as "potter's rot," or silicosis. Josiah believed that new factories and machines could be built on principles informed by science and medicine to make them healthy places to work, generating a revolution not only in new products and consumer spending but in laboring-class standards of living. Such Utopian faith in the future of industry provided a powerful impetus for Josiah to become the biggest and most respected entrepreneur in the world. He would eventually consider the persistence of diseases amongst his workers one of the most disappointing failures of his career.

But at this point, in 1773, in response to charges that his wares might cause those who ate off them to shake, become paralytic, and go toothless, Josiah decided the best strategy was to return to his laboratory. "I will try in earnest," he declared, "to make a glaze without Lead, & if I succeed will certainly advertise it."

Managing the public image of the business—whether in the safety, the color and craftsmanship of the wares, the design of the showroom, or mode of advertising—was always of central concern to Josiah. As his success grew, so did his efforts to protect this image against any threat, whether from doctors or unscrupulous traders. In 1774, he discovered that one of his former modelers, who left Wedgwood's employment to work for Humphrey Palmer, was distributing seals and cameos fraudulently stamped "Wedgwood & Bentley," taking advantage of Josiah's innovative idea to "brand" his own products. Dreading the expense and tribulations of a lawsuit, Josiah attempted "to stop the Rascals career" through an announcement drawing attention to it, including "a description of his Rogueship."

Admittedly, it was time to surprise the world with something new, something his competitors could not imitate, but not at any cost. Even if Josiah could get access to the Cornish kaolin, he would not do what Humphrey Palmer did to him—flagrantly "trespass" the patent and steal the idea. That would reduce him to the level of the "sniveling copyists" he condemned.

In fact, in 1766 Erasmus Darwin wrote to Josiah with news that a French nobleman and "Man of Science, who loves everything English," was seeking to sell "the Secret of making the finest old China, as cheap as your Pots" for £2,000 (assuring him that the materials were in England); but Josiah did not pursue it. Again, years later, when the proprietors of the closing Bow manufactory approached Wedgwood in an attempt to sell their secret to soft-paste porcelain, which they had patented in 1744, he responded unambiguously: "I do not wish to purchase any English process, and much less the Bow, which I think one of the worst processes for china making." Rather, Josiah preferred to rely on his chemical knowledge and embark on an experimental quest to invent something entirely new, which would put his "Cherokee" clay to use. And, as he was finishing Catherine's "Frog Sevice," he reported to Bentley "on some very promising experiments."

⁊❦

Discovering a new "secret of nature" may happen in a flash, but the flash usually occurs after an immense duration of non-eventful work. Tiring work, especially since the complaint in Josiah's eyes, which neither he nor his doctors could diagnose, was still causing him headaches. He spent month after month systematically experimenting with new kinds and proportions of clay, mixing them with chemicals, and test-firing the materials at different temperatures, using small, swatchlike samples. As always, he meticulously recorded each step in secret code in his experiment books. Fatigued and under much stress, he lamented the inconsistent results he was getting and the inevitable sense of distress at not knowing where precisely one was going, or would end up. "I am fairly enter'd into the field," he wrote late one night, "& the farther I go, the wider the field extends before me." In his usual way, Bentley responded with encouraging words, politely if pedantically reminding his partner that it was "bad policy" to hurry things; but that was not what worried Josiah.

He felt he was on the brink of discovery, but he faced constant troubles with the new materials he was using, and problems were arising from being unable to ascertain the heat to which the experimental pieces had been exposed. "Moorstone & Spaith fusible are the two articles I want," he said, referring to China stone and spar (carbonate of barium), "& several samples I have of the latter are so different in their properties that no dependence is to be had upon them. They have plagued me sadly of late. At one time the body is white & fine as it should be, the next we make perhaps, having used a different lump of the Spaith, is a Cinamon color. One time it is melted into Glass, another time dry as a Tob:Pipe." One good result was not followed by another. "I cannot work miracles in altering the properties of these subtle, & complicated (though native) materials," he complained, yet he would not give up. "If I had more *time*, more *hands*, & more *heads* I could do something"; but he had none of these things, and he had more pressing family matters to tend to, which irritated him because they interrupted his concentration. "A Man who is in the midst of a course of experiments *should not be at home* to anything, or any body else but that cannot be my case . . . I am almost crazy."

Sally was heavily pregnant, and her only brother had fallen gravely ill. Among other errands, Josiah traveled to his father-in-law Richard's home in Cheshire, where he lived with Sally's brother (who never married), and called for Erasmus Darwin. The prognosis was not good. Josiah was there for two weeks, comforting his "Aged & affectionate father," who could do nothing but watch his only son, bed-bound, emaciated, "and in the last stage of a worn out constitution," quietly pass away. Josiah worried about leaving his father-in-law alone in the house, where "the place, & the scenes every hour bringing to his remembrance the loss he has sustain'd"—first his wife, then his son. He persuaded Richard to return with him to Etruria.

Meanwhile, "my dear Girl," Sally, "bears this afflicting stroke of providence with that fortitude & strength of mind, which, from other instances, I have reason to say she seems indued [*sic*] with the power of exerting upon every proper & trying occasion." It was a good thing, for the next week, at half past four in the morning, "she gave me a gentle notice to quit her Bed & call the Midwife" ("as usual," he said, it was "very short notice of the approaching critical moment"). Fifteen minutes later, "news was brought me that I had another Daughter, & all was well." They named her Catherine, and Josiah ordered "two Barrels of Good Porter & a Barrel of Oysters" to honor the occasion.

After the oysters it was back to the laboratory, where a frustrated Josiah was determined to make the different materials for his new ware bond successfully. Were he to accomplish this, it would be "a metamorphosis" over which "we should endeavour to throw an impenetrable veil." It was difficult for Bentley to understand exactly what Josiah was up to. Josiah purposely kept him in the dark about his research, fearing their correspondence would be intercepted. With the experience he'd had of his employees' betrayal, there was reason to be suspicious. When Bentley requested particulars he was answered in code, with the information scattered in different letters, since, as Josiah said, "it is too precious to reveal all at once." He frequently offered propitious hints and clandestine commands to discontinue some practice in London, such as enameling certain pieces, because his new secret formula embraced that part of business. The problem was that his new formula was still not yielding consistent results, and nothing could be made public before standardization was achieved; "uniform success," as Josiah called it.

On 18 December 1774, Bentley was given his first glimpse of the products of his partner's toil: "4 black & Blue onyx Intaglios." Josiah was also making medallions, seals, and cameos—smooth pieces of pottery with an image carved (as in signet rings) or in relief (such as the cameos). What made these special was the preparation of the clay. It was hard, durable, but it possessed a translucent quality, like porcelain, and unlike all other pottery, this type was not painted or enameled. Rather, the clay itself had been dyed blue or black with a metal oxide before firing, so that each piece was composed of clay stained all the way through a particular color. Josiah had just introduced colored jasper, "my porcelain."

On New Year's Day, 1775, he gleefully reported to Bentley that he was able to produce this ware in a number of colors in good quality. "The blue body I am likewise *absolute* in of almost any shade, & have likewise a beautiful Sea Green and several other colours" for cameos depicting "the heads of Eminent Men, Greeks, Romans & Moderns," themes of "War—Hunting—Music—& the Arts & Sciences," or they could be catered for certain occasions or country's tastes. The market in Mexico was particularly religious, he was told, so he wanted to produce pictures of "Crucifixes, Saints, &c" for bracelets, lockets, and so on.

There was still some work to be done, but Josiah was once again progressing in leaps and bounds. He ordered 50 tons of white clay from Bruges, with which he hoped to confirm that he could consistently replicate the process, "so you see a spirit is up amongst us which must have consequences, & I hope they will be desirable ones." Josiah's spirits in his newest endeavor were further raised when a visiting Austrian nobleman told him that "the Manufactures of Dresden & Berlin Porcelain both of which he had visited were not, he said, to be compar'd with ours for taste, Elegance of designs, & fine modeling." This gave him the confidence to declare that he was "going upon a large scale" in preparation for the coming winter's show, where they would "ASTONISH THE WORLD ALL AT ONCE, for I hate piddling you know."

Josiah was feeling confident and proud of his invention of jasper, which "nobody," he relished in saying, "but W & B can make." One potter claimed that he had discovered the secret, but, Josiah calmly said, "I would as soon believe he had discover'd the Philosophers Stone." So confident was Josiah in his "victory" that he was happy once again to explore collaboration with his friendly rival, Matthew Boulton, who was "very civil to me." The cameos he was producing were "suitable for setting in boxes, Lockets, bracelets, &c &c," and Boulton, whose metalworks were of course well suited for this, told Josiah that he thought he might have "many opportunities for disposing of some this year."

It would take Josiah slightly longer to introduce his new ware than he anticipated, for he spent the winter on "the completion of the Art of *Jasper making*." But the work, he felt, had paid off. "I believe I can assure you of a conquest," he told Bentley on 14 January 1776, "& a very important one to us."

∂⚭

Although, in the long course of his experiments, Josiah had used an array of different materials to make "my porcelain" unique from anything else on the market, he was sure not to forget one ingredient that made it even more distinct. "I have often thought," he said to Bentley,

> that it may not be a bad idea to give out, that our jaspers are made of the Cherokee clay which I sent an agent into that country on purpose to procure for me, & when the present parcel is out we have no hopes of obtaining more, and it was with the utmost difficulty the natives were prevail'd upon to part with what we now have, though recommended to them by their *father Stewart* [John Stuart], Intendant of Indian Affairs. But then his Majesty should see some of these large fine tablets, & be told this story (which is a true one for I am not joking).... This idea will give limits, a boundary to the quantity which your customers will be ready to conceive may be made of these fine bass reliefs, which otherwise would be gems indeed. They want nothing but *age* & *scarcity* to make them worth any price you could ask for them.

Since his jasper was mainly made from the 50 tons of clay from Bruges, and could in fact be made from English kaolin, for added authenticity Josiah sketched another link between his wares and the Cherokee story. "A Portion of Cherokee clay *is really used* in all the jaspers so make what use you please of the fact."

"A Portion": Bentley was skeptical, not only because the portion would have been so small as to be irrelevant with the quantities he produced but because in Josiah's own formula for jasper the number 23, the secret code for Cherokee clay, was notably absent. Bentley, always prudent and confident that Josiah's jasper was comfortably in a class of its own without the tall tale, kept "the story" quiet, even though now more than ever it was time to talk about scarcity of materials coming from America. The entire trade with America was collapsing.

25

Mad Ministers

"I am no politician," declared Josiah back in January 1775. "All the world are with the Ministers & against the poor Americans. They are all gone mad, & have given them up for incurables." Parliamentary debates and decisions once again worried Wedgwood & Bentley. Ministers were composing the New England Restraining Act, which would restrain colonial trade and commerce to Great Britain, Ireland, and the British West Indies. This was Parliament's answer to the declaration of the Continental Congress the previous October, 1774, wherein colonial delegates attacked what they called "cruel and oppressive acts" by a "wicked ministry" in Britain that was discouraging the settlement of British subjects in America. The Congress angrily declared that "we will not import, into British America, from Great-Britain or Ireland, any goods, wares, or merchandise whatsoever," initiating a "non-consumption agreement" that agitated diplomatic and commercial relations to an unprecedented degree.

For decades, the King of England had ruled over an "empire of goods" that benefited Britain and grew in proportion to the numbers of colonists who, as Benjamin Franklin explained in the wake of the Seven Years War, had affection for Great Britain, and "a fondness for its fashions." This fondness benefited British manufacturers: one third of their customers lived in the American colonies; "around half of all English exports of copperware, ironware, glassware, earthenware, silk goods, printed cotton and linen goods, and flannels were shipped to colonial consumers." For over ten years the manufacturers had been kept on the edge of their benches

hoping that their ministers did not ruin the market by batting their customers away, forcing them to find alternative suppliers or attempt to
manufacture their own goods.

Benjamin Franklin made a point to Parliament that Wedgwood &
Bentley, along with a plethora of other manufacturers, found sympathic.
When explaining why Parliament should repeal the Stamp Act, he said
that colonists purchased three kinds of product: "necessaries, mere conveniences, or superfluities." The first, "as cloth, &c with little industry they
can make at home; the second they can do without . . . the last, which are
much the greatest part, they will strike off immediately." The threat was
that the market for British goods was expendable, and manufacturers
repeatedly pleaded to their ministers to consider the damage that could
be done to Britain's economy if that market collapsed. In January 1775,
William Pitt (Lord Chatham) emerged from retirement to rebuke once
again the government's rash actions toward the American colonies. "To
impose servitude to establish despotism over such a mighty continental
nation must be in vain, must be fatal," he said. Along with the Americans,
Josiah had the chance to cheer his hero, but it looked as if his admonish-
ment was immaterial.

"I have got a whirl in my head," said Josiah, as he traveled around on
business, exposed to all the debates on the "American problem." In
Manchester, he heard one outspoken gentleman who "froth'd at the
mouth," being "exceeding hot & violent against the Americans." His aim
was to put an end to the distribution of petitions against the use of
coercive acts in America—petitions largely supported by Dissenters,
who saw the government's aggression as another unjust extension of its
corrupt powers. The gentleman, who "was so excessively rapid in his
declamations, and exclamations," shouted that he would move "Heaven
& Earth either to prevent their petitioning, or to prevail upon them to
counter petition, in which last," Josiah sadly reported, "I believe he was successful."

Josiah learned that the speaker, whom American sympathizers naturally assumed was an "agent" of the British government, was energetically
traveling from town to town, preaching about the wrongs of Americans
taking arms against the king, and aggressively spreading his counterpeti-
tion to drum up support for the British government. Josiah was alarmed
to find that "his labor has not been in vain. . . . His harangues, & even
those simple queries have had a very considerable effect amongst many,

Dissenters & others . . . I do not know how it happens, but a general infatuation seems to have gone forth & the poor Americans are deemed Rebels . . ."

The official Royal Proclamation of Rebellion came a few months later, in August 1775, by which time preachers and spokespeople for and against the conflict had traveled widely, debating, petitioning, and publishing. Samuel Johnson wrote a pamphlet arguing that taxation was not tyranny. Embracing the point, John Wesley issued a "Calm address to the colonies," a half dozen copies of which Josiah received, "to my astonishment," from the "House of a Noble Lord in our Neighbourhood," who strangely thought that Josiah might sympathize with the minister's arguments supporting the extension of the government's powers over America. "Wesley is not a bad *Cats Paw*," Josiah quipped, "& they seem determin'd to lay hold of him & use him to their best advantage."

Tired of biased newspaper reports and the neglect of the "friends of America" to publish prompt replies to the propaganda, Josiah asked Bentley to "send me half a dozen of the answers & another book or two which you mention'd to me as the best things publish'd upon the American controversy." One answer, which arrived a few months later, was *Observations on the Nature of Civil Liberty . . .* , published by the Dissenting Welsh minister Richard Price, which Josiah devoured, calling it a "most excellent pamphlet." He agreed with Price's moral principles, which posited that "liberty" was a natural and unalienable right to every member of society, and that the principle of liberty included self-direction and self-government. "If the laws are made by one man, or a junto of men in a state, and not by common consent, a government by them does not differ from slavery," Price wrote, going on to develop what would become an immensely popular argument justifying the American Revolution based on liberal principles of civic consensus and representation. He proclaimed that he saw the events in America as "a revolution which opens a new prospect in human affairs, and begins a new era in the history of mankind."

"Those," Josiah announced, "who are neither converted, nor frightened into a better way of thinking by reading this excellent and alarming Book may be given up for harden'd Sinners, beyond the reach of conviction." Josiah then delved into more literature on the concept of liberty and inalienable rights, rereading John Locke—the seventeenth-century patron of the English Enlightenment—and carefully reading Thomas Paine's *Common Sense*, a new publication which forcefully argued for America's complete separation from Britain. This was just the beginning. Over the year 1776, Adam Smith would publish *Wealth of Nations*, which elaborated on Josiah's favorite theme of "self-improvement" by linking it to the growth of commercial society, where (as Smith said) everyone "becomes in some measure a merchant." Also published at this time were the first volumes of Edward Gibbon's *Decline and Fall of the Roman Empire*, which warned against the dangers of idle rulers overindulging in luxury and vice. Josiah and Bentley, with all their friends (and, no doubt, Sally, though she and much of the family were suffering from another "tyrannical" fever), excitedly discussed the new commercial and moral order taking shape around them. It was probably the most intensive reading list and politicized discussion with Bentley that Josiah had engaged in since his reading of Voltaire, Rousseau, and other French *philosophes* a decade earlier.

This time, however, the philosophy of government and individual rights was not a subject raised simply for his own edification. Not only did the "rebellion" have commercial implications that would certainly affect his business, but the prominent reputation he had built for himself prompted ministers to pressure Josiah into helping to promote the government's position. As a well-known and respected manufacturer with a record of representing local interests, he was asked by Lord Gower to solicit public opinion about forming a militia to fight the revolutionaries. The request irritated Josiah, to say the least. He had shown, and would continue to show, his gratitude to a valuable patron "where I can do it without a sacrifice to principle," he said, "which I hold too dear to part with at any price." But why, he wondered, was he approached in preference to the Gilberts, the Beards, the Sparrows—Lord Gower's own agents, lawyers, and associates, "whose devotion is unquestionable." But Josiah knew it was a moot point. "I will not scrutinize into the motives that actuate the great ones of the Earth. . . . I will do what better befits me— Obey—& give the best information I am able."

He mulled over the question Lord Gower posed to him. "How will the people stand with respect to raising the Militia?" "The *common People* I suppose," Josiah responded. "Tradesmen, &c." It was an "evil" idea, he immediately concluded, and he doubted there would be much goodwill in Staffordshire since the last militia that was raised, during the Seven Years War, was promised not to be sent abroad, "but," he remembered, "this promise was basely broken, & the poor Fellows were sent to Gibraltar."

After spending a few days "collecting intelligence," Josiah wrote to Lieu-tenant Colonel Sir John Wrottesley, of Stafford, who was preparing to sail to America with the First Regiment of the First Foot Guards (the "Grenadier Guards"). While the idea of raising a militia to fight America, especially when many of the men would be his own employees, was against Josiah's principles, he found a way of stating his views diplomati-cally by stressing the economics of it, for Josiah knew that ministers were convinced that Britain's ability to win wars was largely attributable to its thriving economy.

"There is no doubt," Josiah noted, "but every Parish would willingly be excused from the expense which raising the Militia will certainly bring upon it; and the Manufacturing Parts, whose rates are already very high, will be the more sensible of any addition to them, especially, if at the same time they feel this new burden, their trade should be upon the decline." That said, he recognized the necessity of telling the "great ones" what they wanted to hear, not least to steer well clear of appearing unpatriotic. However admired he was as a potter, political tensions quickly elevated his status as a Dissenter who had suspect connections to radical philoso-phers and revolutionary sympathizers. Knowing that the great ones would carefully listen to what he had to say, Josiah added that if it became neces-sary "to defend ourselves," he believed the local people "will very readily acquiesce in it when call'd upon to perform that duty."

The economic point, though, was the crucial one. Josiah was not spec-ulating that manufacturers might feel their trade "upon the decline"; they were *already* feeling it. The effect of the war on commerce was dramatic. In 1770, customs and excise officers recorded over 1.2 million pieces of glass and earthenware shipped to America. In 1775, under 139,000 pieces were sent. The Continental Congress had authorized privateer raids on British ships, and, three months before the Declaration of Independence was signed, American ports were officially closed to British trading ships. Manufacturers worried that this was the end of a major artery of trade, but they did not all agree on the principles at stake. Boulton, who was in serious financial trouble following a credit scandal in 1772 and was saved from bankruptcy by borrowed money, despised the American embargo on the grounds that it posed a threat to his business. But other entrepreneurs and manufacturers, particularly in Josiah's circle of Dissenting friends— such as Bentley, Erasmus Darwin, Joseph Priestley, and others—supported the "poor Americans' " cause in the hopes of seeing liberty triumph over tyranny (Boulton, we should remember, was an Anglican). The American cause was only a problem to trade because the mad ministers created an insufferable condition by trying unfairly to extend their rule. It was not dissimilar in principle to the grievances Dissenters had expressed for decades. Whatever the commercial considerations, Josiah was clear in his opinion of "the absurdity, folly & wickedness of our whole proceedings with America."

One unexpected consequence of the war with America was Tom Byerley's return to Etruria. When Tom left for America in 1768, Josiah had shown some frustration with his nephew's peregrinations—at fifteen wanting to be an author in London, at nineteen giving up as an actor in Dublin, then at twenty venturing off to explore America—but Josiah had a weakness for the young man, even though his patience had been pushed to the limits after Byerley arrived in America and had to be bailed out of debtors' prison in 1773.

The next year, Josiah was relieved to learn that Byerley had decided to become a schoolteacher, and implored his nephew to use some "good sense" to satisfy "the Gentlemen who repose so much confidence in you as to place their Children under your care." To help him along a more enlightened path, Josiah sent Byerley two globes and a packet of books for the youths' instruction, assuring him "that I shall at all times receive a particular pleasure in doing everything in my power that may contribute to your real welfare & happiness." But in the gathering storm of 1775, when it looked as if he might need to take up arms against his own countrymen, Byerley decided it was time to return to England, to the great relief of his mother. "She had much rather he should run away," said Josiah, "than stay to fight in so disagreeable a service as he must have been engaged in." Upon his return, Byerley resumed his occasional position as general clerk at Etruria.

Josiah was thankful to have him back at work. With all the pressures of the war, and the demands of inventing new materials and designs (not helped by "the Workmens *unhandiness* & *want of Ideas*"), it was a relief to have someone within the family who, until wanderlust struck again, could manage much of the paperwork. One of the first things Josiah asked Byerley to do was act as "Clerk to the Committee of Potters," which was set up to represent local concerns regarding the prime minister's enquiry as to whether lowering the duty on imported European earthenware—with the expectation of reciprocity in British exports to Europe—would help or hinder their trade.

Josiah was of the immediate opinion that abandoning *all* duties, which were long the subject of his complaints, would allow free trade and encourage open competition. "I should be asham'd to feel anything like a fear in having a free intercourse open'd between Great Britain & all the Potteries in the World," he confidently declared, "we enjoying the like liberty of exporting our Manufactures to other States." When preparing Byerley with the arsenal with which to convince "our Fraternity" of potters to agree, Josiah had a second thought about lowering the duties on the "Asiatic Porcelains," "as we can have no motive or expectation of receiving any reciprocal advantages." In essence, cheaper Asian porcelain would, Josiah feared, kill the home market for English porcelain and, more important, his own new jasper.

Inspired by the prospect of uninhibited trade with Europe, if the prime minister, Lord North, could get the reciprocal agreement of foreign governments, Josiah swiftly began jotting ideas down about what kinds of goods he could send into foreign markets. Bentley thought about inlaying snuff boxes with pictures of kings and queens, an ironic thought that did not escape Josiah's attention. They "will be very good things *for England*," he remarked, and went on to suggest that

> We can make other Kings & Queens, & eminent Heads for other Countries & such subjects will be the most likely to go in quantities, for People will give more for their own Heads, or the Heads in fashion, than for any other subjects & buy abundantly more of them. Henry the 4th, & some others for France for instance & the proper Heads for the different European Markets.

Bentley had just told Josiah of his plans to visit France, and Josiah saw immediately that his learned partner might do a great deal of useful research there.

26

The Philosophes *and Plaster Shops of Paris*

Three weeks after the American Declaration of Independence was signed, Bentley and "my good governess," his wife Mary, arrived in Paris. While socializing with the *ton* in London, Bentley and Mary had regular discussions with people incessantly preparing for their holidays abroad. One frequent customer at Wedgwood & Bentley's showrooms, Elizabeth Montagu, extended a particularly enthusiastic invitation to the couple to visit her on her first trip to Paris. When the Bentleys arrived, they found that she had been showing her collection of their cameos and intaglios "to the Duke or Count of Rochefoucault, to the Popes Nuncio, & many other great personages, who were highly delighted with them." She enjoyed having Bentley on hand as an added attraction to the unique jasper wares. "She is pleased to say she is proud of shewing them," Bentley wrote, "& always observes they are made by her particular Friend."

As Bentley said, his trip was "professedly a journey of expense and amusement"—a sort of belated honeymoon. Like many travelers, he kept a diary, which Josiah was eager to read. Also like many travelers, Bentley was critical of the differences between London and Paris. Everything, he claimed, was "black and dirty. The streets are narrow, dirty, and badly paved, without any side walk for passengers." In the mornings, he ate breakfast at the English coffeeshop and then sat by the Pont Neuf and read English newspapers; in the afternoon, he assessed the architecture. He was disparaging of French ornamental design:

Many of the buildings are *grand*, but few of them *beautiful*. The famous Louvre is an incomprehensible jumble of magnificence and mean-ness—of grandeur and bad taste—and ruins. The Seine at Paris is but a poor dirty river. Their bridges are not worth speaking of. Their gar-dens are in the old Dutch taste; Kensington gardens are infinitely superior either to the Tuileries or Versailles. The palace of Versailles merits the same character as the Louvre. Some parts of it, both within and without, are very magnificent, while others are only fit to excite disgust. The insides of their houses and palaces are almost all in the same style; as much glass and gilding as they can either afford or contrive to put into them; and nothing can be uglier and more tasteless than their chimney pieces, which are all alike, from Calais to Versailles.

Elizabeth Montagu, while finding French women "better informed than the English in general" since informed conversation was not banished "under the notion of pedantry," felt much the same as Bentley about her physical surroundings. "Tell me," she asked Bentley, "whether Paris had more the appearance of a city rising or falling into ruin?" Bentley thought the latter, which unsettled Josiah as he read Bentley's account, thinking the worse of a future market for his goods.

"Your remark that everything is either unfinished, or going into decay, might furnish much speculation," Josiah wrote back. "It seems to indicate great unsteadiness in the nation, & sudden transitions amongst the Great, from Riches to Poverty—from Court Favour to disgrace and obscurity."

Bentley agreed. "The causes," he said, "must be looked for in the char-acter and state of the nation. The French have very magnificent ideals, and it is their delight to be laying magnificent plans. They begin works with a degree of vigour and expense that exhausts both their patience and their finances. They are too lively, too volatile when they have been inter-rupted to return heartily to the same object. . . ." Clearly, both were preoc-cupied by the uncertainty of the future world order, which now swayed like a ship in a storm between opposed political and moral principles.

Bentley recorded his thoughts while watching Jean-Baptiste Pigalle finish his statue of Voltaire, depicted as a naked, frail old man. Though Bentley called it a "fine statue," public opinion was already deeming it an aesthetic failure. Was frailty symbolic of the failure of the eighty-two-year-old's Enlightenment philosophy? Was it symbolic of the failure to create a Panglossian world amounting to "the best of all possible worlds"?

Josiah and Bentley both hoped not. They wanted desperately to believe in their friend Benjamin Franklin's optimistic prediction about the possibilities of improving standards of living in the New World (embodied in Franklin's own rise to fame) and his belief that, owing to the wonders of science and medicine, all diseases, "even that of mortality," would be eliminated. They wanted to believe that Voltaire's own inspired writings promoting tolerance and individual rights still provided the clarion call for positive reform. But ideals, they knew, did not always spawn realities. Uncertainty about how the revolutions afoot would unfold unsettled people like Bentley, who placed so much faith in the theories of the great philosophers. A meeting with one of France's greatest philosophers and one of Bentley's heroes would stabilize his confidence in the future.

Bentley claimed that he was "not made of the stuff" to trouble a person of status without being summoned—very unlike Josiah, who would break in on any conversation in any home to sell his wares or his ideas. But once in Paris, Bentley could not resist the urge to climb uninvited to the fifth floor of a house in the rue Plâtrière, near the Palais-Royal gardens, and leave his card four times, in the hope of meeting one of his favorite authors, sixty-four-year-old Jean-Jacques Rousseau. On his fifth trip up the stairs on a rainy afternoon,

> my heart expanded with joy when Madame his spouse opened the door and desired us to walk in. I found this great philosopher writing or composing music in a small and very homely apartment, and his wife working by his side. He received us very civilly, but as soon as I observed to him that I had the pleasure of bringing some letters and books for him from Mr Day and Mr Williams which I had left a few days ago, I began to fear our conversation would not be very agreeable, not of long continuance . . .

Bentley had earlier delivered to Rousseau's home two publications by two of his friends from England: Thomas Day's 1773 antislavery poem, *The Dying Negro*, and David Williams's *Liturgy on the Universal Principles of Religion and Morality*. Both Day and Williams were part of the loose circle of friends linked to the teachers of the Warrington Academy and entrepreneurs like

Josiah, Boulton, and others, who occasionally participated in the meetings of the self-styled "Lunar Society," the moonlight gathering of like-minded men who privately discussed religion, politics, and science. Both were also founding members, along with Benjamin Franklin and Bentley, of the Margaret Street Chapel, the first Unitarian chapel in London, set up as "a society for a philosophical religion."

Williams, a translator of Voltaire and later the founder of the Royal Literary Fund, penned the liturgy to define and defend their mission to promote public worship, "a form of social worship in which all men may join who acknowledge the existence of a supreme intelligence and the universal obligations of morality." Bentley, who it is suspected co-wrote the *Liturgy* with Williams, thought Rousseau would appreciate their intentions. "Ah yes," said Rousseau, "that is a truly noble and respectable undertaking."

"And sir," said Bentley, "it is not an *idea* or *theory* only. Mr Williams has begun a Church and a course of lectures upon these principles."

"Why do you confine God within the walls of a house," asked Rousseau. "Would it not be better to worship him in the open air under the canopy of Heaven?"

"Not in England," replied Bentley, "it rains too often."

Rousseau smiled, saying it was a "very good answer."

Bentley had also thought that Rousseau would appreciate Day's poem, which was dedicated to Rousseau: a man who "prefers exile, poverty, and obscurity, to all the riches and the honors which ambitious meanness extorts from Kings." The poem cried out against the disgraceful actions of "Christian merchants," who were "annually reducing millions to a state of misery still more dreadful than death itself."

> ARM'D with thy sad last gift—the pow'r to die,
> Thy shafts, stern fortune, now I can defy;
> Thy dreadful mercy points at length the shore,
> Where all is peace, and men are slaves no more;
> —This weapon, ev'n in chains, the brave can wield,
> And vanquish'd, quit triumphantly the field:
> —Beneath such wrongs let pallid Christians live,
> Such they can perpetrate, and may forgive.

However, Day also logically extended his argument to condemn the hypocrisy of the American revolutionaries who were ostensibly fighting on moral principles of inalienable human rights. "Such is the inconsistency of mankind!" Day argued. "These are the men whose clamours for liberty and independence are heard across the Atlantic Ocean! Murmurings and rebellions are the first fruits of their gratitude. . . . Let the wild inconsistent claims of America prevail, when they shall be unmixed with the clank of chains and the groans of anguish. . . . But let her remember that it is in Britain alone that laws are equally favourable to liberty and humanity."

This was the passage that upset Rousseau. It was, he said, an "unjust reflection" upon the Americans, who "had not the less right to defend their liberties because they were obscure or unknown." Bentley learned that Rousseau thought it important at this time to support the American cause, now that "these Americans were able to defend themselves," in spite of the existence of slavery in the colony. The problem of slavery was a moral issue being confronted in the courts of law, Rousseau said, condemning Day for writing "upon subjects that he did not understand."

It was an awkward position for Bentley, who defended his friend's intentions while acknowledging that Day's heated poem was written when "he was something younger than he is now." But, to Bentley's great delight, he and the philosopher continued to converse for hours, discussing the meaning of virtue, goodness, and systems of education reminiscent of what Bentley learned when reading *Emile* years earlier, a system which friends of his actively adhered to when raising their own children. Listening to the author—the great philosopher—made a tremendous impression on Bentley.

As their conversation came to an end, Bentley was absorbed by the friendliness of Rousseau's expression and the earnestness of his manner. When Rousseau said that he would be glad to meet again, Bentley suddenly "felt very foolish." "Something was the matter with my eyes, that I could not very well see how I got through his little antechamber to the stairs, and I quite forgot to take leave of Madame Rousseau."

❧

Josiah, no doubt, shared Bentley's enthusiasm for his discussion with the renowned philosopher. When the two friends had first met fourteen years earlier, Rousseau's *Emile* had just been published and Bentley urged Josiah to read it, introducing him to the world of French philosophy. For years they had debated the concepts and tenets articulated therein; but now, weeks after the Americans asserted a new identity for themselves, the discussions seemed to bridge the gap between the ideal and the practical, the philosophy of reform and the fighting. Bentley's trip may have reached its high point, but it was not over, and he had more practical concerns to address.

Like Josiah's incognito approach to travelers to America when he was considering Cherokee clay, Bentley was discreet when dipping in and out of shops, taking notes, buying specimens, and scouting for casts that could be used for their own decorations. "Upon examination," he wrote, after stepping into a "plaster shop" one afternoon, "I found the things much worse than I expected; the honest man told me they were very good, but I spoiled them with looking at them through my glass. There are but very few *fine* things anywhere." At a shop in the rue Saint-Jacques, he spotted imitation Queen's ware which he learned was manufactured at Montereau, not far from Paris, on the road toward Auxerre, but it was no match for Wedgwood & Bentley's authentic wares. "The models and glaze in general are very indifferent, and the workmanship bad." One place he had to go before he left was France's premiere manufactory—Wedgwood & Bentley's Continental rival—the factory at Sèvres.

It was on the road to Versailles. Supported by the new king, Louis XVI, the few hundred employees worked in a "very magnificent building." "The workshops are very commodious and well fitted up, and there are several fine apartments left for his Majesty when he chooses to visit the manufactory." Bentley took notes on their "déjeuners," teapots, dessert services, terrines, and other table services.

> They have an *immense* number of ornamental vases, highly enriched with enamel and burnished gold; and amongst *several hundreds* there may be about *half a dozen* very elegant forms. All the rest are neither antique nor gothic, but barbarous beyond conception. I must particularly distinguish a *new kind of vases*, intended for some of the royal apartments at Versailles, of which I saw but one. This was in a pretty good form, but its style, if I may use that expression, was charming. White biscuit with bas-relief bays, ornamented and not overdone with burnished gold. These vases are from a few guineas to 50 guineas a piece.

He spied biscuit medallions and figures—one a bust of Voltaire, which Pigalle used to model the face for his own statue—marbled vases and miscellaneous pieces of ornamental and useful wares. He noted the workers' practices—painting, glazing, and pressing their molds. "They turn their plates upon a horizontal wheel," he commented, "very different from any I have seen in England."

He then pocketed his pigskin notebook and courteously bought a few small pieces to take back with him to England. He felt he had learned all he could from the French, which, he added in a condescending tone, was not much. As he looked around, he realized that they had more to worry about in England from French visitors than vice versa. English fashions, he realized, were a bit of a craze. "It is striking and rather flattering to an Englishman to see how fond they are of making almost every thing *à l'anglaise*," he wrote. Indeed, a number of manufactures advertised their wares as "façon de Angleterre" or "a la manière d'Angleterre." Perhaps Josiah was not as paranoid as he sometimes seemed when writing in secret codes and separating the content of his letters to Bentley.

When he got hold of the journal upon Bentley's return in September 1776, Josiah devoured its contents. He had reminded Bentley that among his amusements he must engage in "some useful pursuit," urging his partner to visit foreign ambassadors and take out advertisements for their wares in the papers (he ended up putting a notice in the *Gazette de France*). "I willingly refer myself to your journals," Josiah informed Bentley, "& our future conversations for the particulars of your Tour, as I would wish you to see, hear & memorand all you can, as well for pleasure, & entertainment, as utility." As soon as Bentley returned from Paris, the partners "discuss'd over a Pipe" the particulars of these useful pursuits.

27

A Poor Regiment

Smoking a pipe was, as Josiah exclaimed, "doubly sweet" when it meant face-to-face conversation with Bentley. Anticipating late-night talks about the French expedition, Josiah ordered no less than a crate of wine for himself and his partner—some, no doubt, reserved for Mary, but Sally, forty-two years old and eight months pregnant, probably desisted. This was the sort of indulgence that Josiah and Bentley, both now forty-six, relished. Bentley, with his curly brown hair descending further down the back of his head, had grown rounder about the waist than ever and was suffering from a near-crippling case of the gout. Josiah remained leaner, though his jowls were rounding out and his fingers were thick and coarse. The two partners still corresponded as quickly as the post could deliver their letters between London and Etruria, but with the business growing, there was too much to cover on two sides of parchment.

It was not just the business that was growing and expanding. Sally was about to give birth to their seventh child (including the departed Dicky). With five others tugging at his elbows, Josiah was finding it more tiring to carve out extra time for reading and writing after the workers left the factory and he snuffed out the candles in his laboratory. He had already resorted to writing "before our people are up," but, impressively, his days were as long as ever and as full of new ideas. "Nay, you need not make such a face of wonderment," Josiah said to Bentley, who was just promised some "*quite new*" bas-relief designs (on jasper ware). "I have many ideas & visions crowd in upon me, not only quicker than I can execute them, but faster than I can find time to lay them to rest a while in my Common Place Book."

But while Bentley was away, in the midst of what Josiah called his frantic "visions" of the future, all production suddenly looked as if it was going to ground to a halt. When he finally had time to contact Bentley, Josiah was relieved to be able to share his account of the new problems. Bentley, as usual, provided "a healing Balsam to my mind which is almost distracted & torn to pieces with the Men, & things about me here."

&

The cry "ere comes Owd Woodenleg" alerted the other workers of an imminent inspection of the wares, and it never failed to send a chill up their spines. Mr. Wedgwood emerged from his office, crossed a special bridge connecting it to the first of a line of workshops, and descended a staircase to the factory floor. Scrutinizing works in progress, he would sensationally smash with his stick any object that fell short of his standards, declaring: "This will not do for Josiah Wedgwood." "My name has made such a Scarecrow to them," he told Bentley, "that the poor fellows are frighten'd out of their wits."

He certainly believed in stern discipline; his workshops were run like a military regime. "It is *hard*," he once said, "but then it is *glorious* to conquer so great an Empire with raw, undisciplin'd recruits. What merit must a General have who atchieves such wonders under such disadvantageous circumstances." He was always looking for effective ways of instilling that longed-for discipline among his laborers. He posted "rules of conduct" on factory doors, banning alcohol, "obseen writing" on the walls, and gambling, and he made a spectacle of himself as the master who ruled with an iron hand, or at least a hard wooden cane. While his performance of smashing imperfect pieces had a powerful effect on his authoritarian status—something that rather took Josiah aback, since normally his workers were as willing to give as well as take—its purpose was not primarily to frighten them. All potters smashed up their trial and imperfect pieces, usually by throwing them into shard piles, to keep others from stealing free samples of new products. Josiah, probably impulsively, one day decided to break a piece down on the workshop floor, which turned heads.

Josiah's relationship with his workers went beyond supervising their craftsmanship. He took on apprentices and often had the responsibility of housing, feeding, and ensuring their well-being—which included looking after how the boys and girls developed into men and women. Journeymen, who were intended to develop an intimate role in the running of the business, found their moral conduct under scrutiny. The factory workers formed a close community. Many lived in Etruria Village, rows of neat houses that were now taking shape adjacent to the factory, where their children would grow up and where retired workers could live out the rest of their lives. Josiah's authority was underwritten by an industrial paternalism, wherein his role was to teach obedience, humility, sobriety, and right conduct.

What frustrated Josiah more than anything was his workers' transgressions. In the early 1770s, a senior employee named Ben Mather, who was hired as head clerk to oversee the London warehouses, was corrupting a younger employee, "taking & Keeping him out the Evenings," indulging in "Gallantries & evening rambles." Josiah immediately thought it time to "introduce new regulations," but worried that Mather might also be embezzling from them. "What avails all our industry & care," Josiah asked in aggravation, "if we must finally lodge all the fruits of it in the hands of unprincipled Boys & spendthrifts, who we see are debauching & ruining themselves, & perhaps half a score of their acquaintance at our expence." Josiah volunteered to Bentley that he would be willing to sacrifice some profit in exchange for "a more certain foundation" in the labor of their manufactory. Always committed to the principle of "improvement," Josiah rejected the idea of abruptly dismissing the wayward employee in favor of offering him help. "Charity may incline us to hope that after a little cool reflection & seeing the folly & danger of his past conduct, there is still some chance of his being reclaim'd," he told Bentley. "If he is immediately turn'd adrift, with the total loss of his character, he may probably be driven to a degree of desperation beyond any effort of amendment. He should have *some hope left him* that upon a change of conduct he may still be restor'd to the favour & confidence of his friends."

Hope for future improvement of moral, mental, and even physical health was, fundamentally, the impetus behind the rigorous growth of Wedgwood & Bentley's industry. Rooted in their devotion to Enlightenment theories of progress was the firm's Utopian belief that the money it made, which was reinvested in the business, would provide for the research and development of a better standard of living for those for whom it was responsible. According to this philosophy, conducting chemical research to eliminate lead from glazes, starting a school for the children of Etruria Village, and training the workers with new skills were all part of the panoply of responsibility of "enlightened" entrepreneurs. Essentially growing up without a father, and discouraged in his prospects by the remaining patriarch (his older brother) in his family as a boy, Josiah was determined to provide what he could for the community that he believed could also be improved, just as he had been.

But there was responsibility on both sides. The workers had to cultivate a resistance against the evils and vices in society. They had to learn a new way of life. "They seem to have got the notion," Josiah said after his workers began to live in their new houses, "that they are to do what they please." Part of their reform involved being trained in new ways of working, as well as living. When Etruria opened and Josiah had to recruit new labor, he faced the time-consuming task of training them to make wares that their apprenticeships elsewhere had not taught them how to do. Every new product that Josiah invented required new methods of production—successful jasper ware even required a new kind of kiln to fire it properly. The problem was, complained Josiah, "we have too many *fresh* hands to take in at once, though we have business enough for them, if they knew how, or would have patience to learn to do it, but they do not seem to relish the idea of a second apprenticeship."

This problem never went away. New levels of skill were developed with every experimental achievement. Standardization was crucial for product "quality assurance," as we would call it today. If the color of the wares varied—especially in an item of creamware, where the color was its most desirable aspect—his customers complained. Josiah himself had a difficult enough time with consistency, but to train all his workers to follow suit was a nightmare that needed a remedy.

"A *Waking notion* haunts me very much of late which is the beginning of a regular drawing, & modelling school to train up Artists for ourselves. I would pick up some likely Boys of about 12 years old & take them apprentice 'till they were twenty or twenty one & set them to drawing." He had a similar "scheme for taking Girls into paint," a crucial aspect of his skilled labor force that women excelled at, as they did with "flower dressing," a skill which a certain Mrs. Southwell, a regular visitor to Etruria, demonstrated to Josiah. "I am more & more in Love with her every time I see her," he declared, excited about having "such a Mistress in the Science of flower dressing" to share her talents with his women employees. Whatever resources he created for his workers, though, he needed some assurance that they would put the effort into learning new techniques.

Like any other forward-looking business, Wedgwood & Bentley's had to adapt rapidly to changing fashions to stay alive. Adaptation often required a new specialization in the workforce, a diversification of their skills. Techniques such as lathe operating, glaze mixing, slip casting, and firing at controlled temperatures had to be performed with that unwritten know-how that distinguishes the skilled from the novice, leading to more specialized workshops and a more particular division of labor. Since workers eventually did improve their skills and by extension the particular ware they were manufacturing, they naturally felt they should be rewarded with higher wages. This was what had led to Josiah's latest headache.

ॐ

Josiah was not averse to rewarding his workers as they grew more skilled, even doubling the pay of some from seven or eight shillings a week to fourteen or fifteen for finely executed designs; "improved in their *wages*," as he said, "as well as in their *workmanship*." On the other hand, he drove a hard bargain when he felt his hands were not performing to the mark, especially his painters, who—he had occasion to lament—"have shamefull prices & done shamefull work for it." This reflected a hierarchy amongst the arts, wherein painters customarily demanded more for their work, considering themselves elevated above cruder crafts.

But Josiah, like many other manufacturers, was cautious about the wages he would pay. At face value he could be accused of merely wanting to keep overheads down to maximize profit; this was not the case. He had no problem raising the prices of his wares to earn more, since the bill was paid by the rich, but he would not penalize the poor for profit. Nor did he fall in line with Arthur Young's assessment (repeated by numerous contemporary economists) that "everyone but an idiot knows that the lower classes must be kept poor or they will never be industrious." Rather, he worried about whether the workers recognized the value of money, about what *useful* ends it could be put to, instead of using their higher wages to undiscipline themselves by spending their pay in the pub. This caused resentment amongst workers, who considered it an intrusion on their lives—already uncomfortably regulated by bells and clocks at the factory. That was because Josiah (and, increasingly, other manufacturers) wanted workers to recognize the value of time, by which they were now paid rather than for piece-by-piece productivity.

"Expenses move on like clockwork," noted Josiah, wondering how he could create incentives for his workers, "& are much the same whether the quantity of goods be large or small . . ." Producing as much as possible in a given time was, of course, the desired effect, but expenses persisted regardless:

> Wages to Boys & Odd Men, Warehousemen & Book-keeper who are a kind of satellites to the Makers (Throwers, Turners, &c) is nearly the same whether we make 20 doz of Vases or 10 doz per week, & will therefore be a double expense upon the latter number. The same may be said in regard to most of the incidental expenses, Coals for the workshop fires (no small expense) which must be rather increas'd than diminish'd when the men are idle, in order to keep them warm.

One emerging economic theory that Josiah did appear to sympathize with was that pay itself was not a good incentive to work. In what later became known as "backward bending labour supply," economists reasoned that workers would do *less* work with more money, since they could attain the standard of living they wanted with less labor. Those "who can subsist on three days' work will be idle and drunken the remainder of the week," one government report on taxes read in 1764. "The poor in the manufacturing counties will never work any more time than is necessary to live and support their weekly debauches." Josiah's alternative incentive schemes provided the guarantee of a higher standard of living for his employees. If they remained in his employment, workers could have a home to live in, education for their children, and—a new idea at the time—a share of a collectivized plan of health insurance offering financial security for them or their family in the event of disease or death. It had a long way to go, but Josiah believed in progress. The workers were more difficult to persuade.

৯৯

On a Monday morning in mid-July 1776, just as Bentley was heading off to Paris, Josiah arrived at Etruria's front gate at half-past six in the morning to open the factory and found "all the Men at the Ornamental work were assembled to meet me." They wanted to expostulate about their wages, which at the end of the previous week Josiah had complained "were exorbitant & must be reduced." The men had brooded on this all weekend.

"They determin'd not to begin to work on Monday morning till they had settled this matter with me," arguing that they were doing their best work, that they "work'd late & early & could not work any lower &c &c." It was, Josiah coldly remembered, exactly like the complaint he heard repeatedly from the painters at their Chelsea workshops. Josiah talked to the workers for fifteen minutes, standing his ground, then losing his temper. "I told them we would *make a new sett of hands* which they must be sensible was in my power to do rather than submit to give such prices as must in the end ruin the Manufacture both to us, to themselves & their Children after them. . . ." He suggested that they return to work and he would review their wages and the prices of the products to see if anything could be done; but he made it clear that "if they meant to frighten me into their measures by assembling together in that way they were very much mistaken in their measures."

The workers shuffled but remained in front of him. One of the younger men, who "seem'd to take the lead for the rest, talk'd very pertly," demanding to know why, if the master was unhappy with his work and unwilling to reward him money, he was not dismissed from duty. "The reason," Josiah calmly stated, leaning forward, "was my hopes that he would, as he had often promis'd me, do better," but since the boy suggested he would rather leave his place than mend his work, Josiah gestured to the road. "This stopp'd his mouth," he reported, and prompted the others to go quietly about their work, "& there the matter rests at present." Josiah knew it was not yet settled.

≷➋

The tension at the factory worried Sally. She was concerned it might turn ugly, that the workers' restlessness might turn against Josiah or the managers. As the size of the workforce increased, it was harder for her to acquaint herself with all the employees, and reports of such events made the business feel strange—distant and somewhat dangerous. Her home, Etruria Hall, was only about 200 yards up the hill from the factory, but the work was drifting further from her mind. Listening to these latest incidents, Josiah noticed that "Mrs Wedgwood was not frightened at all," and that late September night, 1776, Josiah learned why.

"A little before 12 she talked of some pains which I thought it would not be in my power to remove, so I immediately sent for better assistance & amongst them they presented me with a fine Girl in her Cap &c before two." Sally was fine, and so was baby Sarah, the newest addition to Sally's own growing army of "Etruscans" whom she supervised.

PART IV
Wealth
1776–1795

28
Arrivistes

I n May 1777, the Trent & Mersey Canal was officially opened. Ninety-three miles of calm water now cut through the crags and chasms of the rugged Midlands landscape that had previously made travel and transportation of goods so difficult. The tunnels, locks, and associated works made it the greatest civil engineering work built in Britain. At a cost of more than £300,000, it was a crowning achievement for the industrializing world, in which Josiah took a small measure of personal pride.

Josiah had already taken the opportunity of enjoying "a very pleasant expedition" along the canal from Cheshire to Manchester, where the "Canal Duke" of Bridgewater was running two passage boats: "one carries Passangers at a shilling each—the other is divided into three Rooms & the rates are 2s 6d per head for the best Room, 18d & 12d & it is the pleasantest, & cheapest mode of traveling you can conceive." Now, as planned, the canal ran right through the heart of Etruria on its route south to Derby, where it met the Trent River. Josiah's sprawling factory, redbrick walls with large windows, was built only yards away, parallel to the bank of the canal, with a level, flagstone embankment where the warehouse men could wheel the crates of goods onto the long wooden boats. It was every bit as dramatic a transformation in the operation and appearance of manufacturing life as Josiah could have envisaged, the epitome of the reformation of life in what was now the industrial Midlands. John Wesley, who once commented on the small town on the top of a hill, did not recognize the place. "The whole face of this country has changed," he said, twenty years after his first visit. "The wilderness is literally become a fruit field.

Houses, villages, and towns have sprung up." Just as the landscape changed, however, so did the atmosphere. With factories and houses came more ovens, workshops, and "prodigious piles of coal burning to coke," as another traveler remarked of the nearby metalworks of Coalbrookdale, shocked by "the furnaces, the forges, and the other tremendous objects emitting fire and smoke to an immense extent, together with the intolerable stench of the sulphur," giving him the uncomfortable feeling "of being placed in an air pump." The sky no longer carried steel-colored clouds. It was now, as Josiah called it, "the Blacklands."

The Burslem potters struggling to make a living up the hill gazed down on Josiah Wedgwood's situation with envy, landlocked and unable—for lack of wealth to build and available land to build on—to follow his example and relocate along the canal. He stood alone as a symbol of the new order of things. He had eclipsed all other potters whose manufactories were only incrementally developing, falling well short of the scale of Etruria. Some potters were still proving strong—Josiah Spode, for instance. Whieldon's talented apprentice, who went off shortly after Josiah arrived as a partner, was one of the best amongst local competition; but with the war and the cost of keeping ahead of the fickle and ever-changing tastes of consumers, the broader level of competition was growing thin.

Now and then Josiah sympathetically reflected on the fate of his competition. After a quick trip to Cornwall in 1775 in search of Cornish kaolin, Josiah expressed his surprise that the potworks of a manufacturer named Nicholas Crisp, who had moved from London to Cornwall in order to manufacture porcelain, was "not in a more flourishing and improved state than we saw it," considering its prime location. Despite the apparent advantages, Crisp died almost penniless. "Poor Crisp haunts my imagination continually," Josiah told Bentley, as he was struggling to perfect his jasper ware. "Ever pursuing—just upon the point of overtaking—but never in possession of his favorite object. There are many good lessons in that poor Man's life, Labours & catastrophe if we schemers could profit by example." A similar example was presented in the debacle of Richard Champion, who engaged in expensive litigation to ensure his rights to the monopoly of the same clay when he bought Cookworthy's patent but failed to extend its life. "Poor Champion, you may have heard, is quite demolished," said Josiah, who was active in getting the court to quash Champion's application. "It was never likely to be otherwise," he continued, "as he had neither professional knowledge, sufficient capital, nor scarcely any real acquaintance with the materials he was working upon."

Without those three qualities—professional skills, money, and scientific knowledge—one was, Josiah was sure, doomed to fail in the modern world of industrial manufacturing. The symbol of success for the previous generation—Long John and cousin Thomas's Big House—was a remnant of a world already lost. It was, literally, a dying family craft. Cousin Thomas had passed away in 1776, after a whole life devoted to his and his brother's pottery. Following in his brother's footsteps, he finally married at the age of sixty-two, and died eleven years later without children. His gravestone in Burslem's St. John's churchyard is succinct: "Here lies the body of Thomas, brother of John Wedgwood."

Josiah knew that his place in history was already secured and that his name would mean much more than an association with the rest of the Wedgwood family. Each new product was, in a sense, a commemorative piece capturing the progress of the art of pottery for which he was responsible. "I have often wish'd," Josiah wrote back in 1774, "I had saved a single specimen of all the new articles I have made to be left as a sacred deposit for the use of our Children & Children's Children with some account of what *has* been done & what *may* be done, some *hints* & *seeds* for future discoveries, might perhaps be the most valuable treasure we can leave them." But as he hadn't, he was resolv'd "*to make a beginning.*" He wondered if there was something more he could do to tell the story of his accomplishments, something artistic. It would help set the record straight about who the real innovators were. And in 1777, one person was inundating Josiah with requests for a particular jasper portrait medallion, working to distort that record.

Paul Elers was the son of John Philip Elers, one of the two Dutch brothers who had made such an impact on Staffordshire pottery manufacture at the end of the seventeenth century. When he learned that Wedgwood & Bentley were producing portraits of "Illustrious Moderns" for those "in all the Courts & Countries of Europe to be immortalized," Elers thought it would be appropriate to have a portrait of his father produced. His father, he was sure, belonged to the illustrious moderns by virtue of the innovations he made in pottery—a particularly appropriate medium, therefore, in which to be portrayed.

Since his "friends are pretty numerous," Elers repeatedly wrote (*"beg[ged] without ceasing*," as Josiah said) asking for more and more copies of the portrait, suggesting some improvements, namely, an inscription engraved on the copper frame to read: *Johannes Philipus Elers—Plasticis Britannicae Inventor* ("Inventor of British Pottery").

"This inscription," an annoyed Josiah wrote, "conveys a falsehood, & therefore can do no honor to the memory of his father, who was not the *inventor* but the *improver* of the art of Pottery, or forming clay in Britain." Josiah then told Bentley the story of the Elers brothers, how they came to Burslem about eighty years earlier, having moved from London to Burslem because "Pottery was carried on there in a much larger way & in a much improved state than in any other part of Great Britain." When they arrived, they made a spectacle of themselves by glazing their wares with the use of salt, but Josiah was uncertain if even this was their own improvement. He asked Bentley to "obtain some intelligence amongst the Potters near London" to see if salt glaze was already being used there, or perhaps in Bristol.

The one "improvement introduc'd" by the Elers brothers that Josiah was prepared to acknowledge was "the refining of our red common clay, by sifting & making it into Tea & Coffee Ware in imitation of the Chinese Red Porcelain." But even here there is no mention of "invention," only "improvement," "refining," and "imitation." They were "ingenious," said Josiah, "but the sum total certainly does not amount to INVENTING THE ART OF POTTERY IN BRITAIN."

Bentley, as usual, suggested ways that Josiah could write to Paul Elers and delicately break the news that he was not prepared to assert such a claim in their portrait. But Josiah was determined to drop the issue altogether, particularly when Paul Elers kept suggesting that Wedgwood & Bentley could rise above producing "trifling trinkets" to manufacture "Bomb proof fortifications" and water pipes—"for London first & then for all the world."

Josiah did not spare much more time for the correspondence since his views about the history of pottery and its improvements were so completely different from Paul Elers's. But these irritations were funneled into creative energy. Josiah began to wonder just what the origin of pottery was, and whether he could represent it in his own way. He had an idea of the kind of story it would be.

∂

... Under the glowing light from a hanging lantern she watches as her lover sleeps, slumped in a chair, head and shoulder resting against the wall. He will soon be gone, off on a long and perilous journey to fight a war in foreign lands. The Greek maiden begins to trace her lover's shadow. His silhouette on the wall will preserve the moment. The woman's father, a potter in Corinth by the name of Dibutade, will use her drawing to model a clay relief, which he will bake in his furnace to create for her a ceramic memento.

This legend of the origin of painting and the invention of the art of modeling bas-relief sculpture was the basis of Joseph Wright's allegorical painting *The Corinthian Maid*. Josiah commissioned the painting from Wright in 1778, the year that a mutual friend of theirs, William Hayley, retold the story in his poem, *An Essay on Painting*. Josiah wanted it to depict the antique origins of his craft, and the progress he had made in that art. The painting helped illustrate to Wedgwood & Bentley's customers that his own pottery, decorated with bas-reliefs, was the aesthetic descendant of ancient attempts to preserve a precious memory.

Wright thought it was a good idea to include pieces of pottery "to mark her father's profession," and Josiah lent the painter some antique vases for him to copy, though he did wonder how his vases "could be supposed to exist in the infancy of the potter's art." But the painter made it a subtle allusion. In the corner of the ancient pottery stood an earthenware vessel, while in an adjacent room the embers in a fiery kiln glowed.

Wright was already well known for painting scenes of scientific experiments, philosophical lectures, and industrial work. Throughout the 1770s he had produced a series of paintings depicting progress in industrial and entrepreneurial pursuits—from new machines being used in *An Iron Forge* to hammer form into glowing galena to the oblique detail of skilled craftsmanship: the shiny buckles and buttons or the fine silk and lace-edged kerchiefs—items of mass production from the Midlands metalworks and textile mills—that were worn by well-to-do patrons of his art.

His paintings illuminated the dusty corners of workshops and the candlelit smiles of satisfaction on the faces of natural philosophers and inventors. Wright showed England's entrepreneurs at work, chasing their dreams of manufacturing a better Britain. And Wedgwood's choice of artist established Etruria among the triumphs of the new age.

The artist himself was an experimenter, a "mechanical genius," who tested different pigments and materials to render light sources and shadows more effective or dramatic—borrowing technical methods from studies of old masters such as Rembrandt to discover the secrets of their coloring. From a blacksmith illuminated by the white-hot metal on an anvil to a portrait of Richard Arkwright resting next to a model of his patented spinning frame, Wright captured the resourcefulness and versatility in pursuit of the Enlightenment, diminishing the sense of provincial insignificance for humble family manufacturers. His portraits showed that the world owed much to the lives of ordinary people outside the metropolis. He himself gained an international reputation as "Wright of Derby."

His art also told the story of the triumphs of the entrepreneurial and enquiring Enlightenment industrialists like Wedgwood. He masterfully used light sources in his paintings to reveal the moments when those who toil to uncover the secrets of nature strike upon an insight. Josiah was fond of these images, and he considered commissioning Wright for a painting that captured another of his triumphs—teaching his children to have a passion for science.

As the children grew older, Josiah gained new company in his coveted laboratory, where he still nightly conducted his experiments, and where "I can be instructing them, even by way of play & amusement, in the rudiments of chemistry & give them a turn to such studies, & enquiries as are most likely to be of use to them in their particular occupation." Josiah envisaged a portrait of his sons, the future talent of his trade, engrossed and enthralled by experimental enquiry. His oldest boy, twelve-year-old Jack, would be standing at a table conducting a chemical experiment, "mixing fixable air with the glass apparatus &c.; & his two brothers accompanying him." The youngest, seven-year-old Tom, would be "jumping up & clapping his hands in joy & surprise at seeing a stream of bubbles rise up just as Jack has put a little chalk to the acid." Nine-year-old Joss would be sitting "with the chemical dictionary before him in a thoughtful mood, which actions will be exactly descriptive of their respective natures."

The portrait of his sons would epitomize his motto that "everything comes from experiment," a philosophy that was shared by many of Josiah's friends—his collaborators in scientific experiment as well as his entrepreneurial competitors. It also represented a flair for the kind of work that would make the next generation of Wedgwood potters as successful as their father, or at least that was what Josiah hoped. He had a vision of the future for them that was very different from his own life as a child. "Jack," he predicted, "is to be settled as a gentleman farmer in some desirable situation, with as many acres for himself & his tenants to improve as I can spare him. Joss & Tom to be potters, & partners in trade. Tom to be the traveler, & negociater, & Joss the manufacturer." The children, however, were developing their own ideas.

In 1778, Sukey turned twelve years old and was developing into a "womanly, affectionate" daughter, with an excellent education which Josiah was soliciting help from all his friends to improve further. At seven she had been sent to a boarding school in Manchester, but returned home for a summer break so "full of pouks, & boils & humours" that Josiah took her immediately to the Buxton baths to recover. This was what happens "after sitting & sewing at school for 12 months," he spat, agreeing with Sally never to send her to such a place again.

Instead, it was to be home tutoring, with vetted teachers who would be better "than any common Boarding school Master." She spent the next few years learning music, drawing, and geography. She wrote plays with roles for her brothers and sisters, and she played her harpsichord while her sister Kitty sang (another scene that Josiah wanted captured in a painting). At times, Sukey stayed with the Bentleys in London, "who would support her mind" (Josiah was slightly worried about her "journalist" tendencies, thinking that this had led her cousin Byerley astray for so long) and enhance her character. "We know our dear Sukey to be a good & affectionate Girl," Josiah wrote, "and hope, nay are fully perswaded she will deserve this character as well from her Father & Mother Bentley, as she has done from her Father & Mother Wedgwood." Her younger sisters were looked after by a nurse whose "language & manners are very well, & she keeps the children in great order." Sally warmly welcomed the nurse, for keeping control of her Etruscans was getting more difficult than ever now that they had yet another new daughter. The previous August, in 1778, when forty-five years old, Sally had given birth to Mary Anne, their eighth—and last—child. (Always amazed at Sally's fortitude, Josiah described how, after preparing a pot of tea for the family, she "slipt upstairs just before supper," delivered the baby, then "eat [*sic*] her supper, went to sleep." It was all the proof anyone could need, said Josiah, of the "enlightn'd age" they lived in.)

Jack, the next oldest after Sukey, was also sent to boarding school (in Bolton), and showed his bookish interests, which inspired his younger brother Joss. "My dear boy," Josiah wrote to his eldest son when he first went off to school,

> Your brothers often talk of you & seldom omit drinking your health
> at dinner. Joss wants much to go to school with his brother Jackey,
> that he may learn to read & learn so many things out of books which
> he is very earnest to know, but finds there is no other way of gaining
> the knowledge he wants, but by becoming a scholar and reading &
> studying for himself. "Oh I wish I could take up the book, & read the
> story out myself, papa," he cries.

Like Sukey, however, Jack fell ill while at school and Josiah had to rush to Bolton to retrieve him. He was certain that the boy had had too much of what his friend Joseph Priestley referred to as "phlogisticated air" (hydrogen), which contained harmful acids when breathed in close quarters. "I am convince'd," stated Josiah, "that if they are confin'd again to school air, with school discipline, their healths & bodily strength must be diminish'd very considerably, if not totally lost."

While Jack was recovering under the medical advice of Erasmus Darwin, Josiah avowed that he would keep the boys home and have Tom Byerley "give them some lessons in latin, & for English, French, writing, accounts & drawing, we must make the best shift we can amongst ourselves. Riding, running & other bodily exercises make a considerable part of our schooling & entertainment." Josiah felt comfortable knowing that his children could receive proper attention to their minds, morals, and physical health (since, he noted, "their constitutions were not of the Herculean stamp").

Thinking about the future of his seven children, Josiah, in collaboration with Bentley, Darwin, and a new acquaintance introduced through Darwin—the educational writer Richard Edgeworth—developed a detailed plan for their education. Darwin was strongly supportive, as was Edgeworth, who had already asserted his decision to raise his own children on Rousseau's principles. But Darwin gave Josiah some advice about the content of their education, considering it "a very idle waste of time for any boys intended for trade to learn Latin, as they seldom learnt it to any tolerable degree of perfection, or retain'd what they learnt." Josiah was not so sure, even though he felt that modern translations of classical works were adequate for the job of gaining classical knowledge. Generally, the "Etruscan education" drew on more familiar resources. As he wrote to Bentley in November 1779,

> Before breakfast we read English together in the news paper, or any book we happen to have in the course of reading. We are now reading Ferbers travels [*Travels through Italy in 1771 and 1772*], with the globe and map before us. After breakfast they go & write an hour with Mr Swift & with this small portion of time, & writing their french exercises & entering some experiments which they make along with me: all of which I insist upon being written in a fair legible hand, they have improv'd more in writing in these few weeks here, than they did in the last twelve months in Bolton.

Jack, Joss, and Tom then went to stay at Darwin's house in Lichfield for a month, where he had hired a French prisoner to teach them French. "Your little boys are very good," Darwin reported to Josiah, "and learn French and drawing with avidity. . . . Josiah is a boy of great abilities and little Tom has much humour."

While they were away, Josiah took the opportunity to draw up a schedule which all his children, as well as Useful Tom's and the Willets' own children, could follow.

> Susan, John, Josiah, Thomas & Kitty Wedgwood.
> With three boys & a girl at our Mr. [Useful] T. Wedgwoods. . . . One days of schooling for our own five scholars.
> Rise at 7 in winter when I shall ring the school bell, & at 6 in summer.
> Dress & wash half an hour.
> The boys write with Mr. Swift one hour along with Mr T. Wedgwoods (if I approve of company) in some room fitted up for the purpose at the works.
> The little girls an English lesson with their nurse *in the school*, which happens to be a room near the nursery. I would instill an early habit of *going to school at stated times* in the youngest of our scholars as it

will make it so much easier to them by as much as it seems a necessary & connected part of the routine or business of the day. My young men are quite orderly in this respect since I let them know that it was indispensable, & they are very good in keeping my eleventh commandment—*Thou shall not be idle.*

Breakfast—as school boys.

From 9 to 10 French.

From 10 to 11 Drawing

From 11 to 1 Riding or other exercise which will include gardening—Fossiling, experimenting, &c &c.

Susan fills up these intervals with music besides her exercise.

From 1 to dinner at half past 1 washing &c in order to be decent at the table.

Half past 2 Latin one hour.

Then French one hour and conversation in the same, in the fields, garden or elsewhere as it may happen half an hour, to 5 O'Clock.

From 5 to 7 exercise, bagging, &c.

At 7 Accounts one hour—Supper, & to bed at 9.

The little lasses I had forgot they mist have two more English lessons in the school, & Kitty as much French as she can bear.

Josiah's twenty-year career of developing schedules to discipline his workers clearly rubbed off on his (rather unrealistic) plan of schooling—a kind of miniature factory for his miniature Etruscans. One difference, of course, was that they were not yet learning the tools of the trade: these were not apprentices. They were not regulated by a predetermined division of labor to train them with specialized skills; in fact, the opposite was true. Theirs was to be a rounded education, a *liberal* education, previously reserved only for the gentry and above. Josiah's children were the first generation of the entrepreneurial class to be able to afford and desire the gentrified education.

Josiah wanted another portrait to show this, and he commissioned George Stubbs to do it. Although Stubbs was an eminent painter of horses, he was becoming well known for depicting aristocratic families in leisurely rural settings with their horses, and for the last couple of years had started doing oil painting on ceramic plaques for Wedgwood & Bentley.

It was a large family portrait, four feet by five, on a wood panel (which Stubbs preferred to canvas). Josiah and Sally are shown sitting on a white wooden bench that encircled a mature tree on their lawn near Etruria Hall. Josiah, in a beige suit with an orange silk waistcoat, rests his arm on a small, round mahogany table with a black basalt vase on it. Sally is dressed in an elegant, flowing yellow silk dress, gesturing toward their seven children, the older four of whom are sitting on horseback. It is a graceful and tranquil portrait, and it takes an acute eye to spot the small puff of smoke in the background, distantly beyond Josiah's left shoulder, where a kiln is burning: a discreet allusion to the source of the wealth that had elevated the Wedgwoods to their gentrified lifestyle.

❧

Josiah's growing concern over his children's education throughout 1779 occurred at a transitional moment in his life. He was approaching his fiftieth birthday, when "a man is either a fool or a physician," he laughed to his friends. No, answered Darwin, "a fool is a man who never tried an experiment," and while Josiah was no physician, Darwin and all their mutual friends knew that Josiah was no fool.

Sadly, the person who had taught him his early experimental skills, his brother-in-law Reverend William Willets, had recently died. Josiah and Sally were relieved they were there to comfort Catherine, Josiah's beloved sister, who had been so encouraging and supportive of Josiah and Sally in their younger years. Catherine managed to look forward and, with Josiah's help, opened a milliner's shop in Newcastle. He had also recently heard that his last living brother, Richard, who had become a soldier in the Seven Years War, had died. Josiah never talked of him, but knew that his brother's death was the result "of a long course of drinking & irregular living."

At about the same time, Josiah's early partner, Thomas Whieldon, retired. With savings of about £10,000, he was nowhere near as wealthy and accomplished at the end of his career as Josiah already was, but he was comfortable in the Gothic estate he had built near his potworks. His wife had died seven years earlier, and Whieldon spent his time getting involved in local affairs, eventually becoming High Sheriff of Staffordshire.

Now Josiah was at an age and stage of his career where he could think about aspects of life aside from business. After years of neglecting the children to spend time in his workshop and laboratory, they were all old enough that he could look forward to "Fossiling, experimenting, &c &c" with them. For the first time he pursued a hobby. "In turning my back on the pottery," he said to Bentley, "I have got my face over a shell drawer, & find myself in imminent danger of becoming a connoisseur."

He enjoyed being outdoors, digging for fossils and shells with his children, but he longed for the time when, "retir'd from this bustling World," he and his dearest friend Bentley "will enjoy a few of those quiet hours which it has hitherto seem'd impossible for us to find," when they could read books and discuss all that had happened in their lives. Every summer for years Josiah encouraged Bentley to break up his routine and take an excursion into the country. "It is not good for man to continue too long in one place," he said, lest suddenly they find they have become "*an old man*, so take care of yourself, & run away in time, as I do often, & by that means intend to continue young a long time to come."

Tragically, Josiah soon learned that time was running away too fast.

29
Renewed Grief

The year 1780 began with great distress. "My dear affectionate father," as he referred to his father-in-law, Richard, passed away. His portrait, also painted by Stubbs, was just finished, and Josiah thought it "a very strong likeness." It depicted Richard as a frail man in an over-sized coat wearing a fine white wig. His face is lined and his eyes fading, but he possesses a faint, easy smile. At seventy-nine years old, he was complacent, even though his death was brought on by increasingly severe bouts of rheumatism.

Sally was upset, but comforted by the fact that her father had lived a successful and long life. Her sadness grew, however, when, shortly afterward, her uncle, Long John of the Big House, also died. She was now the only one left on her father's side of the family.

Many children attended the funerals—Long John had six children, Josiah and Sally seven, and Catherine Willets three. One of Catherine's daughters, Sukey's best friend Kitty, could not attend due to an increasingly severe case of consumption. Josiah called in Erasmus Darwin to examine the fourteen-year-old child, but Catherine's letters to her brother and sister-in-law painted a grim picture. If anything could upset Sally and Josiah more than the deaths that had already struck their family, it was these letters.

"Dr Darwin has bin here," Catherine wrote to Sally, who was in London with Josiah briefly visiting the Bentleys, "but did not say anything comfortable about her, indeed I was afraid to ask, my own fear suggested enough for me." For the past few days Kitty had been "seized with a violent spitting of blood," which the local surgeon, Mr. Bent, hoped would help turn the humors to her advantage, but her pulse remained extremely weak and low, and she was unable to rest without opium.

Opium was the only drug that Darwin had any confidence in, and he prescribed it as if there were no other options. "All the boasted nostrums only take up time," he declared, always warning others to look out for quacks, "& as the disease is often of a short duration they have gain'd credit which they do not deserve." But Kitty's illness unfortunately did not look as though it would be of a short duration.

"Her Breath is so very short & the Weather continues so bad she cannot get out" for some fresh air, Catherine reported a few days later. A bitter February fog had descended in the valley, crawling along the canal and enveloping the Willets' home. "She is now taking Dr Darwin's prescriptions twice a day." Opium, buttermilk, and chamomile tea was all she could consume, and she continued to spit up blood.

On Mr. Bent's advice, Josiah paid for a two-week treatment at a hospital in Norwich, where Kitty was wrapped in towels and soaked in cold water, which, as uncomfortable as it sounds, Catherine believed might have an agreeable effect on her daughter. After two weeks, however, Kitty was complaining of the soreness in her bones, and Catherine was heartbroken. In the carriage on the way back to Etruria, she cried in a letter to Josiah: "I am sure your ears are open to such & your Heart ready to relieve, I have suffered so much this fortnight at Norwich that it has made me quite low, I found my poor girl in such a low poor way so emaciated & altered that it shocked me & I never got over it." Kitty died before they reached home.

"I have this morning been mingling my tears with my family and friends," Josiah told Bentley. A young man named Caldwall who had been courting Kitty with the hopes of marrying her one day was there, mourning "with almost fantastic sorrow."

> I hoped to have been firm & not to have renewed their grief with my unavailing tears, but the attempt was vain, we yielded to nature and wept over the remembrance of our dear niece & the amiable dispositions of her mind to which we had fondly hoped for a longer date.

Sukey was equally devastated. "I scarcely ever saw her look worse, & am greatly afraid of a course of illness." Sukey, alas, was not the only of his daughters he was worried about.

❧

Two-year-old Mary Anne was suffering terribly. It had started a year earlier, when what Sally and Josiah assumed were teething difficulties since
several of her teeth were "pushing forward at the same time" brought on
convulsions that "lasted thirteen hours without intermission." This attack
was followed by more over the next few days, during which, one morning,
"we found she had lost the use of her arm & leg on one side."

Darwin was promptly called in and "order'd our little girl to be electri-
fied two or three times a day on the side affected, & to be continued for
some weeks." This was a new experimental practice. Theoretically, electric
currents were linked to the concept of "animal electricity"—a vital force
that animates the living—and to fire, reasoning that electricity was a "fluid"
form of fire which, as a vital element in the body, provided the heat in living
things. Though predating Galvani's famous invention of what became
known as the galvanic battery, medical researchers, particularly in France,
were already experimenting with electric currents, generated through the
use of an apparatus, such as the Ramsden hand-cranked plate electrical
machine, which was connected to Leyden jars—specially constructed canisters—that stored electric charge. When a thick conducting wire protruding
through a cork on the jar was brought into contact with a friction device, a
spark from static electricity was discharged.

Electrical experiments with affordable equipment became immensely
appealing to entrepreneurial culture—inventors and entertainers alike.
As many experimentalists discovered, lightning flashes were difficult phe-
nomena to analyze, but "drawing lightning from the clouds to a private
room," reproducing electric sparks on command, had stunned spectators.
In France, one doctor sent an electric shock through a lineup of 180 royal
guards, to Louis XV's amusement. But it also allowed experimentalists
to claim control over the hidden powers of nature. "The fable of
Prometheus is verify'd," proclaimed one to another self-styled "electrician," "what after this can mortals find difficult?" Electrical experiments
were largely what drove Benjamin Franklin to the sanguine conclusion a
decade earlier that "all diseases, even that of mortality," will be eliminated,
and why Priestley was so interested in writing a history of experimental
progress in this area. It is not surprising that Darwin, their mutual friend,

was one of the first to experiment with the use of electrical shock treatment in physiological disorders.

"I am the electrician upon these occasions," said Josiah, who was given some charged Leyden jars and instructed to run a current through the right side of Mary Anne's tiny body, treatment which "the Doctor gives us great hopes of our poor little girls limbs being restored." The electricity, they hoped, would not only restore movement but stimulate the growth of the limbs, preventing them from being shorter, which they believed could result from inactivity. Josiah also lanced her gums with the sharp end of an ivory modeling tool and kept them open, waiting for the teeth to appear.

"I am in great pain for my dear little girl," Josiah wrote, after two weeks of treatment. "She recovers very little use of her hand & leg, & is not quite clear of the spasms in the diseased hand & foot." Josiah could no longer bear to administer the electric shock treatment, and remained disconsolate. After a month, Mary Anne's condition grew worse. Opiates had no effect, and her "convulsions became so incessant, & so violent that we could scarcely hold her in the warm bath." One evening, Sally and Josiah were horrified to find that Mary Anne had gone completely motionless, could not speak, and "did not know any of us, but seem'd quite in a fright when we came near her." From this point on, a morbid pattern emerged. The baby suffered from convulsions, paralysis, slight recovery, then more convulsions. She would never much improve.

In late 1780, George Stubbs was nearing completion of the Wedgwood family portrait when Josiah wrote to Bentley asking him to find someone in London who could make a suitable frame for it. For the past few months, Josiah had been more prolific than usual in his barrage of letters to Bentley, relaying detailed reports of the "scenes of blood & carnage" that returning soldiers had witnessed in America, where battlefields had become "the grave of thousands & tens of thousands of our fellow-citizens." In the wake of this, he described at length the debates in Staffordshire over the controversial decision to raise a local militia, the sudden dissolution of Parliament, and the widespread Gordon Riots, the anti-Catholic riots that erupted following the passing of the Catholic Relief Act. His letters were long, but Bentley's were getting shorter.

5

...

Bentley had been complaining of headaches, recurring bouts of gout, and a persistent cold for weeks, but he managed to stay on top of business, writing succinct updates on the stock of wares and offering his usual encouragement for Josiah's latest design ideas for jasper ware. At the end of October 1780, Josiah was looking forward to a trip down to West London to see how well Bentley and Mary were settling into their new house near Chiswick. "As soon as I think [Stubb's] picture is finished, I will hie away to kiss your hand at Turnham Green," he wrote. He never received a reply.

30
"But Half Myself"

"Our poor friend yet breathes," Ralph Griffiths, their mutual friend and Bentley's neighbor, wrote to Josiah, "but alas! It is such breathing as promises but a short continuance. Almost every hope seems to have forsaken us! I dread the thought of what will be the content of my next."

Josiah was stunned. Nothing had given him any indication that Bentley's illness was so serious, nor, for that matter, was anyone prepared for the worst. Josiah departed on a wintry road for London immediately, arriving the next day, Sunday, 26 November, but he was too late. Bentley died at his home after collapsing from an "apoplectic seizure." His wife, Mary, and their friend Ralph Griffiths were at his side.

❧

Josiah had frequently expressed his deep affection for his friend and partner, letting him know how much his encouragement and sage advice meant to him. He was moved when Bentley expressed much the same. "I have not any friend," wrote Bentley,

> By whose side I have been accustomed to engage & conquer; & who had the same Energy that you constantly possess, when there is occasion for it, either to promote the public good, assist your Friends, or

support your own rights. I fancy I can do anything with your help, &
I have been so much used to it, that when you are not with me upon
these occasions I seem to have lost my right Arm.

Now, with Bentley gone, Josiah felt "but half myself."

Consolations poured forth from grief-stricken friends. "Our esteemed
friend," wrote Bentley's Liverpool partner, Samuel Boardman, "during the
short time he was with us, spent a happy and useful life. He has left us a
noble example of virtue and goodness which I hope will never be forgotten
in our actions, both in public and private life." Others were worried about
the severe effect this would have on Josiah. "Your letter communicating to
me the death of your friend," wrote Erasmus Darwin, "and I beg I may call
him mine, gives me very great concern; and a train of very melancholy ideas
succeeds in my mind. . . ." He recommended "exertion" to help dispossess
"the disagreeable ideas of our loss," and asked Josiah to read the consola-
tory letter the great Roman orator Cicero received from a friend upon his
daughter's death. It began:

> I was indeed as much grieved and distressed as I was bound to be,
> and looked upon it as a calamity in which I shared. For, if I had been
> at home, I should not have failed to be at your side, and should have
> made my sorrow plain to you face to face. That kind of consolation
> involves much distress and pain, because the relations and friends,
> whose part it is to offer it, are themselves overcome by an equal sor-
> row. They cannot attempt it without many tears, so that they seem to
> require consolation themselves rather than to be able to afford it to
> others. Still I have decided to set down briefly for your benefit such
> thoughts as have occurred to my mind, not because I suppose them
> to be unknown to you, but because your sorrow may perhaps hinder
> you from being so keenly alive to them.

Darwin hoped that Josiah would accept that he was not alone in his grief,
and that his friends were available to offer him much-needed support.
Darwin was especially sensible to loss since he was still experiencing difficulties coping with the death of his young son two years earlier. "Pray pass
a day or two with me at Lichfield," Darwin begged. "I want much to see
you." Indeed, Darwin's kind support drew the Darwin and Wedgwood
families closer together than ever.

❧

Thomas Bentley's death was, as Darwin exclaimed, "a public calamity." His role as the public face of Wedgwood & Bentley had gained him many friends and much attention from people of all backgrounds. A day after his death, the St James's Chronicle reported the news, stating that "For his uncommon ingenuity, for his fine taste in the arts, his amiable character in private life, and his ardent zeal for the prosperity of his country, he was justly admired, and will long be most seriously regretted by all who had the pleasure of knowing so excellent a character."

Sir Walter Scott, writing an account of the life of Bentley's niece, the novelist Ann Radcliffe (whose parents were Wedgwood & Bentley's Bath showroom managers), summed up the partnership: "Mr Wedgwood was the intelligent man of commerce, and the able chemist; Mr Bentley the man of more general literature and taste in the arts." It was a simplistic dichotomy, but it captured the essence of a well-balanced partnership that worked wonders.

Bentley's death meant that the business would shrink. Everything Josiah had done for the previous eleven years had been conducted with Bentley's advice and assistance. No one could simply step in and assume Bentley's role. Now, all that they had developed was reduced to a list of the current stock of ornamental wares that was being catalogued so that Mary could realize Bentley's share of the partnership which was bequeathed to her. Josiah decided the most prudent action was to sell the stock and divide the money accordingly. Over a thousand lots of items, ranging from cameos to intaglios, medallions, busts, and statues, were auctioned the next year at Christie & Ansell in Pall Mall, which raised over £2,000, and kept Mrs. Bentley's property "preserved from a considerable diminution." That was the official end of Wedgwood & Bentley.

After the sale, gossip spread speculation on the future of Wedgwood's pottery. Tom Byerley later explained that "a great many discriminating people were so captivated by [Bentley's] intelligence and animated conversation that they believed & propagated the opinion that he was the origin of all the fine works of taste & all which they saw exhibited in our rooms." Perhaps, they thought, with the educated and talented Bentley gone, the business would not survive.

Josiah, though sunk in spirits and in a state of depression not felt since the death of his brother John, was not concerned. He knew he had something ready that would answer the customers' expectations and "surprise the world" once again. In his last letter to Bentley he'd mentioned that he was "contriving some vases for bodies & bodies for vases," referring to his attempts to make ornamental vases with jasper. Despite the difficulties in forming vases with "the most delicately whimsical of any substance I ever engaged with," Josiah had succeeded shortly thereafter. It was too late, of course, for Bentley to see the ornamental item that would sell better than anything else Josiah Wedgwood produced.

Bentley was buried "in a new vault close to the west door of the added aisle" within the parish church of St. Nicholas at Chiswick. Josiah, Joseph Priestley, and two other friends wrote epitaphs for a marble plaque and passed their versions back and forth. When they decided on the inscription, they commissioned the Flemish sculptor Thomas Scheemakers (whose father had made the famous sculpture of William Shakespeare in Westminster Abbey) to carve a neoclassical marble mural and bust, above a plaque engraved by the famous architect James "Athenian" Stuart.

THOMAS BENTLEY,
Born at Scrapton in Derbyshire, January 1, 1730
He married Hannah Oates of Chesterfield in the year 1754,
Mary Stamford of Derby in the year 1772,
Who survived to mourn her loss.
He died November 26, 1780.
Blessed with an elevated and comprehensive understanding,
Informed in variety of science,
He possessed
A warm and brilliant imagination,
A pure and elegant taste.
His extensive abilities,
Guided by the most expanded philanthropy,
Were employed
In forming and executing plans for the public good.
He thought
With the freedom of a philosopher,
He acted
With the integrity of a virtuous citizen.

[295]

31
"A Storm Is Gathering"

After Bentley's death, Josiah had lost his reason to carve out extra time to write long, informed, and energetic letters. Those he did compose were not written with the same bold, clean, and confident penmanship that he'd proudly developed in his youth. His script began to look thin and unsteady, and his letters became empty. He himself suddenly looked tired and aged. In 1782, he commissioned two portraits from Sir Joshua Reynolds—one of Sally, one of himself. Both are distinguished, but somber. His eyes, black as the background, look forlornly into the distance, and he makes no effort to smile.

Thanks largely to Useful Tom's reliability, the business managed to maintain a steady output of useful wares, and Josiah took on Bentley's role of commissioning artists, such as John Flaxman the younger, to design new relief medallions and experiment with new ornamental styles. When Jack, his eldest son, turned fifteen in 1781, the boy began working at the factory, learning various aspects of production and accounting. The factory had twenty-two separate work stations, with skilled artisans supervising the work of each. Over the years, Josiah had invested in improved machinery and increased the number of engine lathes, throwing wheels, and grinding mills.

He himself still worked in his laboratory to improve the machinery and practices of production, wanting to promote efficiency and standardize production as well as possible. His latest pursuit was to perfect a method of accurately measuring the high temperatures in kilns. This had always been one of the most crucial, as well as elusive, aspects of the craft.

No thermometer existed that could withstand such extreme degrees of heat (above 1000°C.), so the regulation of a kiln's temperature depended upon the tacit knowledge of the "fireman," and his ability to observe the color and quantity of the coal.

Josiah was working on a solution with what he first called the "colour thermoscope." He believed that heat could be measured by the changes in the color of clay specimens during firing, and designed a glass tube with a graduated scale that could hold small clay pellets which, when fired at different temperatures, yielded colors from beige to dark brown. Josiah tried to calibrate this range of colors to a particular temperature of the oven. His interpretation of the oven's temperature was based on examining the color of the clay pellets.

He submitted a paper explaining his method to the Royal Society in December 1781, but the president of the society, Sir Joseph Banks, criticized the technique for the difficulties of distinguishing different shades of color and the loose correlation to particular degrees of heat. Josiah was not discouraged. He returned to his laboratory, sought help from Priestley, James Watt, and others, and after many trials and experiments, invented a new measuring device, which he called the "pyrometer." It consisted of a porcelain gauge of his own construction which held specifically sized clay pellets that shrank during firing according to the degree of heat passing through them, a correlation that yielded acceptably consistent results.

In May 1782, Josiah submitted a revised paper to the society describing his new invention. This time, Banks, who praised Josiah for having "turned the art of Pottery into a Science," accepted its scientific conclusions, and almost exactly on his fifty-second birthday, Josiah was elected a Fellow of the Royal Society. It was the most prestigious appointment of his life—a perfect reward for a career committed to the scientific improvement of his craft, and his enduring quest to discover through experimentation the hidden principles of nature.

Josiah felt honored by this appointment, not least because he found in Sir Joseph Banks a new friend and patron who sent Josiah samples of earth he had collected during his travels with Captain Cook. But he was equally pleased to have come up with a device that further mechanized production. Anything to remove the unreliability of human judgment— any way of transferring skill from person to machine—was beneficial in the eyes of the master. The workers, however, feeling that their jobs were at risk with each technological improvement, reacted differently to such innovations.

೭&

On a chilled October morning in 1779, "a most riotous and outrageous Mob" gathered outside Richard Arkwright's Lancashire cotton mill, "armed in a warlike Manner," according to a witness who testified in front of Parliament. They broke down the doors of the workshops and stormed in, smashing new spinning machines and retreating after torching the buildings. They left to hunt down and destroy other manufactories.

Josiah happened to be in Lancashire at precisely this time. From Bolton, just northwest of Manchester, he heard the distant beating of a drum leading the march of, he was told, a force of rioters now eight thousand strong. They had spent the last few days gathering more firearms and ammunition, "melting their pewter dishes into bullets." Already there was blood shed. During an attack on another mill, near the town of Chorley, "two of the mob were shot dead upon the spot, one drown'd, & several wounded." Reinforcements from the militia in Liverpool and Yorkshire were being called in, but one factory owner, Sir Richard Clayton, attempted to defend his property with fifty hired men. They were no match, and were forced to watch "whilst the mob completely destroy'd a set of mills valued at £10,000." This was a determined mob, barreling down the road just behind Josiah as he hurried back to Etruria. Their "profess'd design," he learned, "was to take Bolton, Manchester & Stockport in their way to Crumford, & to destroy all the engines, not only in these places, but throughout all England."

The agitation was worsened since trade was already hurt in consequence of the war with America, and the local landowners—it was alleged in a later newspaper report—may have been slow to come to the defense of the manufacturers since they feared that the poor rates would be burdened with unemployed workers displaced by new inventions. In despair, the laborers assembled to destroy the machines that caused them distress.

The government demanded answers as to what was happening and set up a parliamentary committee to weigh the arguments of the workers and industrialists. The industrialists won, arguing that the economic advantages not only benefited the state but would in turn benefit the workers, since machinery helped expand the trade, ultimately offering more jobs to those willing to operate the machines. But this was precisely what had motivated Wedgwood's workers to strike. They may have been promised employment, but—the workers were beginning to feel—it was unskilled, and therefore dispensable, work.

The all-round worker, once trained to see the process through from clod of earth to packaged product, was rapidly becoming an extinct ancestor of the specialized worker occupying a particular spot in the division of labor on which modern business was built. Far from being knowledgeable of all aspects of the line of production, the laborers had been deliberately isolated in their tastes, making them less likely to relinquish secrets for bribes.

It was because factories were becoming mechanized that visitors were strictly limited in what they were allowed to see of the secret operations inside. While ever conscientious about protecting his trade secrets—especially surrounding the scientific formula of jasper—Josiah occasionally dropped his guard. Not long after finalizing its composition, he sent jasper portrait medallions to the portrait modeler Joachim Smith, who had associations with William Duesbury, owner of the Derby porcelain works and the person Josiah felt was the biggest threat to the future success of jasper. How much, Josiah wondered, had Smith "learnt from seeing our things, & the free conversation we have had with him upon these subjects." And how much, he shuddered to think, was he telling Duesbury.

Suspicions were further aroused when, weeks later, "a Man from the Derby China works" visited Etruria, ostensibly seeking employment, though Josiah was sure that he was "sent to learn something from us." His application was denied, and it became a matter of policy to direct the gaze of all visitors to designated areas. This frustrated the gentry, who had previously enjoyed their freedom to see the ingenious processes at work, and gave some commentators even more cause to be suspicious of the origins of new wealth. Everything is "wrapped up in mysterious darkness," complained Pastor Frederick Wendeborn, when later writing his *View of England* (1791), "and I have been told, that even not all the directors themselves are admitted behind the curtain, or shewn the Caves of Plutus, where the treasures of the Company are deposited." What were they hiding? What was so special about a machine, an engine, or any mechanical contrivance, such visitors wondered, not yet grasping that these were no mere nut and bolt items of furniture but devices with previously unconceived capabilities to harness the hidden powers of nature. Others, of course, knew well that there was something special going on behind closed doors. "We have had several foreigners here lately," said Josiah, "& most of them extremely anxious after the composition of the black of which we make our vases & busts, & quite hurt & disappointed when they are told we do not shew that part of the manufactory."

Workers meanwhile had their own reasons for being "delusioned" (as Josiah put it) in thinking that there was a conspiracy against them. By some accounts, it might appear that they were correct, at least in the ways that their civil liberties or freedom to move in the labor marketplace were being manipulated to protect industrial trade. The General Chamber of Commerce even advocated legislation to prevent the emigration of skilled workers who might be enticed by promises of a better life, in terms of wages and working conditions. This too concerned Josiah, who, following another bout of riots—this time at his doorstep in Etruria—in 1783 issued an *Address to the Workers in the Pottery on the Subject of Entering into the Service of Foreign Manufacturers*.

Lest anyone contemplate emigrating, enticed by seductive stories of life abroad, Josiah felt compelled to inform them of the terrible consequences that fell upon others. Consider John Bartham, the young potter who left Staffordshire to set up his own factory in South Carolina. He spent three months sailing the rough seas to America, arriving debilitated and capable only of watching his men fall sick and die around him. Because of the weather and climate, Josiah stated (following a medical theory expressed by the physician John Arbuthnot among others) that Englishmen were inevitably led to "a disease of the mind, peculiar to people in a strange land; a kind of heart sickness and despair, with an unspeakable longing after their native country." That there was money to be made was a phantom of the imagination; most workers were left in strange foreign lands facing the "hard necessity of begging in the streets."

Contrast this to life in Staffordshire, "a land truly *flowing with milk and honey*." Life was rapidly improving, thanks to the new factory system. "Ask your parents for a description of the country we inhabit when they first knew it," urged Josiah. "Their houses were miserable huts; the lands poorly cultivated and yielded little value for the food of man or beast..." Today, look at the change. "The workmen earning nearly double their former wages—their houses mostly new and comfortable"—an especially celebratory point since he himself built a model community for his employees. What could be the cause of complaint, considering that

"Industry has been the parent of this happy change—A well directed and long continued series of industrious exertions"? Of course, it was no gentrified life, as Wedgwood's was becoming; the employees could never afford to purchase one of Wedgwood's wares, they could only make them, contributing to their sense of alienation. But things were getting better. Couldn't they *see* what was happening? Josiah wondered.

Not everybody needed convincing that the industrial landscape was bearing healthy fruit; one visitor even wrote to Josiah praising Etruria as "that paradise." Perhaps overstated, but it was not far from the vision that Josiah himself was pursuing. Like many of his Enlightened friends—industrialists, doctors, or natural philosophers—he believed that society was inestimably improvable, maybe even "perfectable."

That was a sentiment that found expression in American republicanism after securing independence, which translated into what was called "republican technology," with people including Thomas Jefferson and Franklin insisting upon the interrelationship of freedom, industriousness, and virtue. The revolutions—political, scientific, and industrial—were fundamentally transforming the world into that Utopian future they had so passionately dreamed of decades earlier, when Josiah, Bentley, Priestley, Franklin, and all the others first set out on their journey of hope and glory.

It remained a vision that Josiah was willing to articulate, but privately he was growing despondent about the bright future he once dreamed of. For all the success, wealth, and expansion of the factory, it was evident that the specter of disease still haunted the hills. "Potter's rot" (silicosis) remained the principal cause of death amongst the workers, a sign that the air was contaminated with evil particles—whether from rubbing mold lines off dry figures, smashing imperfect wares, grinding flint and lead, or breathing in the thick atmosphere of coal smoke.

Josiah had hoped that Priestley's pioneering experiments on air might provide a remedy. In Priestley's *Experiments and Observations on Air* (1782)—experiments that followed on from his discovery of the difference between different atmospheric gases, leading to the isolation (or "discovery") of oxygen in 1776—he announced that he could manufacture air that could be purified in such a way as to "prepare it for respiration." Erasmus Darwin, who had been following Priestley's experiments with much interest, had begun his own course of experiments with air, looking for ways it might be used as an antiseptic for the lungs to cure diseases (including consumption and potter's rot) and was soon prescribing "6 gallons of pure oxygene a day" to his consumptive patients.

When Josiah read Priestley's book, it started him thinking. "May not Dr Priestley's experiments of producing pure air be applied to the improving or changing of the air of sick rooms or hospitals?" he wondered? It was easy to imagine all the other places that would benefit from having pure air pumped into them: schoolrooms came to mind, as well as ships and factories. He even asked Priestley for the estimated cost of supplying air to Etruria, but they were stumped on the design for such an apparatus. One solution Priestley devised was to impregnate water with "fixed air," creating carbonated water which he offered to the Royal Navy as a probable cure for scurvy (an idea that soon caught the attention of a Swiss gentleman named Jacob Schweppe).

The "aerial solution" to atmospheric pollution was an idea in gestation that would be pursued for the next decade. In the meantime, Josiah had to assure his workers that things *would* get better, and they had to rely on their "sick club," the scheme by which workers "lay by a little money whilst they are in health & can spare it, & receive it again in time of sickness," something Josiah had occasion to see in operation at Matthew Boulton's factory, as well as in "Female Clubs" when earlier traveling in Cornwall.

Once again, the worried and unsettled laborers returned to their work. Shortly afterward, however, the shortcomings of science and medicine dealt another blow to Sally and Josiah's faith in the "perfectibility" of the world. After enduring emotionally taxing trials of electrocution and years of opium consumption to help ease her repeated fits—the result of a mental imbalance she appears to have been born with—seven-year-old Mary Anne was very ill with a deep fever. On 4 April 1786, Sally and Josiah called in Dr. Darwin, but even he seems to have been at a loss to determine what to do with the girl. "If the ague does not weaken her very much," he said, "I should give her no medicine at all (not even a vomit), except she wants some natural evacuation, a stool daily. If it should continue a month I should then advise to put an issue in the thigh of the affected side." The ague did continue, but Mary Anne did not last a month. She died on 21 April 1786.

Sally and Sukey took it harder than Josiah, who was growing stoical about death. He spent no time grieving, preferring instead to return to his workshop, where he would engage in one last project.

32
"Some Plan of Life"

On the Frascati Road, a short distance from Rome, was a tumulus known as Monte del Grano. Inside the mound was a secret sepulcher, leading to three chambers above. In the largest of these was a sarcophagus, carved with groups of warriors and horses, and an inscription dedicated to the memory of Emperor Alexander Severus and his mother, Julia Mamaea, both of whom met their death during a revolt led by Maximinus the Thracian in A.D. 235. The sixteenth-century antiquary who discovered the sarcophagus pried it open and found what looked like a cinerary urn, with a decoration in relief portraying the young emperor and his mother.

This was one story in the history of the vase that ended up in the library of Cardinal Francesco Barberini, nephew of Pope Urban VIII. It appeared to be black, but when held up against the sun was shown to be a translucent dark blue, leading people to believe that it was carved from onyx. It was not large—less than ten inches high and seven inches wide—but its mysterious history and qualities made the "Barberini Vase" a much-desired object when it was put on sale by the Princess of Palestrina in 1780. She was in need of money to pay off her gambling debts.

The vase was purchased by James Byers, a Scottish dealer in antiquities who had lived in Rome for forty years, and who knew Sir William Hamilton well. When Sir William saw the vase in Byers's collection in 1783, the inveterate collector was awestruck. "Is it yours," he asked, "will you sell it?" Byers agreed to do so, but would only accept the staggering sum of £1,000, which Sir William promptly paid, "tho' God knows it was not very convenient at that Moment."

Shortage of money meant that Sir William rather suffered from his brazen decision to pay out such an extravagant sum for the vase, which he quickly sent to his niece, Mary Hamilton, in London for her to sell on his behalf. As a former lady-in-waiting to Queen Charlotte, she was well placed to find a rich buyer, and interest in the vase was virtually immediate. It started with the queen, who desired to see the vase but made no overtures to purchase it. Another regular visitor to court, however, the Duchess of Portland, was captivated. Through her extensive European travels, she had formed her own museum of natural history specimens, rare manuscripts, and medals. Looking to add some Etruscan vases, she had already bought a number of treasures from Sir William, but the Barberini Vase would be the centerpiece to her cabinet. He offered it to her along with two other items: "the Vase, the Head of Jupiter & my Picture of Correggio are the cream of all the Virtu I have ever possessed in my life," he said, asking £4,000 for the lot. At the beginning of 1784, the duchess snapped it up.

Alas, she did not have long to enjoy it. After her death in 1785, her estate, including her precious cabinet of curiosities, was sold at auction. Given Sir William's opinion that "I do not believe that there are any monuments of Antiquity existing that were executed by so great an artist," it is not surprising that the vase caught the attention of London artists, such as John Flaxman, who then brought it to Josiah's attention. "I wish you may soon come down to see William Hamilton's Vase," Flaxman wrote to Josiah in February 1784, for whom he had been doing some work; "it is the finest production of Art that has been brought to England and seems to be the very apex of perfection to which you are endeavouring to bring your bisque & jasper. . . ." That was enough to stimulate Josiah's creativity and prompt him to strive one last time to replicate a unique piece of history.

Josiah was not the only person interested in the vase. The duchess's son, the third Duke of Portland, had an agent at the auction and was determined to get it, but found a way to ward off any competition from Wedgwood. He offered Josiah the loan of the vase for study and copying so long as he did not bid at the auction. That Josiah was wealthy enough to threaten to outbid a duke on an item of antiquity is remarkable testimony to his success. But Josiah was not committed to owning the piece, and probably agreed that it was only fair it should be kept in the duchess's family. His principal interest was to imitate it. For that he only needed the vase for a relatively short period of time, and was happy to receive it on loan as agreed in June 1786.

"I begin to count how many different ways the vase itself may be copied to suit the tastes, the wants & the purses of different purchasers," Josiah wrote, wasting no time in devising a scheme for reproduction. Like other unique and challenging pieces—whether Queen Charlotte's first order of creamware or Catherine the Great's "Green Frog Service"—he knew that reproducing what he now called the "Portland Vase" would be time-consuming and expensive. He had already hired a modeler named Henry Webber, who according to Sir Joshua Reynolds was "esteemed the first in his profession in England," but it would take a team of modelers, engravers, mold makers, and other artists to make the fine white bas-relief figures and patterns that were to decorate the vase.

Josiah estimated a cost of no less than £5,000 for all the "best artists capable of the work," if they cared to spend the time mastering the techniques involved. He had repeatedly mentioned how difficult jasper was to work with—how delicate the wet clay was when worked thinly to imitate Chinese porcelain—but jasper had "a property peculiar to itself," he noted, "which fits it perfectly for this imitation," since the dark blue, translucent effect could be attained in the same way as his popular light blue jasper ware, the tint darkened merely by the amount of cobalt used in its production.

Josiah had already tried his hand at imitation by copying from an engraving, "but now that I can indulge myself with full and repeated examinations of the original work itself, my crest is much fallen." He confessed his initial shortcomings to Sir William, from whom he sought some "advice & directions" on his plan. The more Josiah studied the vase, the more he found that "the form . . . is not so elegant as it might be made." It seemed the vase's primary feature was its bas-relief decoration, and he speculated that there were two artists involved with the original: the talented sculptor, who carved the precious white figures; and "another artist, of an inferior class," who seemed to have difficulty working with the material from which the vase was made, which many thought was enamel.

Would it, he wondered, be appropriate to render the vase more elegant—more simple and true to the principles of ancient beauty as propagated by Sir William and other virtuosi? In essence, would it be acceptable to *improve* on a celebrated piece of ancient art?

Sir William thought not. "I admire your Enthusiasm on the frequent & close examination of the Vase," he wrote to Josiah, "& am happy that its superior merit is felt by some few in England." However, while he conceded that there were some "little defects" in the production of the original vase, "it would be dangerous to touch that," he said, preferring to see an exact copy of the vase to help "diffuse the seeds of good taste." Josiah gracefully accepted the advice, and set to work on the long process of exact reproduction.

Working on the Portland Vase gave Josiah the perfect opportunity to introduce Joss, now nineteen and working at Etruria, to the different stages of high-end manufacturing—to teach him that innovative skills are developed slowly through trial and error. Jack was in Europe, on a Grand Tour under the supervision of Henry Webber and John Flaxman. Josiah hoped his oldest son would benefit from being in Italy and immersing himself in its artistic culture in order to polish his liberal education and give him the chance to "fix ultimately upon some plan of life." Josiah had sent Webber and Flaxman with him, not only to supervise the boy, but to explore the possibility of setting up an artists' studio there.

Fifteen-year-old Tom was studying at the University of Edinburgh, long a haven for wealthy Dissenters, where Josiah wanted him to receive the best scientific education available. Erasmus Darwin had sent his son, Robert, to medical school there three years earlier, before pulling strings and enrolling him at the more prestigious University of Leiden where he received his M.D. Since Josiah did not seek to manipulate his sons' future as much as his good friend Erasmus, Tom was easily distracted at Edinburgh. Taking after his father, he was enthusiastic about joining the newly founded Philological Society, "in which I must exert all my oratory powers." And as Josiah predicted, Tom pursued experimental science with enthusiasm. "I wish to have some chemical books," Tom wrote to his father at the end of 1786, "& want only a list of what we have at home &

permission to buy others. I think I shall be able with a good deal of reading improve myself greatly in this Science." But Tom did a little bit of
everything. He stayed after class and discussed medicine with the popular
professor Joseph Black, and learned geology from the famous natural historian James Hutton. When Tom returned to Etruria, Josiah hired the
brilliant young Edinburgh mathematician John Leslie as the boy's private
tutor in natural philosophy. It was an indulgence that Josiah hoped would
begin to turn Tom to productive habits.

Sukey was now twenty-one years old, a woman of charm and beauty.
She took after her mother in her interest in politics and literature, and
like her father had a talent for thoughtful provocation in her letters. By
1786, she was traveling down to London to socialize with the *ton*, at one
point teasing her father about drawing-room gossip regarding her family's
religious and political principles. They "cannot be right," Sukey wrote, "or
you would not be acquainted with such a man as—as—Dr Darwin—as for
her Ladyship [Lady Clive, her hostess], she would rather die than have his
advice if there was no another physician in the world."

Catherine and Sarah, the youngest two daughters, were just turning
twelve and ten, respectively, and were following in their older sister's
footsteps, being educated at Etruria and spending all their time with Sally
and a dozen servants, from butler to maids to a coachman. After an
expansion in 1780, when a symmetrical north and south wing were added
to their home, Etruria Hall was, as William Wilberforce (a visitor with
whom Josiah shared a disgust for slavery) said, "rather grand, Pictures,
&c." The paintings were by Reynolds, Wright, and Stubbs; an elaborate
allegorical subject was painted on a salon ceiling by Flaxman, and carved
chimneypieces were inset with Josiah's own fine jasper tablets. In decor
alone, it was certainly grand, and intriguingly, everything had a connection with the business.

Josiah and Joss spent much of their time throughout the next year in
the workshops and the laboratory. It was the most intimately Josiah had
worked with anyone since Sally took notes for him when they were first
married. They were struggling to get their imitation of the Portland Vase
just right—to get the precise shade of dark blue, to prevent the thinly
thrown vase from collapsing or blistering in the intense heat of the kiln.
As Josiah had anticipated, it was frustratingly difficult, and the long hours
soon exhausted him.

ও৶

"My great work is the Portland Vase," Josiah stubbornly insisted, wanting to put off the second stage of a prescription that the eminent London physician William Heberden gave him in answer to Josiah's complaint about a pain in his head and "a general weakness." He had already been blistered and sent to "rest" in London, where he and Sally managed to find some time alone in the apartment above the Greek Street showroom, now under Tom Byerley's management. But he finally conceded that he had to leave the finishing touches to Joss, who wrote regular updates on his progress and the daily maintenance of Etruria.

Never at rest, Josiah took the opportunity while in London to contemplate the best method to publicize the vase. He thought about ways he could use its fascinating history to his advantage. He decided that he should start collecting "all the explications of this vase that have hitherto been published, which I mean to print and deliver with the copies of the vase, that the purchaser may see the whole that has been said upon it, in a small compass." Calling on all his literary and antiquarian connections to help, he began reading through any reference work he could lay his hands on, searching for anything "that I can find quoted or containing any mention of it," taking notes on d'Hancarville's *Collection of Etruscan, Greek, and Roman Antiquities*, Montfaucon's *L'Antiquité expliquée* (which Joss transcribed for him), Caylus's *Recueil d'antiquités*, and others. In a letter to Sir William Hamilton, he listed twenty sources he had already consulted, hoping that Sir William might suggest some yet unknown to him, especially to inform the debate over the fable represented in relief on the vase. Josiah was preparing a lesson in classical antiquity for the enlightenment of his aristocratic—classically Oxbridge-trained—customers.

In his letter, Josiah also took the opportunity to thank Sir William for receiving Jack when he arrived in Naples. The Grand Tour had much impressed Jack, who collected some busts from Sir William's collection that he sent home to Etruria; he was indeed beginning to "fix ultimately upon some plan of life," but it was not quite what Josiah anticipated. In 1788, Jack wrote to his father declaring his intention to stand for Parliament, "unconnected with any party." Josiah sighed. Of his three sons, he had hoped that Jack, as the eldest, would "take some time to consider your own inclination before you gave your final determination," namely, to forego entering the family trade; but Jack's "aversion to the business" remained.

Josiah, irritated but careful not to lose his temper, was hoping that Jack's return from the Continent would change his disposition, "as I believed the ideas upon which that aversion was founded were taken up in your travels. . . ." It was one of many ironies in these latter days of Josiah's career that travel, which stimulated the interest in the products that made Josiah rich, was what quashed his eldest son's interest in taking over the business. By coincidence, the same month that Jack expressed his apathy toward the business, Josiah had to reach a decision about "the proposed scheme of Tom going to Rome." Josiah was beginning to worry that Tom was restless and had no "plan of life." Having received Henry Webber's opinion that "the degree of knowledge he has acquired of the arts . . . has not yet a sufficient stock to be exported to Rome," Josiah decided it was best to keep the boy under closer supervision, which sent nineteen-year-old Tom into a petulant fit. Even more worrying for Josiah was that the only son who was showing an interest in pottery was changing his tune as well.

Joss was making progress on the Portland Vase, reporting on each new attempt as it came out the kiln, and writing some critical comments about how the modelers "undercut" the molds for the pattern. Josiah was impressed with his son's developing skills. He had recently received a flowerpot that Joss had produced entirely on his own and that Josiah thought was "very well executed & a very good thing. . . . These two articles do you credit as a potter, & will help you to gain our confidence on future orders." Josiah studied the details of the piece—the application of the gilt, the shape of the handles, the form of the pot's feet. "Such little touches and finishings shew the master in works of art," he said to Joss, "as minute attentions in behaviour shew the well bred man & polite gentleman." The problem was, Joss preferred the life of a polite gentleman to that of a master artist.

Like Tom, Joss wanted to travel, to be a gentleman engaged in pleasures of the imagination rather than the agent on business Josiah hoped he would become. When Tom Byerley fell ill and Josiah asked Joss to stand in, he agreed, then worried that his father might misinterpret his commitment. "What I mean," Joss said to his father, "is that I would live in the house and take care of the correspondence while Mr B is unfit for it, and do what other business I could, except attending in the rooms any farther than waiting upon some particular people." The last thing Joss wanted was to be seen working behind a shop counter. "I have been too long in the habit of looking upon myself as the equal of everybody to bear the haughty manners of those who come into the shop," he explained.

This disappointed Josiah, especially at a moment when the family had received another unexpected reminder of life's capriciousness.

❦

"Useful Tom" was fifty-four years old, four years younger than Josiah, and had worked as a potter for the past thirty years of his life. For twenty-two years he was in partnership with Josiah, sharing one eighth of the firm's profits, and during that time he proved he could solidly manage the useful works and keep the cash coming in while Josiah and Bentley dreamed up extravagantly expensive ornamental wares, for much greater public recognition. He and his wife Mary had one daughter and three sons.

In 1788, Tom told Josiah he was ready to retire, that he was planning on moving to the Hill Works in Burslem, owned by his father-in-law, to see out the rest of his days, looking after the future of his children. They agreed that his partnership would end eight weeks later, on 11 November 1788. With one month to go, the family was told the shocking news that Useful Tom had accidentally drowned in the canal. He was buried with the other Wedgwood potters in St. John's churchyard.

❦

Josiah was too tired to manage the entire business of which he was now sole proprietor. Therefore, "to ease myself of increasing care in the decline of life," he gave his three sons and Tom Byerley their own shares. Jack, Joss, and Tom each received a quarter share, while Josiah and Byerley split the remaining quarter. The firm was now known as Josiah Wedgwood, Sons, & Byerley. "By this division of the burden," said Josiah, "I hope it will become light to each of us, at least a little less to my share."

Despite the uncertainties surrounding his sons' future interest in the business—and even though the father pointed out that their share of the profits required work on their behalf—Josiah felt it was time to find "a little more quiet for myself." The year 1789 had been a very busy one. After three years, he and Joss had finally perfected the Portland Vase, and one of the first good copies was sent to Erasmus Darwin, with whom Josiah reflected on the latest war to threaten political stability in Europe. "I know you will rejoice with me in the glorious revolution which has taken place in France," he wrote Darwin just after the fall of the Bastille. "The politicians tell me that as a manufacturer I shall be ruined if France has her liberty, but I am willing to take my chance in that respect." Life was full of gambles. Sadly, it looked as if Josiah's luck was about to change.

33
The "Giant Malady"

"**A**FTER an unremitting attention of nearly forty years to a manufactory which I have had the happiness to establish, and to see flourish beyond my most sanguine expectations," Josiah Wedgwood announced to his customers in a printed handbill his "wish to enjoy that ease and relaxation from the severity of business, so necessary in advanced years." Josiah would turn sixty this year, 1790.

The Portland Vase was an immediate success, gaining publicity of the sort that Josiah was now accustomed to each time he "surprised the world" with a new product. Sir Joshua Reynolds, Sir Joseph Banks, and Sir William Hamilton had all publicly praised it, and the historical painter Benjamin West selected the vase as one of the objects illustrating his theme "Etruria" in his painting *Genius calling forth the Fine Arts to adorn Manufactures and Commerce, and recording the names of eminent men in these pursuits* (1791). It became an icon of Etruria's achievements.

After Erasmus Darwin received a Wedgwood copy of the Portland Vase and learned of his good friend's retirement plans, he wasted no time composing his own story about the progress of the arts, writing a poem to celebrate his good friend's achievements. Josiah was touched. "You have been extremely happy in describing the particular excellencies of the ancient Etruscan potters," Josiah said: "whether your prophecies respecting the productions of modern Etruria be as true . . . it will take some time to discover." Indeed, though basking in glory, Josiah was increasingly worried about the future of "modern Etruria."

Jack's return to England did not solve his "aversion" to taking over the business that Josiah had spent forty years building. In fact, as his brother Joss admitted to his father, Jack "disliked it very much." Josiah was disappointed, but willing to support him in his chosen career path, and helped him buy a partnership in the new London banking firm of Alexander Davidson & Co.

Tom, on the other hand, grew more restless and despondent, having a tendency to disappear into his room at Etruria Hall, where he wrote long, philosophical letters about his life. "I know my father is afraid of secluding myself too much from the world, & becoming too hermetical," he wrote to Joss. "I can only say that I think it would be greatly to the advantage of most young people to pass three or four most important years of their life, in a calm retired manner." In 1790, nineteen-year-old Tom proposed that he move out of Etruria Hall and into one of the houses in Etruria Village with his Edinburgh friend John Leslie. Josiah was not encouraging.

While conceding that "an uninterrupted intercourse & conversation with a man of Mr L's extensive learning" could be useful, and certainly supporting the idea of serious study, Josiah worried that Tom was sacrificing family life and sociability to do it. "Even knowledge itself," said Josiah, "if received in exchange for the blessings of society & the family charities would be dearly bought."

Tom did not give up. He picked up a blank invoice sheet from his father's office at Etruria when Sally and Josiah were still in London and penned an emotional note. Under the letterhead "BOUGHT OF JOSIAH WEDGWOOD: POTTER TO HER MAJESTY," Tom scribbled:

> I am well aware that the next three or four years of my life are the most important . . . our passions & affections are all to be moderated & corrected, in the season of youth—whilst the wax is yet capable of receiving impressions—in this crucial moment, I shall strive hard to fashion myself so that I may best perform the grand dutys of this life—I reflect every day on the relation between the creator & creature & hope by these instructive speculations to arrive at the knowledge of the

purpose of creation & hence of what these dutys consist. The Question is extremely intricate & comprehensive. . . . You perceive my tendency to retirement & are uneasy to trust me from under your eyes. . . .

This time, Tom's neo-Lockean philosophy persuaded Josiah, who allowed Tom and his friend to set up a home, providing they did so economically, "with the plainest possible furniture." Tom was delighted—"I am happy that some of my arguments have had some weight." To prove that it was the right move, Tom showed unusual dedication to a particular course of study, and with John Leslie's help, engaged in detailed experiments on the chemical action of light. He wrote up the results in two papers which he submitted to the Royal Society; they were published the following year in the society's prestigious *Philosophical Transactions*. Tom knew this would impress his father, and Josiah could not help but be proud of his boy.

Joss remained, for the time being, at Etruria, managing the factory and proposing ideas to Josiah about what new wares they should produce. He learned quickly, and had his father's sense of timing and politics. In July 1789, he had asked Josiah if they should start producing something "which should relate to the late revolution in France & to the support given to public credit by the national assembly? What do you think of a figure of public faith on an altar & France embracing Liberty in the front?"

Josiah again thought that Joss was adapting perfectly to the business— showing the right instinct for providing mementos of a historical moment, objects that in circulation became pieces of propaganda. Wedgwood manufactured jasper medallions with relief emblems symbolic of the French Revolution—"a cornucopia, a bonnet of liberty on a stick and an olive branch contained within a fleur-de-lis border."

The Revolution became a central topic of discussion in Josiah's letters to Erasmus Darwin, his principal correspondent at this time other than Joss. Darwin and Josiah both celebrated the French Revolution, believing it a just political expression to dispense with a tyrannical regime in favor of equality amongst humankind. In a long poem that Darwin was writing on the history of the world, he waxed lyrical about the progress made in the history of humanity, honoring scientific achievements (Wedgwood's Etruria factory absorbing some of the spotlight), the "liberation of America," and finally the French Revolution, in which the "Giant-form of Liberty" had long

Inglorious slept, unconscious of his chains;
Round his large limbs were wound a thousand strings
By the weak hands of Confessors and Kings . . .
Touch'd by the patriot-flame, he rent amazed
The flimsy bonds, and round and round him gazed.

But the events following the Revolution disturbed democrats such as Josiah and Darwin.

The year Tom was preoccupied with his careful experiments in the laboratory at Etruria, a close family friend was the target of a brutal assault owing to his apparent support for the events abroad.

In 1791, what the Reverend J. Bartlam described as the "bunting, beggarly, brass-making, brazen-faced, brazen-hearted, blackguard, bustling, booby Birmingham mob" was indeed agitated. They had caught wind of the fact that a dinner celebrating the French Revolution was being held in a Birmingham hotel. To the mob, these royalty-hating unbelievers posed a threat to the pillars of established society. They believed the seeds of a revolution at home were being sown in the fiery landscape around them, fueled by the bubbling chemicals and moonlit meetings of radical freethinkers— Dissenters with republican principles.

"A storm is gathering, depend upon it," the Whig curate of Hatton, Dr. Samuel Parr, had written, keeping vigilant of events unfolding in Birmingham. On the night of the infamous dinner, inflammatory scrawls were found on building walls proclaiming "destruction to the Presbyterians" and "Church and King forever." From inside the hotel, chants of "no Popery" were heard and a crowd "some hundreds" strong was gathering in the streets. The mob began marching to a nearby village, to Fair Hill, in Sparkbrook. This was no factory, Dissenting chapel, or industrial estate. In their eyes, it was more seditious and dangerous. They were heading for the home and laboratory of Wedgwood and Darwin's friend, Dr. Joseph Priestley.

Priestley's reputation as an experimental philosopher had spread internationally since his days at Warrington Academy. For over twenty years, he buried himself in philosophical books, surrounded by scientific apparatus with which to conduct experiments. His laboratory instruments included an air pump, a selection of microscopes, and an "electrical machine" ("a pretty good machine," he assured others), which he used to generate sparks, dissolve water into gases, and ponder what Newton was only able to describe as a kind of "aether"—a mysterious universal fluid, the "electric fire" that Wedgwood, Darwin, and many other interested in the secrets of nature were beginning to investigate.

Priestley's experiments seemed immediately promising, and Josiah had long recognized their potential benefits to his own craft. "I am much pleased with your disquisition upon the *Capabilities* of Electricity," he wrote. If he could contribute anything "towards rendering Doctr. Priestleys very ingenious experiments" more useful, he was eager to do so. Throughout the 1760s and 1770s, Priestley, Josiah, and Bentley were in correspondence about a range of applications of electricity, including its use "to decorate . . . tea boards and baubles," something useful not only to Wedgwood but to Matthew Boulton as well. Another potential area of interest was Priestley's work on adding a "metallic tinge to glass," leading Josiah to wonder whether he could conduct "experiments relating to gilding by Electricity." In fact, Boulton was the one to come up with a useful technique for that some years later, but it was the endless possibilities, the wonder of the unknown, explored by Priestley's "delightful and ingenious researches into the secrets of nature," that so appealed to Josiah.

His enthusiasm for Priestley's experiments turned into practical support for the chemist, something for which Priestley was decidedly grateful. "Such is the interest in philosophical discoveries," he said to Josiah, "and such are my numerous obligations to you with respect to those that I had in this business, that I cannot help giving you an early account of everything that I do." Priestley owed Wedgwood a particular debt of gratitude not merely for his close attention to his experiments—subscribing to his work to aid publication and making copious marginal comments—but for his consideration in supplying Priestley with apparatus for him to conduct those experiments. "The Dr seems much at a loss for a mortar, not metal, for pounding in," Josiah noted in his Commonplace Book while reading the latest account of Priestley's work. "Make him a deep one or two." In fact, Josiah gradually supplied a whole range of utilities made from "compact hard porcelain" to his experimentally oriented friends: pestles and mortars, crucibles, and other chemical wares, which, when he later began marketing them, were described as "excellently adapted also for evaporating pans, digesting vessels, basons, filtering funnels, siphons, tubes, such as Dr Priestley uses in some of his experiments," though Priestley received them gratis.

Josiah knew that science, Royal Society style, was governed by great patronage. Priestley confirmed this view when doing his experiments on electricity and writing the history of achievements in that science: "Natural philosophy is a science which more especially requires the aid of wealth." Scientific progress "provincial style" was based on collaboration, trust, mutual solidarity, the exchange of apparatus, and—most controversially—ideas. Priestley's experiments seemed to give birth to *dangerous* ideas, which made him the immediate object of the Birmingham mob's attack.

For years, Priestley had been analyzing the properties of isolated gases and investigating their role in respiration. In gruesome detail, Priestley described his experiments on animals that were forced to breathe "fixed air" (carbon dioxide), noting the different times it took for the life to expire in mice, frogs, and even flowers. Finally, after a decade of laboratory work, Priestley announced that he was now able to convert "*pure water* into *permanent air*," and that this new air could be purified in such a way as to "prepare it for respiration" by measuring the "goodness" (capacity for respiration) of air. What Priestley was ultimately suggesting was a way to manufacture a new atmosphere.

When the conservative MP Edmund Burke read about Priestley's experiments in 1790 while taking a break from writing his anti-Jacobin tract, *Reflections on the Revolution in France*, he was alarmed by what Priestley announced were the implications of his researches. Enlightened, experimental inquiry, said Priestley, was "putting an end to all undue and usurped authority in the business of religion . . . and all the efforts of the interested friends of corrupt establishments of all kinds." Lest anyone miss the point, Priestley spelled it out: "the English hierarchy, if there be anything unsound in its constitution, has equal reason to tremble before an air pump, or an electrical machine"—the most familiar instruments found in a chemist's laboratory. For anyone who knew Priestley—the Unitarian champion of both the American and the French revolutions—there was little doubt that he already detected something constitutionally "unsound" in the English hierarchy.

An agitated Burke quickly returned to writing and launched his *Reflections* with allusions to Priestley, likening the aerated "spirit of liberty" to "the wild *gas*, the fixed air [that] is plainly broke loose." Who else, he wondered, was culpable of spreading such seditious, revolutionary ideas in society?

Suspicious eyes turned toward the Midlands. London prejudices had long catalogued the ways that provincial communities were inherently different from the metropolitan elite. Satirists mocked the Staffordshire dialect, suggesting locals did not know "ow ter toke raight." But throughout the century, they watched as obscure manufactures emerged from the rugged fields, were entertained at court, were buying political patronage, building walls to hide their scientific secrets, and propagating their radical philosophy of equality and freedom of thought.

Since the American Revolution, this had begun to sound familiar, worrying, and suspiciously foreign. Such were the perceived democratizing effects of scientific practices that, especially after 1789, conservative critics were prompted to accuse French "natural philosophers"—philosophers of nature—as being the culprits of the French Revolution, particularly chemists, who believed in gases rather than holy spirits, "the *wrongs* of Providence, and the *rights* of man," as Erasmus Darwin boldly stated. Such expressions agitated the likes of Edmund Burke. "The revolution in France is the grand ingredient in the cauldron," he warned. If the chemists who in Britain were actively organizing themselves into satellite scientific societies and laboring in their seditious laboratories had their way, they would disintegrate society, like the polluted air we breathe, into a "chaos of elementary principles."

Like the collapsed, convulsing cockatoo suffocating in a vacuum at the hands of the experimental scientist in Joseph Wright's *Bird in the Air Pump*, these philosophers—these "fanatics," as Burke called them—"would sacrifice the whole human race to the slightest of their experiments." Something needed to be done to stop this, and the Birmingham mob agreed.

Priestley was warned that a torch-waving mob, inflamed by Anglican preachers and free drink, was descending on his house, and he fled with his family, having no time to gather any personal belongings. His house was ransacked and burned to the ground. His manuscripts, library, and scientific instruments were destroyed in the fire that engulfed his laboratory. Everything, save his and his family's lives, was lost.

≈

"The Birmingham riots are a disgrace to mankind," Darwin told Josiah, but he was careful not to say more. He knew that Priestley's own words solicited the attack against him, and from then on Darwin and his friends were guarded in their opinions about France, science, and the Revolution. Who knew how much each of them had agreed with their friend Priestley. Josiah himself, when applauding Priestley's electrical experiments, had playfully declared, "But what daring mortals you are! To rob the Thunderer of his Bolts—& for what?—no doubt to blast the oppressors of the poor." Priestley's sentiment exactly. Who was to say that Etruria, or Darwin's Derby home, was not next on the hit list?

Josiah warned his son to be on guard. Boulton and Watt armed the men at Soho, but nothing happened to them—nothing physically, at least. The "Church-and-King" riots snuffed out much of their enthusiasm for the latest act of "liberation." It was another warning about the uncertainty of the future, a reminder of the shortcomings of their Utopian dreams that envisioned the "perfectibility" of the world.

Concerned for his family, Priestley sent them off to America. With some financial aid from Josiah and his other friends to help rebuild his life, Priestley soon followed his family, heading for a job as professor of chemistry at "a liberal college in the back settlements of America." As he set sail in April 1794, he left a note for the friends he left behind. "When the time for reflection shall come," he said, "my countrymen, I am confident, will do me justice." Erasmus and Josiah wished they had as much confidence. In fact, just as Priestley left, Josiah had heard that "every name supposed to think different" from the government was put into a doomsday book, "and that if the French land, these recorded gentlemen are to be all imprison'd. . . ." Josiah learned that his name was "high on the list."

≈

Erasmus and Josiah had much to discuss. The bright moment in a dark, turbulent time was when, in 1794, twenty-nine-year-old Sukey and Darwin's twenty-eight-year-old son, Robert, agreed to marriage.

Sukey had been in and out of the Darwin's household since childhood, even giving Robert's older brother, Erasmus, music lessons. Young Erasmus was also infatuated with her. She was "an accomplished lady," he said, in congratulating his younger brother; she was someone "I always much esteemed."

Their fathers were jubilant. Darwin and Wedgwood's long friendship had crystallized in the years following Bentley's death. Erasmus, once merely described as Sally's "favorite Esculapius," had become Josiah's closest friend. The marriage would not be immediate, but knowing that their families would be united through their children gave Josiah a pleasure that could only have been surpassed if Bentley had had children whose names could have been added to the Wedgwood family tree.

Unfortunately, Josiah's other children were not giving him as much pleasure. In 1792, eager to see the Bastille Day celebrations firsthand, Tom joined James Watt's son in Paris. This James Watt was, according to Tom, "a furious democrat—detests the king." Tom's description of the events in France added no relief to Josiah and Sally's worry about their son's travels or the state of affairs in Europe. "French politics as mutable as the wind," he reported. "Watt says that a new revolution must inevitably take place, & that it will in all probability be fatal to the King, Fayette, and some hundred others." This trip marked the beginning of a new passion for travel in Tom, who, the next year, followed his older brother Jack's lead and formally resigned his partnership in the firm of Josiah Wedgwood, Sons, & Byerley.

Josiah worried about the future of the business he'd worked so hard to build. The only hope of keeping it in the family now rested on Joss's shoulders, to whom the factory and all its contents were left in the will that Josiah drew up late in 1793.

❧

Erasmus and Josiah agreed these were depressing times. As the "liberation" of France was transformed into a regime of horror in 1794, their thoughts turned to the "giant malady" that plagued their own lives.

As students of the Enlightenment, who held Rousseau and Voltaire to be their heroes, Dissenters such as Josiah and Darwin had long believed that by studying nature they would effect a revolution in society, which would not only empower people to think and speak freely and allow humanity to prosper but would lead to a healthier world. Priestley's experiments on air gave them hopes for just that, and Darwin himself pursued the medical benefits of administering pure oxygen to patients. Disappointingly, it was precisely where wealth was being created based on scientific innovation that the scourge of environmental disease persisted. It appeared that the ability to manufacture a physically healthier environment still eluded them. "Nothing now remains" in the desire for money, lamented James Watt, "as I find it can neither bring health nor happiness."

In the growing manufacturing regions across the world, consumption—the disease of the lungs that "like war, cuts off the young in their prime of life"—was rife. Josiah and Darwin's own friends and family were affected by it. Richard Lovell Edgeworth had just lost two children from consumption; Joseph Priestley's daughter was suffering from it, as was James Watt's daughter. More personally, Erasmus Darwin's own daughter, Emma, had developed a "nervous cough," and Darwin suspected that Tom, Josiah's own son, was languishing from the disease. Josiah and Erasmus financially supported the research on the treatment of consumption by a bright young doctor, Thomas Beddoes, who was kicked out of Oxford for his outspoken support for the French Revolution. "In a future letter," Beddoes wrote to Darwin, "I hope to present you with a catalogue of diseases in which I have effected a cure." For Darwin, belief in such an optimistic dream evaporated when he was summoned to Josiah's own sickbed.

34
"To Mix Again with Their Original Clay"

S ally and Josiah had returned from London to Etruria by November 1794 when Josiah complained of heart palpitations and general fatigue. Darwin prescribed a mixture of alum and nutmeg with ground rhubarb, along with water treatment at the spas in Buxton. Josiah hoped "taking the waters" would also help relieve pains he had in his joints, which had been irritating him for some time. At first, it seemed to help.

"Your letter gives me great pleasure in assuring me, what your son Josiah had before mention'd, that you have become free from your complaint—the ceasing of the palpitation of your heart and of the inter- mission of your pulse is another proof of your increase in strength," Dar- win wrote that December. Josiah, however, was less confident about his convalescence, complaining of shortness of breath as he climbed up hills, fearing it was asthma. Darwin assured him it was merely his sixty-four years that was slowing him down. "You know how unwilling we all are to grow old," said the doctor, who recommended that Josiah leave off taking his medicine. But his confidence was misjudged.

Days later, Josiah was bed-bound. His face was swollen and he com- plained of acute pain in his jaw, which was attributed to a decayed tooth. When his trusted surgeon, James Bent, arrived to extract it, he found something much worse. He immediately sent for Darwin, saying that Josiah was showing signs of "mortification" and needed urgent treatment.

Darwin rushed to Etruria Hall from Derby. There was nothing that he could do. He remained at Josiah's bedside, where Sally nursed her lov- ing "Joss." Jack and Tom returned to be with the family, as did Tom Byerley, who arrived from London. Young Joss was joined by his wife and their eighteen-month-old daughter, Sarah, Sally and Josiah's first grandchild. Sukey comforted her younger sisters and showed her strength of character. She had "a distinct understanding and an excellent heart during her father's illness," observed the younger Erasmus Darwin, who was there with his brother, Sukey's fiancé, Robert.

Josiah's health deteriorated steadily. "For several days," Tom Byerley reported to an old family friend, "the physicians had declared he could not live two hours—such was the state of his pulse." His throat swelled and he developed an intermittent high fever. He could not talk—Darwin said it was because his jaw had rotted—but he felt comfort from the friends and family that surrounded him. While not able to converse, he had a lifetime to reflect on: falling in love with Sally, with her long fair hair, when they were young; building the confidence to approach Long John and cousin Thomas for help to enter business by himself; the rush of enthusiasm when given the chance to produce a "Sett of tea things" for the queen; the sorrow of his brother John's drowning in the Thames; the thousands of heartening letters he received from Bentley; and the smiles on the faces of his children as they surrounded him.

On New Year's Day, 1795, he slipped into unconsciousness. Two days later, on Sukey's thirtieth birthday, Josiah Wedgwood died.

35

"Unremitting Fires"

"The death of Mr Wedgwood grieves me very much," Darwin wrote to William Hayley, a good friend. "He is a public as well as private loss."

As Josiah was such a well known public figure, newspaper reports across Britain were quick to announce his passing—from the local *Aris's Birmingham Gazette* and *Derby Mercury* to the national *Times*. The eulogies praised both his professional career and his personal benevolence. He was "possessed of great public spirit, and unremitting perseverance, with a mind fraught with general intelligence," said the *Staffordshire Advertiser*, while the *Gentleman's Magazine* commended his promotion of public utilities, such as the canal and turnpikes, and his employment of the "deserving poor." He was ranked amongst the finest chemists by his contemporaries for his untiring and innovative scientific experiments, which yielded such extraordinarily diverse results.

When tourists floated down the Trent & Mersey Canal and passed by Etruria, they were impressed at the sight of the modern factory built along its banks but also knew its special place in history. The buildings, noted John Aikin in his 1795 travel guide to western England, "constitute nearly the whole of the present fine English earthen wares and porcelain, which are now become the source of a very extensive trade, and which, considered as an object of national art, industry, and commerce, may be ranked amongst the most important manufactures of the kingdom." Others agreed. The "ingenious and industrious Wedgwood," said Samuel Parkes, a prominent nineteenth-century chemist, created a manufactory that became "a national source of wealth." His reputation, as other travelers to more distant lands observed, was international.

The Swiss traveler Faujas de Saint-Fond remarked in 1797 that Wedgwood had created "a commerce so active and universal, that in Travelling from Paris to St Petersberg, from Amsterdam to the farthest point of Sweden, from Dunkirk to the southern extremity of France, one is served at every inn from English earthenware. The same fine article adorns the tables of Spain, Portugal & Italy, and it provides the cargoes of ships to the East Indies, the West Indies and America." During his life, Josiah dreamed of conquering the farthest shores. Once, he contemplated whether his wares could be taken by British diplomats and introduced to the market in China. He saw it happen before he died, when in 1793 Lord Macartney presented examples of Wedgwood's vases to the emperor.

Josiah was even more amazed, however, when Sir William Hamilton told him his Etruscan wares and other ornamental pieces "are much admired" and were fetching high prices in Italy. Drawing inspiration from ancient Tuscany and selling his imitation pots back to the Italian marketplace was the ultimate *coup d'état*. In the eyes of some, though not Josiah's, it was even more flattering to see Wedgwood ware being imitated in Italy. As Arthur Young said when he spotted this during his travels, "It is surely a triumph of the arts in England to see in Italy Etruscan forms copied from English models." That he sold his china in China and his Italian vases in Italy was the most ironic expression of Josiah Wedgwood's marketing genius. That his wares eliminated much of the competition in Europe was more proof. By the time of his death, most of the Delft factories were closed—a fate attributed to the introduction of Wedgwood's creamware, which replaced the older-style imitations of Oriental porcelain. Josiah's trade had endured wars, revolutions, privateering, and espionage to become a worldwide success. But the difficult times that the company soon faced, at the beginning of the Napoleonic Wars, once again threatened everything. Josiah's son Joss did not think he had it in him to pull through.

Josiah died a very rich man. His estimated wealth was £600,000. Sally was left £10,000 and Etruria Hall, where she stayed until 1802, when she and her youngest two daughters, who remained unmarried throughout their lives, moved to a comfortable country cottage nearby. Josiah left each of his daughters £25,000. Tom and Jack were each left £30,000.

Joss inherited the majority share of the factory, where he worked for another five years. By 1800, however, with Continental trade devastated from continuing war, he lost his nerve. He saw other European factories on the verge of bankruptcy, including Meissen, which had recently introduced its own imitation *Wedgwoodarbeit*, "Wedgwood-work," in an effort to revitalize its trade.

Thomas Byerley, who was bequeathed another eighth of the business, giving him a full quarter share, held out. After treating his clerkship cavalierly for so many years in his youth, repeatedly abandoning it with the hopes of succeeding in a more "entertaining" life, he was now the only one left who had any faith in Etruria. As good as his intentions were, unfortunately, he could not successfully manage the entire business on his own. Discipline in the factory became slack and the standard of production dropped. Less than five years after Josiah's death, the future of Etruria looked bleak.

In 1800, however, Jack purchased back his share of the partnership in Etruria and in 1804 took a leading role in restoring its fortunes. In 1806, Joss returned to work, and Josiah Wedgwood, Sons, & Byerley regained considerable lost ground. The Wedgwood touch was still alive. Etruria's future suddenly looked brighter. Their young brother's future, however, dampened their spirits.

Addicted to opium, Tom often silently contemplated philosophical questions that he took notes on in his diary. What limit was there to the perfectibility of man or society? What are the true laws of nature? What is the essence of human consciousness? What is the most effective way to relieve human suffering?

These were the ponderings of the man whom the poet Thomas Campbell described as "full of goodness, benevolence, with a mind stored with ideas, with metaphysics the most exquisitely fine I ever heard delivered, a man of wonderful talents, a tact of taste acute beyond description." In 1803, Tom was thirty-two-years old, and chronically ill.

One of his closest friends was Samuel Taylor Coleridge, another chronic sufferer with a passionate philosophical bent. When they were together, the two spent immeasurable hours discussing their dreams and visions, and experimenting with a cornucopia of drugs hoping to relieve their pathological misery. "We will have a fair trial of *Bang*," wrote Coleridge in anticipation of an imminent visit from Tom in 1803, referring to some recently arrived Indian hemp. "Do bring down some of the Hyoscyamine Pills—& I will give a fair Trial of opium, Hensbane, & Nepenthe."

Coleridge, referred to by Wordsworth as "The most intense of Nature's worshippers," in turned referred to Tom as "the benefactor of my intellect," eternally grateful for the annuities he received from Tom, which brought him "tranquillity & leisure of independence" and the ability to "inspire and purify" his poetry.

It was a mission in life that Tom had also settled on. Once, he was the little boy whose father idealized him, "jumping up & clapping his hands in joy" as his elder brother performed chemical experiments. And indeed, like his father, Tom proved to be quite an experimentalist. In a scientific paper he had published just the previous year, in a journal edited by the promising young chemist Humphry Davy, he described how an image can be obtained on a piece of paper when a source of light is projected on a sheet moistened with nitrate of silver. Despite the fact that he knew of no way to "fix" the images, his discovery has been hailed as the invention of photography. But after this, ill health forced him to quit the laboratory.

Joss agonized over his brother's ailing condition. While Joss managed Etruria, Tom searched for his health at home and abroad. His efforts were supported by the companionship of his growing circle of artistic friends, including John Leslie, Coleridge, and a new friend of Tom's, William Godwin, who were in turn supported by Tom, who was, as he confessed, "possessed of a considerable superfluity of fortune."

The group, along with others including the engineer James Watt's son, Gregory, formed a social club in London which one member immodestly described as a "gathering place of brilliant talkers, dedicated to meetings of the reigning wits of London." Among the topics debated by the group was something which Tom and Coleridge had mused about for some time: social progress. William Godwin was particularly outspoken on this subject. He was a radical thinker and author, a Dissenting minister turned atheist and Utopian philosopher, who argued that the abolition of rank and riches would promote the happiness, welfare, and perfectibility of mankind. His was a doctrine of extreme individualism, maintaining that small self-sustaining groups should replace government and social institutions to ensure the future improvement of society. Large forms of social organization—judicial, religious, educational, and so on—were oppressive, Godwin argued; after their removal humankind would be liberated from misery, ignorance, and poverty, and live in a world of uncoerced morality, virtue, and happiness.

Godwin found many disciples in the society of London poets and philosophers, and the Wedgwoods' philanthropy fitted well with his Rousseauian optimism about the benevolence of human nature. So enthused were his friends by this new Utopian philosophy that a number of them—especially the poet Robert Southey, Coleridge, and Tom—drew up plans to emigrate to America to start a Utopian community free from the prejudices of British society. Why not? They even had a role model—Tom's scientific mentor Joseph Priestley, whose new life in the Susquehanna Valley in Pennsylvania they found adventurous and exciting.

But another of Godwin's readers was fiercely skeptical about his philosophy. This was the Reverend Thomas Robert Malthus, who published a response to "the general question of the future improvement of society" entitled *An Essay on the Principle of Population* (1798). In this polemical tract, Malthus mused on the fate of humanity, declaring that "those whose minds are not suited to a purer and happier state of existence, shall perish, and be condemned to mix again with their original clay."

Look around, Malthus demanded: is it right that manufacturers are producing "trinkets and baubles" when disease, warfare, and death still haunt the world? It was a particularly cutting criticism, written in the wake of the "great hunger" that had preceded the French Revolution and amid anxieties caused by the scarcities of 1795 in England. There was not enough food, Malthus warned, so why waste effort producing dinnerware! The "best stimulus to industry," he wrote, was "the hope of bettering our condition, and the fear of want, rather than want itself." As Josiah and Erasmus Darwin had earlier feared, people believed that manufacturers and industrialists were, ultimately, manufacturing dearth and disease; the best way to secure a healthy future, Malthus said, was to encourage agricultural production.

This was not the line of reasoning that the sons (whether Wedgwoods, Darwins, or Watts) of major industrialists and enlightened entrepreneurs were keen to embrace; nor were their friends. Godwin, who corresponded with Malthus (who was ten years younger) about this, stuck by his original argument politely. Behind the scenes, however, the group mocked Malthus's "exceedingly illogical" (in Coleridge's words) argument.

The debates over Utopian philosophy and the emerging critique of manufacturers as represented by Malthus exposed the social tensions that affected the presumed benefactors of industrial triumph which the previous generation had celebrated. Before his death in 1803, Erasmus Darwin wrote paeans to industrial progress in his massive poem *The Botanic Garden*, which applauded the work at Etruria, subtly alluding to the metaphor of divine creation and ancient ideals of perfection:

> And pleased on WEDGWOOD ray your partial smile,
> A new Etruria decks Britannia's isle.
> Charmed by your touch, the kneaded clay refines,
> The biscuit hardens, the enamel shines;
> Each nicer mould a softer feature drinks,
> The bold Cameo speaks, the soft Intaglio thinks.
>
> Whether, O Friend of Art! Your gems derive
> Fine forms from Greece, and fabled Gods revive;
> Or bid from modern life the Portrait breathe,
> And bind round Honour's brow the laurel wreath;
> Buoyant shall sail, with Fame's historic page,
> Each fair medallion o'er the wrecks of age.

However, not all their offspring inherited the optimism of Erasmus's generation. Erasmus's own son appeared to be a successful solicitor—he acted on behalf of the Wedgwood firm—but inwardly deep neuroses were festering. He proved a poor businessman, badly mismanaging his finances while overextending his financial security in buying a beautiful but lavish house, Breadsall Priory, just north of Derby. This was where the forty-year-old Erasmus hoped to relax in early retirement, or where he would "sleep away the remainder of his life," as his father disapprovingly put it, maybe thinking of the listless life of Tom Wedgwood. But it was worse than that.

One month after moving into Breadsall Priory, on 29 December 1799, Erasmus fled from his house in a frantic state, threw himself into the Derwent River a mile's run through his garden, and drowned. On that same day, his father (unaware of his own son's death) wrote a letter to Dr.

Thomas Beddoes in Bristol saying he was "truly sorry to hear Mr T Wedgwood is in so indifferent a stage of health." But Tom managed to hang on a bit longer. He died, emaciated and intoxicated, on 10 July 1805, at the age of thirty-four.

Tom's tragic life had made his friend William Wordsworth ponder. Among the schemes for the "progress of human improvement" that Tom had shown to the poet was his vision of an academy for genius, in which a child would be reared under laboratory conditions, with "plain grey walls with one or two vivid objects for sight & touch . . . the child must never go out of doors or leave his own apartment." Eventually, Wordsworth grew skeptical of the plan. He was, after all, as Tom had later observed, a man who enjoyed meditating on nature "with no other companions, than the flowers, the grass, the cattle, the sheep that scamper away from him when he makes a vain unexpecting chase after them."

Wordsworth also grew skeptical about the benefits to nature that industry promised. He shared his ideas with Coleridge, who earlier had listened to Wordsworth read the first part of his poem, *The Excursion*, in 1797. It was a simple story, in which a man contemplated the difference between the ruined cottage as it appeared before him and as he once had known it, before he was forced to leave in search of work, for war had blighted the rural economy. The transition of the landscape around him was breathtaking.

> at social Industry's command,
> How quick, how vast an increas'
> I grieve, when on the darker side
> Of this great change I look; and there behold
> Such outrage done to nature as compels
> The indignant power to justify herself;
> Yea, to avenge her violated rights,
> For England's bane.—When soothing darkness spreads
> O'er hill and vale, the Wanderer thus expressed
> His recollections . . .

"One of the most beautiful poems in the language," thought Coleridge. But how different was this response to the landscape to that of Tom's father, Josiah Wedgwood, when he first wandered a few miles from his birthplace and cast his eyes over the vast vales. He did not see an area

> O'er which the smoke of unremitting fires
> Hangs permanent

Nor did he foresee "outrage done to nature." Rather, he saw a promising future; a new way of life yet to come.

❧

Tom's death and his friends' Romantic struggles with the transformation of nature and society were a harsh reminder of the trials of new wealth for the next generation, but the spirit of scientific progress that Josiah Wedgwood had so passionately believed in remained alive. Sally lived until 1815, long enough to see all of her nineteen grandchildren begin to grow. Joss's youngest daughter, Emma, was born in 1808. Sukey and Robert Darwin's youngest son was born in 1809. He was Sally's last grandchild, who would eventually marry his cousin Emma. They named him Charles.

Epilogue

J osiah Wedgwood possessed a number of special qualities that enabled him to succeed beyond all expectations, barring his own. It is evident that he could not have accomplished what he did without the support of his family and friends—Sally's dowry and lifelong assistance was essential, Bentley's advice and experience invaluable—but without Josiah's own traits, he would be as lost to history as the imperfect pieces of his pottery that were smashed in a shord pile.

It is ironic that Josiah's own abilities as a master craftsman were not enough to elevate his pottery to international admiration. Struggling with his own physical weaknesses throughout most of his life, it is almost certain that had he relied solely on his own labor—performing all the traditional aspects of the potter's craft in the way his brother was forced to—he would not have survived in business at all. Rather, his crucial skill was getting those he employed to improve the quality of their work to meet his standards. While demanding and stern, Josiah was in many ways a model employer. With a confidence most likely gained from the encouraging education he received from his brother-in-law Reverend Willets, his compassionate mother, and his dedicated friends, Josiah developed an ability to get people to rally around a cause. Having the acute political sense to court action with reward was vital. His workers enjoyed unprecedented guarantees of family housing, health insurance, and retirement benefits in return for their dedication and loyalty to the Wedgwood business.

Timing, of course, cannot be ignored. It was certainly a fortuitous moment to be a manufacturer. In an age when Adam Smith elaborated the principles of the division of labor, when chemists such as Josiah's friend Joseph Priestley were finding new ways to standardize products for consistency, and, in the broader social context, just as a wealthier consumer class grew eager to spend money on home decor—Wedgwood's was the first pottery in England to be bought for display—opportunities for success abounded. But Josiah was willing to take risks with his reputation, his materials, and his money, to capitalize on these opportunities.

Whenever the economy was threatened by another war, or sales were dropping off due to a waning fashion, Josiah put his faith in his experimental trials, spending longer hours in the laboratory working to invent a new glaze or unique characteristic within the clay. Science, he firmly believed, would provide the solution to consumer disinterest. Few of Josiah's contemporaries grasped as quickly as he did the practical implications for business that the "chemical revolution" would offer.

While, late in life, Josiah grew despondent about the problems that existed in the world—war, despotism, disease—things which his youthful ideology had imagined eliminated by Enlightened thought, he could rest proud that his own example of success, created from practically nothing, could inspire others with few prospects before them. The term "tycoon," as Donald Trump recently remarked, "belongs to an era when people outside of aristocracy were able to forge ahead for themselves, which inevitably gives rise to the thought of someone being self-made." Being seen to possess wealth was far less important to Josiah than knowing that through determined inquiry and tenacity one could succeed without aristocratic advantage. "I would imagine," added Trump, "that Josiah Wedgwood would be honored to be so labeled." Indeed, Josiah was proud to have his name symbolize the creation of something desirable from raw, unrefined materials. Though, after his death, the future of the Wedgwood name and firm looked as uncertain as ever.

ॐ

The promising recovery of Josiah Wedgwood, Sons, & Byerley following Jack and Joss's return to the firm did not last long. The last years of the eighteenth century had seen respectable sales—profits for 1800 are estimated at nearly £8,000—and Byerley, keeping with Josiah's spirit of improvement, purchased a steam engine from Boulton & Watt to power some of the factory machinery, which was installed in 1802. The firm employed a workforce of about three hundred people who lived in one hundred houses in Etruria Village (though a few workers preferred living in boats on the canal). But, once again, as so often throughout Josiah's own career, politics and war interfered with business.

War with France was disastrous for Continental trade. During the Napoleonic Wars, exports of Staffordshire pottery were cut in half. Thirty local potteries went bankrupt. Making matters worse, between 1815 and 1820, sales to the United States of America, the largest market, plummeted by 75 percent. "Trade is very bad," reported a worried Josiah Bateman, the firm's senior salesman, "and people everywhere are very low spirited."

At such a moment, Josiah would have spent longer hours in his laboratory, writing cryptic letters to Bentley about a modified design and new kind of material with which he planned to "surprise the world," thus creating a new market for himself to keep the orders alive. But none of the present partners—his two sons, or the dutiful nephew Thomas Byerley—had the creative vision or indefatigable commitment that had previously kept Wedgwood pottery one step ahead of its competitors. While they enjoyed a brief revival of the so-called Egyptian ware, in the rosso antico body (the red paint on black basalts first introduced twenty years earlier), the taste for other styles of pottery had changed. The neoclassical vases that captured public attention when Josiah introduced them were no longer in vogue. More detrimental to the account books was that sales of jasper ware had substantially fallen off.

Rather than working collaboratively to introduce an improvement that might recapture their customers' imagination and orders, the three partners concentrated on their own personal interests and left the pottery in relative neglect. Both Jack and Joss continued to live their lives as country gentlemen. Jack, who before returning to work at the firm had run up a staggering debt by employing a retinue of servants and gardeners to assist him in his hobby of studying botany and horticulture (building greenhouses for cultivating exotic plants and growing tropical fruit), drew far more money from the business than his share of the partnership provided. But the same was true of Joss and Byerley. Joss also had an interest in horticulture, planting 65,000 trees of rare species on his property in one year alone, and traveled around the country "*en prince*." Byerley, meanwhile, was drawing exorbitant funds from the firm to provide for the education of his thirteen children. While none wanted to acknowledge it, the largest problem they had to confront in their ailing business was the debt they were principally responsible for incurring.

The unpleasant extent of that debt was confronted in 1810, when Byerley died and the brothers examined the accounts to pay Byerley's widow her share of the partnership. It was disappointing. His share was assessed at just over £6,300, to be set against his debt to the firm of £8,600. Jack owed the firm just above £11,000; but more alarming still was the discovery that the firm was owed £48,000 in unpaid bills, a figure nearly double the estimated value of the entire business. Never before had the firm fallen so fast toward bankruptcy.

When Joss sent letters to customers announcing Byerley's death and giving notice that business would be continued under the name "Josiah Wedgwood," he devised a plan which he hoped would rescue the firm. However, it required that his partnership with Jack also be dissolved. Jack did not take it well, and wrote a self-deprecating letter to his brother complaining that "all my endeavors to render myself useful to society are vain," adding that he hoped "the dissolution of the partnership should not be put in the Gazette." Agreeing to bow out, Jack, with his wife Jane and their children, thereafter relied on a series of family trusts established by other members of the family. None of Jack's children or descendants ever became involved with the family trade. From the beginning of 1812 until his retirement in 1841, the Wedgwood business was under the primary management of Joss.

In the 1810s, the principal new type of ware that Joss introduced to the market was bone china, a translucent porcelain that other Staffordshire potters had made, but that had never before been undertaken by Wedgwood. It was an unsuccessful venture. Instead, the business was kept alive by the production of common wares—a nineteenth-century variation on the stock-in-trade wares that provided the reliable sales in difficult times for the first Josiah. They produced large quantities of toilet ware—closet pans, urinals, washbasins, and stands.

Joss and his wife, Bessie, had eight children—four daughters and four sons. It was their youngest daughter, Emma, who went on to marry her cousin, Charles Darwin. The boys were all well educated, two sent to Eton and two to Rugby. The three younger boys were then educated at

Cambridge, where they planned to study for the bar. The eldest, Josiah III, was sent to Edinburgh, where he studied chemistry and natural history. Perhaps worried that his son might fall into the desultory habits that afflicted his own generation, Joss wrote to remind him that "You are in a house with tried young men whose fathers are much richer than I am. Do not attempt to vie with them in expense."

While the youngest Josiah managed to stay sober and received an education that would have provided a sound basis for the technical aspects of the potter's craft, his father was as uncertain about who would take over the family business as his grandfather, the first Josiah, had been. "I am very doubtful," he confessed, "if any one of my sons will succeed me in my business." However, in 1823, Josiah did join his father in a partnership, mainly because, in the words of one historian, the boy "showed no particular enthusiasm or aptitude for anything else." In fact, there was little to suggest that this Josiah would offer any useful improvements to the firm's performance. This condition was only moderately improved when Josiah's younger brother, Francis—whom they called Frank—determined that his chances at the bar were less than favorable and accepted an offer to enter into partnership with his brother and father. From 1827, the firm was once again Josiah Wedgwood & Sons.

While business did show signs of progress throughout the 1820s— certainly relative to the slump of the 1810s—it was necessary for Joss to devise new ways of raising money to keep the ailing business afloat. One possible solution was to sell the London showrooms, which he opted for in 1828. Unfortunately, the £16,000 he raised from that sale amounted to a loss when the cost of all the alterations and renovations to the building was included as part of the original investment. Over the next ten months they auctioned off the general stock of useful and ornamental ware, including enameled Queen's ware, stone china, and blue-printed patterns, as well as irreplaceable models, molds, and experimental pieces. With the added money this raised, and without the expense of London staff, the three partners of Josiah Wedgwood & Sons managed to concentrate their resources on the Etruria factory.

In 1841, Joss turned seventy-two years old. His health was deteriorating. Over the past decade he had withdrawn from the business and left the minutiae of managing the firm to his two sons. Taking after his father, Joss was stimulated by parliamentary debates, especially heated during the passing of the great Reform bills, and he became active in politics. He saw the practical impact of the reforms around him. The organization of trade unions was made legal by the repeal of the Combination Acts in 1824, and the period 1831–50 has been described as "the heroic age of trade unionism in the Potteries." The Factory Act of 1833 forbade the employment of children under the age of nine and limited children under thirteen to a 38-hour work week. The simple "rules of conduct" that Josiah had pinned to the factory door no longer acted as the foundation for terms of employment. Etruria, like all other factories that emerged during the age of industrialization, was now regulated by the state.

By the beginning of the 1840s, the firm had been making gross profits in the region of £5,000 a year, enough to allow Joss to retire in peace in 1841, and enough for Josiah III to sell his share of the partnership the next year and retire to his 400-acre estate in Surrey. Joss died two years later.

᠊ᢒᡱ

In 1859, the year Charles Darwin published *Origin of Species*, his cousin, Frank Wedgwood, accepted his own son, Godfrey, into a partnership, thus beginning the fourth generation of Wedgwoods at Etruria. The factory employed 445 people and began what has been described as "a new era of endeavour and development." Besides a number of mechanical modernizations, Godfrey brought new vigor to the production line, and was more committed to design standards and innovation than anyone since Josiah. He hired distinguished artists as decorators and raised the popularity and commercial value of Wedgwood pottery to a nineteenth-century peak. Their new products received critical acclaim at the International Exhibition in London in 1862, a vast improvement on the 1851 "Great Exhibition," where their display was ignored during Queen Victoria's visit to see the best examples of the "industry of all nations." The firm's performance continued to improve.

Part of its growing success in the latter half of the nineteenth century can be attributed to the rediscovery of Wedgwood pottery and the revitalized taste for jasper ware, as well as to heavy investment in hiring the best artists to decorate the new wares. So improved were the accounts of the business that in 1875 the firm was able to reopen showrooms in London. By 1882, twelve years after Frank retired and the business was placed in the partnership of Godfrey and his two younger brothers, Clement and Laurence, Wedgwood recorded profits of £13,600.

In 1884, the fifth generation of Wedgwoods took over Josiah Wedgwood & Sons. However, this was the last generation that would manage the firm as a family partnership that had existed since its foundation 136 years earlier. In 1895, company law reforms required that the firm change from a partnership to a limited liability company. In a personal way, this marked the end of a family saga.

It did not, of course, mark the end of the production of Wedgwood pottery. Indeed, in 1920, Wedgwood expanded to America, while in Britain, it continued to modernize. In 1936, the directors decided to build a new factory at Barlaston, some six miles south of Etruria, where a village for its workers was also built. In an improvement that would have made Josiah proud for its health benefits, this was the first pottery to power its kilns by electricity. It is still the main factory for the production of Wedgwood pottery today.

On 15 June 1950, the date on which, 181 years earlier, Josiah and Bentley ceremoniously opened Etruria by throwing the "First Day's Vases," Etruria was officially closed. To commemorate the event, six "Last Day's Vases"—replicas of the early pieces—were thrown. Sadly, in the 1960s, the original factory was bulldozed to the ground, save one round room that stood at the southeast corner of the building; in its place is now a parking lot next to the Trent & Mersey Canal. If one pulls back the branches of an overgrown shrub on the east side of the canal, a bent, rusted metal sign can be found. It states that this was once the spot of the famous Etruria factory.

Look elsewhere, however, and the Wedgwood name is not hard to find. The well-known pale blue jasper vases, saucers, and bowls, offset by white classical figures, have remained in continuous production since Josiah first introduced jasper in 1774 and are on prominent display in retail shops across the world. The name—and the range of products the company offers—endures from a combination of historical status and commitment to innovative, quality design.

Reaffirming its commitment to the principles that Josiah adhered to—the highest standard of production and untiring search for new designs—the company now, as in the eighteenth century, recruits renowned artists and uses the latest technologies to guarantee accuracy and efficiency. Academics from Harvard Business School use Wedgwood as an example of the first manufacturer "to command widespread consumer recognition and loyalty"; his was the first "brand name," and it became synonymous with fine taste. Much of the continued popularity of Wedgwood pottery derives from customer expectation of this high quality. It comes at an expense (using a composition of 51 percent animal bone in ceramic cups ensures durability, but costs much more than producing thicker, heavier cups composed of more clay), but Josiah Wedgwood was dedicated to prioritizing his patrons' approval over profits. One of Josiah's main competitors, Matthew Boulton—at the height their rivalry in 1771—learned the lesson. "Our pottery does very well," commented James Watt, "tho' we make damned bad ware." Soon after this Josiah received the largest and most prestigious commission of his life—Catherine the Great's "Frog Service"—and announced his "victory" over Boulton and Watt's outfit.

Consistency and quality have been the two key characteristics of the Wedgwood pottery's success. In October 1863, William Gladstone, chancellor of the exchequer, gave a speech to mark the opening of the Wedgwood Institute in Burslem, remarking that Josiah "was the greatest man who ever, in any age or country, applied himself to the important work of uniting art with science." Gladstone was not only recalling the sophisticated manufacturing techniques that allowed Wedgwood to combine artistic craftsmanship with mass production but also establishing Wedgwood's place in history. Like the industrial scenes portrayed on the items of Catherine the Great's "Frog Service," Wedgwood became both a symbol and a product of Britain's innovation and expanding economy. "No one better than Gladstone could have made us understand the true genius of a Wedgwood," remarked Louis Solon, himself a renowned potter of the late nineteenth century. After Gladstone's speech, buying Wedgwood pottery became a matter of national pride. It meant literally possessing a piece of British soil, which through revolutionary innovations was transformed into an elegant and functional piece of art.

It is therefore the history and symbolism that Wedgwood pottery embodies that has made it such a sought-after collectable. In 1903, President Theodore Roosevelt commissioned a 1,300-piece dinner service for the White House, with the U.S. Great Seal hand-enameled on each piece of the service in silver and gold. Since then, a revival of prestigious orders has continued to attract attention. In 1995, a new Russian service was commissioned which rivals Catherine the Great's in importance. The 47,000 pieces—the largest commission for Wedgwood ever—are now in the Kremlin.

But as always, Wedgwood represents elite taste without social prejudice. The name carries the status of an old master, but is accessible to those without aristocratic wealth. Never one to ignore the interests of the "Middling Classes" in favor of the rich, Josiah would be proud to learn of the favorable impression his wares continue to make on customers, whether royalty, presidents, or everyday tourists.

Notes

Anyone who has carefully consulted the Wedgwood archives has noted that, while there are two sources which published a portion of his correspondence, the letters—particularly the Lady Farrer, ed., *Letters of Josiah Wedgwood*, 3 vols. (1904–06)—are badly edited and abridged, arbitrarily eliding much that any biographer would find illuminating of Josiah's thoughts and character. It therefore remains the best policy for clarity and consistency to cite the reference number of the manuscript located in one of the archives listed below, many of which are referred to here for the first time.

One source that is surprisingly underused relating to Wedgwood's extended family—particularly the Wedgwood family of Bignall End and of the Big House, who play a prominent part early on in this biography—is The Potteries Museum Collection at Stoke-on-Trent City Archives, Hanley Library. The catalogue to the collection alone is telling of the kinds of activities they engaged in, especially as small landowners, and I am happy to note that this catalogue has recently begun to go on line, and is growing annually, as part of the "Gateway to the Past" on-line catalogue of the Staffordshire and Stoke-on-Trent Archive Service, located at www.archives.staffordshire.gov.uk. It will prove an invaluable aid to future researchers.

Frequently cited archives:

BL	British Library
CUL	Cambridge University Library
Keele	Wedgwood Etruria and Liverpool Collections at Keele University
PM	Potteries Museum, Hanley, Stoke-on-Trent
RSL	Royal Society London
SOT	Stoke-on-Trent City Archives, Hanley Library
SRO	Stafford Record Office
W/M	Wedgwood/Mosely Collection, Keele University
WSL	William Salt Library, Stafford

xix   Currency conversion and costs ca 1760: Rough averages from figures estimated by Joseph Massie in 1760, full table reprinted in Peter Mathias, *The Transformation of England: Essays in the Economic and Social History of England in the Eighteenth Century* (London: Methuen, 1979), table 9.1, supplemented with particulars I have gathered from the Wedgwood accounts. Expenses from Brian Inglis, *Poverty and the Industrial Revolution* (London: Hodder & Stoughton, 1971). See also John McCusker, *How Much Is That in Real Money? A Historical Price Index for Use as a Deflator of Money Values in the Economy of the United States* (Worcester, MA: American Antiquarian Society, 1992); Council of Economic Advisers, *Economic Report of the*

President (Washington, D.C.: U.S. Government Printing Office, 2000); and Peter Lindert and Jeffrey Williamson, "English Workers' Living Standards," *Economic History Review*, 2nd ser., 36 (1983).

Part One:
1: A Place for Thomas

4 calling himself Thomas of Burslem: Hughes, *Mother Town*, 13. The place name Burslem was ancient, derived from "Barcardeslim" as recorded in the Domesday Book. Strictly, until 1809 when Burslem was made parochial, it was a chapelry in the parish of Stoke-on-Trent, though, as the local historian Greenslade points out, since the sixteenth century it had been referred to as a parish, implying a level of its own administrative autonomy—Greenslade, "History of Burslem," 121.

4 He was born in 1588: See Wedgwood, *History*, 50–55, for Gilbert's background; the next eldest brother married a woman with family wealth.

4 round, blackened oven: Shaw, *History of Staffordshire Potteries*, 101.

5 new interests in coal mining: Hughes, *Mother Town*, 13–14.

5 passed into Wedgwood lands: See below for breakdown of lots of property that ended up in Wedgwood hands in 1670, but note that—as discussed further below—the other 400 acres which Katherine owned were sold and divided up amongst other children of Gilbert and Margaret. The 150 acres or so which Thomas Wedgwood would soon own (in total) represented the largest single landowner at the time.

5 Suddenly, at fifty-two years old...: Margaret's sister was Katherine Colclough; her son, John, had died in 1666. Upon Katherine's death in 1669, most of the property in question was bequeathed to Burslem Wedgwood II (1649–1696), the son of Thomas's older brother, Burslem Wedgwood. But it was a heavily encumbered estate, requiring a massive £950 be raised through sale or rent for future legacies. To meet this, he sold much of the property to Thomas in 1670 and settled for the remainder of his life at Dale Hall. The source is the property deed, Keele E21-17776 and E21-17798; also comments in Ward, *Stoke-on-Trent*, 196. The Overhouse Estate itself was around 100 acres of property.

5 "barns, stables, outhouses...": In the will of Thomas Wedgwood (1617–1679), reprinted in Wedgwood, *History*, III (cited here after as Thomas Wedgwood's will).

6 The more elbow power one had: cf. the analysis of land labor in the early stages of industrialization in Wrigley, *Continuity, Chance and Change*.

6 owned two small potteries: Property deed, Keele, E21-17798; great-grandfather Thomas Wedgwood's will.

6 Crown and Mitre: Hughes, *Mother Town*, 15.

6 "workhouses and pot ovens": Description from a bill of complaint relating to the ownership of the land, 15 June 1640, reprinted as appendix to Wedgwood, *History*, 255. From Thomas Wedgwood's will.

7 "he was apparently content": Wedgwood, *History*, 130. This assessment of father Thomas's talents is widely supported, but more recent scholars have challenged the idea that Burslem at the time was merely "peasant pottery"; see Weatherill, *Pottery Trade*, chapter 4. For my purposes, it is relevant that Josiah himself was critical of his father's achievements.

7 "Men necessary to make...": From "Memorandums relative to the pottery," Keele L96-17695; Josiah calculated annual profits at 46 weeks to the year.

8 "The Wear and Tear": JW's "Memorandums," Keele, L96-17695.

8 average income: See Waterman, *Wages in Eighteenth-Century England*.

8 dusty workshops: Described in Thomas Wedgwood's will.

8 an insatiable maw: The mill is mentioned in Thomas Wedgwood's will, and the process is described in these terms in Graham, *Cup and Saucer Land*, 16.

8   thrower's wheel: Note that much of the information regarding the content and distribution of real and personal property amongst Josiah Wedgwood's family draws from their wills and probate records, including inventories. The wills of Josiah's great-grandfather, Thomas (1687–1739), grandmother Mary Leigh (?-1719), father Thomas (1687–1739), and brother Thomas (1716–1773) are preserved in the Lichfield Record Office. Portions, in full or extract, were first printed in 1908 by Josiah C. Wedgwood, *A History of the Wedgwood Family*, and some of the documents (in full or abridged) have since been put on line as part of the "Wedgwood Family History" site: *www.geocities.com/heartland/3230/alt.html*—along with miscellaneous other documents relating to the transfer or lease of property by the Wedgwood's of Burslem. I have spotted a number of typographical errors (some wrong names, variously incorrect birth/death dates) in the on-line versions, and in such cases I refer specifically to the manuscript sources.

2: A Will and a Prayer

10   the freezing temperatures: Meteorological Office statistics.

10   a twenty-year-old trade agreement: This was the Treaty of Utrecht (1713) that ended Queen Anne's War and permitted Britain to participate in slave traffic in the Spanish colonies.

10   "of great yearly value": See the bill of complaint lodged by the rector of Stoke challenging the ownership of Churchyard House, which was eventually resolved in the Wedgwoods' favor, reprinted in Wedgwood, *History*, 255–68.

10   "convenient": See the discussion in Crowley, "Sensibility of Comfort." For a general sense of the average size of houses in the region at this time, see the discussion in Vaisey, ed., *Probate Inventories*, 23–27.

11   Mary and six of her children: In ascending order, all the living children were Josiah, nine, Catherine, thirteen, Richard, fourteen, Aaron, seventeen, John, eighteen, Margaret, nineteen, Thomas, twenty-three, and Anne, twenty-seven. Anne was already married and living with her husband; Margaret seems not to have been married yet (unlike Anne, whose dowry probably acted as her share of the inheritance, Margaret was still included in her father's will). John had probably already gone to make his living as a merchant in London, and Aaron probably secured his living in Burslem.

11   "intolerable smoke and stink": A complaint from the Norfolk parson, Rev. James Woodforde, quoted in Crowley, "Sensibility of Comfort," who examines common living conditions as recorded in contemporary diaries.

11   the kitchen: Meteyard, *Life of Josiah Wedgwood*, i, 200–01, provides a physical description of the house; she saw the buildings around one hundred years later when they were extended, but she also relies on an oral history from talking to grandchildren of locals.

11   "china" cups: As a general point, here and below the description of any household item is drawn from the probate inventories of Josiah's brother. Thomas: Keele, L96-17800-45, "Accounts, receipts, inventories, letters, abstract of will, relating mainly to Thomas, brother of Josiah Wedgwood." The kitchen contents are specifically described in Keele, L96-17808.

11   the "backhouse": Keele, L96-17811.

12   "They bake 'em in kilns": Trinder, *Industrial Landscape*, 36.

12   Each pannier of coal: The analysis of price of coal in Thomas, *Rise of Staffordshire Potteries*, 68–69.

12   The well next to the churchyard: Warrillow, *Stoke-on-Trent*, 177.

12   evaporating finances: The probate records for Josiah's father begin the story of Thomas's financial struggles: Keele, E22-17930. "Letters of Administration, granted in the consistory court of Coventry and Lichfield, to Mary, widow of Thomas Wedgwood."

12–13   a bakehouse...nineteen alehouses: Description in Greenslade, "History of Burslem," 130.

13   "right" to do this: Steele, "Social Conditions," cites references in the Tunstall Manor Court Rolls of fees of 4s yearly paid for the right to dig, and penalties for failing to fill up the pits.

13   "the greatest pottery they have": Plot, *Natural History*, 422.

13   twelve shillings a week: These wages from Weatherill, *Pottery Trade*, chapter 7.

13   "poor *Cratemen*": Plot, *Natural History*, 124; Meteyard, *Life*, i, 146.

14   "only one horse and one mule": Josiah's "Memorandums relative to the pottery," Keele, L96-17695.

14   the Jolly Potters: See the map of Burslem ca 1750; "Dredge Malt": Plot, *Natural History*.

14   "Up the Potter!": Hughes, *Mother Town*, xviii.

14   "mean and poor": Ward, *Stoke-on-Trent*, 31.

14   "the manners of the inhabitants": Ward, 31.

14   "bull and bear-baiting": Meteyard, *Life*, i, 106.

14   "Coom, sup it Rafy...": This remarkable conversation about Burslem in the 1750s took place in 1810 and was transcribed by the local historian John Ward and printed in his *History of the Borough of Stoke-upon Trent*.

15   "teazed of my life": Josiah to Bentley, 7 August 1765, Keele, E25-18089.

15   "behave and demean himself" and "at Cards, Dice...": Indentures reprinted in Jewitt, *The Wedgwoods*, 66, 93.

16   responsible for supplying bread: From "Churchwardens Accounts of Stoke on Trent," Keele, E49-32807.

16   "one of the gentry": Meteyard, *Life*, i, 193; Reilly, *Josiah Wedgwood*, 2.

16   Throughout January and February: Weatherill, *Pottery Trade*, 94.

16   village had in the past relieved its poor: Greenslade, "History of Burlem," 129, who analyzed the Burslem parish register and Churchwarden's and Overseers' Accounts.

17   first parish "poorhouse": Opened in 1741; it is also referred to as a "workhouse," but I will persist with this term to avoid confusion with the potters' workhouses. See Greenslade, "History of Burslem," 129; Webb and Webb, *English Local Government*; also Crowther, *Workhouse System*, chapter I.

17   "a croft or two": Meteyard, *Life*, i, 193; the price of food from a household account book kept 1738–41 mentioned in Pitt's *Topographical History* is also quoted by Meteyard.

17   "employing class": While I don't think they use that term, I believe it's more appropriate than "middle class" which, with relation to income earned from rents and property, is analyzed by Davidoff and Hall, *Family Fortunes*, 205–07.

17   "they rendered no account": Shaw, *History*, 155. Sometimes the problems were compounded when the customer was given leave to pay on credit, and never paid: Weatherill, *Pottery Trade*, 54.

17   "Money": These tokens had no legal value, but where the issuer (the potter's customer) was well known and trusted, his tokens would be accepted. Different people had distinctive tokens—130 different kinds of tokens have been found by archeologists in Staffordshire. When merchants accumulated enough, they would take them to the issuer and exchange them for silver. See Watkin, "Staffordshire Tokens": Peter Mathias, *English Trade Tokens: The Industrial Revolution Illustrated* (London, 1962).

18   "in the bringing up...": Thomas Wedgwood's will.

18   bound himself for the sum of £50...mortgaged: Wedgwood, *History*, 130; Greenslade, "History of Burslem," 133. Father Thomas refers to the mortgage in his will as part of his debts.

NOTES

3: "Creators of Fortune and Fame"

19 "interest therein determined": Thomas Wedgwood's will, Litchfield; Margaret (Shaw) Wedgwood, will, Litchfield; Wedgwood, *History*, 115.

19 lessons at the school in Newcastle-under-Lyme: Josiah's contemporary cousins attended this school, as discussed below, but the only evidence that Josiah might have gone is the statement by his great-granddaughter Julia Wedgwood in her *Personal Life*, 10.

19 "English Charity Schoole": History discussed in Steele, "Glimpses into the Social Conditions," 28.

19 "a fair arithmetician": Meteyard, *Life*, i, 208.

20 "Blunging": These early stages of the preparation of clay are discussed in Weatherill, *Pottery Trade*, 19–22; "beat it till it be well mixed": Description of process by the contemporary Plot, *Natural History*, 123. Neither of these specifically refers to Josiah, but children of Josiah's age, nine or ten, usually performed such necessary activities.

20 twelve-hour day: Average working hours nationally amongst manufactory laborers in this period (generally 6 a.m.–6 p.m.); Saturdays were often "half-days," ending at 3 p.m. In winter, hours were often from the "spring of the day ... till night of the same day"—see Bienefeld, *Working Hours*, 22–23, 228. In later chapters I mention slightly reformed working hours set by Josiah.

20 Rising food prices: There has been much debate about the agricultural production and the working conditions of laborers moving into the manufactories in the "early" industrial revolution. Josiah's circumstance is a good example of the difficult transition families faced. See the discussion in de Vries, "Purchasing Power," 107, 114–15; Freudenburger and Cummins, "Health, Work and Leisure."

20 "administer all the goods": Keele, E22-17930, "Letters of Administration."

20 "judiciously renounced their right": Keele, E22-17930.

20 a bankrupt estate: Wedgwood, *History*, 132, reasons that they renounced executorships since "there was not enough in the estate to pay the legacies."

21 They "left their father's service": Simeon Shaw, *Staffordshire Potteries*, 157.

22 They had new premises: John Wedgwood's Rent Book, Hanley archives, D4842/14/1/62-75. John Wedgwood property title deeds.

22 "East Indian rareities": Reference to his trade in a letter from J. B. Crafft to Leibniz, 1672, quoted in Elliott, *John and David Elers*, 9; Elliot's study is the best source of information on the Elers brothers. For reference to their uncle, see Edwards, "London Potteries," 18.

23 "tay, alias tee": Advertisement in the *Mercurius Politicus*, 30 September 1658, advertising a new drink at the "sultaness Head, a Cophee-house in Sweetings Rents, by the Royal Exchange, London."

23 "Home—and there find": Pepys's "Potticary" refers to an apothecary.

23 "The drink is declared to be . . .": From "An Exact Description of the Growth, Quality, and Virtues of the Tea Leaf, by Thomas Garway, in Exchange Alley, near the Royal Exchange, in London, Tobacconist, and Seller and Retailer of Tea and Coffee," reprinted in Francis Leggett & Co., *Tea Leaves* (New York, 1900) and reproduced at the book's site: http://www.ibiblio.org/herbmed/eclectic/tea/chapter-ii.html.

23 under 5,000 pounds of the leaf: Wills, "European Consumption," 141; Chaudhuri, *Trading World of Asia*, chapter II.

23 "for health" (Cornelis Bontekoe): Schama, *Embarrassment of Riches*, 172.

23 "base, black, thick": From *The Women's Petition against Coffee, Representing to Publick Consideration the Grand Inconveniences accruing to their Sex from the Excessive Use of that Drying, Enfeebling Liquor* (1678), quoted in Wilson, *England's Apprenticeship*, 307; coffeehouses were made rowdier at about that time when they began selling alcohol as well; see Wills, "European Consumption," 141–42.

24 Holland—which was much more "modern": Wrigley, *Continuity, Chance, and Change*, 103.

24 "The potters made dishes": "Mr Sadler" to the committee on manufactures, quoted in Edwards, "London Potteries," 22.

24 "to bring a person well skilled": Oade, *The Unnatural Parent*, 47.

24 "a society of Experimenters": Joseph Glanvill's "Address to the Royal Society" quoted in Dear, "Totius in Verba," 148.

24 "the misterie of the stone ware": Dwight's patents (1672 and 1684) quoted from Haselgrove and Murray, "John Dwight's Fulham Pottery."

24 experimentally minded Dutch entrepreneur: A sketch of their educational background, including the claim that links them to Becher, is from an account written by David Philip Elers's grandson, reprinted in Elliott, *Elers*, 8.

25 Etruria Formation: For this information I am grateful to Bernard Besley of the Earth Sciences Department at the University of Keele.

25 "their extreme precaution": Stebbing Shaw, *History and Antiquities*, 18.

26 "to intimate the approach": Ibid., 19. The story of the clay "speaking tubes" resurfaced in the twentieth century with alleged proof of their existence: "It is a curious tribute the value of such legends," wrote Josiah C. Wedgwood in his *Staffordshire Pottery and Its History* in 1913. "that, within the last few years, white earthenware voice-pipes have actually been dug up on the site of the Bradwell factory. They did not of course, really extend from Bradwell to Dimsdale, but they went from one part of the factory to another, and were probably devised to secure secrecy rather than modern economy. These pipes are now to be seen at the Hanley Museum" (p. 35); this was reproduced in Wedgwood and Ormsbee, *Staffordshire Pottery* (1947), p. 19, but modern analysis shows that the material composition of these pipes dates them to the later nineteenth century.

26 "The people of Burslem": Wedgwood, *History*, appendix XII.

26 "a soft oar like Clay": Martin Lister to Royal Society, 1693, in *Philosophical Transactions of the Royal Society of London*; their activities also announced in an advertisement in the *Husbandry and Trades Improv'd*, 13 October 1693.

27 "to hinder and restrayne": Suit filed 10 August 1693, quoted in Haselgrove and Murray, "John Dwight's Fulham Pottery," 95. For a later case where Staffordshire potters interact with the Royal Society and patents result in competitive means, see Mountford, "Thomas Briand."

27 the "idiot": From later in the eighteenth century the story went that "Astbury," presumed by many to be the Shelton potter Robert Astbury, pretended to be the idiot (see Wedgwood, *Staffordshire Pottery*, 37 note). Occasionally writers have wrongly assumed it was John Astbury, who would have been too young. Josiah only writes—in his notes on the Elers brothers—that "Astbury of Shelton made white ware with the addition of flint the first in Shelton," but this hardly makes him an idiot. Weatherill, *Pottery Trade*, 32, concedes the possibility that such a type of person might have been employed in an effort to protect trade secrets, but who exactly it was and whether this allowed the Elers business to be penetrated remains a historical enigma. What's important for the purposes of considering Josiah's life is that much contemporary emphasis was put on the possibility of such radical measures of espionage, which was a lesson Josiah never forgot.

27 "unjust and injurious practices": 15 December 1693, quoted in Haselgrove and Murray, "John Dwight's Fulham Pottery," 97.

28 "The Fulhamites can come and go": Quote from the *Stoke-on-Trent Historical Pageant and the Josiah Wedgwood Bicentenary Celebrations* (1930), p. 52.

28 "Where they went": Keele, Josiah's commonplace book, E39-28408, f. 212. They had, in fact, returned to London, where they declared bankruptcy.

28 concealing pieces . . . in the garret: Wedgwood and Wedgwood, *Wedgwood Pedigrees*, 173.

29 "pyrometrical beads": Meteyard, *Life*, i, 159.

29 "the one an excellent thrower": Simeon Shaw, *Staffordshire Potteries*, 157.

29 "a most pertinent illustration": Ibid., 183.

4: A Potter and a Gentlewoman

31   It was a sign of prosperity: Lane, *Apprenticeship in England*, 13.

31   "to Learn his Art": 1744 indenture, Keele, L134-26845, reprinted in Jewitt, *Wedgwood*, 92–93.

32   Josiah's other brother, Richard . . . became a soldier: Wedgwood and Wedgwood, *Wedgwood Pedigrees*, 100.

33   was running one of the most profitable potteries: Josiah estimated that his weekly turnover was £6, the most of any potter in Burslem around 1715; Keele L96-17695.

33   Oldfields . . . Oxley Croft: A list of approximately twenty-one properties that she leased, with notes on the annual value of each, is found in Wedgwood, *History*, 135.

33–34   Aunt Katherine . . . regard: Katherine Wedgwood Egerton's will, copy in Keele, W/M 21-17778.

34   "earnest money": See appendix to Mountford, "Thomas Wedgwood," for examples of wages for apprentices; also, Wedgwood, *Staffordshire Pottery*, 76, for earnest money.

34   preparing to borrow £100: Wedgwood, *History*, 135.

34   Unitarians were different: See Wilbur, *History of Unitarianism*, vol. 2.

34   "two corruptions of Scripture": Newton's *Historical Account of Two Corruptions of Scripture*, published posthumously in 1754.

35   "God that made the World": Bellers, "Essays about the Poor," 105; for the relations between Quakerism and Unitarianism, see the debate expressed in William Penn's *The Spirit of the Quakers Tried* (London, 1672).

35   the eighteen-year-old medical student: The student, Thomas Aikenhead, was hung in 1697—Wilbur, *History of Unitarianism*, 231–32.

35   full "toleration": It came in 1813 with the passing of the so-called Trinity Act.

35   Burslem, and the five small towns: The six towns of Burslem, Tunstall, Hanley, Stoke-upon-Trent, Longton, and Fenton were united in 1910 to form one city called Stoke-on-Trent. Reference to "the Potteries," referring generally to this cluster of towns, emerged in the early nineteenth century, especially with the publication of Simeon Shaw's *History of the Staffordshire Potteries* in 1829.

36   "febrile state": Lobb, *Treatise*, vii.

36   "we dare not eat milk": Comment from Horace Walpole in 1745 referring to the gloom of the period, quoted in Wilson, *England's Apprenticeship*, 243; for discussion of the relationship between smallpox, hunger, and death, see Landers, *Birth and Death*.

36   "never intend that": Crowther, *The Workhouse System*, 20.

36   "as the small-pox in him": Meteyard's description, in her *Life and Works*, i, 220; compare, however, with Reilly's more cautious account, *Josiah Wedgwood*, 4.

37   "It turns many into frightful spectacles": Doddridge, *Case for Receiving the Small-Pox*, 12.

37   "a season of severe bodily affliction": Tom Byerley, Ms "life of Josiah Wedgwood," Keele, W/M 1131.

38   "However ill the practice": From an anonymous tract titled "The origin, object, and operation of the apprentice laws" (1814), quoted in Lane, *Apprenticeship in England*, I.

38   Booth was experimenting: Towner, *Creamware* 23, notes that Booth is usually attributed as having introduced liquid lead glazes, but it is more likely he was one of the first to use the method. Young, ed., *Genius*, 22. Meiklejohn, "successful prevention of lead poisoning."

39   white flint stones created: See analysis in Weatherill, *Pottery Trade*, 25–27.

39   "Any person ever so healthful": Quoted in Meiklejohn, "Successful Prevention of Silicosis."

39   "potter's rot": Ibid. Benson took out two patents for the construction of flint mills, the first on 5 November 1726, the second on 14 January 1732, which improved on the first by substituting iron balls with granite used for crushing and grinding the flint stones. See Weatherill, *Pottery Trade*, 24, 65.

39   "To take, farme, & Rent": Quoted in Mountford, "Thomas Wedgwood," 23.

40   Fortunately for the Staffordshire potters: Young, ed., *Genius*, 10.

40   "mottled" ... "combed": Mottled ware was produced through the application of metal oxides to the ware before glazing, while "agate" ware was formed either by wedging different-colored clays together (known as solid agate) or by using stained surface slip (known as marbled ware). See the description by Plot, *Natural History*, reprinted in Jewitt, *Wedgwoods*, 30–31. Weatherill, *Pottery Trade*, 28, points out that although Plot identifies "magnus" as manganese, it is "more likely to have been the workman's term for iron-ore, for the glaze of black wares contains iron but not manganese."

40   "seated at two corners": Comment by John Fletcher, who was paid four pence weekly to prepare the clay for Josiah and Richard; from Shaw, *History of Staffordshire Potteries*, 180.

41   "was considered a ridiculous expense": Enoch Wood's reporting, quoted in Wedgwood and Wedgwood, *Wedgwood Pedigrees*, 173.

41   "endless illusive projects": A sentiment that Meteyard puts into Thomas's mouth, *Life*, i, 233; but see Reilly's skepticism of the oft-cited allegation of excessive "bitterness" between Josiah and his brother, *Wedgwood*, 8.

41   "No single handed man": Quoted in De Vries, "Purchasing Power," 116.

5: Discipline and Dissent

42   "Tailor, Draper, and Man's Mercer": Simeon Shaw, *Staffordshire Potteries*, 182.

42   "family apartments": Brief description offered by Meteyard, *Life*, i, 235.

42   women "flowerers": Shaw, *Staffordshire Potteries*, 177; Meteyard, *Life*, i, 232.

44   Fearing the subversion: See Gascoigne, *Cambridge in the Age of the Enlightenment*, for discussion of the ways that Dissenting beliefs are aligned with the pursuit of experimental natural philosophy and the associated political prejudices, a general argument that I am adapting to analyze the commitments of provincial Dissenting tradesmen.

44   in the 1750s Staffordshire was not seen: See Hobsbawm, "Methodism and the Threat of Revolution," for related discussion of nineteenth-century sentiments and demography in Staffordshire.

44   prominently so in Josiah's family: In 1747, for instance, Josiah's brother Thomas had voted Whig, and the Whig politics of Josiah himself become increasingly clear as he gets older: Wedgwood and Wedgwood, *Wedgwood Pedigrees*, 101. For the Whig Party suspicions about church authority, see Gilbert, *Religion and Society*, 4, though it is worth qualifying that there was also growing awareness of the gradual secularization of social institutions in the beginning of the eighteenth century.

45   "the aim of business": Courtauld quoted in Davidoff and Hall, *Family Fortunes*, 207.

45   pursuit of "free enquiry": For a catalogue of "social improvers" who shared the Unitarian faith—which addresses not only religious but political views—see Holt, *Unitarian Contribution to Social Progress*.

45   "Potmaking chiefly depends": Long John's essay published as an appendix to Mountford, "Thomas Briand," 96–99. I have altered a sentence to make grammatical sense of it (the original sentence reads "Earth according to ye Chymist principles for in the potters Art it is to be considered in yt [that] light because it undergoes ye operation of fire ...").

46   "one Clear Annuity": Long John's will quoted in Mountford, "Thomas Wedgwood," 28; Long John also supported Dissenting congregations in other nearby areas, giving, for instance, £5 cash to the "Congleton Dissenting Society" in 1758.

46   a man of "good will to Philosophy": Willets to C. Mortimer, secretary to the Royal Society, 20 January 1737/8, BL, ADD Mss 4434, f. 213r.

46   "assured by experiment": Willets to Mortimer, 10 October 1738, BL, ADD Mss 4434, f. 211.

46   that "truly good man": Keele, E25-18837.

46 "great philosophic fact": Meteyard's comment, in *Life*, i, 246–47. She and Josiah's great-granddaughter, Julia Wedgwood, both state that Josiah borrowed books from Willets's personal library, and Meteyard adds a note that the books Josiah personally copied "are now in the possession of Mr. Dingwell, of Edinburgh"—Meteyard, ibid.; Julia Wedgwood, *Personal Life*, 17, citing a later letter where Wedgwood mentions Willets's library. Reilly, *Wedgwood*, 23, questions the way the story was embellished to put Wedgwood on a sickbed and being visited by Erasmus Darwin at the same time, but Willets's intellectual influence seems convincing. "Service to Philosophy" is what Willets declared he was committed to: BL, ADD Mss 4434, f. 213.

47 "secrets" that he knew Josiah alone possessed: The point is raised in Mankowitz, *Wedgwood*, 24.

47 "Pot ovens, houses, Buildings": Indenture reprinted in Mountford, "Thomas Whieldon's Manufactory," 175–81; the article gives an interesting account of the archeological digs carried out in 1968 under the aegis of the City Museum, Stoke-on-Trent.

47 "He was shrewd enough": Summary of the ceramics historian Mankowitz, *Wedgwood*, 24.

47 "from whom he exacted": These were the traits he passed on to his best apprentice. Josiah Spode: Whiter, *Spode*, 17.

48 £106 annual supplement: Weatherill, *Pottery Trade*, 55.

48 called "The Grove": Mountford, "Thomas Whieldon's Manufactory," 171; additional biographical information provided in Morley-Hewitt, "Early Whieldon."

48 "not a very likeable character": Morley-Hewitt, "Early Whieldon," 142.

48 eight shillings a week: For Whieldon's wages from his account book, see Whiter, *Spode*, 5.

48 "6 tenements or dwghoues": From the indentures reprinted in Mountford, "Thomas Whieldon's Manufactory," 173. The point about his workers' housing is on p. 171, where it is noted that Wedgwood is often attributed to doing this for the first time; for his London aristocratic clients, see Mountford, ibid., 173, for Lady Leicester's order.

48 "Visitation returns": Gilbert, *Religion and Society*, 12.

48 "from a delicacy of taste": The quotations in this and the next paragraph are from Doddridge, *Free thoughts on the most probable means of eviving the dissenting interest* (London, 1730), 7–20.

49 "The neglect of the Poor": Sir Francis Brewster, *New Essays on Trade* (London, 1702), 52, 122; Wilson, *England's Apprenticeship*, 350, for the point about "secret weapon." Brewster was arguing that better trade would help secure the nation against growing concern about the commercial power of the French.

49 "parish manufactories": Mackworth's proposals are from the printed *Bill for the Better Relief, Imployment, and Settlement of the Poor, as the same was Reported from the Committee to the Honourable House of Commons* (London, 1704), 3–7; the bill was read on 4 January 1704.

50 turning "Parishes into Ware-houses": Daniel Defoe, *Giving Alms No Charity, and Employing the Poor: A Grievance to the Nation, Being an essay upon this Great Question* (London, 1704), reprinted in Owens, ed., *Political and Economic Writings*, 171–75.

50 "House of Industry": From Webb and Webb, *English Local Government*, 127–28.

51 "the highest wages then given": Whiter, *Spode*, 4.

51 "a Man of Energy": Ibid., 17.

52 "I had already made": This and the following comments are from Josiah's famous "Experiment Book," Keele, E26-19115, f. 71.

53 "block maker": William Greatbatch. It has been generally assumed that an entry in Whieldon's account book referring to "Daniel Greatbachs son" is a reference to William Greatbatch (see, e.g., Towner, "William Greatbatch"): but recently Barker, in his *William Greatbatch*, 29, casts doubt on this. While the evidence is inconclusive, is seems likely that Greatbatch was employed by Whieldon at some point, and it is certain that Josiah had great respect for his talents and they remained close throughout Josiah's life.

53   an "ingenious young man": Opinion of Thomas Byerley, Josiah's nephew, Keele, W/M 1131.

53   "STILE ornament": Keele, W/M 1131 (I've altered the word "e'ware" in the original to "earthenware" here).

54   " 'solid-agate' teapot lids": This list covers some of the things that were excavated during an archeological dig on the Whieldon site, discussed in Mountford, "Thomas Whieldon's Manufactory," 174.

54   "The age is . . . running mad": Johnson quoted in Wilson, *England's Apprenticeship*, 311.

54   "Few countries are equal": Josiah Tucker, *Instructions to Travellers* (London, 1757), 20.

55   "dissent, that religion of trade and manufacturers": Tucker's sentiments expressed in his *A Treatise concerning Civil Government* (London, 1781), 33; the quotation about dissent comes from Wilson, *England's Apprenticeship*, 342, in discussing the evolution of Matthew Arnold's onslaught in his *Culture and Anarchy*.

55   "for the improvement of our manufacture": Keele, E26-19115.

56   "should completely cover the piece": Ibid. "JW": an extant example of a green tea canister from about this period with his initials on its base is at the Victoria & Albert Museum, Arthur Hurst Bequest, C.16-1940; see also Young, ed., *Genius*, 26, illustration B10.

56   "Willy's" sack: Josiah refers to the horse he was to have for the next twenty years, Keele, E26-18862.

6: "Dues & Demands"

57   a stillborn girl: Mountford, "Thomas Wedgwood," 29.

58   "the women to have gloves": Katherine Wedgwood Egerton's will, 9 January 1756, Keele, W/M 21-17778.

58   "with gambling, duelling, sporting": See discussion of "middle class" management of landed property in Davidoff and Hall, *Family Fortunes*, 205, and the uniqueness of a woman in the first half of the eighteenth century performing these sorts of duties.

59   to "tread the wheel": Weatherill, *Pottery Trade*, 32.

60   "all the appearances of a most extensive Laboratory": Shaw, *History*, 30, describing the slightly later potworks of Enoch Wood. The description of the skills involved is nicely summarized by J. G. Crowther in *Social Relations of Science* (New York, 1941), 19, quoted in Clow and Clow, *Chemical Revolution*, 296.

60   "manifestly ineligible": Discussion from G. Rae, *The Country Banker* (1886); see Davidoff and Hall, *Family Fortunes*, 211.

61   "yeoman" son of . . . Jonah Malkin: For the story of Malkin's crisis, I have relied on the information provided in the late Arnold Mountford's unpublished MA thesis from Keele University, "Thomas Wedgwood, John Wedgwood, and Jonah Malkin," to which I would like to register my debt.

61   "His father lent him . . .": Mountford, "Thomas Wedgwood," 39.

62   "J. W. has taken to his Account": Ibid.

62   "It is more money": Ibid., 40.

63   "I saw the field was spacious": Quoted in Reilly, *Wedgwood*, i, 32.

7: The *Racehorse*

64   Ruffley's: The situation is gleaned from Enoch Wood's map of Burslem in 1750; also Josiah's list of potters from his "Memorandum": Keele, L96-17695, reprinted in Meteyard, *Life*, i, 190–91.

65   their first Town Hall: Ward, *Stoke-on-Trent*, 206.

65   his first year's bill £17 6s: Long John's account books reprinted in Mountford, "Thomas Wedgwood," 52.

65 a "potter ambitious to improve": Comment from Reilly, *Wedgwood*, 28, where the family relationship is also stated; Mankowitz, *Wedgwood*, 25, for the "memorandum of agreement."

65 "idle, slovenly, irregular": Meteyard's summary, *Life*, i, 260; Useful Tom's salary from the "Memorandum of an Agreement," Keele, WMS 27-19281, 30 December 1758; Spode's equivalent salary from Whiter, *Spode*, 4; see also Niblett, "A Useful Partner."

66 "a scattered town": Wesley's account of Burslem from Curnock, ed., *Journal of the Rev. John Wesley*, iv, 370–72.

66 "full of fierce Ephesian beasts": Charles Wesley's experience quoted in Meteyard, *Life*, i, 265.

67 "preaching publicly in the streets": The account of the Wesleys' visit and the subsequent riots they caused is from [anon.], *Some Papers Giving an Account of the Rise and Progress of Methodism in Wednesbury in Staffordshire and other Parishes adjacent, as likewise of the Late Riot in these parts* (1744).

68 "Milton for the masses": Roy Porter's phrase to describe Wesley's literary commodities, in his *Enlightenment*, 85; see also his and Dorothy Porter's *Patient's Progress*, 198, for *Primitive Physick*.

68 *Electricity made plain*: See Brooke, *Science and Religion*, 191, for discussion of Wesley's approach to "popular science."

68 the "lathes, whirlers": See Meteyard, *Life*, i, 261; Jewitt, *Wedgwoods*, 130–31.

69 "greengrocery" warts: Reilly, *Wedgwood*, i, 44.

69 pineapple-shaped: Color teapot illustrations of the pineapple wares are found in Young, ed., *Genius*, 26, plates B5/B6; Reilly, *Wedgwood*, i, plate C16, opposite 169.

69 "had other difficulties": Josiah's nephew Thomas Byerley's biographical notes, Keele, W/M 1131.

69 "biscuit ware only": Account of Josiah's Ivy House business from Byerley, Keele, 121-23528; Reilly, *Wedgwood*, i, 44.

69 Josiah's budget: See Barker, *William Greatbatch*, for elaboration.

70 Sarah Muir: An interesting example of a domestic manufacturer's division of labor that includes well-placed positions for the women; see Adams, *Some North Staffordshire Families*, 20.

70 "dealing with customers": This new interpretation of Greatbatch's early career and relationship with Josiah is in Barker, *William Greatbatch*, 46.

70 "without the aid or assistance": Williams-Wood, *English Transfer-Printed Pottery*, 102. An Irish engraver named John Brooks had devised the same technique, independently, a little earlier.

71 "India porcelain": See Young, ed., *Genius*, 27.

71 "Expt No: 406": Experimental page from Keele, E26-19115; the page is photographically reproduced in Reilly, *Wedgwood*, i, 183 (illus. 159).

72 "5 doz 18s": Price, *John Sadler*, 34; Keele, W/M 1431.

72 "Law, Physick, and Divinity": Verse from "The Triple Plea"; a picture of Josiah's mug is reproduced in Reilly, *Wedgwood*, i, 212, illustration 219.

73 "Plates & Drawings!": Sadler to Josiah, 23 February 1764, Keele, W/M 1431.

73 "a blind simpleton": This and Wesley's quote from Colley, *Britons*, 208–09.

73 "very bad things": 25 September 1766, Keele, E25-18129.

74 "The trade of the West Indies": Quoted in Crowhurst, *Defence of British Trade*, 60.

75 "two penny earthen porringer": Franklin quoted in Bushman, "American High-Style," 374; see also the article Franklin wrote in the *Philadelphia Gazette*, 10 July 1732, addressing genteel accoutrements.

75 "Our importation of dry goods": William Smith writing in 1762, *History of the Late Province of New York*, quoted in Breen, "An Empire of Goods," 487, which surveys the literature on colonial consumption.

75 "were more English": James Deetz, *In Small Things Forgotten: The Archaeology of Early American Life* (New York: Anchor Press, 1977), 38.

75 "Our people, both": Breen, "Empire of Goods," 478.
75 "sought English manufactured goods": Lemon, "Spatial Order," 102.
75 Not until after the Revolution: This comment from Rodris Roth, "Tea Drinking in Eighteenth-Century America: Its Etiquette and Equipage," in *Contributions for the Museum of History and Technology, U.S. National Museum Bulletin*, 225 (1961), cited in Breen, "Empire of Goods," 488.
76 "colonists set their tables": McCusker and Menard, *Economy of British America*, 287; see also C. Malcolm Watkins and Ivor Noël Hume, *The "Poor Potter" of Yorktown* (Washington, DC: Smithsonian Books, 1967).
76 "Already" . . . "it is really possible": Gottlieb Mittelberger, German minister, quoted in Breen, "Empire of Goods," 489. In the two decades after 1750, England's exports rose 120 percent (McCuster and Menard, *Economy of British America*, 277), and pottery, along with other "luxury" items such as silk, brass, and furniture, accounted for nearly 40 percent of goods legally exported from Britain to the American colonies in the 1760s, or just under £900,000 of merchandise (Shepherd and Walton, *Shipping, Maritime Trade*, 180–86).
76 *Boston Gazette* was advertising: Mankowitz, *Wedgwood*, 22.
76 *Boston News Letter*: Gorley, *Wedgwood*, 27.
76 £13 million for the year: Anderson, *Crucible of War*, 308–09.

8: By the Docks

77 the most convenient port: See Ewins, " 'Supplying the Present Wants,' " 11; Josiah's interests in Liverpool discussed in Blake Roberts, "Josiah Wedgwood and His Trade Connections."
77 "for 10 pence": Observation of Samuel Derrick, a traveler to Liverpool who left a detailed contemporary account of the community, cited in Roberts and Pigeon, "Biographical Sketch," 68.
77 "The dwelling house": Ibid., 70.
78 The "Old Dock": General description in Smith, "The Past," in J. F. Smith, Gordon Hemm, and A. Ernst Shennan, *Liverpool: Past, Present, Future* (Liverpool: The Northern Publishing, 1948).
78 "You may rest assured": Sadler to Josiah, 11 October 1763, Keele, W/M 1431, Reilly, *Wedgwood*, i, 209.
78 "I have had a good deal of talk": This is the report of a later conversation with Sadler but typical of the level of supervision Josiah had exercised over their professional relationship for the last decade; 12 May 1770, Keele, E25-18299. Reilly and others agree that, contrary to Mankowitz's suggestion that Sadler and Green would send the printed wares back to Josiah for a final firing, they would have for practical reasons finished the job themselves, which would also expedite their export. This further stresses the importance of feeding the foreign market, which has consistently been downplayed in the histories of Wedgwood's pottery.
78 "two glass factories": Roberts and Pigeon, "Biographical Sketch," 69.
79 "Earthen ware manufacture": Statement in connection to Sadler's affidavit, 1756; "all of whom were connected": Both quotes from Boney, *Liverpool Porcelain*, 4.
79 700 annual tons: Ibid.
79 a "Liverpool China Manufactory": Unless otherwise stated, all the information cited about William Reid's Liverpool pottery comes from Boney, *Liverpool Porcelain*, 127–28—a useful source but lamentably brief.
79 "any young persons": *Liverpool Advertiser*, 19 November 1756; for information about the locale of Reid's establishments, see Gatty, *Liverpool Potteries*, and Sir James Picton's map discussed on p. 13 there.

80   rising to anywhere between 6 and 10 percent: An average, from Crowhurst, *Defence of British Trade*, 94–95.

80   "however unable he might be": Park, *System of Law of Marine Insurance*, reproduced in Atkinson, *The Shipping Laws*, 3.

80   "provide a vessel": Atkinson, *Shipping Laws*, 179.

81   "merchants are hospitable": Quoted by Dorothy Wane, *A History of Liverpool* (1910), on line at www.fortunecity.com/meltingpot/park/346/history4.html; Daniel Defoe, *A Tour through the Whole Island of Great Britain* (1724), 88.

81   well over £3 per capita annually: Statistic from Shammas, "How Self-Sufficient," 265.

81   "The territory of Great Britain": Quoted in Crouzet, "Sources of England's Wealth," 61.

81   "France would become dependent": Marquis de Torcy quoted in ibid., 62.

82   "trade, which has made richer": These and the following quotations from French critics from Crouzet, "Sources of England's Wealth," 64, 69.

82   "the prize was usually taken": Information from Crowhurst, *Defence of British Trade*, 16, 34, 37.

83   most ships that sailed from there avoided capture: Ibid., 63. In 1720, Nicholas Magens, an insurance broker who wrote a well-known treatise on British insurance law, commented that "it is notorious to all the mercantile world that as the English insurers pay more readily and generously than any others, most insurances are done in England." Crowhurst points out that because "London dominated the European market for marine insurance . . . many French merchants insured their ventures in London during Anglo-French wars, a practice that was not considered unpatriotic to begin with, for it brought considerable business to London underwriters. When they were forced to pay heavy compensation to French merchants for losses inflicted by British warships public opinion changed . . ." (p. 89). It should also be noted that the French were not the only privateers—the British and Americans were known for privateering during the American Revolutionary War, for instance; see David Starkey, *British Privateering Enterprize in the Eighteenth Century* (Exeter, Devon: University of Exeter Press, 1990).

83   "refuse to pay their said subscriptions": This fascinating case has never—to the best of my knowledge—been linked to Josiah's own export activities, and yet, I believe, it is crucial to explaining his financial difficulties at the time, which has been seen as a puzzling historical incidence. This case not only helps to capture some of the challenges Josiah faced in the first years of his own business but illuminates some of the practices involved with arranging foreign exports. (I disagree with McKendrick, "Commercialisation of the Potteries," 134–35, and Reilly, *Wedgwood*, i, 94, that Josiah's own claim that trade with America was the most important market for him should be treated with "scepticism.") The case I refer to is "petition of Josiah Wedgwood and John Dobson Assignor," BL, ADD Mss 36191, f. 361–64.

84   "an order be had for the Creditors": "Petition . . . ," in BL, ADD Mss 36191, f. 364, and the above quotation.

84   "To be sold": Advertisement quoted in Boney, *Liverpool Porcelain*, 128.

85   He was only able to stay afloat: Josiah needed to hand over goods valued at £5, which was deducted from his rent in 1760; Mountford, "Thomas Wedgwood," 52.

85   "Having considered what you and I": Greatbatch's letter to Josiah, 31 January 1762, quoted in Barker, *William Greatbatch*, 42.

85   "I have four men": Greatbatch to Josiah, end of January 1762, in ibid., 42. See Reilly, *Wedgwood*, i, 188, for account. Josiah, for instance, was buying biscuit teapots from Greatbatch for 3[h]d and selling them for 5d to Sadler to glaze. Adding up a potter's dozen—six pots and six lids—amounted to a profit of about is 6d; he was turning over around a dozen dozen, which gave him about £1 profit per shipment.

86   "Consider the discount": Sadler quoted in Reilly, *Wedgwood*, i, 212.

9: Paradise Street

87 "large oblong dishes": Example of content of crates in invoices from Greatbatch to Josiah; see Barker, *Lillian Greatbatch*, 44.
87 "the ware getting wet": Reilly, *Wedgwood*, i, 214; Sadler to Josiah, 11 October 1763, and Josiah to Bentley, 10 December 1774, Keele, W/M 1431.
87 "I know not . . .": Arthur Young's traveling difficulties recorded in his *Six Months Tour*, iv, 580–85.
88 Since 1755, preparatory surveys had been conducted: Mountford, "Thomas Wedgwood," 33–34; John Phillips, *General History of Inland Navigation* (1792), discusses the 1755 survey; *Derby Mercury*, 7 December 1758, announced Brindley's 1758 survey.
89 Burslem remained the most difficult place: A startling fact, gleaned from the survey in "Turnpike Network," 90; J. Ogilby, *The Traveller's Guide, or Most Exact Description of Roads in England* (London, 1711).
89 "Here let me pause": Young, *Six Months Tour*, iv, 580, 584.
89 Josiah crashed down: For lack of better evidence, this follows Meteyard's (*Life*, i, 299–300) description—essentially repeated in many subsequent biographical accounts—though Reilly (*Wedgwood*, 354, n. 12) points out that no documentary evidence of the exact accident has been located.
90 the "great conflagration": Bentley, *Thomas Bentley*, 17; "Dale Street" in Liverpool: See J. Chadwick's 1725 "Mapp of all the Streets, Lanes, & Alleys within the Town of Liverpool."
90 "a good surgeon": Assessment of his talents by Meteyard, *Life*, i, 300; "very clever indeed": *Historic Society of Lancashire and Cheshire Proceedings and Papers*, v (1853), 147.
90 "young laymen of the like": Kendrick, "A Morning's Ramble," 83; Gibbs, *Joseph Priestley*, 22–23; "anatomy and the theory of forms": His lectures referred to in Roberts and Pigeon, "Biographical Sketch," 72.
90 "varnishes, fumigations": Summary in entry on Matthew Turner in the *Dictionary of National Biography*; "some of the principal Experiments": From course syllabus quoted in McLachlan, *Warrington Academy*, 40.
91 "As near as I can guess": 16 March 1762, Matthew Turner to John Seddon, the chief Dissenting minister at Warrington, explaining his interests in lecturing, quoted in Schofield, ed., *Scientific Autobiography*, 8.
91 "arrangements for obtaining": Description by Dr. William Turner (no relation to Matthew Turner), a former student of Warrington, whose history of the Academy has been reprinted in Turner, *Warrington Academy*; see also Orange, "Rational Dissent," 205–30.
91 "a room was properly fitted up": Warrington Academy's trustees' report for 1763, quoted in Gibbs, *Joseph Priestley*, 23; £100 cost of instruments from McLachlan, *Warrington Academy*, 26.
92 Josiah's "dear girl": Meteyard, *Life*, i, 300.
92 "courtly": Blake Roberts, "Josiah Wedgwod and his Trade Connections."
93 His father was a minor: Biographical information from Bentley, *Thomas Bentley, passim*.
93 James Boardman: See ibid., 25; also *Historic Society of Lancashire and Cheshire Proceedings and Papers*, vi (1854), 42.
93 "persuade the merchants and masters": Boardman, *Bentleyana*, 10.
94 "to take charge": Bentley, *Thomas Bentley*, 10, 15.
95 skilled "mechanist": Roberts and Pigeon, "Biographical Sketch."
95 "The tutors at Warrington": Priestley quoted in Meteyard, *Life*, i, 309.
95 "the serious pursuit of truth": Priestley quoted in McLachlan, *Warrington Academy*, 23.
95 "intended for a life of Business": McLachlan, *Warrington Academy*, 39.
96 "an engraver for the potters": *Historic Society of Lancashire and Cheshire Proceedings and Papers*, v (1853), 148.
95 "without missing a word": Schofield, *Enlightenment*, 7.
95 "furious freethinker" and "not a single pupil": Gibbs, *Priestley*, 10–12.

96 "I greatly admire Mr. Priestley": Turner to Seddon, 16 March 1762, quoted in Schofield, *Enlightenment*, 137.

10: "Improveable Subjects"

97 "much esteemed Friend": Josiah to Bentley, 15 May 1762, Keele E25-18408. A large percentage of the letters from Josiah to Bentley, here frequently quoted, are published in Farrer, ed., *Letters of Josiah Wedgwood*, though, as previously noted, they are poorly edited and abridged; more complete copies are in the John Rylands Library, Manchester. For consistency and clarity, I will cite the original manuscript reference for each letter when possible, particularly as I have tried to draw out comments and sentiments not included in the published versions.
97 "crucible making": From copy of letter from Turner to Josiah, 11 December 1762, commonplace book, Wedgwood Museum, E39-28408, f. 33.
98 "I have told you what a troublesome": Josiah to Bentley, 26 October 1762, Keele, E25-18049.
98 "I have lately purchased": Josiah and Catherine Willets to a "close friend," 8 February 1762, printed transcription in Keele, E25-18051.
99 "Critical and curious": A category of readers used, for example, by the editors of the *Critical Review*, as opposed to "vulgar" readers, blurred boundaries of knowledge and reading habits are discussed Yeo, *Encyclopaedic Visions*
99 "more numerous" than ever before: Donoghue, "Reviews and the Reading Public," 68.
100 "business is so much affected" and "joynot industry": Josiah and Catherine Willets to a close friend, Keele, E25-18051.
100 "those pimps of literature": *Critical Review*, 1763, quoted in ibid., 69.
101 "excellent piece upon *female education*": Josiah to Bentley, 15 May 1762, Keele, E25-18048; "Octagon chapel": See Watts, *Gender, Power and the Unitarians*, for further discussion of Dissenting religious and educational theory linked to Bentley's context.
101 "instinctive goodness" . . . "the finest feelings": Josiah to Bentley, 26 October 1762, Keele, E25-18049.
102 "It is perfect enough": Josiah to Bentley, 26 October 1762, Keele, E25-18049.
102 "I am about to furnish a shelf": Josiah to Bentley, 26 October 1762, Keele, E25-18049.
102 "younger part of our species," "instinct," and "charity" are all used as part of the same discussion, which conveys these points in Josiah's letter to Bentley, 26 October 1762, Keele, E25-18049; I, not Josiah, use the term "self-improvement" to summarize all that Josiah grapples with that is involved in encouraging an "improved human mind" (Josiah's phrase).
102 "Mr Locke's excellent Treatise": From Chambers' *Cyclopaedia* (1728), quoted in Porter, *Enlightenment*, 342.
103 "You cannot think how happy": Josiah to Bentley, 16 September 1769; Keele, E25-18256; see also Uglow, *Lunar Men*, 56.
103 "my Magazines, Reviews . . .": Quoted in Reilly, *Josiah Wedgwood*, 33.
103 "instruct the ignorant": Josiah to Bentley, discussing the futile attempts of a local Dissenting chaplain to get the blessing of the bishop to educate the locals from his newly built chapel using his own prayer books, which he "altered to his own liking," 26 October 1762, Keele, E25-18049.
103 "our most gracious Sovereign": From the Accession Service in the Book of Common Prayer, reach each anniversary of the day of the accession of the reigning sovereign after the Restoration. The Dissenters' objections to the reaffirmation of a fundamental right to rule based on the teachings of this and other services is explored further below; see also Gunn, *Beyond Liberty and Property*.

103 "Submit yourself to every ordinance": First General Epistle of St. Peter, 2:13–16, a text that provides the "crucial foundation" to the tenets of the Church of England in the eighteenth century; see Hole, *Pulpits, Politics and Public Order*, part I.

104 an "excellent little essay": Josiah's description of Willets's piece on "prayers for public worship" in "The Library"; his sarcastic comment which I quote was a lament that there were not more authors like Willets who expressed the "true" Christian spirit. Josiah to Bentley, 26 October 1762, Keele, E25-18049.

104 "There is a clear demonstration": Brady, *Complete History of England* (1685), quoted in Dickinson, *Liberty and Property*, 24–25.

104 "Goddess of Liberty" . . . "On Virtue": Thomson, *Works*, i, 105.

105 "formed a strong desire to educate": Josiah's soon-to-be friend, Richard Lovell Edgeworth, writing about his son's education in 1765—Clarke, ed., *Memoirs*, i, 173.

105 "good or evil, useful": Locke, *Some Thoughts Concerning Education*, in Porter, *Enlightenment*, 340; "we make scientific instruments of ourselves" is my paraphrase of Rousseau's proposal, in *Emile*, that "I want us to make all our machines ourselves," by which he not only meant that we should make (rather than obtain) machines or instruments for investigation, but that our natural enquiries undertaken without manufactured instruments will allow people to develop precision faculties within themselves. "By dint of gathering machines around us," he wrote, "we no longer find any in ourselves"—Rousseau, *Emile*, trans. Allan Bloom.

II: "O Grief of Griefs"

107 "pretty but not expensive": From a Dutch retailer in 1763, in Mankowitz, *Wedgwood*, 31; the following comment about one hundred pieces of pottery per crate a local average calculated by Weatherill, "The Growth of the Pottery Industry," 16.

107 "this rugged Pot-making spot": Josiah to Bentley, 16 June 1763, Keele, E25-18054.

108 "a scattered town": Gurnock, ed., *Journal of the Reverend John Wesley*, iv, 370.

108 "The Trade flourishes": From the printed proposal to Parliament for a turnpike, drafted by Burslem potters in 1762, reproduced by the "history of the borough of Stoke-on-Trent" Web site, http://www.netcentral.co.uk/steveb/borough/008=~turnpike.htm.

108 North Staffordshire [potteries] were the largest in the country: See Weatherill, "The Growth of the Pottery Industry," 22, where this statistic is qualified with the note that there were "few exceptions, such as Leeds."

108 "It might be asked": Josiah's speech copied in his commonplace book, Wedgwood Museum, E39-28408, ff. 193–94.

109 "the ware in these Potteries": The 1762 petition referred to above.

109 "pot-wabblers": See *The Dictionary of the Vulgar Tongue*; also, Porter, *London*, 151.

109 could use as a prototype teapot: Reilly, *Josiah Wedgwood*, 33, refers to Josiah's expenditure on such items for this trip.

110 "Josiah shopped for shirts": Ibid.

110 "sister Willet's little lasses": Josiah to John Wedgwood, 11 November 1763, quoted in Wedgwood and Wedgwood, *Wedgwood Circle*, 18.

110 "This day I had the mortification": Josiah to Bentley, 31 March 1763, Keele, E25-18052.

111 "with candour equal" and "lofty strain": Josiah to Bentley, 31 March 1763, Keele, E25-18052.

111 the powers of excise officers: See, e.g., Watson, *Reign of George III*, 91.

111 "The extension of the excise laws": Josiah to Bentley, 12 April 1763, Keele, E25-18053; later, Josiah conducts his own investigation into how customs officers define "earthen ware" in their records, which he believed was unclear and affected the way their foreign trade was evaluated: Josiah to his brother John Wedgwood, 19 February 1765, Keele, E25-18064.

112   the Brick House: Information on the rent and family from Adams, *Adams Family*, 125–26; see also Turner, *William Adams*.

113   Byerley was one of his eldest sister Margaret's: Reilly, *Josiah Wedgwood*, 38.

113   "trunk came down with all his papers": Josiah to Bentley, 16 June 1763, Keele, E25-18054.

113   "a very good boy": Josiah to Bentley, 28 May 1764, Keele, E25-18057; Josiah to Bentley, 28 May 1764, Keele, E25-18057, for Byerley's attempts to learn French; Keele, E25-18063, Josiah to John Wedgwood, 16 February 1765, for allusion to Byerley's important work on the accounts.

114   "lascivious erudition": I refer to the survey by Tarczylo, "From Lascivious Erudition to the History of Mentalities," for the eighteenth-century context.

114   "and if their imaginations were charmed": *Aristotle's Master-Piece* (1710), 76, quoted in Porter and Hall, *Facts of Life*, 42, which also surveys the popularity and uses of such literature in the period.

115–16   "His head is turned": Josiah quoting Bentley back to himself in reference to an acquaintance's marriage in 1766, in Josiah to Bentley, 11 April 1766, Keele, E25-18143.

116   Remaining single was good for business: These points are discussed in Stone's classic *Family, Sex and Marriage*, 44–46.

116   In 1763, his income . . . : Keele, WMS 32-24293, for his accounts; "Squire Western," from Fielding's *Tom Jones*, the archetypical "Old English gentleman," concerned to marry his daughter off to a wealthy man.

116   to marry a wealthier woman who lived over twenty miles away: Results of a study discussed in Stone, *Family, Sex and Marriage*, 51.

117   exchanging numerous orders a year with them: Josiah's dealings with his cousins is documented in his account books, namely, Keele, 6-30442 and 6-30443, for these dates.

117   in the region of £20,000: Jewitt, *The Wedgwoods*, 157.

117   every other Sunday Josiah rode: Wedgwood and Wedgwood, *Wedgwood Circle*, 13.

117   could offer him £4,000 jointure money: This figure comes from Jewitt, cited with skepticism by Reilly, *Josiah Wedgwood*, 34, 354n.

117   "Reid the Bankrupt": For Josiah's management of the accounts here, see Keele, E54-30700.

118   "Consider my case": Reid to Dobson (who forwarded it to Josiah), 19 April 1763, Keele, E55-30959.

118   "Desire you'l Remit": Greatbatch to Josiah, 30 May 1763, and the two following letters quoted in Barker, *William Greatbatch*, 35.

118   "glazing" . . . "Love": Keele, 11-9272, verso; his debts also named in Keele, 49-29894.

119   "I [would have] acknowledg'd": This and the rest of the letter quoted, Josiah to Bentley, 9 January 1764, Keele, E25-10855.

119   "All things being amicably settled": This and the rest of the letter in Josiah to Bentley, 23 January 1764, Keele, E25-18057.

Part Two
12: Recipe for Success

123   solemnized their marriage: Astbury Parish Registers, microfilm at Cheshire County Council, for which I would like to thank the curator, Paul Newman.

123   "to hear, see, feel" and "Gossiping friends": Josiah's recollections of his desires upon marriage to Ralph Griffiths, 21 December 1767, Keele, E25-18180.

123   to "bundle": Stone, *Family, Sex and Marriage*, 384.

124   "two married lovers": Josiah to Bentley, 28 May 1764, Keele, E25-18057.

124   spending £200 on a new house for the rector: Greenslade, "History of Burslem," 123.

125   The Birmingham iron master Matthew Boulton: His marriage tactics discussed in Uglow, *Lunar Men*, 25.

125   "they made up 20 per cent": Statement from Davidoff and Hall, *Family Fortunes*, 211. Unfortunately this brief comment is about the extent of their analysis of "women as investors." To the best of my knowledge, there has been no historical work looking directly at this issue; the majority of publications tended to concentrate on women as laborers. Studies on women and capitalism that I've looked at, such as . . . Pamela Sharpe, *Adapting to Capitalism*, Roberta Hamilton, *The Liberation of Women*, or Mary Murray, *The Law of the Father?*, frustratingly don't look at women investors. Even Neil McKendrick's "Home Demand and Economic Growth," subtitled "A New View of the Role of Women and Children in the Industrial Revolution," which draws information from the Wedgwood archive, says nothing about how women's wealth can contribute to the industrializing process. I hope I've reviewed the relevant studies, but am confident that much more needs to be written on this.

125   "What forlorn Animals": Josiah to Bentley, 4 November 1766, Keele, E25-18131.

126   "Sally is my chief helpmate": Josiah to his brother John Wedgwood, 6 March 1765, Keele, E25-18070.

126   "I often think . . .": Ibid.

126   Richard Wedgwood began giving Josiah: Account book of Richard Wedgwood, Keele, 32-24293, e.g., f. 183 verso (July 1764), £200; f. 145 verso (1765), £150. Other writers, such as Wedgwood and Wedgwood in *Wedgwood Pedigrees*, 174, followed by Reilly, *Josiah Wedgwood*, 36, refer to a gift of £500 from Josiah's new brother-in-law John, which he used to improve the potworks. Reilly points out that no documentary source was given for this, but no one refers to the money transferred from Richard, which seems to offer a better explanation of where the money came from.

127   a new kind of discipline amongst his workers: Though it principally deals with a later period of Wedgwood's career, McKendrick's "Josiah Wedgwood and Factory Discipline" is a useful source for this issue.

127   "Time wasted is existence": Boney, *Liverpool Porcelain*, 69; Meteyard, *Life of Josiah Wedgwood*, i, 308.

127   "an excellent book": Josiah to Bentley, 28 May 1764, Keele, E25-18057; "Art of the Turner": Charles Plumier, *L'art de tourner* (Paris, new ed., 1749); Meteyard, *Life of Josiah Wedgwood*, i, 338–39.

127   "parallel lathes": For Josiah's thoughts about the Elers brothers role in this, see Josiah to Bentley, 19 July 1777, Keele, E25-18772, which we will return to in a later chapter; for an account of engine turning as it affected Wedgwood pottery, see Appendix C to Reilly's *Wedgwood*, i, 691–93; Meteyard, *Wedgwood*, i, 339, for Turner and Cox.

128   "This branch hath cost me": Josiah to Bentley, 28 May 1764, Keele, E25-18057.

128   "forming a big hoop": Bills for work on his lathe at Keele, E49-29829.

128   "just begun a course of experiments": Josiah to his brother John Wedgwood, 6 March 1765, Keele, E25-18070.

128   Meredith was elected a Whig MP: Information on Meredith's position and glimpses of London life can be gleaned from his correspondence in the BL, ADD Mss 38201 and 38204, letters to the 1st Earl of Liverpool.

129   "in sorting out my 2nd red-ware": Josiah to Tom Byerley, 1 February 1765, Keele, E25-18060— a letter which puts to bed any doubt that Josiah was engaged in this very low end market, which has been reluctantly supposed by a number of scholars. The prices for the goods varied; the full crates which he sent to London, packed with up to ten dozen teapots of varying sizes, were valued at between £5 and £7 each.

129   "If you can spare Tom": Josiah to John Wedgwood, 13 February 1765, Keele, E25-18062.

130   whose £800 sales in 1765: See Mountford, "Thomas Wedgwood," Appendix III, for their accounts, which show they had spent £13,000 on acquiring property in Staffordshire over the previous twenty years.

130 "with my humble thanks": Josiah to Sir William Meredith, 2 March 1765, Keele, E25-18067.
130 "I wish Sir William would give me": Josiah to John Wedgwood, 13 February 1765, Keele, E25-18062.
130 "Cream Colour teapots" for Enoch Booth: Booth to Josiah, 1764, Keele, E11-9280 ("foyer" is "fire" written in the Burslem dialect by Booth); for accounts of the orders of Enoch and George Booth, see Keele, E11-9272–E11-9280 (1762–1765).
130 "trying a trick upon us?": Josiah to John Wedgwood, 13 February 1765, Keele, E25-18062.
131 "small service of printed dishes": Josiah to John Wedgwood, 19 February 1765, Keele, E25-18064.
131 "You have heaped your favours on me": Josiah to Sir William Meredith, 2 March 1765, Keele, E25-18067.

13: Fit for a King and Queen

132 "Sukey is a fine sprightly lass": Josiah to John Wedgwood, 1 February 1765, Keele, E25-18059; Susanna, always called Sukey, was baptized 17 January.
132 "The finest Girl!": Josiah to John Wedgwood, 11 March 1765, Keele, E25-18071.
132 "Tell John Wedgwood": Josiah reporting to John Wedgwood, 1 February 1765, Keele, E25-18059.
132–33 "I shall hardly find time": Ibid.
133 "about eight tons of pot ware": Sir Richard Whitworth quoted in Lead, *Trent and Mersey Canal*, 6: general accounts of the canal movement which are drawn on here include Charles Hadfield, *Canals of West Midlands*, J. Lindsay, *Trent and Mersey Canal*, and S. H. Beaver, "The Potteries." For the particular context of industrialists' activities in building canals, see the discussion in Uglow, *Lunar Men*, chapter 10.
133 "the Uniting of Seas": Josiah to Bentley, 15 October 1765, Keele, E25-18095.
134 "Our gentlemen seem very warm": Josiah to John Wedgwood, 11 March 1765, Keele, E25-18071; information about the Leopold from Hughes, *Mother Town*, xxv.
134 "is undoubtedly the best thing": Josiah to John Wedgwood, 11 March 1765, Keele, E25-18071.
134 "with one Mr. Loyd": Ibid.; the brand-new partnership between John Taylor and Sampson Lloyd, referred to by Josiah, marked the origin of what became, and remains, Lloyds Bank.
135 "freeholders, tradesmen": His letter of introduction copied in commonplace book, Wedgwood Museum, E39-28408, f. 195: "I had the honour": Josiah to Bentley, 20 April 1765, Keele, E25-18075.
135 "*Countenance* is of extreme consequence": Samuel Garbett to Josiah, 18 April 1765, Keele, E25-10875.
135 "I have been waiting upon his Grace": Josiah to John Wedgwood, 6 July 1765, Keele, E25-10880.
136 "for I do not think that that close": Josiah to John Wedgwood, 16 February 1765, Keele, E25-10863.
136 "you have not set the finishing hand": Josiah to John Wedgwood, 25 February 1765, Keele, E25-18066.
137 "Dear Brother": This to the series of questions for Miss Chetwynd in Josiah to John Wedgwood, no date, early July, 1765, Keele, E25-18073.
138 "You may be sure . . . my best endeavours": Josiah to John Wedgwood, 6 July 1765, Keele, E25-18080.
138 "the pleasure of your letter": Josiah to John Wedgwood, 24 July 1765, Keele, E25-18079.

139   "appear to be made for each other": Josiah to John Wedgwood, 6 July 1765, Keele, E25-18080.

139   "night & day": Josiah to John Wedgwood, 22 July 1765, Keele, E25-18082.

139   "preparing sprigs, handles, spouts": Josiah to John Wedgwood, no date, July 1765, Keele, E25-18083.

139   "but suppose we fail": Josiah to John Wedgwood, 6 July 1765, Keele, E25-18080.

139   "the foolish wakes": Josiah to John Wedgwood, 6 July 1765, Keele, E25-18080.

139   "2 Millions of Working People": Henry Pollexfen, *A Discourse on Trade and Coyne* (London, 1697), 50; see related discussion in Thompson, "Time, Work-Discipline and Industrial Capitalism."

139   "I am just teased of my life": Josiah to John Wedgwood, 7 August 1765, Keele, E25-18089.

139–40   "You cannot think how busy" and "that the Queen was impatient": Josiah to John Wedgwood, 24 July 1765, Keele, E25-18100.

140   "take any quantity of leaf gold": Dossie, *The Handmaid to the Arts*, 385–86.

140   "perhaps tell you how": Josiah to John Wedgwood, no date, July 1765, Keele, E25-18083.

140   who helped to double the incomes: McKendrick, "Home Demand and Economic Growth": see also Berg, *Age of Manufactures*, chapter 6, for elaboration of women's work in early industrialization.

140   could not "find any French book": Josiah to Bentley, 2 November 1765, Keele, E25-18096.

140   "For some tryals I made today": Josiah to John Wedgwood, 29 July 1765, Keele, E25-18085.

141   "I will forward the Creamcolour": Josiah to John Wedgwood, 29 July 1765, Keele, E25-18087.

141   "I sent a crate of patterns": Josiah to Bentley, 26 August 1765, Keele, E25-18080.

14: The Vexed and the Virtuosi

142   even the king had expressed admiration for: For King George's "influence on the design of the famous green and gold service," see Ayling, *George the Third*, 204–05.

142   "Dr Swan dined with Ld Gower": Josiah to John Wedgwood, no date, July 1765, Keele, E25-18083.

143   "His Ld Ship said that . . .": Josiah to John Wedgwood, 29 July 1765, Keele, E25-18085.

143   100,000 acres of land stretching across 27 different counties: From Foreman, *Georgiana*, 4.

143   a national curiosity and "madness to gaze": Tinniswood, *The Polite Tourist*.

143   "they have bought some things": Josiah to John Wedgwood, 7 August 1765, Keele, E25-18098.

143   "I sent a parcel": This and the following quotes about executing orders from Josiah to John Wedgwood, 25 November 1765, Keele, E25-18101.

144   "to distribute as occasion serves": An early example is Keele, E25-17831.

144   "trade tokens": See the discussion in chapter 2.

144   "I have this year sent goods": Josiah to John Wedgwood, 2 August 1765, Keele, E25-18087.

144   "for ready money": Information on the payment structure for Josiah's orders explained in Josiah to Bentley, 26 June 1766, Keele, E25-18120, and 18 July 1766, Keele, E25-18123.

145   "astonish'd, Confounded & vexed": This and the following quotes relating to the canal debate in the company of Gower are from Josiah to Bentley, 2 January 1765, Keele, E25-18058.

146   a brand-new light brown wig . . . expensive shave: Details from his account book,
Keele, L47-8673: the "Queen's House": See Wedgwood and Wedgwood, *Wedgwood Circle*,
20, for encounter with the queen; see also the portrait medallion of Josiah in court dress,
illustrated in Reilly, *Wedgwood*, I, 327, plate 416A.

147   "Having already introduced several improvements": Josiah quoted in Barker, *William
Greatbatch*, 21.

147   "if a Royal or Noble introduction": Josiah to Bentley, no date, Keele, E25-18167.

147   "Mr Josiah Wedgwood, of Burslem": *Birmingham Gazette*, 9 June 1766.

147   "Potter to Her Majesty": He was not the first to receive such an honor. In the early
seventeenth century a merchant trader named Thomas Browne is quoted in Herald's *Visitation of London* (1634), referring to himself as "Potter to King Charles": but Josiah boldly
seized the moment. See also Edwards, "London Potteries," 16.

147   "to have the success of all our manufactures": Bentley writing in his journal, following a visit to meet the king and queen with Josiah, 15 December 1770, quoted in Boardman, *Bentleyana*, 17.

147   "Vase maker General": Josiah to Bentley, February 1769, Keele, E25-18232. I confess
to putting this in two years prematurely since, even at this time in Josiah's life, there seems
no more adequate way to describe his ambitions. However, it should also be noted that this
famous phrase was in fact used by Josiah to describe Bentley on the eve of the opening of
Etruria.

148   "I have not a Warehouse in London": Josiah to John Wedgwood, 7 August 1765,
Keele, E25-18089.

148   "I have often mentioned": Josiah to John Wedgwood, 2 August 1765, Keele, E25-
18087.

149   "The demand for this said *Creamcolour*": Josiah to Bentley, no date, Keele, E25-18167.

149   In 1765, over 7 million kilograms: Wills, "European Consumption," 144.

149   "I am quite clearing my Wareho.": Josiah to Bentley, 18 July 1766, Keele, E25-18123.

15: "Exquisite Models"

151   "The mind shudders": Pliny's account quoted from Letts. *The Eruption of Vesuvius*,
contemporary accounts of the story include Fordyce, *Memoirs concerning Herculaneum* (1750).
An inscription found in 1763 revealed the name of Pompeii.

151   "There might certainly": Walpole quoted in Brian Fothergill, *Sir William Hamilton*
(New York: Harcourt, 1969), 121.

152   "While the antiquary investigates": Ibid., 136.

153   "cities of the dead": For accounts of the activities of agents, see Julia Williams, *Gavin
Hamilton: 1723–1798* (Edinburgh: National Galleries of Scotland, 1994), and Lord Edmond
Fitzmaurice, *Letters of Gavin Hamilton* (London, 1879); for excavation activities, see Rodolfo
Lanciani, *New Tales of Old Rome, Profusely Illustrated* (London: Macmillan, 1901).

154   "It is the custom": Moore, *View of the Society*.

154   "who play very well": Burney's account from his *Music, Men and Manners*.

155   "who had travelled in Italy": Cust, *History of the Society of Dilettanti*.

157   it "will tend to": Fothergill, *Sir William Hamilton*, 116.

16: The Creators of Beauty

158   "I have now bought the Estate": Josiah to Bentley, 18 July 1766, Keele, E25-18123.

158   "dirty spot of Earth": Josiah to Bentley, 19 September 1766, Keele, E25-18128.

158   "increased their connections": Josiah to Bentley, 26 June 1766, Keele, E25-18120.

158   "My Sally says": Josiah to Bentley, 15 September 1766, Keele, E25-18127.

159   "Cargoes of Cream colour": Josiah to Bentley, 26 June 1766, Keele, E25-18120.

159   "asked me if I had not sent Mr Pitt": Josiah to Bentley, 18 July 1766, Keele, E25-18123.
160   "The American business": Josiah to Bentley, early [February] 1767, Keele, E25-18186.
160   the Townshend Act: The bill can be read in full on line at http://ahp.gatech.edu/townshend_act_1767.html. Townshend proposed this despite the fact that he had previously supported Pitt's attack on the Stamp Act. For the dynamics of party politics in this period, see John Brewer's excellent *Party Ideology and Popular Politics*. For the politics of British customs and excise, see Ashworth, *Customs and Excise*.
160   "Tho the subject of commerce": Bentley writing in the *Monthly Review*, 35 (December 1766), 439–46.
161   for "Deary's amusement": Written as "amusement of Deary" in Josiah to Bentley, 14 February 1767, Keele, E25-18135.
161   "The bulk of our particular manufacture": Josiah to Sir William Meredith, 2 March 1765, Keele, E25-18067; more information on Bartham in Keele, E14-13490.
162   "Mr Grenville & his party": Josiah to Bentley, 20 May 1767, Keele, E25-18146.
162   "Would you think it": Josiah to Bentley, 23 May 1767, Keele, E25-18147.
162   "which surprised me a good deal": Josiah to Bentley, July 1766, Keele, E25-18119.
162   "kaolin will come out of the fire": See Watt to Josiah, Wedgwood Museum, Keele, E39-28408.
163   "must be got as clean from soil": Josiah to Bentley, 17 November 1766, Keele, E25-18133. Josiah's analogy to the purity of clay with its edibility was apropos, since there was, and apparently remains, a curious custom of people eating kaolin, the type of clay Josiah called Cherokee, which is further discussed in a subsequent chapter.
163   even "kept incognito": Josiah to Bentley, 27 May 1767, Keele, E25-18148.
163   "The Chancellor of the Exchequer might be applyd": Josiah to Bentley, 23 May 1767, Keele, E-25-18147; Josiah's reference to Samuel Garbett is identified by Meteyard, *Life*, ii, 4.
163   "hath resided many years in N.A.": Josiah to Bentley, 20 May 1767, Keele, E25-18146.
164   "downright serious business" plans: This and the following exchange between Bentley and Josiah from Josiah to Bentley, 8 November 1766, Keele, E25-18132, where Josiah quotes Bentley's own words. For stylistic purposes, I have altered Josiah's quotations to put Bentley's words in the first person. The original text of the letter is reprinted (in abridged form) in Farrer, ed., *Letters*, vol. 1, pp. 183–88 (where it is misdated 1767).
165   "Sally and I pronounce'd its doom": Josiah to Bentley, February 1767, Keele, E25-18186.
165   named "Etruria": Technically, at this point he spelled it "Hetruria," but soon corrected the spelling.
165   "This building of houses": Josiah to Bentley, 3 March 1768, Keele, E25-18191.
165   £10,000: The exact estimate was £10,053, discussed further in next chapter; Keele, E43-28632, "first cost of buildings at Etruria."
166   "Indeed" . . . "I am not in possession": Josiah to Bentley, 20 May 1767, Keele, E25-18146.
166   "anything curious in the Pottery branch": Topic of conversation inaugurated in Josiah to Bentley, February 1767, Keele, E25-18137.

17: An Afflicted Heart

167   "Your friend & My poor Brother": Josiah to Bentley, 14 June 1767, Keele, E25-18151.
167–68   "it is indeed too much for me": These and the following quotations in Josiah to Hodgson, 13 June 1767, Keele, E25-18153 and 14 June 1767, Keele, E25-18154.
168   "Monday evening a man . . .": *Lloyd's Evening Post*, Wednesday, 10 June 1767, 551.

168   "I know you will sympathise": Josiah to Bentley, 14 June 1767, Keele, E25-18152.
169   "a Valley of Tears": Josiah to Ralph Griffiths. 4 July 1767, Keele, E25-18157; the printed version misprints "Vale" instead of "Valley."
169   "Besides all pecuniary considerations": Josiah to Bentley, late July 1767, Keele, E25-18159; information on Bentley's business affairs here is sketchy, inferred from what Josiah said and perhaps linked to his activities mentioned in Bentley, *Thomas Bentley*, 33.
169   "Mrs Wedgwood & her Wedgwoodikin": Josiah to Bentley, late July 1767, Keele, E25-18159.
170   "I am now sunk over head": Josiah to Bentley, 24 August 1767, Keele, E25-18164.
170   "Why you never knew": Josiah to Bentley, 8 September 1767, Keele, E25-18166.
170   "every rarity soon grows stale": Josiah to Bentley, 31 May 1767, Keele, E25-18149.
170   "Many of my experiments": Josiah to Bentley, 5 August 1767, Keele, E25-18161.
170   "a mode of introducing": Josiah to Bentley, no date, Keele, E25-18132.
170   "COMMAND SUCCESS": Josiah to Bentley, 27 September 1767, Keele, E25-18168; "if you can make this branch": to Bentley, no date, Keele, E25-18132.
170   "My present business is too good": This and other quotations in the paragraph from: Josiah to Bentley, 3 July 1767, Keele, E25-18160.
171   "may be of use to me in the Antiquities": Josiah to Bentley, no date, Keele, E25-18183.
171   "*written instructions*": Josiah to Bentley, 3 March 1768, Keele, E25-18191.
171   wanting "nothing but arrangement": Josiah to Bentley, 31 May 1767, Keele, E25-18149; see Fontaines, "Wedgwood's London Showrooms," for an excellent survey of his different showrooms.
172   "One of the objects": Josiah to Bentley, 24 March 1768, Keele, E25-18196.
172   "work'd several years": Josiah to Bentley, 21 March 1768, Keele, E25-18197.
172   "several hours" together: Josiah to Bentley, 24 March 1768, Keele, E25-18196.
173   "surprise *the World*": Josiah to Bentley, 31 October 1768, Keele, E25-18212.
173   "almost overwhelm my patience": Josiah to Bentley, 28 April 1767, Keele, E25-18178.
173   "leaving home in a great hurry": Sally to Bentley, 30 November 1767, Keele, microfilm reel ii, p. 85.
173   "about 50 people": Josiah to Bentley, 12 October 1767, Keele, E25-18169.
174   "with good fingers": Josiah to Bentley, 31 December 1767, Keele, E25-18182.
174   "to know when they must begin": Josiah to Bentley, 8 September 1767, Keele, E25-18166.
174   "Root flowerpots . . .": Planned products from Josiah to Bentley, 8 November 1767, Keele, E25-18132.
174   with "hands so cold": Josiah to Bentley, 31 December 1767, Keele, E25-18182.
174   "the hazardous state of my health": Josiah to Bentley, 3 July 1767, Keele, E25-18160; cf. earlier complaints, Josiah to Bentley, July 1767, Keele, E25-18159. The inclement weather is complained about continuously.
174   "over-walk'd & over-work'd": Josiah to W. Cox, 30 April 1768, Keele, 96-17660. Various modern interpretations of the medical condition that led to Josiah's amputation have been proffered. Leonard and Juliette Rakow. "Wedgwood's Peg Leg," summarize it thus: "Small pox products multiple skin vesicles which become secondarily infected. The bacteria from the resultant abscesses frequently enter the blood stream and lodge in the end of long bones where they cause osteomyelitis. . . . The bacteria growing in the ends of the long bones produce bone abscesses [and in certain circumstances] drainage does not occur. . . . The body's immune processes wage a constant war with the infecting bacteria which nest in the ends of the long bones. . . . Unfortunately small injuries to the infected area, excessive use of the extremity and reduction of immune activity for other reasons, all result in moderate or severe flareup of the symptoms" (pp. 11–12). See also Meiklejohn, "English Domestic Medicine," 541–42.
174   "the pain had no soon left my knee": Quoted in Meiklejohn, "English Domestic Medicine," 541.

175   "brotherly love & affection": Josiah to Bentley, June 1768, Keele, E25-18199; various accounts of the amputation stem from Meteyard, *Life*, ii, 40–41.

175   "Your favor of the 26th": 28 May 1768, Keele, E25-18305.

175   "violently seized": Swift writing, 30 May 1768, Keele, E25-18306.

175   "One grain of variolous matter": Darwin, *Temple of Nature*, quoted in King-Hele, *Erasmus Darwin*, 291.

176   "that terrible disease": Information on Josiah's children in letters of 2 March 1767, Keele, E25-18139, and 31 December 1767, Keele, E25-18182.

177   "that it is bringing a Distemper": Doddridge, *Case for Receiving the Small Pox*, quotes from 9, 18, 25.

18: The Arts Reborn

177   "left off my laudanum": Josiah to Bentley, June 1768, Keele, E25-18199.

178   "a wooden-leg maker": Josiah to Bentley, 14 July 1768, Keele, E25-18205; for portraits of him with a straight wooden prosthesis, see Rakow and Rakow, "Wedgwood's Peg Leg."

178   "a long time ago" and "I shall be very glad": Josiah to William Cox, 13 July 1768, Keele, E96-17665.

179   "there are some statues": Montesquieu quoted in Haskell and Penny. *Taste and the Antique*, 73, which provides an excellent account of the spread and lure of classicism throughout this period.

179   "as a Society of Artists": Josiah to Bentley, [February 1769], Keele, E25-18232.

180   It was difficult enough: Josiah to Bentley, 1767, Keele, E25-18132.

180   figurines modeled after Spinario: Haskell and Penny, *Taste and the Antique*, 96, who point to examples in the Victoria and Albert Museum; I'm also grateful to Hilary Young at the V & A for taking the time to show me around and discuss the collections there with me.

180   "in making ornamental Earthenware": Partnership agreement between Josiah and Bentley signed 15 November 1767, Keele, W/M 1826; see Blake Roberts, "Wedgwood and His Partners," and McKendrick, "Josiah Wedgwood and Thomas Bentley."

180   "in the original works of the ancients": Bentley reviewing Hamilton's volumes upon their publication in the *Monthly Review* 42 (1770), 514; see the useful guide to Josiah's and Bentley's book collections, Johnson, "Books Belonging to Wedgwood."

180–81   "I apprehend the Etruscan body": Notes in Josiah's commonplace book, Wedgwood Museum, E39-28408, £ 153.

181   "all my patterns as they arrive": Josiah to William Cox, 31 August 1768, Keele, E96-17667.

181   The Sèvres factory and Capodimonte "china": Haskell and Penny, *Taste and the Antique*, 96.

182   "I have had many *Visions*": Josiah to Bentley, 26 December 1768, Keele, E25-18221.

182   stood at "plinth height": Josiah to Bentley, 25 July 1768, Keele, E25-18205.

183   He "does not seem to consider": Josiah to Bentley, 30 August 1768, Keele, E25-18208.

183   Some six hundred men were busy: Meteyard, *Life*, i, 497.

183   a drying and storage room: The round dome that is today the only remaining fragment of the original Etruria factory may have been used for this sort of storage.

184   "Some of my good Neighbours": Josiah to Bentley, 10 April 1768, Keele, E25-18198.

185   "I believe you will think me": Josiah to Bentley, 24 December 1767, Keele, E25-18181.

185   "He promises to be very good": Josiah to Bentley, 6 July 1768, Keele, E25-18204; E25-18199 for advance of £70.

185   "Mr Cox is as mad": Josiah to Bentley, 21 November 1768, Keele, E25-18215.

186   four "serpent handled antique vases": Peter Swift (with postscript by Josiah) to William Cox on an invoice, 3 September 1768, quoted in Meteyard, *Life*, ii, 69.
186   "I am collecting some figures": Josiah to Bentley, [February 1769], Keele, E25-18232.
187   "new cabinets are opening": Josiah to Sally, 7 March 1769, Keele, E25-18235; for Lady Bessborough and a glimpse of the activities on the Grand Tour of some of Josiah's best customers, see Dolan, *Ladies of the Grand Tour*.
187   "as they will be looked over": Josiah to Bentley, [February 1769], Keele, E25-18232.
187   "Etruscan Vases are the run at present": Josiah to Bentley, 6 February 1769, Keele, E25-18227. For drumming up further patronage, he sent free examples of the new wares to Miss Chetwynd and the Prince of Wales: see letter to Cox with instructions, Keele, L96-17672.
187   "fine old Gentleman": Josiah to Bentley, 7 February 1769, amended to Keele, E25-18227.
187   "Pray do exert yourself": Josiah to Bentley, 14 February 1769, Keele, E25-18229.
188   "works are cover'd in": Josiah to Bentley, 6 November 1768, Keele, E25-18213.
188   "Etruria Village": The cost of the various buildings worked out as: Etruria Hall and offices, £2,660; the house and offices of Mr. JW, £633; the barn, £240; the house Swift lives in, £82; the Inn, £681; the useful works, £2,646; the ornamental works, £1,041; dwelling houses, in no. 42, including the six houses at the works, £1,880; and the Mill,£190—Keele, E43-28632.
188   "I am getting things forward": Josiah to Bentley, 9 April 1769, Keele, E25-18237.
189   "dare not acquaint her": Josiah to Bentley, 18 June 1769, Keele, E25-18243.
189   "slops": See, e.g., Wedgwood and Wedgwood, *Wedgwood Circle*, 42.

Part Three
19: Ingenious Working People and Formidable Opponents

193   "Amid the hoary Ruins": Thomas, *Liberty* in *Works of Mr Thomson*, i, 103.
193   Wedgwood & Bentley's: The most comprehensive study to date of Bentley's influence on Josiah is McKendrick, "Josiah Wedgwood and Thomas Bentley."
193   "In general" . . . "we owe the possession": Young, *Six Months Tour*, iii, 309.
194   "300 houses": Ibid., 306.
194   "narrow selfish views": Josiah to Bentley, 22 February 1768, Keele, E25-18187.
194   "doctrines of *money getting*": Bentley quoted by Josiah in 12 March 1767, Keele, E25-18140.
195   Society for the Encouragement of Arts, Manufactures and Commerce: My discussion here draws from Allan and Abbott, eds., *The Virtuoso Tribe of Arts and Sciences*.
195   "against foreign despotism" and "no truly benevolent": Ibid., xvi–vii.
195   "That the national improvement of skill:" Dossie, *Handmaid*, v.
196   "there is a rivalship": Ibid., 407.
196   totaled £11 million: These figures from Mathias, *Transformation of England*, 125. For discussion of the differences between customs and excise revenue and land assessments, see Mathias and O'Brien, "Taxation in England and France": Brewer, *Sinews of Power*, 100; and Ashworth, *Customs and Excise*.
197   "mechanic invention, toys and utensils": Schofield, *Lunar Society*, 24; Roll, *Early Experiment*, 8. For an updated account of the relationship between Boulton, Erasmus Darwin, and others discussed particularly in this chapter, see Uglow, *Lunar Men*.
197   "industrious, ingenious working people": Franklin quoted in Uglow, *Lunar Men*, 58.
197   "to show the Difference of Workmanship": Franklin quoted in Clark, *Benjamin Franklin*, 147.
198   "My idea was to settle": Boulton quoted in T. H. Marshall, *James Watt* (Edinburgh: Leonard Parsons, 1925), 101.

199 "I intend to ask him" and "He is I believe the first": Josiah to Bentley, 23 May 1767, Keele, E25-18147.

199 "laid the foundations" and "Mr Boulton tells me": Josiah to Bentley, 15 March 1768, Keele, E25-18193.

200 "Mr Boulton is picking up Vases": Josiah to Bentley, 21 November 1768, Keele, E25-18215. Boulton tried to forge a union again at the beginning of January, but Josiah was still uncertain how Bentley would react: Josiah to Bentley, 3 January 1769, Keele, E25-18222.

201 "If Etruria cannot stand": Josiah to Bentley, 27 September 1769, Keele, E25-18261.

201 "It doubles my courage": Josiah to Bentley, 27 September 1769, Keele, E25-18261.

201 "I have got the start of my Brethren": Josiah to Bentley, 9 April 1769, Keele, E25-18237.

202 "No getting to the door": Josiah to Bentley, 1 May 1769, Keele, E25-18240.

20: French Frippery and Russian Husks

203 "I have waited upon Ld Cathcart": Josiah to Boulton, January 1768, "Lunar Society Correspondence," Adam Matthew microfilm.

203 "an East Indian Captain": Josiah to Bentley, April 1767, Keele, E25-18167.

204 "I cannot raise the prices": Josiah to Bentley, April 1767, Keele, E25-18191.

204 "If the Bills are sent": Lady Cathcart to Josiah, quoted by him in letter to Bentley, 4 September 1769, Keele, E25-18250.

204 "We have a large order": Josiah to Bentley, 4 September 1769, Keele, E25-18250.

204 "Ld Barrington is angry": Josiah to Bentley, 12 or 13 September 1769, Keele, E25-18253.

205 "take a little of the weight": Josiah to Bentley, 13 September 1769, Keele, E25-18253.

205 A full-blown retirement scheme: See Priestley's plan, *Lectures on History, and General Policy* (1788).

205 "A Porter has offer'd himself": Josiah to Bentley, 13 September 1769, Keele, E25-18252.

206 "Lazy & fickle": Josiah to Bentley, 9 April 1769, Keele, E25-18237.

206 "several others would fain to hire": Josiah to Bentley, 20 September 1769, Keele, E25-18258.

206 "They must not be *presented*": Josiah to Bentley, 20 September 1769, Keele, E25-18258.

206 "I am on the spot to be of Service": Lady Cathcart to Josiah, 19 March 1771, W/M 1442.

206 "I was not order'd to insure": Josiah to Bentley, 25 September 1769, Keele, E25-18260.

207 "Saturday is the busiest": This and the following quotations relating to Boulton from Josiah to Bentley, 27 September 1769, Keele, E25-18261.

208 "Conquer France in Burslem?": Josiah to Bentley, 13 September 1769, Keele, E25-18252.

208 "for the *Virtuosi* of France": Josiah (repeating Bentley's words) to Bentley, 17 September 1769, Keele, E25-18255; Reilly, *Wedgwood*, i, 98.

208 "The field is vast indeed!": Josiah to Bentley, 1 October 1769, Keele, E25-18264.

208 "Avenue into the Russian Empire": Josiah to Bentley, 2 July 1770, E25-18312.

208 "Ords from Russia this Spring": Josiah to Bentley, 16 February 1771, Ferrer, ed., *Letters*, ii, 13.

208 "What is good will sell here":Lady Cathcart to Josiah, 17 April 1771, W/M 1442.

209 "the Russian trade comes": Josiah to Bentley, 21 April 1771, in Ferrer, ed., *Letters*, ii, 24.

209 "How many Lords and Dukes":Josiah to Bentley, January 1771, in ibid., I.
209 reached £650: Reilly, *Wedgwood*, 31.
209 "Generalissimo" of trade: Josiah to Bentley, 23 January 1771, in Ferrer, ed., *Letters*, ii, 6.

21: Wanting Air for Sally

211 "Sukey & Jack at my elbows": Josiah to Bentley, 22 December 1770, Keele, E25-18333; E25-18329.
212 "we have all things in common": Sally to Bentley, 29 November 1769, Keele, microfilm reel ii, f. 162.
213 "New grates are put up": from Meteyard, *Life*, ii, 95; the household inventory by Cox is at Keele, W/M 1360.
213 "Wet mornings & fine afternoons": This, and the following quotations (until otherwise noted), from Sally to Bentley, 29 November 1769, Keele, microfilm reel ii, f. 162.
213 "If ministers can once usurp": Wilkes quoted in Dickinson, "Radicals and Reformers," 126.
214 "As I am deeply enter'd": And following quotations until otherwise noted, Sally to Bentley, 8 December 1768, Keele, microfilm, ii, ff. 185–86.
215 "such fine things of my Lad" and "Jacks smile Pleased": Sally and Catherine to Bentley, 29 November 1768, Keele, microfilm, ii, f. 162.
215 "I will not trust to writing": Josiah to Bentley, [December] 1768, Keele E25-18216.
215 "My good man is upon the ramble": Sally to Bentley, December 1768, Keele, microfilm, ii, ff. 178–79.
215 "just arriv'd, in good health": Sally to Bentley, December 1768, Keele, microfilm, ii, f. 188.
215–16 meeting "with several accidents" and "I was rewarded" Josiah to Bentley, 11 November 1769, Keele, E25-18268.
216 "They are near": Josiah to Bentley, 1 January 1770, Keele, E25-18280.
217 "My *life*": Josiah to Bentley, 24 January 1770, Keele, E25-18286.
217 "I am often practicing": Josiah to Bentley, 15 January 1770, Keele, E25-18284.
217 "Little Tom, for so they call him": Josiah to Bentley, 15 May 1771, in Ferrer, ed., *Letters*, ii, 29.
217 "a vast deal of *hard weather*": Josiah to Bentley, 22 March 1772, Keele, E25-18358.
217 "removing our Wheels": Josiah to Bentley, 23 April 1772, Keele, E25-18369.
217 "My Landlord is married": Adams, *North Staffordshire Families*, 125.
217 "The sun shines": Josiah to Bentley, 22 March 1772, Keele, E25-18358.
218 "Mrs Wedgwood is Ill": Josiah to Bentley, 22 March 1772, Keele, microfilm, iii, f. 14.
218 "Carried to & from": Josiah to Bentley, 30 March 1772, Keele, microfilm, iii, f. 17.
218 "take an airing on Horseback": Josiah to Bentley, 11 April 1772, Keele, E25-18365.
218 "He says he is afraid": Josiah to Bentley, 30 March 1772, Keele, E25-18360.
218 earth's "central fires": Darwin's interest in Buxton discussed in King-Hele, *Erasmus Darwin*, 245.
218 "patients would have no confidence" and "is not to be trifled with": Both physicians' opinions quoted in Harley, "A Sword in a Madman's Hand," 52.
219 "I believe London will": Josiah to Bentley, July 1769, Keele, E25-18247.
219 "to prepare a sortment": Josiah to Bentley, 22 March 1772, Keele, E25-18358.
219 "mention'd going to Bath": Josiah to Bentley, April 1772, Keele, microfilm, iii, f. 30.
219 "Mrs. Wedgwood has been well enough": Josiah to Bentley, [end April] 1772, Keele, microfilm, iii, 46.
219 "Mrs. Wedgwood is again confined": Josiah to Bentley, 20 April 1772, Keele, E25-18368.
219 "half remov'd": Josiah to Bentley, 12 May 1772, Keele, E25-18373.

220   "I have left them with": Josiah to Bentley, 9 May 1772, Keele, E25-18372.
220   "Coal Carts": Josiah to Bentley, 6 June 1772, Keele, E25-18376.
220   "a very rich shop": This and the following quotes relating to this story from Josiah to Bentley, 6 June 1772, Keele, E25-18376.
221   "Mrs Wedgwoods lameness": Josiah to Bentley, 14 June 1772, Keele, E25-18378.
221   "Mr Willets has just been": Catherine to Sally, 20 May 1772; "Tom grows every way": Catherine to Sally, 6 June 1772; "Tommy has four teeth": William Willets to Josiah and Sally, 12 June 1772; all from Keele, W/M 5.
221   "almost a skeleton": Josiah to Bentley, August 1772 (they returned to Etruria 13 July), Keele, microfilm, iii, 106.
221   "Breeding disease":Josiah to Bentley, 23 August 1772, Keele, E25-18392.
221   "& nothing but the greatest attention": Josiah to Bentley, 7 September 1772, Keele, E25-18399.
221   "a course of steel": King-Hele, *Erasmus Darwin*, 110, where he refers to a three-page letter of advice from Darwin to the Wedgwoods written on 30 September 1772, but this is not printed in King-Hele, ed., *Letters of Darwin*.
222   "the dear Partner": King-Hele, *Erasmus Darwin*, 91.
222   "but I believe I shall not": Josiah to Bentley, 13 September 1772, Keele, E25-18403.
222   had "lost a great deal of flesh" and "a scene of vilany": Josiah to Bentley, 12 October 1772, Keele, E25-18412.
222   "in a very dangerous situation": Josiah to Bentley, 2 November 1772, Keele, E25-18415.
222   "revolution in our household": Josiah to Bentley, 9 November 1772, Keele, E25-18418.
222   "if we can preserve her": Josiah to Bentley, 26 December 1772, Keele, E25-18430.

22: "All the Gardens in England"

223   baking dishes . . . "sortables": Thomas Wedgwood's inventory of earthenware from Keele, L96-17804.
223   amounting to a mere £130: "Inventory of workhouse equipment and values": Keele, L96-17807.
223   "has had vexations": Josiah to Bentley, 3 February 1773, Keele, E25-18442.
224   "Ailments of various kinds": Josiah to Bentley, 3 February 1773, Keele, E25-18442.
224   "ill treated & almost ruined" and "her black misdeeds": Josiah to Bentley, 30 May 1773, Keele, E25-18465.
224   "the foolish talk & behaviour": Josiah to Bentley, 15 March 1773, Keele, E25-18449.
224   received £50 worth of furniture: "An account of the household goods Mrs Wedgwood hath . . . ," Keele, L96-17808.
224   repeatedly needed to borrow money from Josiah: Promissory notes, Keele, L96-17819.
225   "who is not one remove": Josiah to Bentley, 30 May 1773, Keele, E25-18265.
225   "Mrs W has had a good night": Josiah to Bentley, 2 March 1773, Keele, E25-18446.
225   "upon the verge of the Holy Estate": Josiah to Bentley, 23 April 1772, Keele, E25-18369.
226   a Dessert Room with a "dessert Table": Description of the Adelphi showroom in Josiah to Bentley, 4 April 1772, Keele, microfilm, iii, ff. 23–26, and 11 April 1772, Keele, E25-18365.
226   £400 annually: See Fontaines, "London Showrooms," 221, for further discussion.
227   "I like the idea": See Fontaines, "Portland House," for the full story.
227   "simple, beautiful and varied": *Acts of Parliament* (1772). BL 215.i.2 (f. 132).
227   chemical concoction including: See Josiah's patent reprinted in Jewitt, *The Wedgwoods*, 201.
227   "The *selling*": Josiah to Bentley, 25 October 1770, Keele, E25-18328.

228 "clever" enamelers: Josiah to Bentley, November 1770, Keele, E25-18346.
228 "a sharer in the patent": See Reilly, *Wedgwood*, 81, for this point.
228 "There is nothing relating to business": This and the following quotations about "surprising the world" are from a long letter to Bentley, 27 September 1769, Keele, E25-18261.
228 "in order of time he ought": Josiah to Bentley, 1 October 1769, Keele, E25-18264.
228 "Variations" . . . "will produce": Josiah to Bentley, 27 September 1769, Keele, E25-18261.
229 "I am not without": Josiah to Bentley, 11 April 1772, Keele, E25-18365.
229 "my Great Patroness in the North": Josiah to Bentley, 23 March 1773, Keele, E25-18450. Much has been written about this commission, including Williamson, *Imperial Russian Dinner Service*; a useful article which summarizes the story is Kelly, "Wedgwood's Catherine Services."
229 *every piece having*": Josiah to Bentley, 23 March 1773, Keele, E25-18450.
229 "Do you think the subjects": Josiah to Bentley, 29 March, 1773, Keele, E25-18452.
230 "If his Mistress heard": Josiah to Bentley, 30 July 1773, Keele, E25-18484.
230 "not be *fit*": Josiah to Bentley, 5 April 1773, Keele, E25-18454.
230 "the paintings in most" and "the *publish'd views*": Josiah to Bentley, 30 July 1773, Keele, E25-18484; "published views," as Kelly. "Wedgwood's Catherine Services" notes, included well-illustrated volumes such as Bickham's *Beauties of Stow*, Chambers's *Description of Kew*, and so on.
230 "first Empress in the World": Josiah to Bentley, 9 April 1773, Keele, E25-18455.
230 "all of the centuries and styles": From Bentley's catalogue of the service, written in French. The British Library copy of Williamson's book. *Imperial Russian Dinner Service*, contains a full translation of Bentley's original catalogue, BL K.T.C.36.b.9.
231 "it would bring an immense number": Josiah to Bentley, 14 November 1773, Keele, E25-18498.
231 "It consists I believe": From Delany's autobiography, quoted in Jo Dahn, "Mrs Delany and Ceramics in the Objectscape," in the on-line journal *Interpreting Ceramics*, http://www.uwic.ac.uk/ICRC/issue001/delany/delany.htm.
231 "her approbation": Quoted in Kelly, "Wedgwood's Catherine Services," 12.
231–32 just over 16,000 rubles: This is the figure stated by L. N. Voronikhina, in her Russian monograph *The Service with Green Frog*, cited by Kelly, "Wedgwood's Catherine Services," 12. James Harris, an English traveler to Russia in 1779, was shown the "very remarkable service . . . and this led us to a conversation on English gardening, in which the Empress is a great adept"—Malmesbury, the Third Earl. *Diaries and Correspondence of James Harris, First Ear of Malmesbury*, 4 vols. (London: Richard Bentley, 1844), I, 231.

23: "Off for the Cherokee Nation"

233 "a miserable hot": This and all the following quotes relating to Griffiths's journey, unless otherwise noted, from his "Journal of the Voyage to South Carolina, 1767," a transcript of which is in the Wedgwood Museum, Barlaston. I am grateful to their staff for providing a copy and giving and permission to quote from it. It is interesting to compare Griffiths's journey to William Bartram's journey in 1775, discussed in his published *Travels*; see, also, the account by the North Carolina Bartram Trail Society, http://www.ncbartramtrail.org/index.htm. Griffiths's journey has been discussed by Bill Anderson, "Cherokee Clay, from Duché to Wedgwood: The Journal of Thomas Griffiths, 1767–1768," *North Carolina Historical Review* (1976), and in an article by George Ellison in *Mountain Voices*, 7 March 2001, at www.smokeymountainnews.com.
235 an Englishman named Mr Downy: This, I believe, is the same couple who later extended hospitality to William Bartram during his travels.

24: Poison and Porcelain

239   Cookworthy discovered deposits: This, of course, is a much-simplified version of what happened; see Selleck, *Cookworthy*, for a more comprehensive analysis of the unfolding series of events that led to Cookworthy's discovery. Also, Anderson, "Cherokee Clay, from Duché to Wedgwood."

239   enhanced the desired cream color of earthenware: Blake Roberts, "Josiah Wedgwood and Richard Champion," 45.

239   "I apprehend our customers": Josiah to Bentley, 12 December 1774, Keele, E25-18572.

240   "The Great People have had their Vases": Josiah to Bentley, 23 August 1772, Keele, E25-18392.

240   "Few Ladies, you know": Josiah to Bentley, 21 June 1777, Keele, E25-18766.

240   the "present vogue for imitating": *Monthly Magazine* (1763), quoted in Bushman, "American High-Style."

240   they were never his primary market: In another instance, when Josiah was considering resurrecting the agate and green ware that he stopped producing a decade earlier when they dropped out of fashion, he reasoned that "there are, and ever will be a numerous class of People, to purchase *shewy & cheap* things. The Creamcolour is of a superior class, & I trust has not yet run its race by many degrees," 7 March 1774, Keele, E25-18521. A number of recent studies have looked at Wedgwood as a pioneer in marketing and branding: see, e.g., Nancy Koehn, *Brand New: How Entrepreneurs Earned Consumers' Trust from Wedgwood to Dell*, and Regina Lee Blaszczyk, *Imagining Consumers: Design and Innovation from Wedgwood to Corning*.

240   "We have hitherto appeared": Josiah to Bentley, 7 December 1772, Keele, E25-18427.

241   "receive, by the Mouth and Nostrils": Ramazini, *Treatise on the Diseases*, 62. My thanks to Paul Blanc for allowing me to use his library of eighteenth-century medical tracts relating to occupational health, and for his input.

241   "First of all": Ramazini, *Treatise on the Diseases*, 62; Strother, *An Essay on Sickness and Health*, 447, where he essentially repeats the symptoms and recommends "chalybeates and mercurial purges as Remedies."

242   "May it not reasonably": Baker, "An Examination of Several Means," 300.

242   "That part of the old earthenware": Ibid., 359–60.

243   "The very beautiful polish": Thomas Percival, *Observations and Experiments on the Poison of Lead* (London, 1779), 26.

243   "& I told him it was": Josiah to Bentley, 21 July 1773, Keele, E25-18481.

243   "I did not dispute": Josiah to Bentley, 17 August 1773, Keele, E25-18488.

244   "to shew how pernicious": Josiah to Bentley, 22 August 1773, Keele, E25-18490.

244   "it is now very difficult": Benson's patent, quoted in Owen, *The Staffordshire Potter*, 276.

244   "I will try in earnest": Josiah to Bentley, 22 August 1773, Keele, E25-18490; for more on the issue of lead poisoning, see Meiklejohn, "Successful Prevention," 169.

245   "to stop the Rascals career": Josiah to Bentley, 4 December 1774, Keele, E25-18571. A year earlier, Josiah hoped that publishing a descriptive catalogue of their wares would be useful not only as an advertising aid but perhaps as an additional measure to distinguish between their wares and anyone else's. This led to the publication of their first catalogue in 1774, which does not seem to have worked as a deterrent to forgers. Part of the difficulty—as Josiah explained to Bentley—was that some of their smaller pieces, such as seals or cameos, didn't have enough room on the back to add more distinguishing marks and numbers. See Josiah to Bentley, 7 June 1773, Keele, E25-18469.

245   "Man of Science, who loves": Erasmus Darwin to Josiah, 27 April 1766, in King-Hele, ed., *Letters*, i, 40.

245   "I do not wish to purchase": Josiah to Bentley, 6 February 1774, quoted in Blake Roberts, "Josiah Wedgwood and Richard Champion," 45.

245 "on some very promising experiments": Josiah to Bentley, 6 February 1773, Keele, E25-18443.

246 "I am fairly enter'd into" and "bad policy": Josiah to Bentley (and Josiah therein quoting Bentley), 7 March 1774, Keele, E25-18521.

246 "Moorstone & Spaith fusible": Josiah to Bentley, 21 July 1774, Keele, E25-18548. For a further discussion of these experiments, which relate to the creation of jasper, see Reilly, *Wedgwood Jasper*, particularly pp. 70–71, where he discusses the work of William Burton and Sir Arthur Church, who worked out, in modern terms, the chemical properties of jasper.

246 "I cannot work miracles": This and other quotations to "almost crazy" from Josiah to Bentley, 30 August 1774, Keele, E25-18555.

246 "Aged & affectionate father": Josiah to Bentley, 19 November 1774, Keele, E25-18565.

246–47 "the place, & the scenes": Josiah to Bentley, 26 November 1774, Keele, E25-18569.

247 "my dear Girl": Josiah to Bentley, 30 November 1774, Keele, E25-18570.

247 "we should endeavour to throw": Josiah to Bentley, 12 December 1774, Keele, E25-18573.

247 "it is too precious to reveal": Josiah to Bentley, 3 February 1776, Keele, E25-18650.

247 "4 black & Blue onyx Intaglios": See Reilly, *Wedgwood Jasper*, 76.

248 "The blue body": Josiah to Bentley, 1 January 1775, Keele, E25-18578.

248 "Crucifixes, Saints": Josiah to Bentley, 5 November 1774, Keele, E25-18561.

248 "so you see a spirit": Josiah to Bentley, 23 July 1775, Keele, E25-18612.

248 "the Manufacturers of Dresden" and "ASTONISH": Josiah to Bentley, 6 August 1775, Keele, E25-18614.

248 "nobody" . . . "but W & B": Josiah to Bentley, 5 July 1776, Keele, E25-18680.

248 "very civil to me": Josiah to Bentley, 5 July 1776, Keele, E25-18680.

248 "suitable for setting in boxes": It seems the earliest this was proposed was 7 June 1773, Keele, E25-18469.

248 "the completion of the Art": Josiah to Bentley, 14 January 1776, Keele, E25-18642. For Josiah's account of the production of jasper, written in a memorandum on 23 November 1777, see Reilly, *Wedgwood Jasper*, 87–88.

249 "I have often thought": Josiah to Bentley, 15 December 1777, Keele, E25-18802. I add the emphasis here.

249 the number 23, the secret code: Reilly, *Wedgwood Jasper*, 90.

25: Mad Ministers

250 "I am no politician": Josiah to Bentley, 8 January 1775, Keele, E25-18582.

250 "cruel and oppressive acts": "Resolves of the First Continental Congress," 14 October 1774.

250 an "empire of goods": See Breen "Empire of Goods," 498; Franklin from Greene, ed., "The Examination of Benjamin Franklin," 73.

250 "around half of all English exports": McCusker and Menard, *Economy of British America*, 286; Blake Roberts, "Wedgwood to America."

251 "necessaries, mere conveniences": Greene, ed., "The Examination of Benjamin Franklin," 73.

251 "To impose servitude": Lord Chatham in House of Lords, 20 January 1775; see Young, ed., *Genius*, 88.

251 "froth'd at the mouth": Josiah's observations from Josiah to Bentley, 6 February 1775, Keele, E25-18590.

252 "to my astonishment": Josiah to Bentley, 5 November 1775, Keele, E25-18623.

252 "Those" . . . "who are neither converted": Josiah to Bentley, 24 February 1776, Keele, E25-18657; Richard Price, *Observations on the Nature of Civil Liberty, the Principles of Government, and the Justice and Policy of the War with America* (London, 1776), which went through five editions in under two months of first publication and sold over 60,000 copies.

253 "where I can do it without a sacrifice": Josiah to Bentley, 27 November 1775, Keele, E25-18626.

254 "There is no doubt": Josiah to Sir John Wrottesley, 29 November 1775, Keele, E25-18627; for wars and the state of the British economy, see Brewer, *Sinews of Power*, 178–79.

254 In 1775, under 139,000 pieces were sent: Ewins, "Supplying the Present Wants," table 1; Schumpeter, *English Overseas Trade Statistics*.

255 "the absurdity, folly & wickedness": Josiah to Bentley, 3 March 1778, Keele, E25-18815.

255 "the Gentlemen who repose": Josiah to Bentley, April 1774, Keele, E25-18529.

255 "She had much rather": Josiah to Bentley, 23 June 1775, Keele, E25-18603.

256 "I should be asham'd": Josiah to Bentley, 3 February 1776, Keele, E25-18650.

256 "Asiatic Porcelains": Josiah discussing Byerley's letter on behalf of the committee, 7 February 1776, Keele, E25-18652.

256 "will be very good things *for England*": Josiah to Bentley, 2 July 1776, Keele, E25-18679.

26: The *Philosophes* and Plaster Shops of Paris

267 "to the Duke or Count": Quoted in Johnson, *Thomas Bentley's Journal*, 8. The journal was reproduced by Peter France (University of Sussex Library); cited hereafter as Bentley, *Journal*.

257 "professedly a journey": Bentley to Samuel Boardman, 3 October 1776, quoted in ibid., 9–10.

258 "Many of the buildings": Bentley to Samuel Boardman, ibid.

258 "Tell me": Montagu in ibid., 29; Dolan, *Ladies of the Grand Tour*, 131–32; "Your remark that everything": Josiah to Bentley, 8 August 1776, Keele, E25-18687.

258 "The causes" . . . "must be": Bentley, *Journal*, 30.

259 "my heart expanded": This and the following account of his meeting with Rousseau in ibid., 59–61.

260 self-styled "Lunar Society": See Uglow, *The Lunar Men*, and Schofield, *Lunar Society of Birmingham*, for comprehensive discussions of this.

260 "a form of social worship": David Williams, "A Liturgy on the Universal Principles of Religion and Morality" (1776), preface; for more, see David Williams, "Incidents in my Life," Cardiff Central Library, MS 2.191–92.

260 "Ah yes": the Rousseau-Bentley dialogue is recorded in Bentley, *Journal*, 60.

260 "prefers exile, poverty": Day, "The Dying Negro: A Poem" (London, 1773; 3rd ed., 1775), preface.

262 "Upon examination" and the comments that follow: Bentley, *Journal*, 42.

263 "It is striking": Ibid., 11; see also Harris, *Industrial Espionage*, 328.

263 "I willingly refer myself": Josiah to Bentley, 8 August 1776, Keele, E25-18687.

27: A Poor Regiment

264 "before our people are up": Josiah to Bentley (on a Saturday morning), 7 March 1774, Keele, E25-18521.

264 "Nay, you need no make": Josiah to Bentley, 15 May 1776, Keele, E25-18669.

265 "a healing Balsam": This and the following account of the dispute with the workers from Josiah to Bentley, 22 July 1776, in Ferrer, ed., *Letters*, ii, 299–301.

265　"This will not do": Meteyard, *Life*, i, 219.
265　"It is *hard*": Josiah to Bentley, 23 December 1770, Keele, E25-18310.
266　Josiah's authority and industrial paternalism: See Roberts, *Paternalism in Early Victorian England*, for the development of this role. For a view of paternalism in apprenticeships, where the role of the master replaces the "negligence" of local government supervision and care for children, see Ivy Pinchbeck and Margaret Hewitt, *Children in English Society*, 2 vols. (London: Routledge, 1969–1973).
266　"taking & Keeping him out": Josiah to Bentley, 1 September 1772, Keele, E25-18397.
266　"Charity may incline us": Josiah to Bentley, 4 October 1772, Keele, E25-18411.
267　"They seem to have got the notion": Roberts, *Paternalism*, 173.
267　"A *Waking notion* haunts": Josiah to Bentley, 23 May 1770, Keele, E25-18302.
267　"scheme for taking Girls": Josiah to Bentley, 19 May 1770, Keele, E25-18301.
267　"I am more & more in Love": Josiah to Bentley, 25 July 1772, Keele, E25-18382.
268　"improved in their *wages*": Josiah to Bentley, 10 January 1770, Keele, E25-18283.
268　"everyone but an idiot knows": Young quoted in Mathias, *Transformation of England*, 148; numerous comments like this are brought up in Inglis, *Poverty and the Industrial Revolution*.
269　"Expenses move on like clockwork" and the account that follows: Josiah to Bentley, 23 August 1772, Keele, E25-18392.
269　Those "who can subsist on three days' ": Quoted in De Vries, "Purchasing Power," 112.
269　"all the Men at the Ornamental": Josiah to Bentley, 22 July 1776, in Ferrer, ed., *Letters*, ii, 299–300.
271　"Mrs Wedgwood was not frightened": Josiah to Bentley, 25 September 1776, Keele, E25-18699.

Part Four
28: *Arrivistes*

275　In May 1777: Lead, *Trent and Mersey Canal*, 9; cost of canal in Josiah to Richard Lovell Edgeworth, 13 February 1786, Keele, E3-2488.
275　"a very pleasant expedition": Josiah to Bentley, 19 September 1774, Keele, E25-18559.
275　"The whole face of this country": Wesley in 1781, quoted in Hughes, *Mother Town*, 12. An excellent overview of the transformation of the industrial landscape is Trinder, *Making of the industrial Landscape*.
276　"the Blacklands": Josiah to Bentley, 4 May 1776, Keele, E25-18666.
276　"Poor Crisp haunts": Josiah to Bentley, 6 August 1775, Keele, E25-18614. See also Mallet, "Nicholas Crisp," in Allan and Abbott, eds., *Virtuoso Tribe*.
276　"Poor Champion": Josiah to Bentley, 24 August 1778, Keele, E25-18846.
277　"I have often wish'd": Josiah to Bentley, 3 September 1774, Keele, E25-18556.
277　"Illustrious Moderns": Reilly, *Wedgwood*, i, 553.
278　*"beg[ged] without ceasing"*: See Josiah to Bentley, 19 July 1777, Keele, E25-18772, for this and the following account of Elers's ideas, unless otherwise noted.
278　"Bomb proof fortifications": Josiah to Bentley, 1 August 1777, Keele, E25-18775; Reilly, *Wedgwood*, i, 553.
279　"to mark her father's profession": Succinct account of Wright in Daniels, *Joseph Wright*; Josiah to Bentley, 5 May 1778, Keele, E25-18834; quote from Joseph Wright to Josiah, 11 February 1782 (Josiah's initial idea to commission a painting did not further develop until this time), Keele, WMS 1-670; see Reilly, *Wedgwood*, i, 304–07.
280　"I can be instructing them": Josiah to Bentley, 23 November 1779, Keele, E26-18939.

280   "mixing fixable air": Josiah to Bentley, 30 May 1779, Keele, E25-18894.
281   "Jack" . . . "is to be settled": Josiah to Bentley, 19 December 1779, Keele, E26-18946.
281   "full of pouks": Josiah to Bentley, 12 June 1773, Keele, E25-18472.
281   "We know our dear Sukey": Josiah to Bentley, 26 October 1775, Keele, E25-18620.
281   "language & manners are very well": Josiah to Bentley, 11 July 1779, Keele, E25-18909.
282   "slipt upstairs just before": Josiah to Bentley, 19 August 1778, Keele, E25-18845. Josiah's attitude about childbirth had some way to go to be enlightened. When Sally wanted to stay in bed the next night and skip the afternoon meal, he put it down to "a sort of decorum establish'd amongst the sex, originally intended, no doubt, to impose upon us poor men, & make us believe what sufferings they underwent for us & our bantlings."
282   "May dear boy": Josiah to his son John Wedgwood, 1774, Wedgwood Museum, E39-28408, f. 292.
282   "I am convinc'd": Josiah to Bentley, 9 October 1779, Keele, E25-18929.
282   "give them some lessons in latin": Josiah to Bentley, 24 October 1779, Keele, E26-18934.
283   "a very idle waste of time": Josiah relaying what Darwin said to Bentley, 8 November 1779, Keele, E26-19836.
283   "Before breakfast we read": Josiah to Bentley, 23 November 1779, Keele, E25-18939.
283   "Your little boys": Erasmus Darwin to Josiah, December 1779, in King-Hele, ed., Letters, 99.
283   "Susan, John, Josiah": Josiah to Catherine Wedgwood. 27 March 1780, copied into commonplace book.
285   "a long course of drinking": Josiah to Bentley, 7 May 1777, Keele, E25-18755.
285   "In turning my back": Josiah to Bentley, 15 September 1778, Keele, E25-18851.
286   "retir'd from this bustling World": Josiah to Bentley, 23 July 1775, Keele, E25-18612.

29: Renewed Grief

287   "My dear affectionate father": Wedgwood and Wedgwood, *Wedgwood Circle*, 79.
287   "Dr Darwin has bin here": Catherine Wedgwood to Josiah and Sally, February 1780; this and the following quotations from Catherine from a series of letters, all in February 1780, at Keele, W/M 5.
288   "All the boasted nostrums": Darwin quoted by Wedgwood, 12 December 1779, Keele, E26-18943.
288   "I have this morning": Josiah to Bentley, 19 February 1780, in Ferrer, ed., *Letters*, ii, 560.
289   "pushing forward at the same time": Josiah to Bentley, 8 November 1779, Keele, E26-18936.
289   "drawing lightning from the clouds": For electrical machines, see Daumas, *Scientific Instruments*; for uses in medicine, see Rowbottom and Susskind, *Electricity and Medicine*.
290   "I am the electrician": Josiah to Bentley, 8 November 1779, Keele, E25-18936.
290   "I am in great pain": Josiah to Bentley, 17 November 1779, Keele, E26-18937.
291   "As soon as I think": Josiah to Bentley, 28 October 1780, in Ferrer, ed., *Letters*, ii, 603.

30: "But Half Myself"

292   "Our poor friend yet breathes": Ralph Griffiths to Josiah, 25 November 1780, quoted in Bentley, *Thomas Bentley*, 77.
292   an "apoplectic seizure": According to one account—other circumstances have been

posited, including pleurisy and gout. There are no extant sources to throw any more light on the cause of his death.

292 "I have not any friend": Bentley to Josiah, 18 December 1778, quoted in Blake Roberts, "Josiah Wedgwood and His Partners," 18.

293 "Our esteemed friend": Samuel Boardman on 31 December 1780, quoted in Bentley, *Thomas Bentley*, 83.

293 "Your letter communicating to me": Erasmus Darwin to Josiah, 29 November 1780, in King-Hele, ed., *Letters*, 102–03.

293 "I was indeed as much grieved": Sulpicius to Cicero, from *Cicero's Letters*, trans. E. K. Shuckburgh, Harvard Classics, vol. 9, 1909–1914, ed. C. W. Eliot, part 3, letter 13.

294 "For his uncommon ingenuity": Quoted in Boardman, *Bentleyana*, 12.

294 "Mr Wedgwood was the intelligent": Quoted by Peter France in his edition of Bentley, *Journal*, 12; McKendrick, "Josiah Wedgwood and Thomas Bentley," analyzes in further detail the dynamics of their partnership.

294 "preserved from a considerable": Wedgwood quoted in Reilly, *Josiah Wedgwood*, 251.

294 "a great many discriminating people": Byerley quoted in ibid., 252.

31: "A Storm Is Gathering"

296 twenty-two separate work stations: Inventory and description of factory at Keele. W/M 1578; also William Heath's notebooks on the maintenance of Etruria, 1782, Keele, W/M 1818.

297 "colour thermoscope": The best account of the development of what becomes known as Wedgwood's pyrometer is in Reilly, *Wedgwood*, i, 130–35. For this and other aspects of Josiah's experiments in chemistry, see Schofield, "Josiah Wedgwood, Industrial Chemist."

297 "turned the art of Pottery": Banks to Josiah, 6 February 1792, quoted in Gascoigne, *Joseph Banks*, 180.

298 "a most riotous and outrageous Mob" and the quotes that follow: Josiah to Bentley, 9 October 1779, Keele, E26-18929.

300 "We have had several foreigners": Josiah to Bentley, 1 August 1779, Keele, E26-18912.

300 "a disease of the mind" and the quotes that follow: Wedgwood, *Address to the Workers*, 2–6.

301 to "prepare it for respiration": For an elaboration on the concerns over industrial disease and the chemical researches on air, see Dolan, "Conservative Politicians."

302 "May not Dr Priestley's experiments": Commonplace book, Wedgwood Museum, WMS 39-28408.

302 with "fixed air": Carbonated water; see Gibbs, *Priestley*, 57–59, and Golinski, *Science as Public Culture*, 115.

302 "lay by a little money": Josiah's observations of the "Female Club." recorded in his travelogue of his Cornish tour, are reprinted in the *Proceedings of the Wedgwood Society*, 2 (1957); see also Posner, "Eighteenth-Century Health," and Stuart, "Service of Truth."

302 "If the ague dies not weaken": Erasmus Darwin to Josiah, 4 April 1786, in King-Hele, ed., *Letters*, 149–50.

32: "Some Plan of Life"

303 the "Barberini Vase": The early history of the vase is still a matter of controversy, but according to Reilly and Savage, *Dictionary of Wedgwood*, 276, it is more likely an ancient Roman vase representing the marriage of Peleus and Thetis. The history of the vase is summarized in Beeson, "Reproductions of Documents Concerning the Slate

Blue Wedgwood Copy of the Portland Vase"; Wilcoxen, "Peregrinations of a Letter from Sir William Hamilton," is also relevant.

303 "Is it yours?": Sir William Hamilton relaying the story to Josiah in a letter of 24 July 1786, reprinted in Wilcoxen, "Peregrinations."

304 "the Vase, the Head of Jupiter": Dolan, *Ladies of the Grand Tour*, 196.

304 "I do not believe": Hamilton quoted in Fathers, II, *Sir William Hamilton*, 192.

304 "I wish you may soon": John Flaxman to Josiah, 5 February 1784, quoted in Reilly, *Josiah Wedgwood*, 315.

305 "I begin to count": This and the following quotes until otherwise indicated are from Josiah to Sir William Hamilton, 24 June 1786, Keele, E26-18976.

306 "I admire your Enthusiasm": Sir William Hamilton to Josiah, 24 July 1786, reprinted in Wilcoxen, "Peregrinations," 36–37.

306 "diffuse the seeds of good taste": The expression is Josiah's in his previously cited letter to Sir William, 24 June 1786.

306 "I wish to have some chemical": Tom Wedgwood to Josiah, 30 December 1786, Keele, W/M 12.

307 They "cannot be right": Sukey to Josiah, in Wedgwood, *Personal Life*, 360.

307 "rather grand, Picture, & c": Wilberforce quoted in Reilly, *Josiah Wedgwood*, 289; see p. 333 for the following description of the contents of house.

308 "My great work": Josiah to Heberdeen, 25 April 1788, Keele, uncatalogued letter.

308 "all the explications": Josiah to William Hamilton, 1787, BL, ADD Mss 40717, f. 230.

308 but it was not quite what Josiah: For Josiah's sons' attitudes toward the family business from which the following two quotes come, I am indebted to Robin Reilly's account in *Josiah Wedgwood*, 335–40.

309 "as I believed the ideas": Josiah to Joss, 16 April 1788, Keele, E26-18976.

309 "the proposed scheme of Tom": Ibid.

309 "the degree of knowledge": Ibid.

309 "very well executed & a very": 16 April 1788, Keele, E26-18976, appendix.

309 "What I mean" and the quotes that follow from Reilly, *Josiah Wedgwood*, 338–40.

311 "I know you will rejoice": Josiah to Erasmus Darwin, July 1789, Farrer, ed., *Letters*, iii, 90.

33: The "Giant Malady"

312 "AFTER an unremitting": Notice dated 18 January 1790, reproduced in Reilly, *Josiah Wedgwood*, 332.

312 "You have been extremely": Josiah to Erasmus Darwin, July 1789, Farrer, ed., *Letters*, iii, 91: Darwin's interpretation of the scene is discussed in Mankowitz, *Portland Vase*, 58–59; King-Hele, *Erasmus Darwin*, 244 and 391n, notes that there were forty-four interpretations of the meaning of the depiction.

313 Jack "disliked it very much": Joss to Josiah, 16 April 1793, in Reilly, *Josiah Wedgwood*, 339.

313 "I know my father is afraid": Tom Wedgwood to Joss, 27 April 1790, Keele, W/M 12.

313 "I am well aware": Tom Wedgwood to Josiah, 8 May 1790, Keele, W/M 12.

314 "I am happy that some of my arguments": Tom Wedgwood to Josiah, *ca* 11 May 1790, Keele, W/M 12.

314 "which should relate to the late revolution": Joss to Josiah, 28 July 1789, Farrer, ed., *Letters*, iii, 95.

314 "a cornucopia, a bonnet": Dawson, *Masterpieces of Wedgwood*, 63.

315 "Inglorious slept": Darin, *The Economy of Vegetation* (1792), Canto II, lines 378–80; 385–86; King-Hele, *Erasmus Darwin*, 261.

315 "bunting, beggarly; brass-making": Quoted in Rose, "The Priestley Riots," 70.

316 "I am much pleased": Josiah commenting on the early results of Priestley's experiments to Bentley, 9 October 1766, Keele, E25-18130. Priestley had received an honorary doctorate from Edinburgh for his well-received *Chart of Biography*.

316 "delightful and ingenious researchers" and the quotes that follow: Cited in Gibbs, *Joseph Priestley*, 34.

317 "to prepare it for respiration": Priestley writing in 1782 while preparing his *Experiments and Observations on Air*; for an elaboration of the following few paragraphs, see Dolan, "Conservative Politicians, Radical Philosophers."

318 Priestley was warned that a torch-waving mob: The best study on Priestley and the "Church-and-King" riots of 1791 is Kramnick, "Eighteenth-Century Science and Radical Social Theory."

319 "But what daring mortals": Josiah to Bentley, 9 October 1766, Keele, E25-18130.

319 "a liberal college in the back settlements": Priestley, letter dated 16 May 1793, printed in J. F. Marsh, "On Some Correspondence of Dr Priestley Preserved in the Warrington Museum and Library," *Transactions of the Historic Society of Lancashire and Cheshire*, 7 (1855), 71.

319 "every name supposed to think": Erasmus Darwin quoting Josiah, in King-Hele, *Erasmus Darwin*, 295.

320 "an accomplished lady": Erasmus Darwin quoted in ibid., 303.

320 "a furious democrat": Tom Wedgwood to Sally and Josiah, 7 July 1792, Keele, W/M 12.

321 "Nothing now remains": Quoted in King-Hele, *Erasmus Darwin*, 248.

321 "In a future letter": the Beddoes quoted in Dolan, "Conservative Politicians," 97.

34: "To Mix Again with Their Original Clay"

322 "Your letter gives me": Erasmus Darwin to Josiah, 9 December 1794, in King-Hele, ed., *Letters*, 269.

323 "a distinct understanding": Quoted in King-Hele, *Erasmus Darwin*, 303.

323 "For several days": Tom Byerley to Samuel Boardman, 18 January 1795, the only contemporary account of Josiah's last days, printed at length in Reilly, *Wedgwood*, i, 142.

35: "Unremitting Fires"

324 "The death of Mr Wedgwood": Erasmus Darwin to William Hayley, 21 January 1795, in King-Hele, ed., *Letters*, 274.

324 "possessed of great public spirit": More obituary reports were collected by Rodney Hampson in "Josiah Wedgwood: 1795 Obituaries," *Northern Ceramics Society*, 96 (1994), 8–9.

324 He was ranked among the finest chemists: See Samuel Parkes's encomium in his *Chemical Essays* (London, 1815), i, 47; also Schofield, "Josiah Wedgwood, Industrial Chemist," assessing his scientific achievements.

324 "constitute nearly the whole": John Aikin, *Description of the Country 30 to 40 miles round Manchester* (London, 1795), 535.

324 "ingenious and industrious Wedgwood": Parkes, *Chemical Essays*, 47.

325 "a commerce so active": Quoted in Reilly, *Wedgwood*, i, 143.

325 "are much admired": Hamilton in Wilcoxen, "Peregrinations," 37.

325 "It is surely a triumph": Quoted in Hudson, ed., *The Grand Tour*, 25.

325 His estimated wealth was £600,000: "Examination of the Estate of Josiah Wedgwood," Keele, W/M 989; probate copy of the will of Josiah Wedgwood, E26-19108. According to "assets of Josiah Wedgwood," he left £153,800 cash in legacies; much of his money was in stock (India bonds) and real estate.

326 *Wedgwoodarbeit*: Reilly and Savage, *Dictionary of Wedgwood*, 236.

326   Etruria's future suddenly looked brighter: Production at Etruria remained active until 1949, when the new works at Barlaston, Staffordshire, were completed. The original buildings of Etruria were demolished in 1965, and sadly only one small round original brick building survives today.

326   "full of goodness, benevolence": Litchfield, *Tom Wedgwood*, 128.

327   "We will have a fair trial": Coleridge quoted in Ashton, *Life of Samuel Taylor Coleridge*, 215.

327   In a scientific paper: See Litchfield, *Tom Wedgwood: The First Photographer*.

328   producing "trinkets and baubles": For Malthus's attack on manufactures, see Dolan, *Malthus, Medicine, and Morality*, chapter 1.

329   "exceedingly illogical": Coleridge quoted in James, *Population Malthus*, 103.

329   "And pleased on WEDGWOOD": Quoted in Reilly, *Wedgwood*, i 110.

330   "at social Industry's command": William Wordsworth, *The Excursion* (1814), written in 1797 and tentatively titled *The Ruined Cottage*, II. 1–2, 27–31.

330   "One of the most beautiful poems": Coleridge quoted in Stephen Gill, *William Wordsworth: A Life* (Oxford: Oxford University Press, 1989), 133.

331   "O'er which the smoke": Wordsworth, *The Excursion*, II, 9–10.

Epilogue

332   The most thorough account of the history of the Wedgwood firm following Josiah I's death is provided by Reilly, *Wedgwood*, ii, which covers in some detail the developments in the business right up to 1986. I am indebted to Reilly's study from which this summary is largely drawn.

333   "tycoon": Donald Trump to Brian Dolan, personal communication, 14 July 2003.

338   "to command widespread": Koehn, *Brand New*, 42.

339   "Our pottery does very well": Watt quoted in "Capital and Labor—The Invention of the Steam Engine: Roebuck," at www.history.rochester.edu/steam/lord/4-2.htm.

339   "was the greatest man": Gladstone, W. E., *Wedgwood: An Address by the Right Hon. W. E. Gladstone, Chancellor of the Exchequer, and MP for the University of Oxford London* (London: John Murray, 1863), 3.

Bibliography of Works Cited

Adams, Percy. *A History of the Adams Family of North Staffordshire and of Their Connection with the Development of the Potteries.* London: St. Catherine Press, 1914.
————. *Notes on Some North Staffordshire Families, Including Those of Adams, Astbury, Breeze, Challinor, Heath, Warburton.* Tunstall, Staffs.: Edwin Eardley, 1930.
Aikin, John. *A Description of the Country from Thirty to Forty Miles Round Manchester.* London, 1795.
Allan, D. G. C. " 'The Present Unhappy Disputes': The Society and the Loss of the American Colonies, 1774–1783," in D. G. C. Allan and John L. Abbott, eds., *The Virtuoso Tribe of Arts and Sciences.* Athens, GA, and London: University of Georgia Press, 1992.
Allan, D. G. C., and John L. Abbott, eds. *The Virtuoso Tribe of Arts and Sciences: Studies in the Eighteenth-Century Work and Membership of the London Society of Arts.* Athens and London: University of Georgia Press, 1992.
Anderson, Fred. *Crucible of War: The Seven Years' War and the Fate of Empire in British North America 1754–1766.* London: Faber & Faber, 2000.
Anderson, William L. "Cherokee Clay, from Duché to Wedgwood: The Journal of Thomas Griffiths, 1767–1768," *North Carolina Historical Review,* 63 (1986), 477–510.
Anon. *Stoke-on-Trent Historical Pageant and the Josiah Wedgwood Bicentenary Celebrations,* 19–24 May 1930.
Ashton, Rosemary. *The Life of Samuel Taylor Coleridge: A Critical Biography.* London: Blackwell, 1996.
Ashworth, W. J. *Customs and Excise: Trade, Production and Consumption in England, 1640–1845.* Oxford: Oxford University Press, 2003.
Atkinson, George. *The Shipping Laws of the British Empire: Consisting of Park on Marine Insurance and Abbott on Shipping.* London: Longman, Brown, Green, & Longmans, 1854.
Ayling, Stanley E. *George the Third.* London: Collins, 1972.
Baker, George. "An Examination of Several Means, by which the Poison of Lead may be supposed frequently to gain admittance into the Human Body, unobserved, and unsuspected," *Medical Transactions of the College of Physicians, London* (1768).
Barker, David. *William Greatbatch: A Staffordshire Potter.* London: Jonathan Horne, 1991.
Beaver, S. H. "The Potteries: A Study in the Evolution of a Cultural Landscape," *Transactions of the Institute of British Geographers,* 34 (1964).
Beeson, Dwight. "Reproductions of Documents Concerning the Slate Blue Wedgwood Copy of the Portland Vase." Privately printed in Birmingham, Alabama, 1964.

Bentley, Richard ["R.B."]. *Thomas Bentley, 1730–1780: Of Liverpool, Etruria, and London*. Guildford: Billing & Sons, 1927; Wedgwood Society of New York, 1975.

Bentley, Thomas. *Journal of a Visit to Paris 1776*, ed. Peter France. Brighton: University of Sussex Library, 1977.

Berg, Maxine. *The Age of Manufactures: Industry, Innovation and Work in Britain 1700–1820*. Oxford: Basil Blackwell, 1985.

Berg,, Maxine, Pat Hudson, and Michael Sonenscher, eds. *Manufacture in Town and Country Before the Factory*. Cambridge: Cambridge University Press, 1983.

Bienefeld, M. A. *Working Hours in British Industry: An Economic History*. London: Weidenfeld & Nicolson, 1972.

Blake Roberts, Gaye. "Josiah Wedgwood and His Partners," *Ars Ceramica*, 13 (1996), 14–23.

———. "Josiah Wedgwood and His Trade Connections with Liverpool," *Proceedings of the Wedgwood Society*, 11 (1982), 72–80.

———. "Josiah Wedgwood and Richard Champion, Adversaries and Friends," *Ars Ceramica*, 17 (2001), 43–53.

———. "Wedgwood Showrooms in London During the 18th Century," *Ars Ceramica*, 2 (1985), 3–6.

———. "Wedgwood to America: Trading Concerns During the 18th Century," *Ars Ceramica*, 4 (1987), 4–8.

Blaszczyk, Regina Lee. *Imagining Consumers: Design and Innovation from Wedgwood to Corning*. Baltimore and London: Johns Hopkins University Press, 2000.

Bloch, Raymond. *The Etruscans*. New York: Frederick & Praeger, 1958.

Boardman, James. *Bentleyana: or, A Memoir of Thomas Bentley, Sometime of Liverpool, with Extracts from His Correspondence*. Liverpool: Wareing, Webb, 1851.

Boney, Knowles. *Liverpool Porcelain of the Eighteenth Century and Its Makers*. London: Portman Press, 1989.

Breen, T. H. " 'Baubles of Britain': The American and Consumer Revolutions of the Eighteenth Century," in Cary Carson, Ronald Hoffman, and Peter Albert, eds., *Of Consuming Interests: The Style of Life in the Eighteenth Century*. Charlottesville and London: U.S. Capitol Historical Society and the University Press of Virginia, 1994.

———. "An Empire of Goods: The Anglicanization of Colonial America, 1690–1776," *Journal of British Studies*, 25 (1986), 467–99.

Brewer, John. *Party Ideology and Popular Politics at the Accession of George III*. Cambridge: Cambridge University Press, 1976.

———. *The Sinews of Power: War, Money and the English State 1688–1783*. London: Routledge, 1989.

Brewer, John, and Roy Porter, eds. *Consumption and the World of Goods*. London: Routledge, 1993.

Brooke, John Hedley. *Science and Religion: Some Historical Perspectives*. Cambridge: Cambridge University Press, 1991.

Burney, Charles. *Music, Men and Manners in France and Italy, 1770, Being the Journal Written during a Tour through Those Countries Undertaken to collect Material for a General History of Music*. London: Eulenburg Books, 1969.

———. *Music, Men and Manners in Italy, 1770 (The Present State of Music in France and Italy)*, intro. E. Edmund Poole. London: Folio Society, 1969.

Bushman, Richard. "American High-Style and Vernacular Cultures," in Jack Greene and J. R. Pole, eds., *Colonial British America: Essays in the New History of the Early Modern Era*. Baltimore and London: Johns Hopkins University Press, 1984.

Chaldecott, J. A. "Josiah Wedgwood (1730–95): Scientist," *British Journal for the History of Science*, 8 (1975), 1–16.

Champion, Richard. *Considerations on the Present Situation of Great Britain and the United States of America, with a View to their Future Commercial Connexions*, 2nd ed., London, 1784.

Chaudhuri, K. N. *The Trading World of Asia and the English East India Company 1660–1760*. Cambridge: Cambridge University Press, 1978.

Cheyne, George. *An Essay on Health and Long Life*. Bath, 1725.

Christie, Ian. "A Vision of Empire: Thomas Whately and 'The Regulations Lately made Concerning the Colonies,' " *English Historical Review* (April 1998), 54–82.

Clark, George N. *Guide to English Commercial Statistics, 1696–1782*. London: Royal Historical Society, 1938.

Clark, Ronald. *Benjamin Franklin: A Biography*. London: Weiderfeld and Nicolson, 1983.

Clarke, Desmond, ed., *Memoirs of Richard Lovell Edgeworth: Begun by Himself and Concluded by His Daughter Maria Edgeworth*. 2 vols. Dublin: Shannon, 1969.

Clow, Archibald, and Nan Clow. *The Chemical Revolution: A Contribution to Social Technology*. London: Batchworth Press, 1952.

Colley, Linda. *Britons: Forging the Nation 1707–1837*. New Haven and London: Yale, 1992.

Cookson, J. E. *The Friends of Peace: Anti-War Liberalism in England 1793–1815*. Cambridge: Cambridge University Press, 1982.

Crouzet, F. "The Sources of England's Wealth: Some French Views in the Eighteenth Century," in P. L. Cottrell and D. H. Aldcroft, eds., *Shipping, Trade and Commerce: Essays in Memory of Ralph Davis*. Leicester: Leicester University Press, 1981.

Crowhurst, Patrick. *The Defence of British Trade 1689–1815*. Folkestone, Kent: Dawson, 1977.

Crowley, John E. "The Sensibility of Comfort," *American Historical Review*, 104 (1999), 749–82.

Crowther, M. A. *The Workhouse System 1834–1929: The History of an English Institution*. Athens, GA: University of Georgia Press, 1982.

Curnock, Nehemiah, ed. *The Journal of the Rev. John Wesley, A.M.* 8 vols. New York: Eaton & Mains, 1913.

Cust, Lionel. *History of the Society of Dilettanti*. London, 1898.

Daniels, Stephen. *Joseph Wright*. London: Tate Gallery Publishing, 2000.

Daumas, Maurice. *Scientific Instruments of the Seventeenth and Eighteenth Centuries and Their Makers*. London: Portman Books, 1989.

Davidoff, Leonore, and Catherine Hall, *Family Fortunes: Men and Women of the English Middle Class, 1780–1850*. Chicago: University of Chicago Press, 1987.

Dawson, Eileen. *Masterpieces of Wedgwood*. London: British Museum, 1995.

De Vries, Jan. "Between Purchasing Power and the World of Goods: Understanding the Household Economy in Early Modern Europe," in John Brewer and Roy Porter, eds., *Consumption and the World of Goods*. London: Routledge, 1992.

Dear, Peter. "Totius in Verba: Rhetoric and Authority in the Early Royal Society," *Isis*, 76 (1985), 145–61.

Defoe, Daniel, *Giving Alms No Charity* (1704), in W. R. Owens, ed., *Political and Economic Writings of Daniel Defoe*. London: Pickering & Chatto, 2000.

Dickinson, H. T. *Liberty and Property: Political Ideology in Eighteenth-Century Britain*. London: Weidenfeld and Nicolson, 1977.

Dickinson, H. T. "Radicals and Reformers in the Age of Wilkes and Wyvill," in Jeremy Black, ed. *British Politics and Society from Walpole to Pitt 1742–1789*. Basingstoke, Surrey: Macmillan, 1990.

Doddridge, Philip. *The Case for Receiving the Small-Pox by Inoculation, Impartially Considered, and especially in a Religious View*, ed. David Some. London, 1750 (published posthumously).

Dolan, Brian. "Conservative Politicians, Radical Philosophers, and the Aerial Remedy for the Diseases of Civilization," *History of the Human Sciences*, 15 (2002), 35–54.

———. *Exploring European Frontiers: British Travellers in the Age of Enlightenment*. Basingstoke, Surrey: Macmillan, 2000.

———. *Ladies of the Grand Tour*. London and New York: HarperCollins, 2001.

———. "Representing Novelty. Charles Babbage, Charles Lyell and Experiments in Early Victorian Geology," *History of Science*, 36 (1998), 299–327.

Dolan, Brian, ed. *Malthus, Medicine, and Morality: "Malthusianism" After 1798*. Atlanta and Amsterdam: Rodopi, 2000.

Donoghue, Frank. "Colonizing Readers: Review Criticism and the Formation of a Reading Public," in Ann Bermingham and John Brewer, eds., *The Consumption of Culture, 1600–1800.* London and New York: Routledge, 1995.

Dossie, Robert. *The Handmaid to the Arts.* 2 vols. London, 1758.

Edwards, Clive. *Eighteenth-Century Furniture.* Manchester: Manchester University Press, 1996.

Edwards, Rhoda. "London Potteries circa 1570–1710," *Journal of Ceramics History,* 6 (1974), 1–30.

Elliott, Gordon. *John and David Elers and Their Contemporaries.* London: Jonathan Horne, 1998.

Erdman, David. "Coleridge, Wordsworth and the Wedgwood Fund," *Bulletin of the New York Public Library,* 60 (1956), 425–43; 487–507.

Ewins, Neil. " 'Supplying the Present Wants of Our Yankee Cousins': Staffordshire Ceramics and the American Market 1775–1880," *Journal of Ceramic History,* 15 (1997), 1–42.

Farrer, Lady (Katherine Euphemia), ed. *Letters of Josiah Wedgwood.* 3 vols. [1903–6]. Manchester: E. J. Morten & The Wedgwood Museum, 1973.

Fontaines, Una des. "Portland House: Wedgwood's London Showrooms," *Proceedings of the Wedgwood Society,* II (1982), 10–18.

———. "Wedgwood's London Showrooms," *Proceedings of the Wedgwood Society,* 8 (1970), 193–212.

Fordyce, W. *Memoirs concerning Herculaneum, the subterranean city, lately discovered at the foot of Mount Vesuvius, giving a particular account of the . . . buildings, statues, paintings, medals, and other curiosities found there.* London, 1750.

Foreman, Amanda. *Georgiana, Duchess of Devonshire.* London: HarperCollins, 1998.

Freudenberger, Herman, and Gaylord Cummins. "Health, Work, and Leisure Before the Industrial Revolution," *Explorations in Economic History,* 13 (1976), 1–12.

Gascoigne, John. *Cambridge in the Age of the Enlightenment.* Cambridge: Cambridge University Press, 1989.

———. *Joseph Banks and the English Enlightenment: Useful Knowledge and Polite Culture.* Cambridge: Cambridge University Press, 1994.

Gatty, Charles T. *Liverpool Potteries.* Liverpool: T. Brakewell, 1882.

Gibbs, F. W. *Joseph Priestley: Adventurer in Science and Champion of Truth.* London: Nelson, 1965.

Gilbert, Alan. *Religion and Society in Industrial England: Church, Chapel, and Social Change 1740–1914.* London and New York: Longman, 1976.

Golinski, Jan. *Science as Public Culture: Chemistry and Enlightenment in Britain, 1760–1820.* Cambridge: Cambridge University Press, 1992.

Gorley, Jean. *Old Wedgwood.* New York: Wedgwood Society, 1945.

Graham, Malcolm. *Cup and Saucer Land* [1908]. Staffordshire and Stoke-on-Trent Archive Service, 2000.

Greene, John. *American Science in the Age of Jefferson.* Ames, IA: Iowa State University Press, 1984.

Greene, John, ed. "The Examination of Benjamin Franklin in the House of Commons, February 13, 1766," in *Colonies to Nation: 1763–1789.* New York: McGraw Hill, 1979.

Greenslade, M. W. "A History of Burslem." *The Victoria County History of Staffordshire,* Vol. 8, 1963. Staffordshire and Stoke-on-Trent Archive Service, 2000.

Greenslade, M. W., and G. C. Baugh. "Stebbing Shaw and the History of Staffordshire," in M. W. Greenslade, ed., *Essays in Staffordshire History.* Staffordshire: Staffordshire Record Society, 1979.

Gunn, J. A. W. *Beyond Liberty and Property: The Process of Self-Recognition in Eighteenth-Century Political Thought.* Kingston and Montreal: McGill-Queen's University Press, 1983.

Hadfield, Charles. *Canals of the West Midlands.* Newton Abbot, Devon: David & Charles, 1974.

Hamilton, Roberta. *The Liberation of Women: A Study of Patriarchy and Capitalism.* London: George Allen & Unwin, 1978.

Hampden, John. *An Eighteenth-Century Journal, Being a Record of the Years 1774–1776*. London: Macmillan, 1940.

Harley, David. "A Sword in a Madman's Hand: Professional Opposition to Popular Consumption in the Waters Literature of Southern England and the Midlands. 1570–1870," in R. Porter, ed., *The Medical History of Waters and Spas,* essays in the special issue of *Medical History,* 10, (1990).

Harris, J. R. *Industrial Espionage and Technology Transfer: Britain and France in the Eighteenth Century.* Aldershot, Surrey: Ashgate, 1998.

Haselgrove, Dennis, and John Murray. "John Dwight's Fulham Pottery 1672–1978: A Collection of Documentary Sources," *Journal of Ceramics History,* 11 (1979), 140–62.

Haskell, Francis, and Nicholas Penny. *Taste and the Antique: The Lure of Classical Sculpture 1500–1900.* New Haven and London: Yale University Press, 1981.

Hobsbawm, Eric. "Methodism and the Threat of Revolution in Britain," in Hobsbawm, ed., *Labouring Men: Studies in the History of Labour.* London: Weidenfeld & Nicolson, 1964.

Hole, Robert. *Pulpits, Politics and Public Order in England, 1760–1832.* Cambridge: Cambridge University Press, 1989.

Holt, Raymond. *The Unitarian Contribution to Social Progress in England.* London: George Allen & Unwin, 1938.

Hudson, Pat. "Financing Firms, 1700–1850," in Maurice Kirby and Mary Rose, eds., *Business Enterprise in Modern Britain from the Eighteenth to the Twentieth Century.* London and New York: Routledge, 1994.

Hudson, Roger, ed. *The Grand Tour 1592–1796.* London: Folio Society, 1993.

Hughes, Fred. *Mother Town: Episodes in the History of Burslem.* Burslem, Staffs.: Burslem Community Development Trust, 2000.

Hutchinson, Sidney. *A History of the Royal Academy 1768–1968.* London: Chapman & Hall, 1968.

Huxham, John. *An Essay on Fevers, and their Various Kinds.* London, 1750.

Inglis, Brian. *Poverty and the Industrial Revolution.* London: Hodder & Stoughton, 1971.

James, Patricia. *Population Malthus: His Life and Times.* London: Routledge, 1979.

Jewitt, Llewellynn. *The Wedgwoods: Being a Life of Josiah Wedgwood.* London, 1865.

Johnson, Harwood A. "Books Belonging to Wedgwood and Bentley the 10th of August 1770," *Ars Ceramica,* 7 (1990), 13–23.

———. "Thomas Bentley's Journal of His Visit to Paris in 1776," *Ars Ceramica,* 9 (1992), 8–13.

Jones, S. R. H. "The Origins of the Factory System in Great Britain: Technology, Transaction Costs, or Exploitation?" in Maurice Kirby and Mary Rose, eds., *Business Enterprise in Modern Britain from the Eighteenth to the Twentieth Century.* London and New York: Routledge, 1994.

Kasson, John. *Civilizing the Machine: Technology and Republican Values in America, 1776–1900.* New York: Hill & Wang, 1976; 1999.

Kelly, Alison. "Wedgwood's Catherine Services," *Ars Ceramica,* 8 (1991), 6–13.

Kendrick, James. "A Morning's Ramble in 'Old Warrington,' " *Transactions of the Historic Society of Lancashire and Chesire,* 7 (1855), 82–96.

King-Hele, Desmond. *Doctor of Revolution: The Life and Genius of Erasmus Darwin.* London: Faber & Faber, 1977.

King-Hele, Desmond, ed. *The Essential Writings of Erasmus Darwin.* London: MacGibbon & Kee, 1968.

——— *The Letters of Erasmus Darwin.* Cambridge: Cambridge University Press, 1981.

Klingender, Francis. *Art and the Industrial Revolution,* rev. and ed. Arthur Elton. London: Paladin, 1973.

———. "The Industrial Revolution and the Birth of Romanticism," *Apropos,* 4 (1945), 20–24.

Koehn, Nancy. *Brand New: How Entrepreneurs Earned Consumers' Trust from Wedgwood to Dell.* Boston: Harvard Business School Press, 2001.

Kramnick, Isaac. "Eighteenth-Century Science and Radical Social Theory: The Case of Joseph Priestley's Scientific Liberalism," *Journal of British Studies,* 25 (1986), 1–30.

Landers, J. *Birth and Death in the Metropolis: Studies in the Demographic History of London 1670–1830.* Cambridge: Cambridge University Press, 1992.

Lane, Joan. *Apprenticeship in England, 1600–1914.* London: UCL Press, 1996.

Lawson, Philip. *The East India Company: A History.* London and New York: Longman, 1993.

Lead, Peter. *The Trent and Mersey Canal.* Wilts.: Cromwell Press, 1980; 1993.

Lemon, James. "Spatial Order: Households in Local Communities and Regions," in Jack Greene and J. R. Pole, eds., *Colonial British America: Essays in the New History of the Early Modern Era.* Baltimore and London: Johns Hopkins University Press, 1984.

Letts, C. F. C. *The Eruption of Vesuvius. Adapted from the Letters of Pliny with Notes.* Cambridge: Cambridge University Press, 1937.

Levere, Trevor. *Poetry Realised in Nature: Samuel Taylor Coleridge and Early Nineteenth-Century Science.* Cambridge: Cambridge University Press, 1981.

Lewis, Lesley. *Connoisseurs and Secret Agents in Eighteenth Century Rome.* London: Chatto & Windus, 1961.

Lincoln, Anthony. *Some Political and Social Ideas of English Dissent 1763–1800.* Cambridge: Cambridge University Press, 1938.

Lindsay, J. *The Trent and Mersey Canal.* Newton Abbot, Devon: David & Charles, 1979.

Litchfield, R. B. *Tom Wedgwood: The First Photographer.* London: Duckworth, 1903.

Lobb, Theophilus. *A Treatise on the Small Pox.* London, 1741.

Mankowitz, Wolf. *Wedgwood.* 3rd edn., London: Barrie & Jenkins, 1980.

Marsh, J. F. "On Some Correspondence of Dr Priestley, preserved in the Warrington Museum and Library," *Transactions of the Historic Society of Lancashire and Cheshire,* 7 (1855), 65–81.

Marshall, Dorothy. *The English Poor in the Eighteenth Century,* London: Routledge, 1926.

——. *Industrial England, 1776–1851.* New York: Charles Scribner's Sons, 1973.

Mathias, Peter. *The Transformation of England: Essays in the Economic and Social History of England in the Eighteenth Century.* London: Methuen, 1979.

Mathias, Peter, and Patrick O'Brien. "Taxation in England and France 1715–1810: A Comparison of the Social and Economic Incidence of Taxes Collected for the Central Governments," *Journal of European Economic History,* 5 (1976), 621–53.

Matthew, Adam (Publications). *Industrial Revolution: A Documentary History. Series One: The Boulton & Watt Archive and the Matthew Boulton Papers. Part I: Lunar Society Correspondence.* Keele University, microfilm.

Mayer, Joseph. "On Liverpool Pottery." *Transactions of the Historic Society of Lancashire and Cheshire,* 7 (1855), 178–210.

McCusker, John J., and Russell R. Menard. *The Economy of British America, 1607–1789.* Chapel Hill and London: University of North Carolina Press, 1985.

McKendrick, Neil. "Home Demand and Economic Growth: A New View of the Role of Women and Children in the Industrial Revolution," McKendrick, ed., *Historical Perspectives: Studies in English Thought and Society, in Honour of J. H. Plumb.* London: Europa, 1974.

——. "Josiah Wedgwood and Factory Discipline," *Historical Journal,* 4 (1961), 30–55.

——. "Josiah Wedgwood and Thomas Bentley: An Inventor-Entrepreneur Partnership in the Industrial Revolution," *Transactions of the Royal Historical Society,* 14 (1964), 1–33.

——. "Josiah Wedgwood: An Eighteenth Century Entrepreneur in Salesmanship and Marketing Techniques," *Economic History Review,* 2nd ser., 12 (1960), 408–33.

——. "The Role of Science in the Industrial Revolution." in M. Teich and R. Young, eds., *Changing Perspectives in the History of Science.* London: Heinemann, 1973.

McKendrick, Neil, John Brewer, and J. H. Plumb. *The Birth of a Consumer Society: The Commercialisation of Eighteenth-Century England.* London: Hutchinson, 1983.

McLachlan, H. *Warrington Academy: Its History and Influence*. Manchester: Chetham Society, 1943.

Meiklejohn, Andrew. "English Domestic Medicine in the Eighteenth-Century from the Letters of Josiah Wedgwood," *Post-Graduate Medical Journal*, 26 (1950), 541–43; 598–602; 663–64.

———. "The History of Occupational Respiratory Disease in the North Staffordshire Pottery Industry," in C. David, ed., *Health Conditions in the Ceramic Industry*. Oxford: Pergamon Press, 1969.

———. "The Successful Prevention of Lead Poisoning in the Glazing of Earthenware in the North Staffordshire Potteries," *British Journal for Industrial Medicine*, 20 (1963). 169.

———. "The Successful Prevention of Silicosis Among China Biscuit Workers in the North Staffordshire Pottery Industry," *British Journal for Industrial Medicine*, 20 (1963), 255.

Meteyard, Eliza. *The Life of Josiah Wedgwood from his Private Correspondence and Family Papers*. 2 vols. London: Hurst & Blackett, 1865: 1980.

Mingay, G. E., ed. *Arthur Young and His Time*. London: Macmillan, 1975.

Moore, John. *A View of the Society and Manners in Italy*. London, 1781.

Morley-Hewitt, A. T. "Early Whieldon of the Fenton Low Works," *Transactions of the English Ceramic Circle*, 3 (1954), 142–54.

Mountford, Arnold. "Thomas Briand—Stranger." *Transactions of the English Ceramic Circle*, 7 (1969), 87–99.

———. "Thomas Wedgwood, John Wedgwood, and Jonah Malkin." Unpublished M.A. thesis, 1972, Keele University, Staffs.

———. "Thomas Whieldon's Manufactory at Fenton Vivian," *Transactions of the English Ceramic Circle*, 8 (1972), 164–82.

Murray, Mary. *The Law of the Father? Patriarchy in the Transition from Feudalism to Capitalism*. London and New York: Routledge, 1995.

Niblett, Kathy. "A Useful Partner—Thomas Wedgwood 1734–1788," *Journal of the Northern Ceramic Society*, 5 (1984), 127–41.

Oade, Thomas. *The Unnatural Parent*. London, 1718.

Orange, Derek. "Rational Dissent and Provincial Science: William Turner and the Newcastle Literary and Philosophical Society," in Ian Inkster and Jack Morrell, eds., *Metropolis and Province: Science in British Culture, 1780–1850*. Philadelphia: University of Pennsylvania Press, 1983.

Owen, Harold. *The Staffordshire Potter*. London: Grant Richards, 1901.

Owens, W. R., ed. *Political and Economic Writings of Daniel Defoe*. Vol. 8: *Social Reform*. London: Pickering & Chatto, 2000.

Parkes, Samuel. *Chemical Essays*. London, 1815.

Parreaux, André. *Daily Life in England in the Reign of George III*, trans. Carola Congreve. London: George Allen & Unwin, 1969.

Peck, T. Whitmore, and K. Douglas Wilkinson. *William Withering of Birmingham*. Bristol: John Wright & Sons, 1950.

Peel, Derek. *A Pride of the Potters*. London: Arthur Barker, 1957.

Percival, Thomas. *Observations and Experiments on the Poison of Lead*. London, 1774.

Plot, Robert. *Natural History of Staffordshire*. London, 1686.

Porter, Dorothy, and Roy Porter. *Patient's Progress: Doctors and Doctoring in Eighteenth-Century England*. Stanford, CA: Stanford University Press, 1989.

Porter, Roy. *English Society in the Eighteenth Century*. London: Penguin, 1982; 1990.

———. *Enlightenment: Britain and the Creation of the Modern World*. London: Penguin, 2000.

———. *London: A Social History*. London: Hamish Hamilton, 1994.

Porter, Roy, and Lesley Hall. *The Facts of Life: The Creation of Sexual Knowledge in Britain 1650–1950*. New Haven and London: Yale, 1995.

Posner, E. "Eighteenth-Century Health and Social Service in the Pottery Industry of North Staffordshire," *Medical History*, 18 (1974), 138–47.

Price, Jacob M. "The Transatlantic Economy," in Jack Greene and J. R. Pole, eds., *Colonial British America: Essays in the New History of the Early Modern Era*. Baltimore and London: The Johns Hopkins University Press, 1984.

Price, Stanley. *John Sadler: A Liverpool Pottery Painter*. West Kirby: Gould's, 1949.

Priestley, Joseph. *Autobiography*, ed. Jack Lindsay. Bath: Adams & Dart, 1970.

Rakow, Leonard, and Juliette Rakow. "Wedgwood's Peg Leg Portraits," *Ars Ceramica*, 1 (1984), 10–13.

Ramage, Nancy H. "Owed to a Grecian Urn: The Debt of Flaxman and Wedgwood to Hamilton," *Ars Ceramica*, 6 (1989), 8–12.

——. "Publication Dates of Sir William Hamilton's Four Volumes," *Ars Ceramica*, 8 (1991), 35.

——. "Restorer and Collector: Notes on Eighteenth-Century Recreations of Roman Statues," in Elaine K. Gazda, ed., *The Ancient Art of Emulation: Studies in Artistic Originality and Tradition from the Present to Classical Antiquity*. Ann Arbor: University of Michigan Press, 2002.

Ramazini, Bernardino. *A Dissertation on endemial Diseases . . . Together with a treatise on the diseases of Tradesmen*, trans. Friedrich Hoffmann. London, 1745.

Raynes, Harold. *A History of British Insurance*. 2nd ed., London: Pitman, 1964.

Reilly, Robin. *Wedgwood*. 2 vols. New York: Stockton Press, 1989.

——. *Josiah Wedgwood 1730–1795*. London: Macmillan, 1992.

——. *Wedgwood Jasper: with Over 600 Illustrations*. London: Thames and Hudson, 1994.

Reilly, Robin, and George Savage. *The Dictionary of Wedgwood*. Woodbridge, Suffolk: Antique Collectors' Club, 1980.

Roberts, David. *Paternalism in Early Victorian England*. London: Croom Helm, 1979.

Roberts, W. J., and H.C. Pigeon. "Biographical Sketch of Mr John Wyke, with some remarks on the Arts and Manufactures of Liverpool from 1760–1780," *Historic Society of Lancashire and Cheshire Proceedings and Papers*, VI (1854), 66–76.

Roll, Eric. *An Early Experiment in Industrial Organisation: Being a History of the Firm of Boulton and Watt, 1775–1805*. London: Frank Cass & Co, 1968.

Rose, Mary. "The Family Firm in British Business, 1780–1914," in Maurice Kirby and Mary Rose, eds. *Business Enterprise in Modern Britain from the Eighteenth to the Twentieth Century*. London and New York: Routledge, 1994.

Rose, R. B. "The Priestley Plots of 1791," *Past and Present* 18 (1960), 68–88.

Rosenblum, Robert. "The Origin of Painting: A Problem in the Iconography of Romantic Classicism," *The Art Bulletin* (December 1957), 279–90.

Rousseau, Jean-Jacques. *Emile; or, On Education*, trans., intro., and notes Allan Bloom. New York: Basic Books, 1979.

Rowbottom, Margaret, and Charles Susskind, *Electricity and Medicine: A History of Their Interaction*. London: Macmillan, 1984.

Scarratt, William. *Old Times in the Potteries*. [1906] East Ardsley, Yorks: S. R. Publishers, 1969.

Schaffer, Simon. "Natural Philosophy and Public Spectacle in the Eighteenth Century," *History of Science*, 21 (1983), 1–43.

Schama, Simon. *The Embarrassment of Riches: An Interpretation of Dutch Culture in the Golden Age*. London: Fontana, 1991.

Schofield, Robert E. *The Enlightenment of Joseph Priestley: A Study of His Life and Work from 1733 to 1773*. University Park, PA: Pennsylvania University Press, 1997.

——. "Josiah Wedgwood, Industrial Chemist," *Chymia*, 5 (1959), 180–92.

——. *The Lunar Society of Birmingham: A Social History of Provincial Science and Industry in Eighteenth-Century England*. Oxford: Clarendon Press, 1963.

Schofield, Robert E., ed. *A Scientific Autobiography of Joseph Priestley (1733–1804): Selected Scientific Correspondence*. Cambridge, MA: MIT Press, 1996.

Schumpeter, Elizabeth. *English Overseas Trade Statistics 1697–1808.* Oxford: Clarendon, 1960.

Selleck, A. Douglas. *Cookworthy 1705–80 and His Circle.* Plymouth, Devon, 1978.

Shammas, Carole. "How Self-Sufficient Was Early America?" *Journal of Interdisciplinary History,* 13 (1982), 247–72.

Sharpe, Pamela. *Adopting to Capitalism: Working Women in the English Economy, 1700–1850.* Basingstoke, Surrey: Macmillan, 1996.

Shaw, Simeon. *History of the Staffordshire Potteries; and the Rise and Progress of the Manufacture of Pottery and Porcelain.* Hanley, self-published, 1829; Newton Abbott, Devon: David & Charles, 1970.

Shaw, Stebbing, *History and Antiquities of Staffordshire.* London: Robson, 1798–1801.

Shepherd, James F., and Gary M. Walton. *Shipping, Maritime Trade, and the Economic Development of Colonial North America.* Cambridge: Cambridge University Press, 1972.

Smith, D. M. "Industrial Architecture in the Potteries," *North Staffordshire Journal of Field Studies,* 5 (1965), 81–94.

Steele, H. J. "Glimpses into the Social Conditions in Burslem During the 17th and 18th Centuries," *North Staffordshire Field Club Transactions,* 78 (1943–44), 16–39.

Stone, Lawrence. *Family, Sex and Marriage in England 1500–1800.* Hammondsworth: Penguin, 1979.

Strother, Edward. *An Essay on Sickness and Health . . . in which Dr. Cheyne's mistaken opinions in his late essay are occasionally taken notice of.* London, 1725.

Stuart, Denis. "Service of Truth: Early Quaker Poor Relief in Staffordshire to the Mid-Eighteenth Century," in Philip Morgan and A. Phillips, eds., *Staffordshire Histories: Essays in Honour of M. Greenslade.* Keele: Staffordshire Record Society and Centre for Local History. University of Keele, 1999.

Tait, Hugh. "The 'Etruscan Service' of King Ferdinand IV and Josiah Wedgwood," *Ars Ceramica,* 3 (1986), 31–34.

Tarczylo, Théodore. "From Lascivious Erudition to the History of Mentalities," in G. S. Rousseau and Roy Porter, eds., *Sexual Underworlds of the Enlightenment.* Manchester: Manchester University Press, 1987.

Thomas, John. *The Rise of the Staffordshire Potteries.* Bath: Adams & Dart, 1971.

Thompson, E. P. "Time, Work-Discipline and Industrial Capitalism," reprinted in Thompson, *Customs in Common,* London: Penguin Books, 1993.

Thomson, James. *The Works of Mr Thomson.* 2 vols. London, 1738.

Tinniswood, Adrian. *The Polite Tourist: A History of Country House Visiting.* London: The National Trust, 1998.

Towner, Donald. "William Greatbatch and the Early Wedgwood Wares," *Transactions of the English Ceramic Circle,* 5 (1963), 180–93.

———. *Creamware.* London: Faber, 1978.

Trinder, Barrie. *The Making of the Industrial Landscape.* London: J. M. Dent & Sons, 1982; 1997.

Tringham, Nigel; A. G. Rosser, and R. N. Swenson, eds. "The Turnpike Network of Staffordshire, 1700–1840: An Introduction," *Collections for a History of Staffordshire* 13 (1988), 122–53.

Turner, William, *William Adams, an Old English Potter.* London: Chapman, 1904.

Uglow, Jenny. *The Lunar Men: The Friends Who Made the Future.* London: Faber & Faber, 2002.

Vaisey, D. G., ed. *Probate Inventories of Lichfield and District 1568–1680,* Staffs.: Staffordshire Record Society, 1969.

Walvin, James. *The Quakers: Money and Morals.* London: John Murray, 1997.

Ward, John. *History of the Borough of Stoke-upon Trent.* London, 1843.

Warrillow, E. J. D. *History of Etruria: Staffordshire, England 1760–1951.* Stoke-on-Trent: Etruscan Publications, 1953.

———. *A Sociological History of the City of Stoke-on-Trent.* Newcastle: Ironmarket, 1977.

Waterman. Elizabeth. *Wages in Eighteenth-Century England.* Cambridge, MA: Harvard University Press, 1934.

Watkin, E. A. "Staffordshire Tokens and Their Place in the Coinage of England," *North Staffordshire Journal of Field Studies*, 1 (1961), 1–25.

Watson, J. Steven. *The Reign of George III 1760–1815*. Oxford: Clarendon Press, 1960.

Watts, Ruth. *Gender, Power and the Unitarians, 1760–1860*. London: Longman, 1998.

Weatherill, Lorna. *Consumer Behaviour and Material Culture in Britain, 1660–1760*. London: Routledge, 1988.

———. "The Growth of the Pottery Industry in England, 1660–1815," *Post-Medieval Archaeology*, 17 (1983), 15–46.

———. *The Pottery Trade and North Staffordshire 1660–1760*. Manchester: Manchester University Press, 1971.

Webb, Sidney, and Beatrice Webb. *English Local Government: English Poor Law History*, Part I. London: Longmans, Green & Co. 1927.

Wedgwood, Barbara, and Hensleigh Wedgwood. *The Wedgwood Circle 1730–1897.* New Brunswick, NJ: Eastview, 1980.

Wedgwood, Josiah G. *A History of the Wedgwood Family*. London: St. Catherine Press, 1908.

———. *Staffordshire Pottery and Its History*. London: Sampson Low, Marston & Co., 1913.

Wedgwood, Josiah G., and Joshua G. E. Wedgwood. *Wedgwood Pedigrees: Being an Account of the Complete Family Reconstructed from Contemporary Records*. Kendall: Titus Wilson & Son, 1925.

Wedgwood, Josiah G., and Thomas Ormsbee. *Staffordshire Pottery*. London: Putnam & Co., 1947.

Wedgwood, Julia. *The Personal Life of Josiah Wedgwood*, rev. and ed., C. H. Herford. London: Macmillan, 1915.

Whiter, Leonard. *Spode: A History of the Family, Factor and Wares from 1733 to 1833*. London: Barrie & Jenkins, 1970: 1989.

Wilbur, Earl Morse. *A History of Unitarianism in Transylvania, England and America*. 2 vols., Cambridge, MA: Harvard University Press, 1952.

Wilcoxen, Charlotte. "The Peregrinations of a Letter from Sir William Hamilton to Josiah Wedgwood," *Ars Ceramica*, 17 (2001), 36–45.

Williamson, George Charles. *The Imperial Russian Dinner Service*. London: George Bell, 1909.

Williams-Wood, Cyril. *English Transfer-Printed Pottery and Porcelain: A History of Over-Glaze Printing*. London: Faber & Faber, 1981.

Wills, John E., Jr. "European Consumption and Asian Production in the Seventeenth and Eighteenth Centuries," in John Brewer and Roy Porter, eds., *Consumption and the World of Goods*. London: Routledge, 1992.

Wilson, Charles. *England's Apprenticeship 1603–1763*. 2nd ed., London: Longman, 1984.

Wrigley, E. A. *Continuity, Chance, and Change: The Character of the Industrial Revolution in England*. Cambridge: Cambridge University Press, 1988.

Wylie, Ian. *Young Coleridge and the Philosophers of Nature*. Oxford: Clarendon Press, 1989.

Young, Arthur. *A Six Months Tour through the North of England*. 4 vols. London, 1770.

Young, Hilary, ed. *The Genius of Wedgwood*. London: Victoria & Albert Museum, 1995.

Index

Act of Toleration (1698), 48
Adams, William, 112, 217
Aikin, John, 95, 324
Alders, Thomas, 42–43, 47, 52
Alexander Severus, Emperor, 303
America:
  colonial unrest in, 160–61, 249, 250
  Declaration of Independence, 254, 257,
    262
  Great Seal of U.S., 339
  Griffiths's trips to, 163–64, 185, 232, 233–37,
    238
  kaolin of, 162–63, 185, 232, 236–37, 238, 239,
    245, 249, 262
  slavery in, 259–61
  taxation on, 160–61, 162, 197, 250, 251–52,
    254
  trade with, 74–76, 77, 149, 159–60, 161,
    197–98, 204, 250–51, 254, 256, 259, 334
  at war with England, 250–55, 290, 298, 318
  Wedgwood expansion to, 338
Arbuthnot, John, 300
Arkwright, Richard, 280, 298
Ashenhurst, Mrs., 158, 166, 173–74
Attakullakulla, Chief, 234

Baker, George, 241–42
Banks, Sir Joseph, 156, 297, 312
Barberini, Cardinal Francesco, 303
Barberini Vase ("Portland Vase"), 303–6, 308,
  312
Bartham, John, 300
Bartlam, Rev. J., 315
bas-relief sculpture, history of, 279–80
Bateman, Josiah, 334
Beddoes, Thomas, 321, 330

Benson, Thomas, 39, 244
Bent, James, 174, 218, 219, 221, 287, 322
Bentley, Mary Stamford, 225, 291, 292, 294
Bentley, Thomas, 92–96, 97–104, 114
  aging of, 264, 286, 291
  early years of, 93
  on education, 101–2, 171
  and Etruria, 174, 183, 184, 188, 189, 193, 205,
    212
  in France, 257–63
  illness and death of, 292–93, 294, 295
  intellectual salons of, 94–96, 99, 254, 260,
    301
  Josiah's correspondence with, 97, 98, 99,
    102–3, 119, 147–49, 158–59, 160–63,
    169–71, 177, 181, 187, 207, 211, 221, 246,
    247, 264, 286, 290–91, 332
  on lead poisoning, 243
  on marriage, 115–16, 119–20, 225
  partnership with Josiah, 148, 158–59,
    164–66, 172, 174, 180, 182, 193–96, 200,
    201, 204, 206, 207–10, 219, 226, 228,
    246, 256, 264–65, 266, 294
  personal traits of, 92, 94, 101, 294
  and slave trade, 93, 259–61
Bessborough, Lord, 187
Birmingham riots, 318, 319
Black, Joseph, 307
Blunt, Thomas, 19
Boardman, Samuel, 164, 293
Booth, Enoch, 38, 130
Boswell, James, 199
Böttger, Johann, 238
Boulton, Matthew, 125, 197–202, 255, 260,
  302
  business expansion of, 197, 198, 202

Boulton, Matthew (*continued*)
  "Church-and-King" riots and, 319
  as competitor, 196, 201–2, 206, 207,
    209–10, 220, 229, 339
  doing business with, 199–201, 248
  metalworks of, 197, 199, 229, 248
  technology and, 198–99, 316
Boyle, Robert, 24
Brady, Robert, 104
Brewster, Sir Francis, 49
Bridgewater, Duke of, 133–36, 144, 145, 162, 163,
    275
Brindley, James, 88–89, 133–34, 145
Burgess, Thomas, 152
Burke, Edmund, 317–18
Burney, Charles, 154–56
Burslem, 12–14
  growth and development of, 194, 225,
    275–76, 318
  potters in, 12, 13–14, 28, 39–41, 70, 91, 108,
    139, 180, 241, 244, 276
  "potter's rot" in, 39, 40, 244, 301–2
  poverty in, 16–17
  roads and canals to, 87–89, 107–12, 133–36,
    144–46, 148, 184
  Wedgwood family in, 4–6, 10–11
  Wedgwood Institute in, 339
Burslem, Margaret, 5
Burslem, Thomas, 5
Bute, Lord, 111, 115
Byerley, Thomas, 282, 322–23
  in America, 185, 188–89, 205, 255
  death of, 335
  restlessness of, 185, 255, 281
  as Wedgwood employee, 113, 129, 130,
    255–56, 308, 309
  as Wedgwood partner, 310, 326, 333–35
  on Wedgwood quality, 69, 294
Byers, James, 303

Capodimonte "china" factory, 181–82
Cathcart, Lady Jane, 172–73, 178–79, 203–4,
    206, 208–10
Catherine II (the Great), 173, 203, 208, 210,
    229–32, 245, 305, 339
Chairs, Sir Henry, 186
Chambers, Sir William, 186
Champion, Richard, 276
Chandler, John, 27
Charlotte, queen of England, 137–41, 142–43,
    146–47, 304, 305
Chetwynd, Deborah, 137, 138, 140, 178
"Church-and-King" riots, 318, 319
Cicero, 293
Cider Bill (1763), 110–11
Clayton, Sir Richard, 298

Coleridge, Samuel Taylor, 326–27, 328, 329,
    330–31
Cookworthy, William, 239, 276
Cox, William, 128, 178, 181, 185, 186, 187, 205,
    207, 212
Crisp, Nicholas, 276

Darwin, Charles, 331, 335, 337
Darwin, Emma, 321
Darwin, Erasmus, 216
  death of, 329
  experiments of, 198, 289–90, 301–2, 316
  family of, 217, 306, 319–20, 321, 329
  and French Revolution, 314, 318, 319, 320
  and Josiah's business, 245, 329
  and Josiah's death, 323, 324
  Josiah's friendship with, 199, 217, 254, 293,
    307, 311, 312, 319–20
  philosophy of, 197, 254, 285, 318, 319, 320–21
  as Wedgwood family doctor, 175–76, 218,
    219, 221–22, 224, 246, 282, 288, 302, 321,
    322–23
  on wife's death, 222
Darwin, Erasmus (son), 217, 320, 323, 329–30
Darwin, Robert, 217, 306, 319–20, 323
Davidson, Alexander & Co., 313
Davy, Humphry, 327
Day, Thomas, 259–61
Defoe, Daniel, 50
Devonshire cider, lead traces in, 241, 243
Dilettanti ("virtuosi"), 149–50, 155–57, 171,
    172–73, 179, 186–87, 200
Dissenters, 44, 46, 48–49, 90–92, 93, 95, 97,
    101, 103–4, 176, 195, 251–52, 254–55, 306,
    320–21, 327
Dobson, John, 84–85, 118
Doddridge, Philip, 49, 176
Dossie, Robert, 140, 195–96
Duché, Andrew, 239
Duesbury, William, 299
Dwight, John, 24–27, 28

East India Company, 23, 26
Edgeworth, Richard, 282, 321
Egerton, Rowland, 33
electric shock treatments, 289–90
Elers, David, 22–28, 43, 70, 278
Elers, John Philip, 22–28, 43, 70, 277–78
Elers, Paul, 277–78
Enlightenment, 102–6, 153, 156, 258, 266–67,
    280, 282, 301, 320
Etruria:
  changes through the years, 337–40
  closing of, 338
  employees in, 205, 219, 265–70, 297–302,
    334, 337, 338

move to, 217, 220
name of, 180
opening of, 186, 188–89, 194, 196, 338
plans for construction of, 158–59, 165–66,
    173–74, 183–84
Portland Vase as icon of, 312
production at, 227
progress in construction of, 182–85, 188,
    200, 205, 212
purposes of, 193, 194–95, 301
reputation of, 280, 324–25, 326, 337
state regulation of, 337
steam power for, 199
trade secrets protected in, 299–300
Etruria Formation, 25
Etruria Hall, 188, 212, 216, 217, 222, 225, 307,
    325
Etruscans, 152–53
art of, 153, 156, 173, 178–79, 180–81, 189,
    242, 304
reproducing the antiquities of, 170–71, 173,
    178–82, 184, 185–87, 189, 201–2, 209,
    227–29, 312, 325

Factory Act (1833), 337
Falconer, William, 219
Flaxman, John, 296, 304, 306, 307
France:
    Bastille Day in, 320
    Bentley in, 257–63
    commercial interests in, 81–82, 143, 179, 181,
        262–63
    markets in, 207–8, 256
    Napoleonic Wars, 334
    philosophers of, 105–6, 259–61, 318, 320
    privateers from, 82–85
    reign of terror in, 320–21
    revolution in, 311, 314–15, 318, 319, 320, 321
    Sarah and Catherine in, 212–15
Franklin, Benjamin:
    on increasing wealth, 74–75, 259
    Poor Richard's Almanac by, 3
    scientific interests of, 68, 198, 241, 259, 289
    on transatlantic trade, 197–98, 250, 251, 259
    Unitarianism and, 260
    Utopia and, 301

Galvani, Luigi, 289
Galway, Thomas, 23
Garbett, Samuel, 134–35, 145, 163, 200
Gay, John, 148
George III, king of England, 73, 99, 103, 110,
    156, 250
Gibbon, Edward, 253
Gilbert, John, 144
Gilbert, Thomas, 144–46

Gladstone, William, 339
Godwin, William, 327–28
Gower, Lord, Granville Leveson-, 133–36, 142,
    143, 144–46, 148, 253
Grease Bill (1763), 111
Greatbatch, William, 53, 69, 70, 85, 109, 110,
    118
Grenville, George, 160, 161–62
Griffiths, Ralph, 158, 179, 213, 292
Griffiths, Thomas, 163–64, 185, 232, 233–37,
    238

Hamilton, Gavin, 153
Hamilton, Mary, 304
Hamilton, Sir William, 153–57
    and Barberini/Portland Vase, 303–4, 305–6,
        308, 312
    and Dilettanti, 155–56, 157, 179
    as envoy to Naples, 153, 172, 308
    and Etruscan art, 156, 173, 178, 180, 189
    intellectual salons of, 154
    and neo-classicism, 153–54
    personal collection of, 153, 155, 156–57, 180,
        227
    publications by, 153, 156–57, 173, 178, 179, 187,
        189
    and Vesuvius, 154–55
    on Wedgwood business, 325
Harrison, John, 43, 47, 52
Harvard Business School, 338
Hayley, William, An Essay on Painting, 279
Heberden, William, 308
Henshall, Hugh, 183
Hodgson, William, 166
House of Industry (child labor), 50–51
Hume, David, 3
Hutton, James, 307

Italy:
    Barberini Vase from, 303–6
    markets in, 202, 325
    Monte del Grano in, 303
    Vesuvius eruption in, 151, 154–55

Jefferson, Thomas, 301
Johnson, Samuel, 54, 198, 252
Josiah Wedgwood, 335
Josiah Wedgwood & Sons, 336–38
Josiah Wedgwood, Sons, & Byerley, 310, 320,
    326, 333–35
Julia Mamaea, 303

Kay, John, 3

Lancashire, worker riots in, 298
Leigh, "Ralphy," 14–15

Leslie, John, 307, 313, 314, 327
Liberty (Thomson), 104–5, 193
Lloyds of London, 80, 134
Locke, John, 105, 252
Louis XVI, king of France, 262
Lunar Society, 260

Mackworth, Sir Humphrey, 49–50
Maidmont, James, 85
Malkin, Jonah, 61–63, 85
Malkin, Sara Wedgwood, 61, 63
Malthus, Rev. Thomas Robert, 328–29
Marlborough, Duke of, 143
Mather, Ben, 266
Maximinus the Thracian, 303
Mayer, Daniel, 42
Meissen ware, 326
Meredith, Sir William, 128–31, 143, 144,
    161–62
Methodism, 66–68
Michelangelo, 152–53
Mitchell, John, 163
Montagu, Elizabeth, 257, 258
Montesquieu, Baron de, 179
Mount Vesuvius, 151, 154–55
Mulligan, Hugh, 95

neo-classicism, 153–54, 179
New England Restraining Act (1775), 250
Newton, Sir Isaac, 46
North, Lord, 256

Oates, Elizabeth, 94
Overhouse Estate, 5, 6, 16, 19, 21, 32–33, 58–59,
    223, 224

Paine, Thomas, *Common Sense,* 252–53
painting, origin of, 279–80
Palmer, Humphrey, 181, 227–28, 245
Parkes, Samuel, 324
Parr, Samuel, 315
Pelhams, 100
Percival, Thomas, 242–44
Pickford, Joseph, 165–66, 173, 182–83, 185
Pitt, William the Elder, 76, 159–60, 251
Pliny the Younger, 151
Plot, Robert, 13, 14
Plumier, Charles, 127–28
Pollexfen, Sir Henry, 139
Pompeii, 151–52
Poor Laws, 49–50
Pope, Alexander, 114–15
porcelain, history of, 238–40
Portland, Duchess of (mother), 304
Portland, Duke of, 304–6
Powell, Charles, 195

Price, Richard, 252
Priestley, Joseph:
    attack on property of, 318, 319
    on Bentley's death, 295
    as Dissenter, 95–96, 214, 254
    experimental ideas of, 98, 181, 205, 214, 289,
        297, 315–19, 333
    Josiah's friendship with, 94, 95–96, 98, 242
    move to America, 319, 328
    pure air experiments of, 282, 301–2, 317,
        321

Racehorse, 76, 81, 83–85, 117
Radcliffe, Ann, 294
Ramazini, Bernardino, 241
Reid, William, 76, 78–81, 83–84, 117–18
Reynolds, Sir Joshua, 156–57, 305, 307, 312
Rhodes, David, 172, 189
Roosevelt, Theodore, 339
Rousseau, Jean-Jacques, 105–6, 253, 259–61,
    320, 328
Royal Literary Fund, 260
Royal Proclamation of Rebellion (1775), 252
Royal Society, 46, 297, 317
Russia, markets in, 203–4, 206, 208–10,
    229–32, 339

Sadler, John, 70, 73, 78, 85, 87
Sadler & Green, 70, 72, 86, 89, 128, 209
Saint-Fond, Faujas de, 325
Schaw, Sir William, 172
Scheemakers, Thomas, 295
Schweppe, Jacob, 302
Scott, Sir Walter, 294
Seddon, John, 95
Sèvres factory, 179, 181, 262–63
Shrigley, John, 112
Smith, Adam, *Wealth of Nations,* 253, 333
Smith, Joachim, 299
Society of Dilettanti, 155–56
Southey, Robert, 328
Southwell, Mrs., 267
Spencer, Lord, 143
Spinario, 180
Spode, Josiah, 51–53, 65, 276
Sprimont, Nicholas, 112
Staffordshire pottery, 4–6, 12
    black ware, 7–8, 34, 53, 300
    blue ware, 42
    Burslem production of, *see* Burslem
    clay for, 25, 27, 28
    competition in, 39–40, 54–55, 108–9,
        181–82, 184–85, 196, 199–202, 207,
        209–10, 229, 262–63, 299, 339
    creamware, 38, 72, 86, 130, 138, 142, 143, 170,
        179, 239, 305, 325

as dying family craft, 277
English porcelain vs., 40, 54, 239
export, 53, 74–76, 129, 159–60, 161, 197,
  250–51
fruit-shaped vessels, 126
green earthenware, 53, 159
green glazes, 56, 69
health problems and, 39
kaolin in, 162–63, 185, 232, 239, 245, 249,
  276
lead glazing of, 39, 241–45
Red China ware, 28, 53, 278
salt glaze, 26, 29, 38, 43, 53, 71, 180, 278
solid agate, 53
status of the industry, 193, 195, 276–77,
  336–39
taxation and, 111, 161, 196
teapots, 23–27, 29, 69, 85, 130, 149, 278
tortoiseshell ware, 43, 52–53, 126
Wedgwood, *see* Wedgwood pottery
white glaze, 126, 128, 162
yellow-orange glaze, 69
Stamp Act, 160, 251
steam engine, creation of, 198–99
Stringer, Samuel, 20, 34–35, 44, 194
Stuart, Charles Edward, 32
Stuart, James "Athenian," 295
Stuart, John, 234, 249
Stubbs, George, 284, 287, 290, 307
Stukeley, William, 152
Swift, Peter, 175, 186

Taylor, John, 128
Tellwright, John, 14–15
Thomas of Burslem, 4, 5, 7
Thomson, James, 104–5, 193
Townshend, Charles, 160, 162, 163
Townshend Act, 160
Treaty of Paris (1763), 109
Trent & Mersey Canal, 144–46, 163, 183,
  184–85, 275–76, 324, 338
Trump, Donald, 333
Tucker, Josiah, 54
Turner, Matthew, 90–92, 94, 96, 97

Unitarianism, 34–35, 44, 260
Urban VIII, Pope, 303
Utopia, 244, 258, 266, 301, 302, 319, 327–29

Vernon, Edward, 50–51, 74, 159
Voltaire, 3, 82, 253, 258, 259, 260, 262, 320

Walpole, Horace, 152, 156
Walpole, Sir Robert, 100
Warrington Academy, 90–92, 94–96, 97, 127,
  259

Watt, Gregory, 327
Watt, James, 162, 198, 199, 297, 319, 320, 321,
  339
Webber, Henry, 305, 306, 309
Wedgwood, Aaron (brother), 18
Wedgwood, Aaron (uncle), 21, 22, 27, 28, 29, 65
Wedgwood, Burslem (Gilbert's son), 5
Wedgwood, Catherine (sister), *see* Willets,
  Catherine Wedgwood
Wedgwood, Catherine "Kitty" (daughter), 247,
  281, 307
Wedgwood, Ellen (cousin), 134
Wedgwood, Francis "Frank" (grandson), 336,
  337
Wedgwood, Gilbert (great-great-grandfather),
  4–6, 12
Wedgwood, Godfrey (great-grandson), 337
Wedgwood, Isabel (Thomas's wife), 32, 41
Wedgwood, Jane Richards (Thomas's wife), 41,
  223–24
Wedgwood, John (brother), 18, 113, 126,
  130–31, 132
  death of, 167–69, 294
  as London agent, 110, 129, 131, 144, 148
  and queen's service, 136–39
Wedgwood, Long John (cousin), 20–22, 70,
  188
  children of, 225, 287
  death of, 287
  essay by, 45–46
  as fireman, 28, 29
  Josiah's arrangement with, 56, 57–58, 59–61,
    63, 65, 85, 107
  Malkin and, 61–63
  pyrometrical beads invented by, 29
  religion and, 46, 49
  success of, 21, 29–30, 39, 41, 45, 130, 277
  transportation and, 88–89, 133–34, 184
Wedgwood, John (great-uncle), 6, 33
Wedgwood, John "Jack" (cousin), 117, 188,
  246
Wedgwood, John "Jack" (son):
  birth of, 158
  childhood of, 207, 215, 220, 221
  education of, 220, 282–85
  and family business, 296, 320, 326, 334–35
  and father's experiments, 280–81
  and father's illness and death, 322, 326
  on grand tour, 306, 308
  political interest of, 308–9
Wedgwood, Josiah:
  adapting to change, 149–50, 170, 179, 228,
    239, 268, 295, 312
  advertising by, 147, 149, 240, 245, 263
  aging of, 264, 285–86, 296, 310, 312, 322
  apprenticeship of, 31–32, 34, 37–38, 39, 40

Wedgwood, Josiah: (*continued*)
aristocratic clients of, 137–41, 142–44,
146–47, 172–73, 186–87, 204, 208–10,
219, 229–32, 239, 253, 257, 277, 305, 308
birth and childhood of, x, 3, 11, 18, 19
and Brick House/Bell Works, 112–13, 123,
127–31, 174, 217
and Catherine's Ware/Green Frog Service,
ix–x, xi, 229–32, 305, 339
at Cliff Bank, 42–43
death of, 323, 324–25
in discussion groups, 94–96, 98–99, 253
employees of, 67, 68–70, 127, 139, 205–6,
244, 247, 265–70, 297–302, 332
and Etruria, *see* Etruria
experiments of, 43, 44, 46–47, 55–56, 69,
71–73, 91, 97–98, 109, 125–26, 128, 162,
169, 170, 176, 180, 182, 194, 232, 244,
245–46, 247–49, 280–81, 296–97, 333
exports of, 74–76, 77, 79–80, 81, 83–85,
129, 149, 159–60, 161, 197, 203–4, 206,
256
and family business, 15–17, 18, 19–22, 30, 38,
40–41, 107, 109–10, 320; *see also*
Wedgwood pottery
and father's death, 3, 11, 18
as Fellow of Royal Society, 297
and finances, xvii, 7–8, 18, 59–60, 85–86,
112, 144, 185, 186, 194, 196, 209, 211,
325–26
and fleshly lusts, 113–16, 123
health problems of, 36–38, 40, 57, 176,
216–17, 246, 308, 322–23
as Her Majesty's potter, 147, 149
and Ivy House Works, 59–61, 64–66,
68–70, 74, 75, 87, 112, 113, 184, 197
jasper developed by, 247–49, 276, 299, 305
labeling his wares, 56
and leg amputation, 175, 176, 177–78, 238
leg injury of, 89–92, 174–75
in Liverpool, 70, 75–76, 77–81, 84–85, 86,
89–96
London business of, 70, 109–12, 148–50,
171–72, 185–87, 225–27
moving on, 41, 42
partnership with Bentley, *see* Bentley,
Thomas
personal traits of, 41, 51, 57, 60, 138, 294,
332–33
political interests of, 109, 110–12, 196,
251–55, 256, 290
and Portland Vase, 305–6, 307–8, 309,
310–11, 312
portraits of, 284–85, 296
and religion, 35, 44, 46, 67–68, 194–95

reputation of, 129, 136, 147, 179, 204, 244,
253, 265, 277, 280, 324–25, 339
retirement of, 312
and Ridge House Estate, 158–59, 165–66,
173–74, 183
on roads and canals, 108–12, 134–36,
145–46, 183, 184–85, 275–76
and Royal Pattern/Queen's Ware, 137–41,
142–43, 147, 149, 170, 208, 239, 240,
243–44, 262, 305
and Sally, *see* Wedgwood, Sarah "Sally"
science as interest of, 47, 91, 95, 100, 194,
245, 280, 296–97, 319, 320
on self-improvement, 99–106, 107, 211, 253,
332
unique style of, 69
wealth of, 325–26
and Whieldon, 47–48, 51–55, 59
Wedgwood, Josiah "Joss" (son), 188
childhood of, 207, 221, 280, 282
death of, 337
and family business, 306, 307, 308, 309–10,
314, 320, 325, 326, 334–35, 336
family of, 335–36
and father's illness, 323
health of, 336
political interest of, 336–37
retirement of, 337
Wedgwood, Katherine (aunt), 33, 58–59,
124
Wedgwood, Margaret (aunt), 18
Wedgwood, Margaret (sister), 11, 18, 113, 202
Wedgwood, Margaret Shaw (great-
grandmother), 10, 19
Wedgwood, Mary (niece), 41
Wedgwood, Mary Anne (daughter), 281–82,
289–90, 302
Wedgwood, Mary Hollins (aunt), 29
Wedgwood, Mary Stringer (mother), 18, 92,
124, 132
and husband's death, 3, 11
and Josiah's illness, 36–37
and Unitarianism, 34–35, 44
Wedgwood, Richard (brother), 11, 18, 32–33,
40, 285
Wedgwood, Richard (cousin), 132, 188
aging of, 246–47
death of, 287
influence of, 128
and Sally's marriage to Josiah, 116–18
wealth of, 30, 58, 116, 117, 126
Wedgwood, Richard "Dicky" (son), 169–70,
174, 175–76, 264
Wedgwood, Sarah (daughter), 271, 307
Wedgwood, Sarah (granddaughter), 323

Wedgwood, Sarah (niece), 41
Wedgwood, Sarah "Sally" (cousin, wife), 30, 58,
    59, 92
  children of, 132, 158, 169, 174, 175, 188, 207,
      217, 221, 247, 264, 271, 281–85, 287,
      325–26
  and Etruria, 211, 216
  and family business, 124, 125–26, 139, 177,
      211–12, 216, 270
  grandchildren of, 331
  health of, 217–19, 220, 221–22, 225
  holiday with, 212–15, 221
  homes of, 158–59, 188, 212, 217, 325–26
  and Josiah's death, 325–26
  and Josiah's health, 175, 216, 322
  and marriage to Josiah, 116–20, 123–24
  personal traits of, 124
  portraits of, 284–85, 296
  wealth of, 116, 117, 125, 126, 184, 332
Wedgwood, Susanna "Sukey" (daughter):
  birth of, 132
  childhood of, 207, 217, 219, 221, 281
  marriage of, 319–20
  social life of, 307
Wedgwood, Thomas (brother), 116, 124
  and Churchyard Works, 9, 11, 12, 17, 22, 32,
      33, 34, 40, 59, 223
  illness and death of, 223–25
  Josiah apprenticed to, 31–32, 34
  and Overhouse Estate, 58–59, 223, 224
Wedgwood, Thomas (father):
  and Churchyard Works, 6–9, 12, 17
  and finances, 17–18, 20, 32, 59
  funeral of, 3, 9
  Puritanical values of, 15–16
Wedgwood, Thomas (grandfather), 7–8, 9, 16,
    33
Wedgwood, Thomas (great-grandfather), 5–9,
    10–11, 19
Wedgwood, Thomas (nephew), 32, 34, 41, 224
Wedgwood, Thomas (of Big House), 21–22,
    70, 188
  death of, 277
  Josiah's arrangement with, 56, 57–58, 59–60,
      85, 107
  Malkin and, 61
  success of, 21, 29–30, 39, 41, 45, 130, 277
  as thrower, 28, 29
  transportation and, 88–89, 133–34, 184
Wedgwood, Thomas (son):
  birth of, 217
  childhood of, 221, 280, 283
  death of, 330, 331
  education of, 283, 306–7, 309
  and family business, 313, 320

  and father's illness and death, 322, 326
  opium addiction of, 326–27
  restlessness of, 309, 313–14, 320, 329
Wedgwood, Thomas "Useful Tom" (cousin):
  death of, 310
  in family business, 65, 68, 92, 113, 184, 187,
      205, 219, 296
  family of, 283
  retirement of, 310
Wedgwood & Bentley, 193–96
  adapting to new markets, 239
  and Bentley's death, 294
  and Catherine's Ware, 229–32
  competition of, 199, 201–2, 206, 207,
      209–10, 229, 245, 339
  formation of, 180, 182, 193–94, 196
  growth and success of, 202, 204–6, 208–9
  London facility of, 226–27
  and patents, 227–28
  and transatlantic trade, 250, 251
  see also Etruria; Wedgwood pottery
Wedgwood & Bliss, 110
Wedgwood family:
  background of, 4–6
  branches of, 16, 21–22, 30, 33
  children of, 11, 18, 280–81, 282–85
  in Churchyard House, 10–11, 17, 33
  family tree, xix
  Overhouse Estate of, 5, 6, 16, 19, 21, 32–33,
      58–59, 223, 224
  philanthropy of, 328
  pottery business of, 4–6, 12, 39–41, 44, 277,
      281
  Puritanical values of, 15–17, 19, 44–45, 194
  Stubbs portrait of, 284–85, 290
Wedgwood Institute, 339
Wedgwood pottery:
  artistry of, 40, 69, 337, 338
  Bath showroom, 219, 220, 294
  black and mottled ware, 7–8, 34
  cameos and intáglios, 201, 247–49, 257
  changes through the years, 276–77, 335–40
  common wares, 335
  company law reforms and, 338
  decline of, 334–35, 336
  electric power in, 338
  Encaustic Painting of, 227, 242
  enduring name of, 338–40
  at Etruria, see Etruria
  expansion to America, 338
  financial matters in, xvii, 12, 17–18, 126
  flower dressing of, 267
  jasper ware, 247–49, 257, 264, 267, 276, 277,
      299, 305
  Joshiah's descendents in, 337–38

Wedgwood pottery: (*continued*)
    Josiah's sons and, 310, 313–14, 326, 334–36
    lathe turning of, 127–28, 130, 138, 194
    lead poisoning from, 243–44
    management innovations in, 126–30,
        296–97, 333–34
    ornamental vases with jasper, 295
    patents for, 227–28
    production of, 8, 13–14, 19–22, 28–29, 40, 45
    public image of, 244, 245, 294
    quality assurance in, 267, 338–39
    tiles, 85
    transport of, 76, 80–81, 87–88, 107–12
    "The Triple Plea," 72–73
    see also Staffordshire pottery
Wendeborn, Pastor Frederick, 299
Wesley, Charles, 66–67
Wesley, John, 66–68, 252, 275
West, Benjamin, 312
Whately, Thomas, 160
Whieldon, Thomas:
    and employee housing, 48, 51, 65, 188
    Josiah's work with, 47–48, 50, 51–55, 59, 69,
        70, 149, 228
    relaxation of, 54, 55, 56
    retirement of, 285
    and social organization, 51, 91
    "Tortoiseshell" ware of, 43, 52–53
    and transportation, 133, 134
Wilburforce, William, 307

Wilkes, John, 114–15, 213–14
Willets, Catherine Wedgwood, 124–25
    childhood of, 11, 18
    family of, 211, 219, 221, 283, 287–88
    in France, 212–15
    and husband's death, 285
    in literary discussions, 98, 125
    marriage to William, 46
Willets, Jenny, 211, 219, 283
Willets, Kitty, 211, 219, 283, 287–88
Willets, William, 46–47, 113
    death of, 285
    as Dissenter, 46, 92, 103, 104
    and experimental philosophy, 125, 194, 332
    family of, 211
    in literary discussions, 98, 125
    marriage to Catherine, 46
Williams, David, 259–60
women, roles of, 125
Wood, Aaron, 53
Wood, Ralph, 53
Wordsworth, William, 330
Wright, Joseph, 307
    Bird in the Air Pump, 318
    The Corinthian Maid, 279–80
Wrottesley, Sir John, 254
Wyke, John, 95, 127
Wynn, Sir Watkin Williams, 156, 187

Young, Arthur, 88, 89, 193, 194, 268, 325